AND MILES TO GO
BEFORE I SLEEP

But I have promises to keep,
And miles to go before I sleep

Stopping by Woods on a Snowy Evening
by Robert Frost

AND MILES TO GO
BEFORE I SLEEP

A British Vet in Africa

Hugh Cran

MERLIN UNWIN BOOKS

To Berna

First published in Great Britain by Merlin Unwin Books, 2007

Published by:
Merlin Unwin Books
Palmers House
7 Corve Street
Ludlow
Shropshire SY8 1DB
U.K.

www.merlinunwin.co.uk

Designed and set in Sabon by Merlin Unwin Books
Printed in Great Britain by Biddles Ltd

ISBN 978 1 873674 96 3

CHAPTER ONE

In early December in the Year of our Lord 1966, while Britain lay blanketed in snow and darkness I boarded an East African Airways jet and was flown in moderate discomfort from London to Nairobi.

I had never flown before and perhaps it was fortunate that I hadn't, as the novelty of the experience had the concentrating effect of preventing me from brooding on whether I was really doing the right thing. I knew that most people back in Scotland thought I was mad to be going off to the land of the Mau Mau, to a country hissing with man-eating lions, gin-swilling colonials and machete-swinging natives, abandoning a solid, safe career in solid, safe Scotland, not to mention the wilful desertion of my recently widowed mother, left to fend for herself in the wilds of Edinburgh.

I told people that I was only going for a trial period, perhaps a year at most, just to test the waters. They laughed. They were right to laugh – it was to be eleven years before I saw the grey roofs and jagged skyline of Edinburgh again.

I was 26 and single, and, for the past three years I had, since graduation from the Royal Dick School of Veterinary Studies in Edinburgh, worked as an assistant veterinary surgeon in a large-animal practice in the north-east of Scotland. The land was bleak, treeless and windswept. The people were equally bleak and windswept, suspicious of strangers, although hospitable and kind in a dour and introspective way. The winters were hard and cold with icy winds and heavy falls of snow which often lay for weeks before melting. Sometimes when going out to a distant farm on a winter's night, when the snow lay deep and banked in the fields and the wind was blowing and the snow ploughs not out, I could not be sure of returning before dawn as the roads filled with snow behind me. Then I had to spend the night in my freezing car or seek refuge in a farm-house.

Winter and summer the leaden cloak of the lowering sky seemed to sink ever closer to the brooding earth until, by the itme I left, I felt I could almost touch it. In their squat cottages, the present-day Picts sat and supped their porridge. I liked porridge, but I hankered after a slice of paw-paw for breakfast. Stocks of fresh paw-paw were scant in rural Aberdeenshire and I would have to venture forth if I were to find some.

But the work was rewarding and my employer and other colleague in the practice were of inestimable value in consolidating my knowledge and furthering my experience. Sheep, pigs, dogs, cats and black Angus cattle made up the bulk of the animals in the area. During the lambing season, hundreds of visits would be made to farms to attend to ewes or their lambs. The workload was heavy and demanding; the experience gained, invaluable.

The thought of practising tropical veterinary medicine had, however, for a long time lain dormant in my mind and, after an offer of a post as a veterinary officer in Uganda had fallen through because of a lack of funds, I applied for a job in a practice a hundred miles from Nairobi. After a brief correspondence I was on my way. No interview, no phone call, just a couple of blue see-through aerogrammes and that was it. The job was mine.

The plane flapped and rattled through the night. It made an unexplained detour to Rome – presumably to refuel. I studied my fellow-passengers, of which there were few – the plane was half empty. Apart from a couple of pallid tyros like myself, the rest were a mixture of well-dressed Africans, turbaned Asians and sunburnt Europeans. To my ingenuous eyes the latter looked distinctly bizarre, especially as it had been snowing when the plane left London. The men were wearing khaki, sleeveless bush jackets sporting dozens of bulging pockets containing I knew not what. Their wrists were hidden beneath copper bangles, wiry bracelets which I later learnt were made from the hairs of an elephant's tail, and the sort of beaded things I imagined might look better on a Maasai warrior. The women were raw-boned, sun-bleached and rather less flamboyant than the men. I fervently hoped that they were the exception rather than the rule as far as white Kenyan females were concerned. My visions of Ava Gardner look-alikes in damp linen slacks slinking through the bush had taken a bit of a knock.

My preparations for life in the tropics had been scant. A shot against yellow fever, a vague directive from the quack about malaria and that was it. My wardrobe was even more destitute and had nothing in it at all suitable for the tropics. Shorts were not on the shelves in Aberdeen in December, and Ambre Solaire was not an item in much demand in the north of Scotland at any time of year, let alone mid-winter. Sartorially and medically I was singularly ill-equipped.

My African experience was limited to student trips to Morocco, and Algeria during the last frantic years of the French occupation. Once again I had the disturbing feeling that I was an innocent abroad.

The thoughts which passed through the brain of my future employer as he penned his advertisement will never be known, but it can plainly be stated without fear of contradiction that they were not of a philanthropic or benevolent nature. A large man of about sixty, supporting a well-established paunch, his prominent blue eyes glared aggressively and resentfully at the world around him. To compare his bald dome with that immortal structure built by Sir Christopher Wren would be to cast a monumental slur upon the latter.

I arrived at the old Embakasi airport soon after dawn and, having passed through customs, scanned the crowd for Arthur Owen-Jones, my new employer. He found me, probably recognising me as a new boy to Africa by the pallor of my epidermis and by the fact that my nether limbs were encased in grey flannel trousers. Old Africa Hands tend to wear shorts, an open-necked shirt, safari boots, and are burnt by the sun to the colour of lightly-done toast, the lot being surmounted by a well-bashed and fairly shop-soiled bush hat. Owen-Jones broke all of these rules, despite the fact that he had been living in Nakuru, the former capital of the White Highlands in the Great Rift Valley, for over eight years. He wore a loud checked shirt, his cavalry twill trousers were suspended by a pair of braces, on his feet he wore a pair of elastic-sided boots, while his bald head, exposed to view, shone in the rays of the early-morning sun now streaming through the plate-glass windows of the airport.

After establishing identities and after Owen-Jones had enquired as to whether I was suffering from anaemia, we repaired to the Simba Grill, on the second floor of the airport, for breakfast. Just below the window stood a flat-topped acacia, the archetypal tree of East Africa. The Athi Plains stretched away, grey and brown, to the horizon.

During the course of the meal, Owen-Jones berated the waiter in what I later learned was execrable Swahili but which seemed to my then untutored ears to be a fluent rendering of an exotic African tongue. Delivered in a loud Welsh accent, Owen-Jones seemed to derive much satisfaction from this, and, belching contentedly, settled back in his chair.

Following the meal, I collected my unaccompanied baggage from the customs shed. It included my climbing gear – ropes, ice-axe, crampons and boots. Having done some mountaineering in Scotland and the Alps, I hoped to be able to pursue my hobby, in a modest way, among the mountains of East Africa. I shouldered these items with what I hoped was a nonchalant air, but the smirks and mocking grins cast in my direction by other baggage collecting passengers suggested that I was not altogether successful in my endeavour. I loaded my things into Owen-Jones' Peugeot

404 station-wagon and we set off.

Later, on the road to Nakuru, my employer expounded at length on the innumerable imperfections of the native population, their inherent unreliability, their indolence, their ability to swing the lead on every possible occasion, while comparing and contrasting them with their erstwhile colonial masters. Having been reared on a diet of David Livingstone and Mungo Park, I was stunned by this outburst and remained silent.

Built by Italian prisoners during the Second World War, the road from Nairobi wound its way upwards through the country of the Kikuyu to the edge of the Rift Valley Escarpment. Narrow, unsurfaced, rust-red tracks snaked across the densely populated hills, green even in December, when usually little or no rain falls. Banana plantations sprouted everywhere. Copses of tall blue eucalyptus bent in the wind on the skyline. Lorries belching stygian clouds of diesel fumes groaned up the incline ahead of us. Mouthing fearful oaths, Owen-Jones overtook these monsters, headlights blazing, horn blaring. Battered buses, bursting with passengers, top heavy with luggage, crates and wickerwork containers crammed with poultry, hurtled downhill towards Nairobi. 'Matatus', small privately-owned commercial vehicles with a body built onto the back and a couple of benches inside, supplemented the buses and replaced taxis. Normally designed to hold about a dozen people, they usually contained double that number. So overloaded were they that the front wheels in many cases appeared to be barely in contact with the road. Sometimes the chassis would be broken so that the vehicle appeared to be moving sideways like a crab, an alarming spectacle to a newcomer used to the orderly procession of roadworthy motors along the highways and byways of Britain. A wild eyed youth was usually perched on the back step of the matatu, ready to leap off at each stop to cram more passengers into the fetid interior, rather like a professional pusher on a Japanese railway station during the rush hour. When obliged to move inside because of inclement weather or for fear of his own safety, the wretched turn-boy, as he was called, was obliged to stand crouched in a sort of vertical foetal position, as normally every seat was occupied.

Weaving through the potholes we passed the road to Limuru, a township hemmed in by tea and coffee plantations. Heavily laden donkeys tottered along the roadside. Kikuyu women, bent almost double under enormous loads of firewood or drums of water held in place by a leather strap across the forehead, plodded by. Boys leaned out from the grass verge, proffering plums, pears, baby rabbits and chickens to passing vehicles, holding them aloft as though they were sacred tribal totems, and whistled in derision as we swept by.

To the south and left of the road the four-peaked ridge of the Ngong Hills crouched, looking down on Nairobi. Clumps of thatched huts lurked in patches of maize surrounded by litters of hairy sheep, speckled goats, and small, hump-backed cattle. The road passed through plantations of pine and then suddenly, without warning, emerged onto the lip of the escarpment. Two thousand feet below lay the tawny floor of the Rift Valley. Forty miles to the west could clearly be seen the blue-black wall of the opposing Mau Escarpment, covered with a shaggy pelt of forest. The extinct volcanoes of Longonot and Suswa rose from the plain, which, from this altitude, appeared level and featureless, broken only by the green of vegetation along watercourses or the red of a dirt track. The air was crystal clear, the breeze cool and refreshing, the sky dotted with fleecy white clouds. I felt as though I could launch myself into space.

As we descended the wall of the escarpment, the features of the floor of the valley came into sharper focus. Apparently flat when seen from a height, it was rolling and undulating, covered at this point with scattered low thorn trees, cut by rust-red ravines, dry and apparently waterless. Beside the road at the foot of the escarpment stood a tiny chapel, built by the Italian prisoners of war who had laboured on the road. A few antelope and gazelle could be seen grazing in the distance. The head of a giraffe reared above the thorns. Birds of prey perched on the telephone poles, gazing into the far distance. Black and yellow weaver birds crossed our bows, diving into adjacent thickets. A brightly coloured lizard darted into the grass. My companion stared ahead, apparently oblivious to the passing scene, answering my eager questions in a cursory manner. Perhaps it's just his way, I thought, a rough diamond with a heart of gold, beating strong and true beneath his rough-hewn carapace, or perhaps it was due to his having had to rise at 4am to meet me at the airport.

Presently the road rose to a saddle lying at about 7,000 feet, between the 9,000 foot high crests of Mt. Longonot and the eastern wall of the Rift Valley. Fringed by papyrus swamps and tall fever trees, Lake Naivasha lay sparkling in the sun. One of the largest of Kenya's freshwater lakes, it supported large numbers of tilapia and introduced black bass, and the sails of fishing boats could be seen dotted about on its limpid blue surface.

We were now in what was known as, until independence in 1963, the White Highlands. Most of the land surrounding Lake Naivasha in late 1966 was owned by white farmers and indeed at the time of writing most of the land around the lake is still farmed by Europeans. Much of the land near the lake was irrigated and grew flowers and vegetables for sale in Nairobi or for export to Europe. Some of the larger farms grew lucerne which was fed to herds of dairy cattle – Friesians, Ayrshires, and Guernseys.

Naivasha township lies about fifty miles from Nairobi. It was then a grey, nondescript collection of stores and fly-blown hovels, scoured by a gritty, eye-searing wind, blowing clouds of dust and litter before it, and quite unworthy of the dramatic and beautiful country surrounding it. A few Indian-owned shops, some African stalls selling fish, a small hotel, a gust of desiccating breeze and we had left Naivasha behind and were soon crossing the muddy Malewa river, which loses itself in the papyrus swamps encircling the lake. The river has its origins in the Aberdares, a range of mountains rising to over 13,000 feet in the peak of Satima, and forming part of the eastern edge of the Rift Valley. Clothed in dense forest and bamboo up to 10,000 feet, it afforded refuge and shelter to Mau Mau guerrillas during Kenya's euphemistically-termed Emergency. Above the forest lie vast areas of moorland, broken by rocky outcrops, thickets of giant heather and expanses of bog and tussock grass. Overshadowed by the bulk of Satima, 10,000 foot Kipipiri in some lights is difficult to distinguish against the bulk of the range behind it. Covered in dark, almost black forest, it dominates the Wanjohi valley and the surrounding area, former home of the often unjustly maligned Happy Valley set.

About twenty miles beyond Naivasha we reached the little town of Gilgil which, to my appalled gaze, was even more of an eyesore than the rural slum we had left behind. The surrounding country was rolling ranch-land, much of it covered in grey leleshwa scrub and owned by wealthy white farmers, many of them titled. The area between Nakuru, whither I was bound, and Gilgil and Naivasha, appeared to be regarded with especial favour by Counts and Lords of the Italian and English aristocracy.

The road now dropped over another escarpment and below lay another lake, Elementaita, shallow and alkaline, the southern shore bespeckled with white outcrops of soda. To the west, Lord Delamere ranched some 50,000 acres of mostly open plain. The eastern shore was presided over by Arthur Cole, whose father, Galbraith, was one of the very early pioneers. Scattered drifts of flamingos lay on the water's limpid surface. To the south of the lake a number of dramatic volcanic remnants broke the surface of the plain-cones, craters and combinations of both. One, called the Sleeping Warrior or less flatteringly, Lord Delamere's Nose, appeared to be a single, knife-edged ridge. In fact, this is only one side of its circular crater. Further south, the land reared up to the forested crest of Eburru, a spur of the western wall of the Rift Valley, here known as the Mau Escarpment. The lower slopes of Eburru, first explored by the Scot, Joseph Thomson, at the end of the 19th century, are peppered with steam jets, and have no running water. Water for stock has to be condensed from the steam and led through aluminium pipes to distant troughs. Despite the lack of surface water, game is plentiful and the area is much frequented by buffalo, eland, warthog, dik-dik, and impala. A railway, part of the Lunatic Line to Uganda, used to run along the foot of Eburru before turning north to Elementaita and Nakuru, and one night, many years later, I came across a leopard in one of the old railway cuttings.

Baboons perched on fence posts watched us with an indifferent eye as we descended the escarpment. Others were too intent upon their social grooming to spare us a glance.

Presently the bulk of Menengai, the extinct volcano overlooking the town of Nakuru, rose ahead. To the left, the low ridge of Lion Hill hid the famous lake. When it eventually came into view, I could see that its shores were indeed fringed with pink – the famous flamingoes I had read about. Above the lake, flights of pelicans soared and circled with majestic ease, turning in unison on thermals of warm air. The far shore was hemmed in by broken cliffs which opened out to the south into wooded plains. The nearer shore was darkly forested and looked lush and faintly sinister, suggesting pythons lurking in the undergrowth and apes chattering in the branches.

A hot, acrid wind, heavy with the aroma of soda and bird droppings, blew in through the open car window. A few miles before Nakuru we turned off at a place called Lanet. Brown and dusty, it was a suburb of the town. Numerous bungalows, each surrounded by several acres of tree-shaded land, lay on either side of the bumpy road. On top of a low hill stood Owen-Jones' house, red-roofed and white-walled. A copse of tall blue eucalyptus trees lay behind it, bending in the strong breeze. Before it sloped several acres of open land covered in wiry brown grass.

The barking of dogs from behind a high wooden palisade indicated the presence of the boarding kennels which Owen-Jones had mentioned during the drive from Nairobi. I was to become familiar with the finer details of its management sooner than I expected.

A few tired-looking flowers and shrubs grew in front of the house. There was no garden.

An elderly gap-toothed African came down the steps grinning broadly. 'Jambo, Opondo,' said Owen-Jones. 'Kwisha lete daktari mpya.' (I've brought the new doctor). Opondo was a Luo from Nyanza Province on the shores of Lake Victoria. Aged about sixty, he had worked for Owen-Jones and his wife for the past five years as cook and general house-servant. He rushed forward and grabbed my bags and staggered into the house with them. Owen-Jones smiled fondly at his retreating figure.

Gwyneth, Owen-Jones' wife, appeared. Tall, pale, with dark-dyed hair greying at the roots, in her late forties, she exuded an air of business-like efficiency. Smiling genially, she ushered me into the house. I was shown into a small bedroom set aside for me. After scraping off the by now well-risen field of bristles from my chin, watched with some curiosity by a bushbaby in a huge wire netting enclosure, which seemed to occupy most of the available space in the bathroom, I joined Mr and Mrs Owen-Jones in the lounge. A large black labrador lay snoring on the parquet floor. Another occupied most of a sagging sofa. The room was sparsely

13

furnished, the walls almost devoid of pictures. The windows looked out over the desiccated acres of withered brown grass. Birds chirruped in the gum trees. Unknown and unseen insects could be heard through the open windows which were meshed on the inside with a wire grill.

Over a refreshing glass of passion fruit juice and ice, Owen-Jones summarised the work of the practice. He had a surgery in town, his wife acted as secretary cum book-keeper, he employed a Goan clerk, a lay assistant to help him during calls and while doing operations, and an office 'boy' aged about 45. He seemed to cover a vast geographical area dealing mostly with cattle and horses. Nearly all the farms were still owned by European settlers although a buy-out scheme financed by the British Government was in operation. Their stock appeared to be under constant attack by a frightening number of hideous diseases – East Coast Fever, Anaplasmosis, Heartwater, Sweating Sickness, Contagious Bovine Pleuropneumonia, Babesiosis – the list seemed endless. Ticks and tsetse flies sucked their blood from without while intestinal parasites assailed them from within. Their sheep were attacked by flies which deposited their larvae in their nostrils. Midges brought Bluetongue during the rains and ticks were the bearers of Nairobi Sheep disease. Rift Valley Fever, a viral disease affecting both sheep and cattle and occasionally man, and carried by mosquitoes and other insects, appeared periodically during years of heavy rain. Horses regularly succumbed to African Horse Sickness while pigs were virtually impossible to keep because of African Swine Fever. Dogs were under constant threat from Tick Fever.

'Ye Gods,' I thought, 'I'll never master this lot!'

Then there was the matter of communication with the local people. The lingua franca was Swahili, widely spoken all over East Africa and of which the only word I knew was 'jambo'. This wasn't going to get me very far.

With a plethora of unknown diseases facing me and unable to converse with most of the local inhabitants, it didn't look as though I would be of much use to my employer for a long time to come.

The town of Nakuru lay at an altitude of 6,000 feet. To the east and west the land rose to even greater heights. In between was some of the finest farming country in Kenya, fit to rival the best in Britain. Dairy and coffee farms abounded. Wheat and maize flourished. Most of the farmers were British but there was a sizeable Danish and Italian contingent. Many had come to Kenya after the last world war, encouraged to do so by the British government and had learned the rudiments of agriculture at Egerton College near Njoro, a small town about a dozen miles from Nakuru. Confident and self-reliant, their independent way of life was coming to an end. Uhuru had come to Kenya and the exclusive White Highlands were no more. Africans were buying farms, either as individuals or as companies and the Europeans were leaving, going to Australia, New Zealand, Britain, Southern Africa, even South America, taking their knowledge and hard-won expertise with them. A few of the white farmers had become Kenya citizens and were determined to stay and brave the difficulties ahead.

The African farm workers came from several different tribes, because before the arrival of the white man, this area had been almost empty of people, except for the nomadic Maasai herding their cattle on the plains and the Wanderobo hunting game and searching for wild honey in the forests. Most of the people today were Kikuyu and Kalenjin, with smaller numbers of Luo, Abaluya and Maasai.

The Kikuyu, numerically the largest tribe in the country, were Bantu and came from the highlands to the west and south of Mt. Kenya, stretching in an arc to the northern outskirts of Nairobi. Mentally agile and quick to realise the advantages to be gained by adopting the new ideas and methods introduced by the Europeans, many were progressive farmers and businessmen, administrators and politicians.

Kalenjin is a generic name for a group of separate Nilo-Hamitic peoples living in north-west Kenya, from the escarpments overlooking Lake Victoria to the arid plains north of Lake Baringo. Mainly pastoral by inclination, they included the Kipsigis in the green tea country around the town of Kericho, the fierce Nandi on their hills overlooking the steaming Nyanza plains, the Tugen of the mountains and plains to the south and west of Lake Baringo and the nomadic Pokot to the north, herding goats and camels across their semi-deserts. All spoke a similar if not identical language.

The Luo, of Nilotic origin, came from the province of Nyanza on the shores of Lake Victoria. Second in number only to the Kikuyu they were easily recognisable by their strong build, greater than average height, dark complexion and jutting upper front teeth with frequently a gap between the lower incisors, a relic of the days when tetanus was common and victims had to be fed through a gap in their clenched jaws. Great fishermen and cultivators, their country is one of the most densely populated areas of Kenya.

The Abaluya are a large Bantu group comprising various groups such as the Bukusu, Tiriki, and Maragoli who live to the north of lake Victoria and west to the Uganda border. Short of stature, cheerful and hardworking, they often found employment on farms or in towns, working as domestic servants or as waiters in hotels.

The Maasai are probably the best known tribe in Kenya, certainly to outsiders, partly because of their reputation as warriors, their good looks and their way of life. They are Nilo-Hamites and live in south-west Kenya down to the border with Tanzania which bisects their territory. Formerly they also lived in Laikipia, an area north of the Uganda railway, but in

15

1911 the northern Maasai were forcibly moved south to be united with those in the Southern Reserve, as it was then called. Much of Maasailand is fertile and well watered and in recent years has attracted the attention of wheat farmers. It is also home to Kenya's finest game reserves. The Maasai were never hunters, except perhaps for eland which they regarded as wild cattle, or for lion which the young men hunted as proof of manhood. They lived for their cattle and in harmony with their surroundings. Those who left Maasailand to come to the farms and towns of the Highlands often worked as herdsmen or watchmen.

All this information was not acquired until later in my career. Meanwhile Owen-Jones announced with jocular pride that his own knowledge of Swahili was still at a very rudimentary stage, despite his eight years in the country. He employed an excellent African lay assistant, a Kikuyu called Moses Mwangi, to help him on his rounds and during operations. Moses spoke good English and helped his master to communicate with those whose knowledge of English matched his master's own deficiencies in Swahili. I apparently would have to do without such assistance but I would be able to turn to *Up-Country Swahili*, a slim volume written by an ex-Indian Army colonel for the benefit of soldiers, settlers, miners and their wives, a copy of which Owen-Jones handed to me. I noticed that several pages were missing and hoped that no vital information had been contained therein. Glancing through it I observed useful phrases such as 'Boy! You have been using my razor again! There are black hairs in it!' and 'Sergeant Major, give that man ten strokes with the kiboko. He has been caught stealing sugar for the third time this week!' This, I could see, was going to help me immensely.

Owen-Jones had bought a second-hand Volkswagen Beetle for me to use, and had rented a cottage about ten miles from Nakuru for 300 Kenya shillings per month. With the cottage went a cook cum house-servant and two aged gardeners. The former received a monthly emolument of 119/- and the latter the princely wage of 53/- per man. How they were expected to survive on such a miserly sum beggared my imagination but Owen-Jones, with a hearty guffaw, dismissed the subject with a reference to the smell of the proverbial oil rag.

'Well, there's work to do I'm afraid,' Owen-Jones suddenly said. 'An African farmer at Rongai, about twenty five miles from here, phoned up while I was collecting you from the airport. He's got a cow stuck calving. Probably been on the go for a couple of days so God knows how long it might take. Afraid we'll have to have lunch when we get back.'

As it was only about noon, this didn't strike me as an undue hardship, but little did I know then just how long a really difficult calving in Kenya could take. The journey, however, a fifty mile round trip, seemed vast. In Scotland the furthest we ever travelled from base was 17 miles.

16

In this, too, the scales were soon to be lifted from my as yet uninitiated orbs. Immense distances separated farms, towns and settlements. The roads were relatively unfrequented and a journey which in Britain would be considered a weekend expedition, would often be completed in a few hours in East Africa.

We drove through Nakuru, first along an imposing avenue lined by lovely lilac-blossomed jacaranda trees, past the impressive railway station, skirting the bazaar and on to the metalled road which led towards distant hills. The bulk of the town lay out of sight over a rise which sloped down to the lake. Dust rose in the air. The smell of sewage and rotting fruit mingled with other unidentifiable odours. Kites circled over the buildings, calling plaintively. Pied crows perched on rooftops squabbling with each other.

The pavements were crowded. Colourfully clad African women, their men more soberly dressed in European clothes, rivalled their Indian cousins in their brilliant saris. Settlers in khaki rubbed shoulders with long-lobed, shaven-headed Maasai. Turbaned Sikhs drove like demons possessed down the streets. Country buses, bursting at the seams, heads protruding from every open window, their roofs a mountain of luggage, bags of charcoal, and wicker baskets full of squawking chickens, rattled over the potholes.

The town behind now, the road rose over breezy uplands. An immense blue sky dotted with fleecy white clouds covered the landscape like a huge dome. Nearby farms looked neat and well-ordered. Feathery grey gum trees lined the roads and surrounded the farm buildings. The trough of the Rift Valley stretched immeasurably into the distance, mysterious and inviting. Ahead loomed the forested bulk of Mount Londiani.

As we approached the base of the mountain we turned left onto a dirt road. After a couple of miles a farm track forked to the right. A sagging sign said 'Mbama Farm.' Owen-Jones swung the wheel and the car lurched and rocked over the ruts, jets of fine dust appearing from several points until it lay thickly over the dashboard and seats.

'Good cars, Peugeots,' Owen-Jones grunted. 'Best car by far for this country, but they have two faults. One is letting in the bloody dust. The other is that the bloody exhaust pipe is always breaking on rough roads, with the result that the car sounds like an old traction engine. It's high time the Frogs did something about it.'

I made sympathetic noises.

Owen-Jones explained that the farm we were approaching was owned by a co-operative, run by a committee of elected members with certain individuals made responsible for various selected tasks. In theory it appeared to be an excellent idea, but frequently in practice that necessary feeling of personal involvement, so vital to the land-owning African, was lacking, leading to a gradual abrogation of responsibilities and a slow but inevitable decline in farming standards.

We passed the farm-house once occupied by the former white owners and turned into a small field where stood a small wooden dairy with a corrugated iron roof, built on a rough plinth of stone blocks. It was unlike anything I had ever seen before and apart from the modern refinement of the tin roof, brought to mind something I had come across in one of the novels of Thomas Hardy describing rural Dorset in the mid-1800s. No rustic swains or apple-cheeked milkmaids were in evidence here, however. Instead there was a small group of Africans hunkered down under a thorn tree, apparently awaiting our arrival. One, the headman or neopara, as he was called in Swahili, came forward. His earlobes had been perforated and the greatly distended loops were snugly coiled ever the tops of his ears. The effect to my ingenuous eyes was bizarre, as it gave the impression that the lower halves of his ears had been cut off.

'Jambo, daktari,' he said to Owen-Jones.

'Jambo,' Owen-Jones replied. 'Wapi ngombe nashinda kusaa?'

(Where is the cow which is unable to calve?)

'Inakuja,' the headman answered. (It's coming).

'So's Christmas!' muttered Owen-Jones, not under his breath.

A man appeared driving an Ayrshire cow through a gate. The 'gate' was a flexible antediluvian affair consisting of several vertical strips of wood connected with fencing wire. It was closed by inserting the endmost strip of wood into a wire loop projecting from the bottom of the gate post and looping another circle of wire over the top of the post. In years to come I was to curse these gates with much fervour. They would either be constructed in such a way that one needed the strength of Samson to open them, or they were ramshackle affairs festooned with spaghetti-like hanks of rusty barbed wire which took interminable minutes to unravel, with the ever-attendant risk of shredding vital digits in the process.

The cow staggered up to the dairy, pausing at regular intervals to arch her back and strain with grim concentration. Each time she did so she uttered a hoarse bellow. Her tail was raised and over her hindquarters hung a cloud of buzzing flies, which circled and dived like a swarm of miniature predatory birds.

'Jok! Jok!' one of the men cried, referring to the yoke in the dairy. The cow compliantly put her head through the wooden bars which were then closed with a metal rod inserted into a hole in the yoke.

'Naweza shika mkia? Can you hold the tail?' Owen-Jones asked one of the labourers, who obediently hoisted the tail skywards. A large nose and two hooves projected through the patient's vulva, which looked small and under considerable tension. Owen-Jones had by now donned a pair of wellington boots and a waterproof calving overall. He soaped his left arm vigorously and then applied a layer of grease from a large tin proffered by one of the Africans. The disintegrating label proclaimed it to be milking salve for the lubrication of cows' teats.

'I always use this stuff when calving cows,' Owen-Jones grunted as he inserted his large hand into the vulva. He seemed to be having some difficulty as several minutes elapsed before it vanished from sight. A light film of perspiration glistened on his bald pate.

'It's damned tight in here,' muttered Owen-Jones. 'There's a hard, fibrous ring just inside the vulva and it shows no sign of relaxing.'

After another twenty minutes of effort he managed to get a calving rope made of soft cotton onto each foreleg but the head remained immobile. The ends of each rope had loops which were slipped over a couple of batons of wood, two to three feet long and about the diameter of a broomstick. Two men pulled on each leg alternately.

Slowly each leg emerged as far as the elbows and then a few inches more. The head however refused to budge. Two nostrils protruded from the vulva, but, despite strenuous efforts by the pullers, further progress appeared impossible.

Owen-Jones withdrew his arm and washed his hands, with difficulty removing the milking grease. Without uttering a word he walked to his car and rummaged in his surgical bag. He returned carrying a scalpel. Still without speaking, he inserted the blade above the calf's nose and suddenly cut upwards through the cow's vulva.

I watched horrified as the calf's head came into view. It was obvious that as soon as the men resumed their pulling, the incision would rupture upwards into the rectum and that a monumental recto-vaginal fistula would be created. And that is just what happened. The men pulled, the calf slowly emerged, dead now, the incision widened and then split upwards through rectum and anus.

Owen-Jones watched unmoved, re-washed his hands and arms, and returned his scalpel to his bag. He made no attempt to stitch the wound and when I offered to do it for him I was brusquely informed that once I started doing my own calvings I could stitch them up myself. In other words shut up, mind your own business or do things my way.

'I don't think she'll recover,' Owen-Jones told the headman, 'so you'd better get hold of a butcher. Even if she does, it's unlikely she'll be able to conceive or calve again.'

And with these words we took our leave of Mbama Farm, bumping our way back down the rutted track. I wondered what I had come to, and I also wondered about my new employer and his seemingly brutal brand of veterinary medicine and what the future would hold. But I had been in the country less then twelve hours so I decided to hold my peace and wait and see.

CHAPTER TWO

One month after my arrival in Kenya, Arthur Owen-Jones and his wife announced their intention of taking three weeks' vacation at the Coast.

This came as something of a shock.

From the moment I had stepped onto the tarmac at Nairobi Airport I had been fully occupied in attempting to assimilate the mass of new information with which I had been bombarded.

This I had barely swallowed, far less digested. Now I had to put it to the test.

It all seemed a bit premature.

The second-hand Volkswagen formed my transport. Although robust and basically reliable, it was not the most ideal of vehicles for veterinary work. The boot, in which was kept the bulk of my drugs and instruments, occupied that space which in most cars is filled by the engine. The boot's cubic capacity, as a result, was niggardly in the extreme and, when reaching to the farthest depths to retrieve some much-needed item, one was in constant danger of dismemberment or decapitation from the collapse of the precariously supported lid.

The roads, deep in dust and cratered with potholes, were less than kind to the engine. When moving at slow speeds, easing one's way into and out of the yawning cavities which littered the highways and byways like something out of a dentist's nightmare, the car was frequently overtaken by its own cloud of choking dust, which slid over and down the domed roof and into its moving parts. This at times would interrupt one's journey in a way which would have been irritating enough in more sophisticated corners of the globe, but here, it was calculated to raise one's blood pressure to dangerous heights. After a while I began to accept these little annoyances with a degree of qualified resignation, enabling me to observe with a cynical smile those slogans so often painted on lorries in Kenya – 'No Hurry In Africa' or even, if the sign-writer was less linguistically gifted, 'No Harry In Africa.'

A close study of *Up Country Swahili for Soldiers, Settlers, Miners and their Wives* enabled me to communicate in a fashion, albeit rather a basic one, with those members of the animal-owning public whose main language was not English.

Of almost equal importance was the problem of navigation. Although most European-owned farms had a plough disc emblazoned with the owner's name positioned at the farm entrance or at the nearest road junction, few Africans had then reached this level of erudite advertisement. So I had to rely either upon verbal or written instructions from others who had gone before, or make enquiries once I was within what I hoped was striking distance of my destination. With my level of Swahili this was no mean feat.

A further difficulty arose from the fact that local knowledge, especially among the peasantry, appeared to be pretty sparse. If one was within spitting distance of one's objective and asked a fellow hoeing his beans in the shamba next door where so-and-so lived, it was ten to one he would reply with the stock answer 'Sijui', (I don't know) even if one was referring to his next door neighbour.

A scrutiny of the available maps, including a large scale one produced during the Emergency, did help, at least in ensuring that I set off in approximately the right direction.

For about 10 days I accompanied Mr Owen-Jones on his rounds and as a result I was able to obtain some idea of the extent and form of the practice area. It extended from Lake Naivasha in the south-east to Londiani township in the north-west. Both areas were about 45 miles from Nakuru and between them lay a great variety of farming country lying at altitudes of six to ten thousand feet. The south-westerly limit was bounded by the airy upland district of Mau Narok, rich in wheat, sheep and cattle, on the western wall of the Rift, about thirty miles away. To the north-east, the practice area extended to Rumuruti on the edge of the Laikipia plateau, sixty miles from base. This was a semi-arid region whose undulating plains, covered in scrub and whistling thorn, stretched from horizon to horizon.

From my arrival in the country, until their return from their coastal holiday, I lived in the Owen-Jones' house at Lanet. This was because, during their absence, in addition to my veterinary duties, I was required to attend to the canine and feline inmates of their boarding kennels, which lay adjacent to the house.

Christmas came and went. Things were fairly quiet, due in part to the plethora of public holidays during December and to the annual migration of European farmers and their families to the sun-drenched beaches of Mombasa and Malindi.

Owen-Jones seemed keen to get away to the seaside.

On the Monday morning of his departure to the Coast he came to the surgery, accompanied by his wife. Exuding an air of bonhomie and goodwill to all men, he burst through the swinging door into the waiting room. His elastic-sided boots sparkled in a shaft of sunlight. Opondo had obviously put his back into it on this particular morning. His braces gamely took the strain over his freshly filled paunch, clothed in a suitably summery shirt, while his nether limbs were covered in the inevitable but well-pressed cavalry twill. His bald head gleamed as though Opondo, finished with the boots, had spent twenty minutes polishing his master's cranium.

Observing that all members of staff were present and correct, he bade us farewell in characteristic fashion.

'Over to you!' he bellowed, 'and the best of luck!' and, clambering into his 404, gunned the motor, and was gone.

We (or rather I) were on our own.

No sooner had his car disappeared round the corner than the telephone rang.

I jumped.

I had hoped for at least a few minutes' respite before the onslaught – perhaps twenty minutes or half an hour in which to prepare myself for the struggle which I envisaged lay ahead.

Vincent, the Goan clerk, answered it. As he spoke in English I assumed that whoever was at the other end of the line was European. Perhaps it's only advice he's after, I thought hopefully, or perhaps he's placing an order for drugs.

Vincent replaced the phone on its cradle.

'That was Claus Jorgensen from Njoro,' he said. 'He's got an Ayrshire cow with what he thinks is cancer of the eye. He wants you to go out and have a look at it and if necessary operate on it – remove the cancer, or, if that's impossible, take its eye out.'

I gulped. Cancerous eyes were a rare condition in Scotland. In fact I had never even seen one, let alone operated on one. I had enucleated a dog's eye once, so I presumed the principles were the same. I hoped so.

Claus Jorgensen was a tall, good-looking Dane in his late 40s. He spoke excellent English with a strong Danish accent and had a son and a daughter by his stunningly attractive wife. Although his hair was snow white he had a commanding presence and an ever-ready eye for the girls. Before moving to Njoro he had farmed on the Kinangop plateau. Life there, he later told me, was a never-ending round of all night parties. So much so that he got into the habit of visiting his dairy just before dawn, on his return from the latest carousel, in order to ensure that his workers were doing what he paid them to do. On these occasions Claus was invariably clad in dinner jacket and tie. As he never attended the evening milking, his

22

dairy workers concluded that this was his normal and only garb.

The farm lay just beyond the township of Njoro on the murram road to Egerton College, which had been established to train fledgling colonial farmers. Leaving Moses behind to assist in dealing with any clients who might call in at the surgery, I chugged off in my Beetle.

As it was only about half past eight, it was much too early for Claus to be out and about, but his headman was waiting in the dairy. He shuffled over as I drove into the yard. He gave me a grin, revealing an alarming collection of umber tusks. One eye was a sinister milky-blue. His hair was grey and brushed the wrong way, back to front. He looked like a black, middle-aged Shock Headed Peter and not the sort of person one would want to bump into on a dark night.

His command of English was impressive and vastly superior to my primitive grasp of Swahili and his manner, I was relieved to note, was friendly and welcoming.

'Are you the new daktari?' he asked.

I explained that I was.

'Jambo, kijana!' (Hello, young fellow!) His fangs shone in the sunshine.

'Karibu!' (Welcome!)

'Where's Ndegwa?' Seemingly this was the title bestowed upon Mr Owen-Jones by the local Africans and meant something like 'big bull' on account of his impressive bulk and aggressive manner. I sympathised with their choice of title and wondered what they might call me.

I said that Mr Owen-Jones and his good wife were even now en-route to Mombasa to enjoy a spell of well-earned rest and relaxation and that I was in charge during what I hoped would be their brief absence, and where was the cow?

In the crush, he said.

So we walked through the dairy and out into a small field on the other side where a short, wooden, cattle race had been constructed next to a fence. Its framework was of a form seen all over Kenya and was one which never failed to irritate me. Whether by design or because it was easier to build it that way, the sides, instead of being driven vertically into the ground, were inserted at an angle, so that the crush had a V shape, narrower at the bottom than at the top. Examining an animal in such a crush was a laborious business. If an animal became cast it was often extremely difficult to get it back onto its feet. On some occasions the crush had to be partially dismantled in order to extricate a fallen animal. It was obvious that it was much less demanding to drive the side-posts in at an angle, but a good cattle crush should be just wide enough to accommodate a fairly large animal and have solid, vertical sides. Some of the jerry-built structures I saw later would have made one weep – ramshackle contraptions made of discarded off-cuts, tied together with pieces of string and wide enough for an elephant to turn round without touching the sides.

On this occasion the crush was reasonably robust. The patient was standing at the far end. She was a large Ayrshire cow with a white head.

A pair of hadada ibis suddenly flew overhead. Their harsh cries sounded over-loud and mocking in the still morning air and lingered in the soft sunshine long after the birds had disappeared.

I walked round to the front of the crush and my heart sank. A mass about the size of a large strawberry protruded from the inner aspect of the cow's eye. It was growing from the nictitating membrane, or third eyelid, and closer examination revealed that it had spread along the inner surfaces of both upper and lower eyelids and onto the cornea. The animal's eyelids were pink and non-pigmented. The tumour, for such it was, was a squamous cell carcinoma, a malignant growth induced in this case by the continuous effects of the ultra violet rays in the tropical sunshine on the non-pigmented skin surrounding the eye. Well, this was no quick-snip job. The eye would have to come out.

I returned to the car.

My employer had left me his surgical bag and instruments for the duration of his leave and I selected what I judged I would need – cotton wool, bandage for packing, local anaesthetic, syringes, gentian violet spray, artery forceps, scissors, Allis tissue forceps, suture material and Dettol solution. I hoped it would be enough, as once begun I wouldn't be able to nip back to the car to replenish my supply. I also brought a cotton rope which I fashioned into a halter. Ropes always seemed to be a rare commodity on farms in Kenya. With the amount of sisal grown in the country one would have thought that every farm would have been well endowed with them. Such was rarely the case and unless one provided one's own, one was left kicking one's heels and grinding one's teeth, while a couple of incompetents constructed a rope by tying together lengths of binder twine and twisting them together into something resembling a giant hank of spaghetti and of about equal strength.

By this time three other men had appeared.

One held the cow by the nose while I slipped the halter over her head. The headman brought a bucket of warm water from the dairy, into which I sloshed some Dettol. After having scrubbed the patient's eyelids and surrounding skin with a wad of cotton wool, I filled a 10 ml syringe with local anaesthetic and injected several mls around and under both eyelids. This done, I waited for a few minutes before anaesthetising the muscles attached to the eye itself. Finally, using a long needle, I injected several more mls at the back of the orbit to desensitise the optic nerve.

I arranged my instruments on a clean towel laid on the grass and waited for 15 minutes. This was partly in order to allow time for the anaesthetic to work but mainly to give me time to formulate the finer details of my plan of attack.

My rustic assistants lay or lolled about, chattering to each other, seemingly confident that I knew what I was about.

My companions were lightly clad in rags. I felt over-warm in gum boots and overalls.

The time had come.

I instructed the men to hold on tight, seized my instruments and set to work. First I clipped the eyelids together with a couple of tissue forceps in order to tighten the skin and maintain traction on the eye. Then I made two elliptical incisions in both upper and lower eyelids enclosing the tumour and meeting on either side. The skin above and below both incisions was then grasped with tissue forceps whose handles I gave to one of my assistants. As forcefully as it was politic to do so, I requested him to hold the handles only, not to pull them and to please keep his filthy fingers out of the wound.

I next began to dissect the skin back to the rim of the bony orbit and almost at once cut through a major artery. The blood struck me in *my* eye. Temporarily blinded, I blinked furiously. I grabbed a pair of artery forceps and clipped off the severed vessel. Feeling even warmer, I continued by making a circular incision within the orbit, close to the bone but outside of the eyeball, severing the muscles attaching it to the skull. Finally, with a long pair of curved scissors, I cut through the remaining muscles at the back of the eye and snipped through the optic nerve.

The patient suddenly struck me as being ominously still.

I glanced up.

Four black faces, eyes goggling, mouths open, stared at me as though hypnotised. None was paying any attention to the patient. The men on the rope appeared to be in a trance, still hauling on the cow's head and neck. She was prevented from moving forward out of the crush by two wooden poles across the front and her head had been pulled over the upper of these – and pulled and pulled by my open-eyed but unseeing assistants until she had lost consciousness and was on the point of choking to death. Her head hung over the pole, jugular veins bulging.

It was my own fault. I should have been watching more closely.

'Toa miti mara moja!' I bellowed. What little Swahili I did know was being put to use. 'Get that pole out at once!' I yelled.

My roar galvanised the men into action. Like a group of robots lying limp and inert until the switch is pressed, they sprang to life, seized the pole and tore it to one side.

The cow dropped to her knees, shaking and trembling, her one good eye blinking convulsively.

Blood began to pump into the empty socket of the eye just removed, as of course it should have done, immediately it had been enucleated, had she not been in a state of near-asphyxia at the time. I grabbed a handful of cotton wool and thrust it into the gaping cavity. Within seconds it was soaked in blood.

The patient staggered to her feet, shaking her head and spraying everyone with blood. I was glad of my overall. My assistants weren't quite so fortunate. I saw them looking ruefully at their bespattered raiment.

I seized a handful of artery forceps and began clipping off the sources of supply. It was like working at the bottom of an inkwell. The crimson flood seemed never-ending. A mutilated fragment of *Macbeth* rose to mind – 'Yet who would have thought the old cow had so much blood in her.' At this rate she'll be dying from exsanguination, I thought. What a splendid start to my tropical career!

I shoved in a few more artery forceps for good measure and then began, not without difficulty, to tie off the major offenders. All the while the pool of blood at my feet grew larger and larger. After a while the flow began to ebb and finally slowed to a trickle. At first I thought she had run out of blood, but she still looked hale if not exactly hearty.

As rapidly as I could I folded a bandage concertina-wise, sprayed it with gentian violet from an aerosol can and inserted it into the socket, leaving about twelve inches protruding from the inner corner. I then stitched the skin edges together with monofilament nylon – actually strong, sterilised fishing line – leaving an extra-long stitch closest to the protruding bandage. I trimmed this to a more manageable length to prevent it from snagging on long grass or bushes.

I instructed the headmen to remove the single long stitch after four days and thereafter every day to pull out and cut off about twelve inches of the bandage folded within the socket until none was left. I would return after two weeks to remove the remaining stitches.

He appeared to understand. I hoped so. The patient had by now recovered from her ordeal by garrotte and stood quietly in the crush while I gave her an intra-muscular injection of antibiotic. Upon being released she strolled out into the field, put down her head and started grazing.

I walked back to the car with my toes curled up inside my boots, wondering just what Claus Jorgensen would have thought, and said, if he had come up to the dairy after a late and leisurely breakfast to be informed that the cow the young vet had come to operate on was dead – choked to death in the crush. I went hot and cold in rapid succession. They say that a miss is as good as a mile but that was a pretty close shave. It just showed that one should never relax while on the job. Eternal vigilance must be the watchword from now on.

✳ ✳ ✳ ✳ ✳

Back at the surgery, which was conveniently sited in Club Lane and separated from the rather splendid club buildings by a high thorny hedge, I found the doorway blocked by a knot of blanket-clad Maasai. Insinuating my way through the crowd and through an almost palpable miasma of equal parts of the ripe smell of sheep's fat, body odour and je ne sais quoi, I pushed open the chest-high swing door into the waiting room.

Moses was conversing with an individual who appeared to be the spokesman of the group. He was a tall, lean fellow wrapped in a coarse, hairy blanket, his hugely distended, perforated ear lobes sagging beneath the weight of copper ornaments. On his head he wore a knitted woollen cap resembling a tea-cosy.

'Jambo, Moses,' I said. 'What do these chaps want?'

'They're Maasai from Mau Narok and they want vaccine for their cattle. Several big calves have died recently and from what they say it sounds like blackquarter.'

Both Moses and the Maasai were familiar with the symptoms of the more common diseases and the means of their prevention.

Blackquarter is an unpleasant bacterial disease causing gas gangrene in living muscle, most commonly in young cattle and the spores responsible are picked up by mouth from the ground in which they can lie dormant for years. Death usually occurs within 12 to 48 hours so treatment is not usually an option.

In Kenya, years might pass without the disease being seen in a certain district. Then, without warning, cases would occur simultaneously over a large area, sometimes also affecting older animals. Why this should be was difficult to explain – perhaps some particular combination of climatic conditions, temperature, humidity, soil acidity or alkalinity favoured the organism and its ability to invade healthy living muscle. Perhaps it was associated with certain facets of ruminant digestion.

Whatever the reason behind these periodic outbreaks of blackquarter, their occurrence meant a heavy loss to livestock owners. Although large doses of penicillin were occasionally curative, the disease was so acute that it was rarely possible to start treatment soon enough to be effective.

An excellent vaccine was available, however. This gave protection for twelve months. The Maasai knew this, but like people world-wide, they tended to get rather slack when things were going well and frequently neglected to vaccinate their stock on a routine basis.

The Maasai explained that several well-grown calves aged between six and nine months had died suddenly. One had been seen to be acutely lame in a hind leg before it, too, had died, and when a rudimentary post-mortem was carried out swollen, gaseous, blackened areas were found in the heavy muscles between the hock and the hip.

'A hind leg was very swollen, and there was a blackened area, with

27

gas and the whole thing stank to high heaven!': Moses did the translation.

'OK,' I said 'It sounds like blackquarter all right. They seem to know what they're talking about. How many doses do they want? I presume they've got syringes and needles.'

They had, and after interminable discussions and arguments between themselves in Maasai, the lop-eared spokesman said they had approximately 300 susceptible cattle, spread between several manyattas in their area of Mau Narok.

'That'll be 6 bottles and the dose is 2ccs for each animal, irrespective of age or size, injected under the skin behind the shoulder. Boil the syringes and needles for 10 minutes before they use them. And it might be a good idea to wash their hands as well – dirt and sheep fat don't mix well with vaccines. And tell them to vaccinate everything between 3 months and 3 years from now on. Don't wait until they start dying.'

Moses translated this to the Maasai, who nodded sagely. Vincent looked up the price of the vaccine in his list. A grand total of 105 shillings.

The Maasai tut-tutted and shook their heads at this colossal expense.

'Iko discount?'

That was one English word they did know.

I ignored this impertinence and gave them some free advice instead, suggesting that they also purchase a bottle of penicillin. The vaccine would not be effective until about 10 days had elapsed after inoculation and in the meantime, should other animals be taken ill, there was always a chance, albeit a small one, that a hefty shot of penicillin, given early enough, might save a life, or two.

In other countries, such as Britain, the veterinary and legal authorities frowned on the use of antibiotics, especially injectable ones, by anyone other than a veterinary surgeon. In a case such as this, in Africa, where these Maasai lived fifty miles from a town and several miles from the nearest road, one used a combination of common sense and discretion, within the framework of the veterinary regulations. I soon became adept at recognising requests for drugs which I suspected would not be put to veterinary use. M&B693 .5gm tablets were a firm favourite when it came to the treatment of infected initiates of locally conducted circumcision ceremonies. Almost without exception, lack of foresight on the part of the would-be purchaser to concoct a suitably convincing tale about sick calves or lambs, led to the discovery that some wretched victim of an unclean, and probably blunt, knife or razor blade, was suffering from a severe malaise of the most vital of all his organs.

The chief Maasai delved beneath his shaggy blanket and, from somewhere in the region of his left armpit, produced a large greasy, leather wallet, slung across his torso on a long cord. Holding this close to his chest, rather like a gambler with a good hand of cards, he withdrew two one hundred shilling notes from what was obviously a very large wad.

I gave him his receipt and change. I had asked Moses to pack the vaccine and antibiotic with ice cubes in a plastic bag and suggested to the Maasai that if it was not possible to get the cattle vaccinated later that day, to keep the drugs cool by immersing them in one of the numerous cold streams flowing off the Mau. These Maasai lived at an altitude of between eight and nine thousand feet, so it should be cold enough. No wonder they wrapped themselves up in hairy blankets.

◈❘◈❘◈❘◈❘◈

From the adjacent kennel-room came the sound of barking. Five wooden kennels allowed owners, if the vet happened to be out when they called, to leave their animals while they went about their business in the town. It was a convenient system, suiting owners and animals, especially during hot weather when the temperature inside a vehicle could rise to lethal heights. Clients brought dogs, cats, birds, sheep and small, and not so small, wild animals from as far away as 150 miles, travelling over rough roads. In such cases, the owner often preferred to spend a night in town before returning home, or might even be driving to Nairobi. The animal would be left in a kennel overnight or even for several days.

Two dogs had been brought in while I had been wrestling with Claus Jorgensen's cow – a dachshund and a ridgeback.

The dachshund dwelt on the shores of Lake Baringo, some sixty miles away. According to the cryptic message left by the owner, several lumps had appeared on various parts of the dog's body. Otherwise the dog was eating and behaving normally.

The patient, a young black and tan fellow with a friendly, alert expression, stood quietly on the surgery table while I examined him. The lumps were there and I counted thirteen of them, ranging in size from one the size of a garden pea to others as big as a large marble. They were scattered over his chest, legs and back.

'What the hell?' I thought.

They looked like boils. I looked at them more closely and in the centre of each I could see a small dark hole.

I gave one of the swellings an exploratory squeeze. The dachshund flinched slightly. Slowly a maggot, dull white in colour, emerged from the hole and then suddenly popped out.

I regarded it with some astonishment.

I had seen maggots in animals before, mainly in sheep, or in open, infected wounds, but never like this.

There was an ancient dust-covered volume of *Monnig's Veterinary Helminthology and Entomology* lying on a shelf in the surgery. I consulted it, riffling through the yellowing parchment-like pages, and discovered that this was the larva of the mango or tumbu fly, an insect rejoicing in the resounding name of *Cordylobia anthropophaga*.

I flushed the remaining larvae from their lairs by a combination of firm but judicious pressure on the swellings and by seizing them with a pair of rat-toothed forceps as they emerged. After their removal, I disinfected their erstwhile homes with antiseptic and gave their unwilling host an intramuscular injection of penicillin to ward off infection.

The adult mango fly feeds on fruit, and also, less delightfully, on animal excreta. About the size of a house fly and dull-brown in colour, the female lays three to four hundred eggs on sand or dry soil, where animals have been sleeping, or where there is contamination with dung or urine. After two to four days, the larvae hatch and if they come into contact with the skin of a suitable host, be it man, dog, rabbit or some other domestic animal, they latch on. They penetrate the skin, forming the boil-like swellings, wherein they lie snug for the next eight to fifteen days until they mature. Then they wriggle out and drop to the ground. After three to four weeks pupation in the soil, a brand new mango fly emerges, ripe and ready to play its disreputable role in the great outside world.

The largest number of maggots I saw in a dog was 27. Cases seemed to occur in batches. For weeks on end I had the impression that every second dog I saw was peppered with the revolting things. Then a year might elapse before I saw another case.

The maggot breathed through its air hole, and when pressure failed to persuade the little devil to emerge, application of vaseline or liquid paraffin, by cutting off its source of oxygen, would induce it to stick its backside out into the wind, whereupon the cunning surgeon would seize it in his forceps and draw it out.

These procedures were wont to cause not a few clients to swallow convulsively and, on the odd occasion, to depart from the scene of operation in some haste.

Not infrequently, people, most often children, were affected by these unpleasant pests. Those foolish enough to dry their clothes after washing, by spreading them out on grass or soil, invited trouble as, when they donned the aforesaid garment, a few mango fly larvae might well be attached and waiting to pounce.

One victim was a friend of mine.

His house-servant had laundered his foundation garments and had left them on the lawn to dry. He had donned them shortly afterwards in the usual way. A few days later he felt an unaccountable and unpleasant sensation in the region of his gluteals and, upon examining his backside in the mirror, was horrified to find both cheeks covered in a multitude of angry looking boils. Rushing off to his medico, he discovered that the dreaded mango fly had struck – and at one of the more sensitive parts of his anatomy. This was bad enough but he was a crop spraying pilot and spent most of his working day sitting on that area now infested with maggots. For the next week or so he flew his Pawnee cushioned by a six-inch layer of foam rubber.

Needless to say, his experience was the source of much mirth and ribaldry, which, to his great credit, he bore with manly fortitude.

As did another client and friend, a Scots agricultural contractor, who also came in for a spot of buttock bashing, although of a different kind. During the course of a fairly rowdy Saturday night party, in which the main source of protein came from bottles of Whitecap and Johnny Walker whisky, he had the misfortune to tumble backwards through a plate glass window, gashing his derriere in several places. Being pretty numb all over at the time he paid scant attention to this minor inconvenience and carried on raising his elbow in the standing position.

On his return home in the small hours he decided to apply some first aid to his injured bum. Dropping his shorts he squinted over his shoulder into the bedroom mirror, and proceeded to affix pieces of sticking plaster to his lacerated rump, following which he retired to his couch for what remained of the night. Upon rising later that morning, he glanced at his bleary image in the glass. He had some difficulty in seeing himself clearly, partly because of a fearful hangover, but mostly because the mirror was covered with small pieces of sticking plaster which, in his befuddled state, he had stuck to the glass instead of to his backside.

The next patient, which was owned by a client from Naivasha, was brought in from the kennel room. This was a large, year old, tan-coloured Rhodesian ridgeback dog. His owner wished him to be registered as a pedigree with the East African Kennel Club in Nairobi and this could only be done if the animal was certified as being free of a dermoid sinus by a veterinary surgeon.

In my feverish reading since my arrival in the country, I had actually come across this condition and so was rather more prepared than I had been for *Cordylobia anthropophaga*.

Many dogs native to Africa have a whorled ridge of hair running down the middle of their backs. Why this should be so, I have yet to discover, but some dogs with this ridge are born with a tube-like sinus descending from the skin to the tough, external covering of the spinal cord. The condition is an inherited one and its possession by any Rhodesian ridgeback prevents it from being registered as being pedigreed or being

31

used for breeding purposes. The sinus can be removed surgically in a prolonged and frequently tedious operation.

Ridgebacks are often nervous, irritable animals, never completely trustworthy with strangers, quick to snap or bite if cornered. So we took precautions and Brutus of Bulawayo was securely muzzled before he had a chance to leap for my jugular. A prolonged and careful palpation of Brutus' neck and back failed to reveal any sign of a dermoid sinus.

I made out a certificate to that effect and asked Vincent to give it to the owner when he returned.

The telephone shrilled again.

An African farmer at a place called Kabatini about eight miles from Nakuru had a cow with milk fever. Or at least that was what the message suggested.

'Praise the Lord,' I thought, 'at least that's something I'm familiar with. Surely that can't be any different from all the cases I've seen in Scotland.'

Milk fever, or *hypocalcaemia*, usually affects cows producing large volumes of milk, often at, or shortly after, calving. There is trembling, a general lack of muscle tone, and eventual collapse and coma, which if not treated with injections of calcium borogluconate, will in due course result in death. Intravenous infusion of the aforesaid calcium borogluconate usually effects a rapid and often dramatic recovery. The name 'milk fever' is a misnomer. There is no fever – quite the reverse.

'OK, Moses, I think you'd better come with me,' I said. 'I haven't a clue how to find this place. Can you check to make sure there's a flutter valve and some calcium in the car.'

Kabatini lay north-east of Nakuru, not far from Solai, a fertile valley rich in coffee and dairy farms. We drove out of Nakuru, the metallic clatter of the Volkswagen echoing back from the jacaranda trees which lined the road out of town. The Solai road was glorious, smooth tarmac and we fairly tore along. To our right was open grassland, to our left the bulk of Menengai, the dormant volcano, which rose 1,500 feet above the town.

All too soon we turned off to the right onto a dirt road. Along this we bumped for about five miles towards the eastern wall of the Rift. Suicidal sheep and goats rushed across the track as we approached. Snotty-nosed urchins howled with delight as we passed, screaming 'Mzungu! Mzungu! Mzungu!' (European! European! European!), leaping up and down in ecstatic frenzy, and turning somersaults in the dust. It appeared there wasn't a great deal of local entertainment in these parts. I felt we were providing a much needed social service.

The potholes deepened, the dust thickened, clouds of it billowed in through the open windows, settling on everything. Uncle Remus was sitting beside me, eyes and teeth flashing. Moses, his hair and eyebrows thickly powdered, appeared to have aged about thirty years. He grinned through the fog.

We came to a crossroads, turned left, and after about half a mile, a faint track led upwards to a cluster of thatched huts and a house roofed with corrugated iron. As we bumped towards them, the smooth belly of our chariot rasping on the boulders cunningly concealed in the middle of the track, which seemed to my jaundiced eye to be more suited to the passage of goats than to vehicular traffic, a ragged figure appeared running over the brow of a hill from behind the huts. It tumbled down a ditch, into and out of a thicket and through a barbed wire fence, virtually debagging itself in the process, and materialised into a wide-eyed panting youth who flagged us to a halt.

Moses translated.

'The cow has finished falling into the river! She's almost dead! Come quickly!'

He tore off up the track, his bare feet pounding in the dust. I followed him up to the huts and stopped the car.

'What the hell's going on?' I thought.

The scarecrow disappeared back over the brow of the hill. We hurried after him. From the top of the hill a field sloped down to a stream, which ran between steeply shelving banks covered with low trees and dense vegetation. At what appeared to be either a ford or watering place, a group of men was clustered knee and thigh deep in the soupy water, supporting something which lay almost submerged.

I ran down the hill.

My patient lay supine and awash in the stream, with only her head, propped up by several perspiring peasants, above the surface.

A grizzled Kikuyu, gasping from his exertions, explained that the cow, a Friesian of about seven years, had calved in the night, and had been turned out with her calf into the field shortly after dawn. At about mid-morning she was observed to be staggering stiffly around the paddock and before anyone could prevent her, had tottered down the greensward and into the stream, where she promptly and inconveniently collapsed. The owner, bellowing for assistance, had rushed after her, plunged into the water and seized her by the horns just before her head went under. His son, the tattered individual who had met us on the road, ran like a stag to the nearest telephone a mile away and contacted the surgery. Meanwhile, several of the farmer's neighbours had come to his help and were at this moment straining their sinews to the utmost in the flood.

I asked Moses to bring a flutter valve, a calving rope, a 14 gauge needle and a bottle of calcium borogluconate from the car. He sprinted back over the hill and returned a few minutes later with the requested items.

Taking off my shoes and socks, I waded into the murky water. Luckily I was wearing shorts. Moses had to roll up his longs to well above his knees.

Slow, intravenous infusion of calcium borogluconate into the jugular vein was the desired method of treatment. But with only the cow's head above the surface, unless we could raise her sufficiently to expose at least a few inches of her neck, treatment would have to be submarine, which, in view of the opacity of, and the particulate matter in the water, was something to be avoided if at all possible.

She was lying in a sort of trough in the bed of the stream. Struggling mightily, we managed to drag her partially out of this and a little way towards the bank. I slipped the calving rope round her neck, which was well below the surface. By raising her head, with its open, unblinking eyes, at last sufficient jugular vein was exposed to enable me to whack the needle into it. Thick, dark venous blood trickled out of the hub. Moses had the 450cc bottle ready, with flutter valve attached.

Holding the bottle up, I slowly ran the calcium into her blood. Every few minutes, I checked that the needle was still in the vein by lowering the bottle, so that the blood ran back down the tube and past a glass window in the rubber.

Almost before the infusion was completed, the cow's eyes closed, then opened wide as though registering surprise at where she was, all but drowned in an African stream. Her ears flicked. Her breathing deepened and steadied. In the rush to get her treated, I had paid little attention to the state of her respirations, apart from checking that she was still alive.

Suddenly she shook her head, showering everyone with water, appeared to sit up, and then, like a breaching whale with the ocean cascading off its back, staggered to her feet, and stood there in mid-stream, legs quivering and muscles twitching.

Gasps of incredulity greeted this almost miraculous rising of the near-dead.

Ten minutes later, aided and supported on either side by our motley crew, she plodded slowly out of the stream, up the bank and into the field. Her calf was there, lying hidden in a corner.

I explained to the owner, the grizzled ancient who had greeted our arrival, that moderation in milking for the next few days was essential to avoid a recurrence.

The old fellow was touchingly grateful, wringing our hands and vocalising about the powerful dawa the daktari had injected into his cow. His stooped and wrinkled wife appeared out of one of the huts carrying a tray bearing two tin mugs and a large, battered, green metal teapot. With a beaming smile which exposed her toothless gums, she filled each mug with a steaming cascade of milky brown fluid. In African fashion, tea, hot water, sugar and milk (also hot) had been mixed together in the pot. To my palate it tasted overly sweet and sickly but, not wishing to give offence, I sipped bravely away.

The gang of helpers stood around us, maintaining a respectful silence, punctuated by the odd 'aiee!' of stupefaction at the patient's seemingly amazing recovery. Indeed I was fairly amazed myself, for when I worked in Scotland it was a rare event for a cow to respond so dramatically to treatment. I often had to resort to cocktail solutions containing phosphorous and magnesium in addition to calcium, and even then some animals took hours or days before they stood up. In some cases they didn't get up at all. This was probably due to the unnatural diet forced on milking cattle in Britain, the stress they suffered pumping out milk, day in day out, and the smothering of their pastures with an excess of fertiliser.

Whatever the cause, I was grateful for such a clean cut case with such a satisfactory outcome. And so was the owner, for he paid his bill of 91 shillings with a will, and as we were leaving, his wizened bed-mate rushed over with six eggs wrapped in a cabbage leaf.

Well, although it was such a simple undertaking, I felt, as yet more metal was being rasped off the belly of my employer's car, that something worthwhile had been accomplished back there. There's nothing like a quick, dramatic, successful treatment to cement good relations between client and vet.

Milk fever cases in Kenya were like that. Almost without exception, they responded with extraordinary speed to treatment, leaving everyone smiling happily. Which was just as well, because the other side of the coin, as far as other diseases were concerned, could be a good deal less sunny.

Provided the animal hadn't succumbed to bloat or inhaled rumen contents into its lungs, it never ceased to amaze me just how long a cow could remain comatose under the tropical sun, flies crawling over her glazed corneas, and still get up.

Perhaps the most bizarre example I later saw of this was when I was called to attend to a case of milk fever in a cow owned by an African politician on a farm at Rongai.

As I approached the spot where I had been told the cow was lying unconscious in the grass, the farm headman ran onto the road and flagged me down.

'Sorry, Bwana, the cow has finished dying. There's nothing to be done.'

He was adamant that there was no point in my inspecting the corpse. This I knew was mainly because the owner was well known for his reluctance and frequent downright refusal to pay his debts and obviously didn't see why he should pay for what in his view would be a totally unnecessary post-mortem in addition to the cost of the mileage.

35

So, silently, and later when out of earshot, not so silently, cursing him for not having bothered to phone to inform me of the animal's demise, I turned the car round and drove back to the surgery.

Two days later there came a telephone call from the same farm with the startling information that the cow was in fact not dead after all, was still lying in the same spot, and would I come as soon as possible – 'You are rushing to the farm immediately, isn't it?' I noted the absence of that little word, 'please'.

Incredulous, I did indeed rush immediately to the farm. This I had to see. How could the cow be alive when two days previously I had been informed that she was dead? I knew that the identification of certain diseases could be a tricky business but surely they could tell the dead from the living.

Apparently not, for I was led to where a large black cow lay snoring peacefully in a bed of knee-high grass. She was quite invisible from a few feet away. Was it the same cow? I was assured it was.

Under normal circumstances a dead animal would have been skinned and eaten by the farm populace in double short order. What had happened in this case?

It turned out that the milker responsible for that particular cow had told the headman that the cow had died, when in reality it was stretched out comatose with milk fever. He had then gone on leave. No one else had been informed. The headman, taking the milker at his word, had told me and had then promptly forgotten all about it, presumably having more pressing matters on his mind.

It was not until a woman fossicking around for firewood stumbled upon her that she was discovered – two days later.

I didn't hold out much hope for her recovery, even if she did respond to the calcium injection, as the possibility of inhalation pneumonia or nerve damage due to body pressure, was pretty high. However, recover she did, reacting with incredible rapidity to the life-restoring fluid as it mixed with her blood, and fifteen minutes later was on her feet, tottering about the paddock like a well-lubricated Member emerging from the Holy of Holies, the Men's Bar of the Club.

I always tried to impress upon African farmers the necessity of propping cows up on their chests should milk fever develop, and not allowing them to flop onto their sides, thereby incurring the additional risk of death from bloat or inhalation pneumonia. Instead of using something soft but firm, such as straw bales, or sacks filled with grass, they invariably opted for boulders or stone blocks which they shoved against the unfortunate flanks of their wretched animals and then looked surprised and hurt when I hit the roof. This seeming indifference to the discomfort of their beasts can in part be explained by the conditions of hardship under which their owners and, more particularly, their herdsmen, lived. Many of these latter were Turkana from the far north who had come south in search of work. They were often paid far less than the minimum agricultural wage, and, as a result, lived at a pretty basic level. Coming from the baking, desiccated country to the west of Lake Turkana, they were noted for their indifference to their surroundings. Cattle rustling, the skewering of their opponents on long slender spears, the thrusting of ivory plugs through their lower lips and the use of bone-hard wooden neck rests as pillows – these pastimes were not the marks of an effete people. So it was hardly surprising that tender, loving kindness towards the beasts of the field could not be numbered among their attributes.

◎◎◎◎◎◎

By the time we got back to the surgery it was almost one o'clock and I was looking forward to a bite of food.

Appetite well-honed, the luncheon hour at hand, I entered the surgery.

As I did so, one Mohanbhai Patel rose to confront me.

'Good day, young man,' he said. His large head wobbled alarmingly from side to side.

'My dog is having fight with another and has sustained injuries requiring your knowledgeable expertise to return him to former high state of health.'

A gust of curry and garlic-laden breath almost brought me to my knees.

He, at least, had dined, and richly, by the smell of it.

For the next hour, I dealt with Mr Patel's large brindle hound whose general appearance was more akin to that of a hyena than most dogs I was familiar with. He had done battle during the night and had come off rather the worse for wear.

In addition to several puncture wounds, there was a V-shaped gash on the top of his head and another in his axilla. In a tractable patient these could have been stitched under sedation and local anaesthesia.

This, however, was an Asian-owned guard dog, savage and unpredictable. Kept locked up in kennels during the day and released at night to patrol his master's walled compound, this dog was not a pet. Muzzling was mandatory before any examination. Such dogs were rarely handled by their owners. African servants were employed to do that. Occasionally the owner might be in attendance, usually standing nervously to one side, perhaps extending a tentative, loose-wristed pat to indicate that despite appearances he was really quite fond of his dog. Round the animal's neck would be fastened a chain of incredible length and weight, which made a fearsome din as it clanked and clattered on the surgery table.

This dog came up to the mark, putting up a fierce struggle before being brought under control with a computed dose of intravenous pentobarbitone.

I was inserting the final stitches as Vincent opened the door to release the log-jam of waiting clients.

A horse-faced, middle-aged European woman with long yellow teeth strode in, dragging a Dalmatian behind her on a choke chain. Her name was Spence and she wanted her dog vaccinated against rabies. Her hair was thin and lank and greying, her face blotched with brown marks from too long exposure to the sun. Her patrician stare registered surprise and irritation on realising that I was not her usual veterinary attendant.

I had met her kind before.

'Play it cool,' I told myself. 'Don't let her get up your nose.' Hers, meanwhile, flared like that of a nervous thoroughbred.

She had a curious accent which I couldn't place. It sounded part Scandinavian, part Dutch with perhaps a trace of German. It was, I later learned, a Kenyan accent, one peculiar to Europeans who had been born and raised in the country. Her sentences were peppered with Swahili words like 'kali' – fierce, 'watu' – Africans in general, 'posho' – mealie meal, 'sindano'– needle, and so on. I was soon to learn that one could pick out long-time residents by the way they pronounced the names of certain towns, always placing the emphasis on the penultimate syllable. Mom*ba*sa, Nai*ro*bi, Nan*yu*ki, were prime examples. Recent arrivals, or those not knowing any better, placed equal emphasis on all syllables, a grave mispronunciation in the ears of the pundits.

Thanks to the imposition of a strict vaccination and quarantine policy, there was no rabies at that time in the Nakuru district of the Rift Valley Province.

The available vaccine was a live one, grown in chick embryos and produced at the renowned Veterinary Research Laboratory at Kabete. Given by intra-muscular injection it was designed for dogs over six months only. Mrs Spence's Dalmatian fell within this category.

Under her beady gaze, I withdrew a single dose vial of the powdered vaccine from the fridge, reconstituted it with 3mls of sterile diluent and injected her dog in the heavy muscles of the thigh.

I signed the dog's certificate and told her that as her dog had, according to the certificate, been vaccinated within the past three years it should, within the limits of any vaccine, be protected with immediate effect for a further three years. In young, unvaccinated dogs, immunity did not take place until a month after injection.

I bade her good day and opened the door for her. Her frosty veneer briefly cracked, her features momentarily relaxed, and her unpleasing visage split horizontally into the semblance of a smile. Then the mask dropped and she departed, her pet at her heels.

There was an almost palpable lightening in the atmosphere as she left – a bit of sunshine breaking through a dark, sullen cloud.

By now there was an impressive mob of clients in the waiting room. Some were standing outside on the pavement. This latter was really a misnomer, as it was composed of beaten earth. Dogs were barking. Cats were complaining. People were laughing and talking loudly. It sounded more like a cocktail party than a vet's waiting room. A clump of Africans stood crammed together in the doorway waiting for advice or drugs. High pitched Indian voices rose and fell.

Aberdeenshire was never like this. There was invariably a reverent hush in the waiting room, a gloomy silence, a feeling of bored resignation. People sat immobile and rigid as though afraid to move for fear of becoming a focus of attention. Eyes studied tweed-covered knees or the pattern on the linoleum or past copies of *The Farmer* and *Stockbreeder*. An air of stupefied tedium hung everywhere like a miasma. People seldom laughed or joked, and, if they did, there wasn't much humour in it. Perhaps all this was due to the harshness of their lives, or to the flat, cold, treeless landscape. Whatever the cause, life for them was a grim and serious affair.

On the surface this did not seem to be the case in Kenya, although I have no doubt that for many people life was as difficult, if not more so, as it was for those dour Aberdeenshire farmers. Maybe the light and the sunshine and the warmth, the spectacular landscape and the kaleidoscope of various peoples made them see life through different eyes.

I closed the door behind each client to deaden the Babel of sound. The cases came in thick and fast – dogs to vaccinate against distemper and leptospirosis, dogs to have their nails clipped, a tom-cat to be castrated, an Alsatian with canker of the ear, an old dachshund to have its tartar-covered teeth scaled and cleaned.

Two Africans brought in a yellow mongrel, leading it by a piece of string. There was a flourishing trade in dogs between Kenya and Uganda. The Ugandan buyers were keen to have large, strong dogs as guards or pets, but before they could cross the border each dog had to be accompanied by a valid rabies certificate, a health certificate and a movement permit issued by the Veterinary Department. It was the second of these three items which was required on this occasion. The dog was strong and healthy and fit to travel. I signed the certificate, they paid the 5 shilling fee and departed for the District Veterinary Office.

Clients arrived requesting medicines for deworming their stock, intra-mammary preparations for treating cows with mastitis, ophthalmic ointments for treating infected eyes, vaccines for sheep and cattle.

The white farmers were generally in a hurry, knew what they wanted and could be dealt with speedily and efficiently.

The Africans were often quite the opposite. Before one could reach a tentative diagnosis and suggest a treatment, a lengthy interrogation was frequently required merely to get an outline of the bare bones of the problem. My infantile knowledge of Swahili didn't help either.

At first I thought it was because of my Scottish accent or my primitive command of the language but whenever I asked an African farmer a question he would answer, ''eh?' Then I thought it might be due to some inherent deafness to certain sound-waves, a bit like my inability to hear bats on the wing. Finally I realised that in many instances it was just an automatic reaction to any question because if I waited patiently and said nothing, the listener would eventually reply without further prompting.

This sort of thing didn't make for short, snappy conversations.

I would spend half an hour getting to the root of a problem, discussing how to treat it and how to prevent it, only to have the wretched recipient of my wisdom and knowledge say that that was all very well but as he didn't have two cents to rub together there wasn't much he could do about it. As an exercise in applied frustration it couldn't be bettered.

By the time the afternoon drew to a close I was feeling fairly ragged round the edges, as I battled to maintain some semblance of control on the more or less constant flow of people bringing in animals for attention, others requesting drugs, and yet others asking for advice on conditions of which I was barely aware, far less qualified to pontificate upon. I had to ensure that everything was written down, that those who had no accounts paid cash and were given receipts, that those who did, signed their invoices.

The pangs of hunger which had gnawed at my vitals earlier in the afternoon had subsided. My stomach merely felt as though it had contracted to the size of a walnut.

Fortunately everything on that first afternoon was of a fairly routine nature. No knotty problems required my attention. Neither was I haled over hill and dale to attend to some animal disaster in the furthest corner of the practice. These were reserved for later, although not as late as I hoped. Compared to what did come later, that first day could almost have been described as quiet and restful. It was its novelty and my inexperience which made it seem so long

The last straggler departed, I switched on the outside security light, bade the staff good-night, and, as swiftly as the road surface and traffic regulations would allow, drove to my employer's residence at Lanet. It was 6pm. This gave me approximately 45 minutes in which to inspect the inhabitants of the kennels which lay behind the house.

James and Karanja, the kennel men, were hard at work feeding the dogs when I arrived. The noise was horrific. It reverberated against the high, wooden stockade which surrounded the kennels, like that of an amplified pack of bloodhounds giving tongue as they pursued some wretched, escaped convict through the marshes. By the time I had finished checking that all inmates were present and correct, my head was swimming. They had been fed on a mixture of cooked meat and maize meal. I was glad I didn't have to eat it. It looked revolting.

It was almost dark.

I could smell something succulent cooking in the kitchen and my salivary glands, which I feared might by now have atrophied through lack of use, secreted furiously.

I tottered into the bathroom, and under the beady gaze of the now alert bushbaby, sluiced limbs and torso in the coffee-coloured water which gushed in fits and starts from rusted taps. The bushbaby peed on the palms of its tiny hands and hurled itself around its cage.

I had to get out of the bath only once to answer the telephone and it cut off just as I was about to lift it off its cradle.

The evening meal was prepared and presented by old Opondo. It consisted of asparagus soup, boiled fish and pineapple fritters. How I came to hate those pineapple fritters! Opondo had been taught how to concoct these culinary horrors shortly before the Owen-Jones' departed coastwards and thereafter, as far as desserts were concerned, his cooking horizon was to shrink and narrow until he could think of nothing else. Occasionally there might be a lapse in which fruit salad would appear, but then it was back to the fritters again.

The Owen-Jones' had locked their drinks cabinet before they left and the fridge was innocent of alcohol. So, instead of cleansing my tainted palate with a great tankard of ice cold Whitecap, I had to content myself with orange juice and water.

Before he went off duty, having cleared the table and washed the dishes, Opondo handed me a large, round, old fashioned alarm clock, asking me to set it for half past five, which was the time he started work. I did so and wound it up.

'Ta lete chai saa kumi na mbili? Shall I bring tea in the morning at six?'

It was less a question than a statement.

I wearily nodded assent.

'Kwaheri bwana.' (Goodnight, sir).

'Kwaheri Opondo.'

He shuffled out.

I perused the Owen-Jones' rather meagre library, and skimmed through a week old copy of the *Tropical Enquirer*.

I idly turned the pages. The paper was thick and rough, the type uneven and blotchy. Dramatic headlines leapt at the reader – 'Suspect cannibals arrested', 'Woman exhibits bitten off ear lobe' – wrapped in tin foil and hidden in her bra! – exhibit number one in a Nairobi court case. Apparently the biting off of ears was a not uncommon occurrence in Kenya, especially when beer parties got out of hand.

Ye Gods, I thought.

I moved on to the parliamentary section.

A Mr Mayega was quoted on the possible introduction of high-speed trains into the country, saying that this would not be an immediate undertaking – 'With speed trains one would arrive at one's destination too early. At the present you get to your destination just at the right time,' he added.

I could hardly believe my eyes, which by now were barely capable of focusing on the printed page.

I pressed on.

'Ant victim gets fresh start'. 'Discipline wild sect'. What could these mean? And what was 'Thin lips and killer apes' all about? 'Kenyans thrown to sharks' screamed another headline.

With material such as this, who needed books?

The correspondence columns were also crammed with fascinating vignettes. A few mysterious lines swam into my ken. 'There would be lesser risks as some boys end up with their private organs completely chopped off'! Strip show – 'Some girls strip themselves naked at the shores of Lake Victoria in Homa Bay. People pass here in big numbers'. This cri de coeur came from one Anthony Obombo.

I could take no more.

I could barely keep my eyes open. Outside the crickets were in full cry, filling the night with harsh sound.

An even harsher sound was the sudden, strident shriek of the telephone.

'God rot Alexander Graham Bell!' I muttered.

An aristocratic female voice haw-hawed at the other end of the line, enquiring whether horse-sickness vaccine was available, as she wanted me to come out to her place at Bahati to inoculate her string of thorough-breds, as soon as possible please, so that they would be protected before the onset of the rains in March. I told her that we had plenty in stock and that I would come out sometime next day. She thanked me and I replaced the receiver.

I felt shattered. It was time to hit the hammock.

There were mosquitoes in the bedroom. I knew because of the raised bites on my face and arms the following morning. But I didn't feel them at the time because I was fast asleep.

CHAPTER THREE

I had been in Kenya rather less than 14 months. The date was 7th February 1968 and I was on my way to examine a herd of cattle suspected of being infected with breeding disease. The farm was owned by an Italian Count and was approached by a narrow dirt road lined with tall blue gumtrees, which bent and swayed and hissed in the wind. Looking back, the deep hollow in which the town lay could be seen over the lip of the hillside upon which spread grey-green pastures and rust-coloured soil, newly-turned in preparation for planting. It was early in the morning and I manoeuvred my well-worn Volkswagen Beetle over the single line track of the Uganda railway which crossed the road to the farm and bumped over the potholes towards distant buildings.

At 7,000 feet the air was crisp and fresh. The sky was cloudless and light blue and the eastern edge of the Rift Valley thirty miles away could be seen with amazing clarity. My thoughts turned to my forthcoming trip up Mt. Kenya later in the month and visions of snow and glaciers scintillating on the equator sent a surge of vitality through my veins.

My Beetle chugged on up the track past some farm workers who waved as I drove by.

'Jambo! Habari gani!' (Hello! How are you!)

An ox-cart came creaking down the road and I hugged the verge to let it past.

'Jambo! Jambo!'

Not for the first time I thought, hey, if this was Scotland, all I would get would be a hard stare and an 'Aye! Aye!' – if I was lucky.

A young African carrying a tall whip with the thong trailing in the dust walked beside the massive lumbering wagon which was piled high with firewood and drawn by six enormous oxen, huge humped beasts, brindled, brown, black and cream. The tracks made by the great, iron-shod wheels snaked behind in the dust like those made by a pair of drunken cyclists.

In one of the fields, a pair of crowned cranes strutted regally over the pasture. Cape rooks chuckled conversationally to each other from the tops of fence posts. Iridescent starlings trotted cheekily along the road before flying off. A small flock of cattle egrets glided gracefully down to execute a perfect two-point landing beside a group of grazing cows.

I drove into a jacaranda-flanked avenue leading to the home of farm manager Enrico Fornari, and his well-fleshed wife, Rosanna. The house was spacious and fronted by an extensive garden, full of exotic shrubs and flowers. I carefully parked the car at the back of the building, well clear of wires stretched between trees to which were chained a pair of ferocious German Shepherds. The dogs' chains were clipped to the wires allowing them to run their full length. Another pair of dogs was on running wires at the front of the house so the whole place was virtually surrounded by these alarming beasts. Woe betide the luckless stranger who had the misfortune to approach the house unaware of their presence. More than one unfortunate wanderer in search of employment had been seen legging it across the fields minus segments of his nether garments.

'Buon giorno, dottore!' beamed Enrico as I got out of the car, keeping one eye on the nearest canine which was having a noisy paroxysm at my arrival.

Dottore! In darkest Aberdeen-shire, where I had last worked, I had been called many things, but never doctor. My professional thorax swelled with pride.

Enrico was about 50, muscular, built like Mussolini, but unlike El Duce he sported a solid shock of iron-grey hair. He wore a checked shirt, sleeves rolled up to reveal brawny forearms, burnt to the colour of mahogany. Round his waist was a broad leather belt supporting a pair of ancient corduroy trousers, while his feet were encased in massive army boots. A glint of gold chain could be espied beneath the frayed shirt collar, the bearer of a crucifix or some religious medal. Captured by the British forces in Ethiopia during the war, Enrico had been interned for a time in a P.O.W. camp at Gilgil, in Kenya's Rift Valley, before being sent to work on a settler's farm near Thomson's Falls. When the war was over, Enrico decided to stay on in East Africa and after working on a number of farms, came to Njoro. He had married Rosanna by proxy after a lengthy correspondence with friends, relations and clergy in Italy. The daughter of one of his uncle's best friends, she had known nothing either of Enrico or Africa other than what she had been told or what she had read. Luckily this matrimonial shot-in-the-dark had turned out well and the marriage was a happy one.

Unlike many Italians of long standing in Kenya, both Enrico and Rosanna spoke fluent, if ungrammatical, English. Until my Swahili became more fluent, communication with some of the less linguistically-gifted members of the Italian community had to be conducted virtually in sign language. Curiously, their knowledge of Swahili was usually excellent.

The farm was a mixed one, growing wheat and maize and running dairy cattle and sheep on pastures of star grass, kikuyu grass and rhodes leys. The dairy herd, which I had come to see, was predominately Ayrshire, but Enrico also had a hump-backed zebu Boran bull which he kept for use on those cows which proved more difficult than average to get in calf. Consequently a small proportion of the herd was now half-bred – excellent animals when conditions were harsh, but often possessing an uncertain temperament, especially where strangers were concerned.

Recently the conception rate in the herd had been giving cause for concern. At first Enrico was not overly worried but when more and more animals came on heat and the bull began to lose weight from a surfeit of receptive females, he deemed it time to seek advice.

The description given suggested either vibriosis or trichomoniasis. Both are venereal diseases transmitted by infected bulls. One method of diagnosis is to take samples of cervical mucus and subject them to an agglutination test in a laboratory.

I explained this to Enrico as we approached the dairy and also that, should one or other of these diseases be confirmed, the bull could be treated with various drugs, but that a switch to the use of artificial insemination in the adult herd would be the method of choice.

Enrico grunted like a rutting warthog and pushed open the wicket gate into the dairy. This consisted of a large paved area with an open wooden dairy at one side: simply a dozen partitions fronted by a narrow trough. The low, corrugated iron roof was supported by massive wooden pillars. Each stall held a single cow restrained by a yoke with a wooden bar behind her hind legs. Most of the cows were Ayrshires but some, I noticed, were cross bred zebus.

A few milkers awaited our arrival. They were mostly Kalenjin-Kipsigis and Nandi tribesmen from the highlands overlooking the steaming plains bordering Lake Victoria. Their coppery skins, perforated ear lobes and slender frames revealed their Nilo-Hamitic ancestry.

'First rate cattlemen, ze Kips,' Enrico extolled their virtues, at the same time no doubt closing his eyes to the disappearance of the odd calf and the adulteration of his milk with water. Nevertheless, their reputation as stockmen was excellent, being sympathetic to and having an affinity for their animals.

'Much better than ze Kikuyus,' said Enrico. 'Someting to do viz being cooped up in ze forests for hundreds of years with nothink but goats and monkeys for company, while ze Kips and Nandi were out in ze open studying ranch management and dairying!'

The swabs which I was using consisted of a small roll of sterile gauze to which a string about 18 inches long was attached. The swab was held inside a tough tube made of a black PVC material containing a wooden rod which was used to extrude the swab into the forward part of the cow's vagina.

I pulled on a pair of wellington boots and donned a calving overall in order to protect my person from the dung and urine which bovine patients seemed to void in unnecessarily large amounts whenever I approached them from the rear. I assembled the dozen swabs in their holders and started moving along the line of selected cows, all repeat breeders which had continually returned on heat after having been presumed to be in calf. One herdsman held the animal's tail while another cleaned the vulval area with a cloth dipped into a bucket of warm water, carried and guarded with assiduous care by a spindly youth with knees like a pair of sun-blackened King Edward potatoes.

The ninth animal was a brindled beast with a small hump, her head in the yoke, and a bar behind her hind legs which were tied together above the hocks with a short leather thong.

I stepped behind the animal, the herdsman elevated her tail and I reached forward with the swab in order to insert it into her vagina as I had done with the previous eight animals.

There was a fearful crash, a blow like a sledge-hammer full in my face, everything went momentarily dark, and I was propelled backwards with frightening force and uncanny precision, full square into one of the massive wooden supports holding up the corrugated iron roof. I regained whatever consciousness I had lost as I slid slowly to the foot of the pillar. Dazed and groggy, I felt as though I was surfacing after a general anaesthetic, wondering where I was, not knowing what had happened and unable to think clearly or to focus my gaze on any one particular object. A babble of voices sounded in my ear and I felt myself being lifted to my feet, strong arms supporting me. A sharp and agonising stab of pain shot through my right leg which collapsed when I tried to place it on the ground. The dairy and its occupants, animal and human, leapt about like a sort of demented equatorial aurora borealis.

When things had sorted themselves out and returned to their normal positions, I found Enrico before me as I stood, Long John Silver-like, on my one good leg, propped up on either side by a couple of sinewy Nandi milkers, whose close proximity was a powerful reminder of the often taken-for-granted advantages bestowed on society by the makers of Imperial Leather bath soap.

Enrico was staring at me with a look of some concern on his weather-beaten features. In his right hand he held a tumbler which was three-quarters full of an amber-coloured fluid. It struck me as being rather early in the day to be quaffing spirits, but when another shooting star of agony exploded in my leg I did not refuse the proffered glass.

'That cow, as you come on her from behind, she jump forwards into ze yoke and kick up and backwards at ze same time weeth both legs tied together. Boom! She kick you full in ze face and you fly backwards and hit your back-side on ze wood and fall down. Your face it looks O.K., a bit bloody perhaps, but your leg I tink is hurt, maybe broken. Best if we take you to ze hospital in Nakuru.'

Despite my predicament I noted that in the general excitement Enrico's command of English had dropped a notch or two.

By this time I was beginning to think it might be best as well, as my leg was beginning to throb in a rather unpleasant, rapid, rhythmic fashion and my foot, still encased in its wellington boot, felt several times its normal size.

Enrico rushed off and jumped into his Peugeot 404 pick-up, which he backed up to the wicket gate. His wife and a house-servant laid a mattress in the back, together with a blanket and pillow. It must have looked quite cosy but at the time I was in no condition to appreciate it. In excruciating slow motion I hobbled across the yard and was winched onto the mattress by several men.

I knocked back another slug of Scotland's Best, Enrico got behind the steering wheel and we set off for Nakuru. A flop-eared Kipsigis called Kiprotich jumped up beside me, presumably to prevent my ending it all en-route. Nakuru was twelve miles away, part of the way being on a dirt road. So, what with the vibration of the vehicle, the occasional jolt into a pothole, the rattling over the railway line, and the general swerving about to avoid stray dogs, jay-walking pedestrians and vehicles approaching on the wrong side of the road, the journey as far as I was concerned was not a happy one. But I am glad to say that my passage through country and town apparently did help to enliven the otherwise routine day of those who observed my passing. At least this is what I was later told. At the time I was in no state to take note of the reaction of the various bus drivers, minibus passengers, cyclists and pedestrians, goggling at the sight of a European with blood all over his face, lying on the back of a pick-up, apparently being carted off to hospital and looking like the survivor of a Mau Mau attack.

During moments of clarity, my main concern was that I might not be completely fit for my trip up Mt. Kenya in a couple of weeks time. But I felt sure that once I had been attended to by the medico, by some miracle of modern healing I would be out and about in no time. My present discomfort was due to severe bruising and concussion, that was all.

Eventually the pick-up turned into the drive of the Nakuru War Memorial Hospital, an imposing complex, stone-walled and red-roofed, built in the form of an open-ended-square. The pick-up stopped opposite a concrete ramp. My foot, still encased in its wellington boot, felt hot and

47

swollen to several times its normal size. Enrico hopped out, rushed off, and soon returned, followed by a couple of hospital orderlies pushing a stretcher on wheels, and behind them, proceeding at a more leisurely pace, as befitted his professional status, was Dr Satchwell, an ancient choleric Irishman with whom I had a nodding acquaintance.

I raised my arm in salutation, to be met with a hoarse bellow from Satch. 'What the divil de ye think ye're doin'? Ye're supposed to have a broken collar bone!'

It transpired that Mrs Fornari had phoned the hospital to warn the staff of my imminent arrival. The combination of excitable Italian volubility, and a telephone system seemingly designed in the Dark Ages, coupled with the inability of the African receptionist at the other end of a crackling line to comprehend more than one word in two of Mrs Fornari's machine-gun fire English, had led to the mistake.

Satchwell peered over the tailboard and paid no further attention to my shoulder after I had brusquely informed him that there seemed to be something amiss with my right leg and that my foot felt about the size of a prize vegetable marrow.

Just then a dazzling apparition in female form, clad in spotless white, glided up, seized my wrist, and, scrutinising a watch pinned to her shapely bosom, proceeded to count my pulse. Satchwell watched, and apart from an occasional grunt, said nothing. Obviously I wasn't on the critical list.

The wheeled stretcher was taxied alongside and, still on my mattress, I was lifted onto it. Up the ramp we went, along a verandah with a stone balustrade and then round a corner and down a long corridor. Being recumbent, I was afforded a good view of the ceiling and was relieved to note that the corners were dust and cobweb-free.

We entered a ward. I knew this by the fact that the African orderlies, with admirable precision, thrust the bows of the trolley, which were next to my skull, through a pair of swing doors, rather like a gunman in the Old West bursting through the batwing doors into a crowded saloon. A bed was approached round which a screen had been drawn. An ominous sign I thought. My apprehension was justified when I was lifted from the stretcher and dropped from what seemed like a height of two feet onto the bed. A loud, crunching, grating noise emanated from my upper right thigh, which I was later told had been heard at the other end of the corridor, and the discomfort was considerable. My Mt. Kenya mountaineering prospects suddenly appeared rather less rosy.

The angel in white reappeared. She was the theatre sister and her name was Heather Forbes. Her husband worked for the East African Power and Lighting Company, more usually referred to by the general public as the Power and Darkness, a name apparently bestowed upon it by some jaundiced devotee of Shakespeare because of the regular power cuts and

48

sudden plunges into darkness which afflicted those whose premises were wired up to the grid. She told me that a Mr Thakkar, a surgeon, would be along to examine me soon. Meanwhile, was I a fully paid-up member of the National Hospital Insurance Fund? This was a scheme whereby the employer deducted a minimal sum every month from his employee's salary, with which he bought a stamp from the N.H.I.F. This he affixed to his employee's card. Presentation of this card upon admission to hospital entitled the bearer to substantial reductions in charges. I professed my ignorance regarding the fund but presumed that my honourable employer Arthur Owen-Jones had the matter well in hand.

I had, in my naivety, assumed that a fellow member of my own profession, and especially my own employer, would indeed behave in an honourable fashion. I was soon to be disillusioned. Not only had he done nothing about National Hospital Insurance Fund contributions, neither had he provided for any insurance cover in case of an accident sustained by any of his employees during the course of their work.

As we talked, a member of the lower echelons was scissoring my good grey flannels from ankle to hip, my wellington boot having been removed as it had been giving olfactory offence to adjacent patients. Massive contusion and swelling came into view. A nurse gave me a sedative by injection and about an hour later Mr Thakkar strode briskly into the ward, accompanied by Miss Brown, the matron.

Mr Thakkar was a middle-aged Asian, inclining towards corpulence. His shrewd black eyes moved constantly as he questioned, prodded and probed. Miss Brown was an elderly Scottish spinster. Seemingly humour-less, her rigid features betrayed none of her thoughts. Her gimlet-like orbs bored like laser beams through the helpless and hapless patient, who, even if he was not guilty of some major or minor infringement of the rules, felt sure that he must have offended in some way against hospital etiquette and might as well confess and get it off his chest before he found himself in even hotter water.

Later in the morning I was wheeled down to the X-ray room to have some pictures taken of my leg. They revealed that I had multiple fractures of my right femur – one spiral fracture and three parallel fractures – and the lesser trochanter, a knobble on the bone, had been sheared right off. *Great,* I thought, *bang goes my trip up Mt. Kenya.*

Back in the ward a tubular splint was fitted to my offending limb as a temporary measure until a more permanent solution could be found. Called a Thomas splint, I assumed it had been named after the man who had invented it. I also assumed that he had never had the misfortune to have had one fitted to one of his own limbs. The upper part consisted of a ring which fitted over the thigh. This was a cause of some discomfort, as every now and again its pressure on the muscles caused them to violently contract, bringing the ends of the broken bone into exquisitely unpleasant juxtaposition. On such occasions, Thomas was my least favourite disciple.

In the afternoon my employer and his wife Gwyneth came to see me, the first of four such visits I was honoured to receive during the next three months. By this time, a huge, blackish-purple bruise had formed over my upper thigh. This much aroused Mr Owen-Jones' professional curiosity. Strangely enough, my face, which had borne the full brunt of my patient's horny feet, remained unmarked, a fact which was the cause of much wonderment and hilarity.

Mr Thakkar returned and informed me that my evening repast would be a light one, as the following morning he intended to investigate my condition more closely under general anaesthesia and that if more radical treatment was indicated, would proceed forthwith, with my agreement of course. As is usually the case, the patient, when confronted by such a situation, nods with bovine acceptance of his fate, knowing full well that he has little choice in the matter and that any querying of the sawbones' views would be futile. The patient at the time is often in no fit state to engage in the cut and thrust of surgical debate with his medical adviser. So it was with me.

That evening a non-meal of soup, ice cream and cocoa was dished up by a lugubrious African ward attendant. Soon afterwards, the two night sisters made their appearance, probably alerted by the rumblings of my stomach. They were both Irish nuns – Sister Borgia and Sister Fidelma.

The former – her name filled me with a certain foreboding – was middle-aged, stout, cheerful and alarmingly competent. The latter was young, slim, coquettish and good-looking. Both spoke with a soft, soothing, southern Irish brogue.

Sister Fidelma seemed to enjoy a certain malicious satisfaction as she withdrew a syringe full of amber-coloured sedative from a curiously shaped vial and slid the needle, with a practice obviously borne of long experience, into my unresisting upper arm.

The following morning, a cheerful gang of grinning African attendants wheeled the mobile stretcher up to my bed and with admirable expertise, rolled me onto it. I was wearing one of those hideous, green hospital gowns taped up the back and manufactured specifically to project one's rump into the passing breeze. As I was trundled off to the operating theatre I cursed the buttock-fetishist who had designed this ghastly garment. The anaesthetist shoved his needle into a vein on my forearm and intoned his over-worn mantra – 'Now count up to ten....'

After what seemed like a few minutes I was being lifted back into my bed in the ward. The surgeon, Mr Thakkar and theatre sister Heather Forbes supervised the manipulations. I was conscious that the foot of the bed had been jacked up on blocks to what seemed like an extraordinary height, so much so that my head was a good deal lower than my feet. A long stainless steel rod protruded from either side of the upper part of my tibia, just below the knee – it went the whole way through. Stuck on either end of the rod were a pair of large corks and on each side of the rod, next to each cork, a cord was attached. Somewhere about the level of my ankle the two cords were knotted together and a single cord ran over a pulley bolted to the iron frame of the bed. At the end of the cord was suspended a metal hook holding a pile of weights. They looked identical to those used by a butcher or greengrocer to weigh one's weekly scrag-end or poundage of potatoes. All that was missing was an adjacent pile of *Daily Mirrors* or *News of the Worlds*. My personal poundage was twelve.

Mr Thakkar explained that it had proved to be impracticable to plate or pin my fractured femur. As the fractures were all in the upper third of the bone, with little displacement and with reasonable alignment apart from a degree of over-riding, he had decided to opt for a conservative approach by keeping my leg in extension and traction. The theory behind the weights was that they should gradually correct the over-riding. This would be done by slowly adding to the weights already hanging at the end of my bed. Apart from a feeling of pressure on the pin through my tibia, there was no pain or discomfort.

The bed felt singularly firm compared with others I had slept in. A quick feel with my hand beneath the mattress revealed solid wood – bed boards! Wonderful! As my leg was in extension and festooned with rods and weights, I was unable to turn over. I would be obliged to sleep on my back – and tilted upwards to boot. Other more intimate problems sprang to mind. And there was always the nagging matter of payment.

There was no National Health Scheme in Kenya.

I asked the surgeon how long it would take before I would be fit for work. About three months in hospital plus another three on crutches, he said. That, in his opinion, would be the minimum period. Well, I thought, that pretty well wraps things up for the next six months. There's no point in worrying about it. Just relax and enjoy the attention while it lasts.

CHAPTER FOUR

Contrary to my expectations I found that my sojourn in hospital, like the curate's egg, was not wholly unpleasant.

Until the tight fitting, spasm-producing, Thomas splint had been replaced by a larger model, and was finally removed, my first ten days were not particularly comfortable, but thereafter things gradually improved.

It took some time before I became accustomed to the bed boards, the rubber undersheet, the tilting of the bed, and the pile of weights attached to my leg.

Clamped to the bed was a rather primitive scaffolding constructed of tubular metal. Suspended from one of the upper cross members was a strong chain with a wooden handle at its lower end. By means of this device I was able to raise myself off the bed in order to allow the nursing staff to perform such essential tasks as changing the sheets. It also helped to aerate my frequently numbed gluteals.

Sleep did not come easily o'nights. This was partly due to my enforced position on my back, unable to turn onto my side, but more to the proximity of the railway station to the hospital. Almost every night, usually between 2-4am when life, and that included mine, was at its lowest ebb, the earth-shattering screech of a train's whistle would erupt into my sub- or unconscious state. It was so loud that it sounded like a ship steaming up the Channel in thick fog, siren booming. I once woke up, sweating, from a nightmare in which the hospital was a drifting iceberg, being rammed by the Titanic with its foghorn trumpeting like a charging bull elephant, while I clung like a marooned mariner to the berg's slippery sides. It was just another train.

The signalmen and level-crossing keepers at that time of the morning, although supposedly on duty and alert to approaching trains, were invariably asleep. As a result a short peep on the whistle was deemed insufficient to rouse them. It had to be a decent three minute blast.

Not that the engine drivers were blameless. Whether they lacked that delicate touch on the throttle, which I had always assumed was necessary to bring the wheeled monster gliding smoothly and softly into the station, or whether it was due to inattention or drowsiness, I do not know, but they invariably hit the buffers with a crash that seemed to rock the hospital to its very foundations. Heaven knows what it did to the passengers and freight.

So, in spite of the sleeping tablets which I thrust nightly, on medical insistence, into my reluctant maw, under the stern gaze of the current night sister, my slumber was often fitful. Creaking floorboards, the whine of dive bombing mosquitoes, the ringing of the night bell as some bed-bound patient desperately signalled that his bladder was on the point of rupture and could someone please bring one of those revolting tell-tale enamel flasks into which he could relieve himself in shameful secrecy under the bedclothes, all added to the initial difficulties in nodding off.

After a while I found that these auditory disturbances faded into the background and I almost missed them if they weren't there. If the 3.30am blast on the train whistle wasn't on time, I found myself wondering if there had been some fearful derailment further up the line. I envisaged concertinaed wagons, the hiss of steam escaping from ruptured boilers and the yells of passengers trapped in the wreckage. And if old Smith-Dobson didn't ring his bell, had his bladder finally burst with a muffled report, leaving him to expire alone and unnoticed by an uncaring world?

The surgeon, possibly in a moment of mental aberration, casually mentioned one day that, as I was otherwise fit and apparently healthy – apart from my leg of course – a bottle of beer a day would not be contra-indicated. Indeed, it might be a valuable method of boosting my depleted protein reserves. I eagerly concurred with his advice, and, nodding sagely, told him that I would act upon it with dispatch.

Beside the bed was a wooden locker and into this, visiting friends deposited their offerings of Pilsner, Tusker and Whitecap. Many a convivial evening was spent quietly imbibing the best that Kenya Breweries could offer. Tankards were in short supply. Only one tooth glass was available but after a hard day's work on the farm none of my visitors complained about that. These friends would silently slip into the ward after dark when the matron had gone off duty. About half a dozen cronies would gather round my bed, and, while the night sister turned an understanding blind eye, a pleasant evening would be passed. I wasn't ill, so no harm was done, and as my locker was invariably full, it was nice to be able to offer something to those kind enough to take the trouble to come to the hospital.

One morning the matron, Miss Brown, materialised in the ward at an hour much earlier than was her normal wont. She moved steadily and remorselessly in my direction, stopping for a few minutes at the beds of the other patients in the ward as she did so.

Had she noticed, as I had just noticed, that the lads of last night had neglected to remove their empties from the window ledge where they had so carelessly left them? I, being attached by various weights, pulleys and ropes to the bed, was unable to reach them. It wasn't unusual for the odd dead man to be left behind, but as the matron normally didn't appear in the ward until the morning was well advanced, there was plenty of time in which to persuade one of the lower nursing orders to pop it into my locker. But on this particular morning there were at least a dozen assorted beer bottles of various brands staring the bright new day, and, very shortly, the matron, shamelessly in the face.

I felt trapped, as indeed I was. I was like a rabbit mesmerised by an approaching serpent.

I studied that morning's *Tropical Enquirer*, which had been brought to the hospital by an itinerant news vendor, with more than usual interest, while covertly watching the matron's inexorable advance.

Perhaps she hadn't noticed the bottles and our conversation would pass lightly from how I had slept, to any problems I might be currently experiencing, and from there to the subject of the present unusually heavy rain, at which point she would bid me a cheerful good day.

'You're looking a bit peaky this morning, Mr Cran!'

Miss Brown's voice boomed in my right ear.

I jumped, or as much as it was possible to jump in my position.

'Yes, Matron. Didn't sleep too well. Those sleeping pills I was given last night didn't seem to work. Perhaps they should be changed for something else.'

'Hmm. You wouldn't be suffering from a hangover by any chance would you?'

She glanced pointedly at the row of bottles sitting on the window shelf like jury members who had just decided on their verdict. I knew only too well what that verdict would be.

'Good grief, no, Matron. Although possibly one or two of my friends might be!'

I gave a hollow laugh.

She grunted.

'Well, when your friends come back tell them to take their bottles away. I don't want to see them in this hospital ever again. Do I make myself quite clear? In the meantime let's get them out of sight. This happens to be a hospital, not a drinking den.'

To my horror she seized my locker, obviously intending to turn it, the easier to put the empties inside. Her protuberant eyes widened in astonishment as she attempted to move it. From her struggles it looked as though she was trying to move a cast iron safe. Her face turned an alarming shade of mauve and I feared she might have an apoplectic fit. She bellowed like a Boran bull for a nurse, who scurried into the ward, obviously expecting, from her expression of concern, to find one of the patients suffering from some serious medical emergency.

'Help me turn this locker round, nurse,' the matron gasped. 'I want to find out what's inside. It's so heavy I wouldn't be surprised if Mr Cran's been storing gold bullion in it.'

I felt this to be an unwarranted intrusion into what little privacy I was afforded in the hospital, and intimated my view politely and diplomatically to Miss Brown, who made a noise like a dyspeptic wildebeest.

They got the locker turned and the matron opened the doors with a triumphant flourish.

She found what I knew she would find – scores of full and empty beer bottles, with the odd bottle of whisky standing aloof amid the plebeian crowd.

Miss Brown's features became suddenly unpleasantly mottled and her jugulars stood out on either side of her sinewy neck like a pair of purple hosepipes. She reminded me of an unfortunate turkey whose corpse I had recently dissected in an effort to determine the malady from which it had succumbed.

I will draw a veil over the proceedings of the next few minutes, but for several nights thereafter I suffered from dreams of a terrifyingly vivid nature in which I was a helpless prisoner, gagged and bound to a chair, being interrogated by the matron dressed in Gestapo uniform, riding crop in one hand and thumbscrews in the other, while a blinding spotlight bored into my eyes.

My friends, of course, were untroubled by such nightly disturbances, and continued to ferry their offerings to the hospital, but, after relating my horrifying experience, they were kind enough to exercise a modicum of discretion.

Our evening sessions continued, albeit at a more subdued level.

🏛✕🏛✕🏛✕

One afternoon about a week later, while immersed in an improving book, I was visited, outside official hours, by a client.

A genial bachelor of about 40, Percy Cameron worked for an insurance company, and kept border collies as pets.

On this particular occasion, although the weather was wet, it hardly justified the tweed jacket he was wearing. We were, after all, only 10 miles south of the equator.

I noticed that his embryo beer belly had grown considerably since I had last seen him and that, instead of being smooth and round, it appeared to be angular and active.

Percy approached the bed with a conspiratorial grin.

He opened his jacket and revealed a young border collie.

'Ye Gods, Percy!' I whispered. 'If the matron comes in we're both for the high jump!'

My recent brush with authority was still fresh in my mind.

'It's OK. It's her afternoon off. I checked before I came in. I'd just like you to have a look at Jock's skin. He's itching like crazy. The hair on his back is dry and falling out, especially in front of his tail.'

Jock wriggled and twisted in his master's arms. I shot a nervous glance towards the door of the ward and then glanced at the other beds. Their occupants appeared to be either asleep, dozing or dead.

'Let's have a look.'

Percy set Jock down on the counterpane on the left-hand side of the bed, the other side being obstructed by my pinioned nether limb. As he did so a flea leapt onto the sheet and vanished. A frantic search beneath the bedclothes found the brute hiding under my pillow. He was silently and summarily executed and his body thrown into the waste paper basket.

The thought of a nurse reporting the finding of a flea in Cran's sleeping quarters made my blood run cold. In the absence of an entomologist how was I to prove it wasn't mine and if it wasn't mine then how did it get there? The ramifications didn't bear thinking about.

'For God's sake don't let that happen again!' I hissed at Percy as though he was personally responsible, which of course he was.

Jock had a dermatitis affecting his lower back and the root of his tail. The hair was dry, thin and broken with areas of inflammation where he had been biting and rubbing the skin. On the inside of his hind legs and on the ventral pelvic area where the hair is normally sparse there were several pink spots and papules. A few fleas could be seen slipping through the foliage, vanishing into the thick mat of black hair over his chest.

'Well, Percy', I said, 'I don't think there's any doubt that Jock's got a flea bite dermatitis.'

I went on to explain that this is caused by a hypersensitivity to flea bites and to the saliva in the creatures' mouth parts.

Percy's own mouth parts writhed in an involuntary rictus.

'You must keep Jock flea free,' I went on. 'If you do, this condition will clear up and his skin will be as good as new. It's essential to get rid of all the fleas. Even one or two are enough to bring about a relapse.'

Percy nodded.

I mentioned the names of a few proprietary dog washes which I knew were reliable and could be purchased without prescription in the town.

Percy was most grateful for the advice and assured me he would act upon it.

I asked him why he hadn't taken Jock to the surgery instead of going to all the trouble of smuggling him into the hospital.

'Well, I've always found your employer rather brusque and somewhat lacking in the social niceties. Also, I prefer my vet to at least give the impression that my dog's problems are uppermost in his mind when he's examining him and not those of the next in the queue. Besides you did a bloody good job on Fergus when he had epilepsy last year.'

Fergus was his other border collie.

As Percy crept out, tweed jacket well buttoned up, my thoughts turned to some of the other worthies who had swum into my ken during my short time in the country.

✿✿✿✿✿

My days in hospital were long and I had plenty of time to reflect on the colourful characters I had met in my first year in Nakuru.

There was Torquil Ridley-Pike, whom I had met when I went to his small farm at Bahati to treat one of his cows, which had mastitis. Torquil had been a squadron leader in the RAF during the War. Tall, lean and elegant with a silk cravat knotted immaculately round his patrician throat, he and his wife Lydia kept a few Guernsey cows, mainly to provide themselves and their immediate friends with fresh milk.

It was just after ten in the morning and Torquil had as yet not partaken of breakfast.

'Come up to the house, old boy, and have some bacon and eggs,' Torquil insisted.

I left my dusty boots at the door and followed Torquil into the dining room.

The wooden floor gleamed with polish. The dining table, which was made of some lovely dark timber, shone like a mirror. Six high backed chairs were ranged neatly round it. Hunting prints hung on the walls. A bowl of fruit stood on a sideboard.

A tall servant, clad in a spotless white kanzu with a red fez on his head, entered, and started silently and smoothly laying the table for breakfast.

Beside Torquil's place he placed a bottle of gin and a tonic water.

The solid section of the meal consisted of avocado pear, bacon, fried egg, sausage, and toast and marmalade. Torquil washed his portion down with copious draughts of gin. I stuck to tea.

Lydia drifted in halfway through the meal and nibbled at a piece of toast. Inserting a cigarette into a 6-inch long ivory holder she languidly drew in a lungful of smoke and let it trickle out of her fluted nostrils.

The conversation was witty and amusing, but the mixture of early-morning gin and tobacco fumes swirling over the bacon made me glad at

57

last to escape into the open air.

Torquil was a first class pilot, even in his cups. And so too had been Robin Torrance, the vet in Nakuru prior to the arrival of my employer.

On one occasion Torquil, Robin, and Pete McCrae, a farmer from Bahati, had been drinking heavily at the Njoro Club. It was a Sunday afternoon, all three had been propping up the bar since mid-morning and all three were very merry.

Torquil and Pete had been given a lift to the club by a neighbour driving on to Mau Narok.

'Time to go!' Pete suddenly boomed. ''smilking time an' if I'm not there in person half my milk will disappear down the throats of my bloody workers! Come on, Torquil, get your aristocratic arse off that stool and let's hit the road.'

'No can do, old fruit,' Torquil slurred. 'You're forgetting that we've no transport until old what's 'is name gets back from Mau Narok.'

Pete gave way to his frustration with a fearful oath which had the heads of hardened drinkers swivelling in his direction all along the bar.

'But there's no problem, me old hearties,' Robin interjected. 'The Old Bag's sitting out there on the strip. We'll have another round and then I'll fly you up to Bahati and land in that big field behind Pete's house. Barman!'

The Old Bag was Robin's trusty Tiger Moth, a fabric-covered biplane in which he was wont to fly to far flung clients.

'If my memory serves me aright,' Pete enunciated with difficulty, 'that thing that you are pleased to call a flying machine has only two seats and we be three.'

Pete was right. The Tiger Moth has indeed only two seats – or rather, two open cockpits, one behind the other. It is now a vintage aeroplane, redolent of helmets, goggles, and scarves streaming out in the wind. The pilot normally flies this plane from the rear seat. Unlike most modern aircraft, which have a nose wheel, the Tiger Moth has a tail wheel. This results in the plane sitting in a nose up position on the ground, and when taxiing the pilot has to weave from side to side in order to see where he is going. Take off and landing also present problems not encountered in nose wheel aircraft, and getting into and out of the cockpit requires physical attributes normally only found in Olympic gymnasts and double-jointed circus artistes.

Robin appeared to be sunk in what was either deep thought or alcoholic stupor, or a combination of both.

'You know how to ride, don't you Pete?'

'Well, I've done a bit of hacking now and again, but I wouldn't call myself an accomplished horseman. So what?'

'Because there's a saddle with all the necessary accoutrements right here in the Club. We'll fasten it to the fuselage behind the rear cockpit and Bob's your uncle. You're the lightest anyway.'

Pete appeared not to be as enthusiastic about this arrangement as Robin and Torquil, but after he had been informed that he would be supplied with reins, hunting cap and riding crop he entered into the situation with all the vim that his inebriated state would allow.

All three tottered out of the Club, down the steps and wove their way across to the strip. A bearer had been commandeered to carry the riding equipment.

The saddle was strapped by its girth to the fuselage behind Robin's seat. The reins were attached to the safety harness mountings of the rear cockpit.

By this time an interested throng of Club members and curious African onlookers had gathered to watch the proceedings.

Willing hands lifted Robin and Torquil into their respective cockpits.

Pete came next.

With his hunting cap set at a jaunty angle, riding crop tucked under his left armpit and reins professionally gathered in his hands, Pete cut a dashing figure. He adjusted his stirrups, jockey style.

'Take up the girth a couple of notches, will you,' he requested a bystander. 'We don't want the saddle slipping half way home, do we?'

Robin produced a small hunting horn from the pocket of his Harris tweed jacket and gave an ear-piercing blast.

Someone swung the propeller. The engine burst into life.

Robin ran through the checks, scrutinising the few dials on the panel with grim concentration, adjusting the fuel mixture, checking carburettor heat and both magnetos. Finally, after making sure that ailerons, rudder and elevator were all functioning normally, he opened the throttle and, lurching from side to side to see where he was going, taxied onto the runway.

A quick glance at the windsock to make ensure he was taking off into the wind and Robin swung the Old Bag up the centre of the runway, throttle fully open, engine blaring. Pete shortened his reins and hung on like grim death, his cap jammed down over his eyebrows.

Robin shoved the stick forwards, the Tiger Moth's tail rose off the ground and she was airborne.

The spectators cheered wildly and then turned back to the Club to drink to three friends whose drinking days were obviously over. Seconds later they were scattering for cover as the Tiger Moth howled over them, its wheels barely clearing the roof of the Club. Pete could be seen lashing the fuselage with his riding crop in an apparent attempt to induce the Old Bag to go a bit faster.

The biplane soared over the trees and rapidly contracted until it was a tiny buzzing speck in the far distance.

Fifteen minutes later, after circling the chosen field, Robin side-slipped the Old Bag down to make a perfect three-point landing behind Pete's house.

African workers, their eyes protruding like organ stops, goggled in amazement.

Pete, his own eyes somewhat more bloodshot than usual, swung himself stiffly to the ground and wrung Robin's hand. Torquil, a rather more elegant figure, cocked a leg over the side of the cockpit and dropped onto the grass.

Pete, at least, was now stone cold sober. He marched off towards the dairy, still wearing his hunting cap and slapping his leg with his riding crop.

The milkers bent their heads and milked frantically into their buckets.

They were never known to steal again.

Torquil meandered off quietly towards Pete's house to relax with a gin and tonic until Pete, his supervision of the milking over, could drive him home.

Robin taxied the Old Bag to the far end of the field.

Relieved of her passengers she was airborne within a few seconds of the throttle being opened and rapidly disappeared in the direction of Njoro.

✕✖✕✖✕✖✕

At the lower end of the Solai Valley lay the property of Franz Shroeder.

Franz was a splendidly jovial Teuton married to a rather serious and staid Ulster-woman of indeterminate years. Her placid, bovine temperament was in complete contrast to his friendly hail-fellow-well-met approach to everyone he came across.

His thick, iron-grey hair was cropped short. He invariably wore a pair of baggy, creased, khaki shorts and he walked energetically and urgently as though pressing business required his immediate attention.

Franz had a loud booming voice which enabled him to conduct one-sided conversations at ranges normally only audible to Kalahari bushmen and Australian aborigines.

Passing down the Solai Valley with its well-ordered farms, neat plantations of coffee, maize fields, and manicured paddocks full of sleek dairy cattle all grazing tidily in the same direction, one suddenly came to what appeared to be an extension of the Tugen reserve. The dirt road narrowed until it was a slender car-width thread snaking its way through dense bush. To the far right the thatched roofs of a Tugen homestead could be seen clinging precariously to the precipitous slopes of the escarpment. To the left the view was obscured by a wall of featureless scrub.

If you knew where to look, a plough disc, all but overgrown with thorny vegetation, would eventually be espied.

Faded letters stated 'F. Shroeder Kasanga Farm'

One had reached Franz's domain.

The farm always appeared to be in a state of benign neglect. What little fencing there was served merely to indicate the rough outline of fields and paddocks. Fence posts leaned at all angles, including the horizontal, the wires sagging sadly groundwards or lying looped in coils upon the dusty earth.

Negotiating the farm tracks in dry or wet weather could be a trying business.

Numerous well-camouflaged potholes lay in wait to trap the unwary. Depending on the degree of recent precipitation these were either filled with a mixture of glutinous mud and water, or with fine choking dust. The presence of a boulder added spice to any visit to Kasanga Farm.

The tracks on Franz's farm were much favoured by ant bears. In them they dug their deep burrows. Perhaps there was a proportionate number of burrows scattered over the rest of the farm, but to my jaundiced eyes they seemed to be concentrated in front of my car wheels. If one had the misfortune to drive into one of these deep, sharp edged holes and no immediate help was available, extrication could be attempted by a number of methods. One was to jack the vehicle up until the offending wheel was level with the lip of the hole and then drive the car off the jack, usually doing a fair amount of damage to jack and car in the process. Another was to jack the car up and fill the hole with stones until they supported the weight of the wheel. The only trouble with this method was that when one wanted stones there were usually none to be found.

Franz dairy-ranched a motley herd of Ayrshires, Red Polls, Borans, and their assorted cross-bred offspring. They wandered through the bush and blighted paddocks, nibbling at whatever edible fare came their way.

Dairy ranching involved milking the cows once a day only. During the rest of the day the calves suckled their mothers at will.

Franz's house was surrounded by tall shade trees and hidden behind a high kei apple hedge. The place was an oasis of greenery, thanks to a tiny rivulet which trickled past the house to vanish into a nearby swamp.

One approached from the rear and entered through the kitchen, a dark cavern in which the dimly visible figure of the cook lurked amid his pots and pans. In order to reach the living room one had to grope one's way along a succession of gloomy corridors.

At the front there was an apology of a garden, a few acres of rank grass under the trees with an ornamental pool in the centre, surrounded by a wall of rough hewn stones, its surface covered with water lilies.

Here Franz dwelt in glorious disorder. The chaos in which he lived appeared to be total. But no matter. It was obvious to all that here was a happy man. And the fact, extraordinary to some, including myself, that he was Vice-Chairman of the Kenya Agricultural Association, no doubt added to the sum of his contentment.

One afternoon, after having completed the examination and treatment of some of Franz's cattle, he invited me in for a cup of tea.

I followed Franz down the cobwebby corridors and into the cluttered living room.

In the far corner Mrs Shroeder was comfortably ensconced in her armchair, all but hidden behind a mixed pack of dogs and cats and knitting something from a ball of what looked like purple pasta.

I sensed that there was something about the room which was not quite right. Suspended over Mrs Shroeder's cranium was some kind of whitish canopy.

I glanced up. The ceiling had partially collapsed. Where I stood at the door it remained at its former height of about ten feet. From here it inclined steeply downwards until it met the opposite wall at about five feet from the floor. In the far corner at its lowest point only a three foot dwarf could have stood erect beneath it.

The collapse did not appear to have occurred recently. Neither Franz nor his wife behaved as though anything was amiss and poured their tea and munched their biscuits as if it was the most natural thing in the world to have their ceiling sloping earthwards at an angle of forty five degrees.

❄ ❄ ❄ ❄ ❄

On the edge of the Bahati Forest, in Kabatini district, was the farm of Max Stadden, chairman of the Kenya Agricultural Association.

Max, of Austrian Jewish descent, was lively, intelligent and articulate. Middle-aged, but as active as a man twenty years his junior, with curly, receding hair and the nose of his ancestors, Max was as often off his farm as on it, travelling in various parts of the country on official business, chairing meetings in Nakuru and Nairobi, and leading delegations to Europe and America. As a result of this constant movement the farm was sadly neglected.

At an altitude of 7,000 feet it received an above average rainfall. During wet weather the Kabatini road and the track to Max's farm could be virtually impassable. The former acted as a drain for all the rain falling on the escarpment behind the Bahati forest. After the mud had been churned up by a few tractors and milk lorries, one's forward motion was either sideways in top gear up the middle of the road, grinding along the ruts in low gear, or no motion at all in the ditch, wheels spinning, clutch burning, the air thick with oaths and muttered imprecations. Fortunately the area was heavily populated and help was always at hand to push one from the mire.

The track to Max's farm was heavily overgrown with encroaching vegetation. The final section was very steep and usually had to be attacked at speed to avoid sticking. Unfortunately a number of exposed tree roots crossed the track at this point and rocketing over them at 40mph, while preventing one from becoming embedded in the morass, did nothing to improve the suspension of one's vehicle.

The stock on the farm included Friesians and Ayrshires. Max also cultivated a market garden, growing, among other things, strawberries for the Nairobi shops and hotels.

When there was a glut, or when the road was so bad that they couldn't be moved off the farm, large quantities were fed to the cows at milking time. Great mounds of strawberries were shovelled into the feeding troughs. What effect this had on the flavour of the milk I was never sure. It must have been beneficial. When strawberries were in ample supply, it was usually wet; the dairy, if such it could be called, was hock deep in mud, the milkers' hands didn't bear inspection, and what water was available for cleaning udders was the colour and consistency of oxtail soup.

It was when I saw Max's cows being milked one soggy afternoon that whatever little attraction milk had hitherto held for me took a steep downward turn.

The cattle dip on the farm was located in the corner of a field and was surrounded by dense thickets of eye-high stinging nettles. It lacked a roof and because of frequent dilution with rain the acaricide frequently fell to levels which failed to kill ticks. The addition of quantities of mud carried in on the animals' hooves hastened this process. As a result, cases of tick-borne disease, such as Anaplasmosis, Redwater and East Coast Fever were common.

It always amused me that the two most important members of the Kenya Agricultural Association should have such ill-managed farms, and that, in this former British colony, both should be of Germanic origin.

※※※※※

Across the road from the surgery stood the Club, and within its hallowed walls, accessible to male members only, lay that inner sanctum, that Holy of Holies, the Men's Bar. Here gentlemen members could relax, talk, and above all, quaff the juice of the barley unmolested by wives and mistresses in particular, and women in general. Any woman who had the temerity to set foot within the shrine was hauled before the all-male committee, heavily fined and given a severe warning regarding her future conduct. Needless to say, such violations were extremely rare.

Farmers from outlying districts often made it their practice to wend their way to the Men's Bar after having completed the bulk of their chores in town. Here they would meet other farmers and discuss business, argue over the price of stock and crops, commiserate over the latest drought, flood or outbreak of rust in the wheat or foot and mouth disease in the cattle, and arrange when next to go to the Coast or to Lake Rudolf to catch that marlin or Nile perch which was going to beat the All-Africa Record. Indeed, some made such a habit of this that they referred to the place as 'The Office'.

Most frequenters of the Men's Bar would spend the lunch hour there over a bottle or two of Tusker or Whitecap and a sandwich. For others the lunch hour might stretch on into the middle or late afternoon. Eventually these latter would emerge, like troglodytes from their cave, blinking in the still fierce sun, weave their way unsteadily to their various vehicles, and, in vino veritas, drive carefully or erratically away.

As the surgery was so close to the Club it was a convenient stopping point to discuss veterinary matters with the present incumbent.

Consulting hours were between 2-3.30pm. During that period most routine cases involving dogs and cats were attended to.

And it was during the latter half of this time, when things were at their busiest, that Leo Foster of Rongai would make one of his regular entries.

Leo managed a large wheat, maize and dairy farm at Rongai. He was a good farmer, regularly producing bumper crops, and sending between two and three gallons of milk per cow to the Kenya Co-operative Creameries in Nakuru.

Most of the time Leo behaved like a perfectly normal, rational human being. Then suddenly he would start drinking heavily and become almost impossible to deal with. He would spend the night drinking in one of the African beer halls in Rongai, get himself arrested for riotous behaviour, be bailed out by one of his sympathetic neighbours, appear in court, pay a fine, and then return to normal – until the next time. During a brawl his upper front teeth had been knocked out. He got some dentures fitted, but soon discarded them and his cheerful gap-toothed grin became a landmark in the district.

Leo was small and stocky, burnt dark by the sun under which he spent most of his working hours. He rarely, if ever, wore socks and his normal footwear was a pair of well-worn flip-flops, made from car tyres.

By the time he made one of his periodic afternoon visitations to the surgery he had done a morning's work in the mud or dust and his feet and ankles were invariably caked in a malodorous layer of something resembling dried cow dung – and probably was.

The sight, sound, and smell of this wild figure, hair awry, minus important sections of his denticulation, legs black from the calves downwards, obviously inebriated, bursting through the swing door, did nothing for client relations.

Nervous Asians and genteel ladies waiting for attention shrank backwards as Leo surged forwards, seeming to fill the entire waiting room with his all-too-overpowering presence, a visitor not from another planet, but from the Men's Bar.

❋ ⛎ ❋ ⛎ ❋

The Men's Bar could be a dangerous place.

One Saturday afternoon a rancher friend from Rumuruti asked me to meet him there to discuss his favourite domestic animal, the camel.

I met him in the Men's Bar shortly after 1pm.

At 4pm I tottered down the Club steps and crept slowly home with every intention of spending the next few hours prone on my bed.

Five minutes after achieving this position the telephone rang.

Arthur Mbogo, a farmer at Mbaruk, about 15 miles from Nakuru, had a cow stuck calving.

The message was transmitted in Swahili of which I had by now acquired a basic smattering. To the question 'naweza kuja?' – (can you come?) – I was able to answer 'ndio' – (yes) – without stumbling over a single syllable, a not inconsiderable achievement for one in my condition.

I donned a large straw hat, very carefully got into my car, pulled the sun-visors down as far as they would go without actually tearing them from their mountings, and pointed the vehicle in the direction of Mbaruk. I took my time. For one thing I didn't want to drive off the road and for another there was always the chance that the cow might have calved before I arrived.

No such luck. She was standing in a small one-cow crush next to the house. A small crowd of Africans - men, women and children, looked expectantly in my direction as I drove into the yard.

The daktari had arrived.

Very gently I got out of the car. The still-powerful sun smote my straw-covered skull with stupefying force. In slow motion I donned calving overall and wellington boots. Observing that a bucket of water, soap and towel had been brought for my use I got my calving ropes from the car and prepared to do battle.

I had considerable difficulty with the soap, which kept slipping from my fingers, and shooting into the dirt, to be retrieved by one or more of the children. Their numbers seemed to wax and wane in an alarming fashion. I was having trouble focusing and at one point I saw the backsides of three cows facing me in the crush. I chose the one in the middle.

Arthur Mbogo, a kindly and soft spoken Kikuyu, a pillar of his local church, held the tail while other members of his family, and friends, helped as the delivery proceeded. Fortunately for all concerned the calving was straightforward and without major difficulty. The calf was alive and the mother well, which was more that could be said for me.

The fact that I had remained mute from start to finish did not appear to upset Arthur or his family in the slightest.

Perhaps they thought I was a bit peeved at being called out on a Saturday afternoon or that I was naturally rather uncommunicative.

I hoped so.

After all, I wouldn't have liked them to have thought that I was inebriated.

❖❘❖❘❖❘❖❘❖

Other individuals came to mind.

Dickie Edmondson was one, soon to enter the ward as a patient himself for a couple of weeks.

Dickie bore a remarkable resemblance to the late Toulouse-Lautrec, although his legs were of normal length. He wore a square black beard, wire rimmed spectacles, and a large felt hat, and was only about 5 feet tall. Dickie had a small farm on the edge of the sisal country in the Solai Valley, but spent most of his time working on a range management scheme in the arid bush to the south of Lake Baringo.

His house had mud and wattle walls and a thatched roof. Dickie's father had at one time been Chief Veterinary Officer and had come to Kenya at the turn of the 19th century.

Although possessing an active and intelligent mind, at once obvious from his lively and witty conversation, Dickie appeared to prefer the simple life. He dwelt in his rustic mansion, living off the land and, even, it would seem, doing his own cobbling. During one visit to the farm to dehorn some Boran bulls with horns like those of an African buffalo, I happened to glance down. The soles and uppers of Dickie's extraordinary boots had been stitched together with wire.

Old Jack Evans lived on his farm at Rongai. His wife had long since died, and instead of a male house servant to attend to his domestic affairs two ancient Kikuyu beldames ran his household. He probably paid them a pittance and the result was much as one might have expected. The house was dark and dingy, dust lay thickly everywhere, the floors were unpolished and chickens scuttled about under the tables and chairs. Two tame genets peered down from the rafters.

Despite the basic conditions in which he lived, Jack was in fact very wealthy, but, like many wealthy people, he was reluctant to part with his money. His battered straw hat had lasted him many years and now an ominous tide of mildew was beginning to eat into the crown. His trousers, held in position by a well-worn leather belt, hung at half-mast above his scuffed safari boots.

Jack's parsimony extended to his use of razor blades and his narrow pointed chin seemed to be permanently covered in a three-day stubble.

When Jack went on one of his infrequent trips to England, he carried all of his personal effects for the visit, which might last three or four weeks, in a medium-sized kikapu – an open straw basket – disdaining the suitcases and trunks used by more effete members of society.

At the other end of the social spectrum were those members of the aristocracy who lived in this part of Kenya – Austrian and Italian counts, English and Danish barons, viscounts, dukes and lords.

One aristocrat was Compte Phillipe Belanger de la Tour. Married to a minor English blue-blood, he lived on a small property together with sundry dachshunds, Guernsey cows and thoroughbred horses. The cares of the world always seemed to lie heavily on Phillipe's sloping shoulders. The cows had mastitis, his wife's horse was lame, the dachshund had canker, the house-servant had just smashed their most valuable piece of porcelain. Despite his beautiful house, full of lovely furniture and paintings, surrounded by closely cropped lawns sloping down to the picturesque stream with its waterwheel, which flowed through the garden, a surfeit of insoluble problems were Phillipe's lot.

His blue eyes bulged, his face reddened and he gobbled like a turkey cock as he narrated the most recent disaster. Most people were inclined to retreat in the face of this verbal barrage, but Phillipe was undeterred. He would follow his victim until they were standing only inches apart. Should the latter take refuge in his car, Phillipe would stick his head through the window and continue his relentless monologue. The recipient's next move was usually to surreptitiously slip the car into first gear and to very gently release the clutch, quietly moving forwards. Phillipe would keep pace alongside, barely drawing breath as he continued with his tale and only when he had almost broken into a canter with the car in second gear, would he withdraw his head.

On one occasion Phillipe came into the surgery just as I was leaving for a dental appointment. He followed me outside into the street and round the corner, talking furiously. His troubles had increased. He had lost his farm. His wife had left him. Everything was going wrong.

The dentist's surgery was on the other side of the main street. The traffic whizzed by. I was already ten minutes late.

Phillipe chattered on.

There was a lull in the traffic and I nipped out into the road, Phillipe at my elbow.

Suddenly he grabbed me by the arm, effectively arresting my progress and repeated everything he had just said. Buses and cars roared down upon us, horns blaring, drivers gesticulating, missing us by millimetres. Phillipe stood there, totally unconcerned, completely immersed in the torrent of his own verbosity.

With difficulty I escaped his clutches, darted across the street and up the stairs and into the dentist's waiting room, Phillipe hard on my heels.

Like most other people I do not normally enter a dental surgery with any degree of alacrity but on this particular day I fairly shot into the dreaded chair as soon as my time came.

Light years away from Phillipe's ethereal world, in Njoro's so-called industrial area, which consisted of a single unpaved street, punctuated at uncertain intervals by noisome alleys, dwelt Ram Dass.

Ram Dass was almost unique in that, being an Indian, he was married to an African woman. Both were elderly. He was a low caste Hindu, possibly an untouchable, a Harijan. She was a Nandi. Where he had come from no one seemed to know, and, as far as I could ascertain, he had no contact whatsoever with the Asian community.

He ran a posho mill, grinding maize into flour, and always wore wide, shapeless, baggy trousers and a loose shirt with the tails hanging out. Because of his occupation he often looked older than he was, as did his workers, as they were all invariably dusted with a light covering of flour.

Ram Dass was a cheerful, friendly, humble person, as was his wife. They would offer me a cup of tea when I had completed my work and were always grateful for what I had done. Mrs Dass' dress was a long, shapeless Mother Hubbard dress which reached to her ankles.

Despite their obvious poverty they paid their bills with a promptitude which would have put many of my more affluent clients to shame.

Then there was Charles Ojoung, manager of a European-owned farm on the northern shores of Lake Nakuru.

Charles was a tall Jaluo and he looked after the farm as though it was his own. Cross-bred Borans and Sahiwals were milked in portable wooden dairies beneath the ancient fever trees beside the lake. At all hours of the day and night Charles was to be found on duty, supervising the milking, feeding the calves, checking the fences, paying the workers, dipping the cattle. The owner was frequently away, and without Charles the whole enterprise would have collapsed.

Charles was the most consistently cheerful person I have ever met. Always smartly dressed in starched shorts and knee-length stockings, his ebony countenance was split into a permanent smile, revealing his gleaming white teeth.

One particular phrase which he was very fond of using when agreeing with something one had said was 'Quite right!' He used this phrase so often that he was known far and wide as Mr Quite Right.

There were others like him. Old Abdi, Count Maurice Coreth's Somali headman at Subukia was one. Kahugu, Molly Hodge's chief syce, also of Subukia, was another. Muturi, head syce at Kay Spier's stud at Njoro, was yet another.

Numbered among this company were those yeoman African farmers, who, having newly acquired properties in the former White Highlands, were determined to make a go of it and prove by getting their hands dirty that they could farm at least as well as their erstwhile colonial masters.

Alas that their initial enthusiasm and momentum could not be maintained, due, in many instances, to outside forces beyond their control.

CHAPTER FIVE

Although I had not appreciated it at the time, my employer going on leave so soon after my arrival in East Africa had prepared me for what lay ahead.

I had been thrown into a small pool. The result was that when I was tossed in at the deep end later in my career, I was able to swim with some confidence.

Meanwhile I was on my own, and, being cast on my own resources, learned fast. By day I worked. By night I studied my Handbook of Tropical Diseases.

When time allowed I swotted up my Swahili.

During the late Sixties the British buy-out scheme, designed to purchase mixed farms owned by British citizens, was in full swing, and everything on farms for sale had to be valued by an agent appointed by the government. On the basis of his valuation, which was often below the current market price, he then made an offer to the owner.

In the course of this procedure all the cattle had to be examined and this entailed a great deal of work for the vet concerned, which was where I came in.

All of the cattle had to be minutely inspected to ensure that they were in good health, fit to breed, good milkers, and disease free. Individual animals could be rejected for various reasons without affecting the sale of the herd as a whole. Old cows with broken teeth, cows with only two functioning teats, the chronically lame, or those with only one eye were unlikely to be accepted.

The cows bought were to be the foundation stock of the African farmers who would be running the farm in the future, whether that farm remained in the same form as in the past, or whether it was to be divided into smaller units.

So the examination had to be done with great care. If any errors were made they would inevitably come to light sooner or later.

The buy-out scheme, although on the whole fair to all parties concerned was, to the British farmers whose properties were being bought, the end of an era, the finale to ten or twenty years' or even a lifetime's endeavour in a land they loved. Although the money they received for their farms might be repatriated, this could not compensate for the fact that the glorious life they lived, despite all its difficulties and setbacks, farming in one of the most marvellous countries in the world was, for the majority, at an end.

So, in many cases, the work of examining the stock was tinged with an air of sadness. One way of life was ending. Another was beginning. The White Highlands were no more and the hewers of wood and drawers of water were at last inheriting their birthright and, in many cases, a little more besides.

The stress and strain of seeing their possessions, animate and inanimate, being prodded, poked, and examined, sometimes magnified the minor eccentricities of some farmers until they became the dominant features of their characters.

A few days after my employer's departure, Bill Dickens, the auctioneer at the Nakuru branch of the Kenya Farmers Association, came into the surgery.

Bill was an officially appointed valuer. A large, middle-aged man, with a full auburn beard, Bill was great fun to work with and had a wicked sense of humour. In his job he needed it.

Bill spent much of his time selling cattle to the highest bidder. Most of the buyers were African, many speaking no English and it required a good man to be able to deal with them efficiently and fairly and command their respect.

I was attending an auction once when a steer was driven into the ring. The animal was being belaboured by a pock-marked Kikuyu, who was driving it around the ring with the aid of a heavy cudgel.

'Don't hit it like that. It's not your wife!' roared Bill in Swahili.

This brought an appreciative burst of laughter from the crowd of Africans watching the proceedings.

The steer-beater retired, abashed and discomfited.

Most of the auction rings were rough and ready affairs and the only person shaded from the burning sun was the auctioneer himself, who conducted his business from a little platform with a thatched roof.

Terms were cash only. Once a buyer had disappeared with his cattle he was probably gone for ever.

'Hello there,' said Bill as he walked in. 'I'd like you to come out and examine a herd of Friesians at Kampi ya Moto. They're owned by a fellow called Tim Bramson. He's normally the mildest person you could hope to meet but having his farm sold has turned his head. I was out at his place

71

yesterday having a look round. Tim drove me in his pick-up. There was a crate of beers on the bench seat between us and by the time lunch time came around I was up to my knees in empty beer bottles and Tim was as pissed as the proverbial newt and barely capable of keeping the car on the road.'

Tim had recently come into the surgery to buy some worm tablets for his dog. I remembered him as a tall chap with long sideburns. When I went out to the farm I barely recognised him. His luxuriant foliage had gone and his hair had been cropped to a convict stubble. He had a hunted look about him. He was obviously taking this pretty badly. In his hand he had a three foot length of plastic piping, which from time to time he swished ominously in the air.

Moses came with me to write down the details of the animals as I inspected them. Bill Dickens was waiting on the farm with a sheaf of official-looking forms.

We drove out to the field where the cattle were waiting. It had been decided to examine the cattle in their portable wooden bails, as it was easier to inspect them there than in the crush.

Tim sat at a little wooden desk, normally used by the milk recorder when writing down the morning and evening yield of each cow. He fished a little notebook out of his pocket, scribbled something in it, and glowered in our direction.

Four milking bails had been drawn into a square. Each held six cows. There were 120 in all to examine, a fair morning's work. I rectally examined each animal. Apart from recently calved cows, the majority were pregnant. I checked the teats and quarters of each cow and as I did so, the previous day's milk yield was noted down, together with any defects discovered. The workers seized each animal by the nose so that I could look at the teeth and also examine the eyes.

Moses wrote in his triple-leaved notebook. Bill filled up his forms. Tim scratched away at his desk, occasionally rising to pace like a caged tiger to a milk churn, from which he refreshed himself with a dipper hanging from the rim.

The beers were all finished.

I soaped my arm and passed on to the next cow.

Suddenly and without provocation Tim leapt to his feet and before I realised what was happening Moses was being closely pursued round the bails, the plastic pipe whistling past his ears. Moses seemed to realise that Tim was just working off suppressed emotions because as he shot past, his assailant hard on his heels, he gave me a grin. The milkers assisting us didn't seem too concerned either. After a couple of rounds of the bails Tim returned to his seat and the work continued as though nothing had happened.

By mid-day the work was almost finished.

My left arm, despite its initial liberal coating of milking grease to ease its passage in and out of 120 bovine recta, felt as though it had been rasped by sandpaper down to the subcutaneous tissues and the muscles of my hand and forearm ached from the strain. The sun was at its zenith and everyone was beginning to wilt in the heat. Tim, bloated with milk and thankfully slumped in a stupor, appeared to have nodded off. Bill and Moses wrote on. It was vital not to make a mistake. A clerical error could cost the farmer a lot of money.

I scraped and washed the dung off my arm, told Tim and Bill that I would leave them both a signed certificate in the surgery, climbed somewhat stiffly into the Beetle and drove off. Tim asked me to come to the house for a drink but I knew that work, perhaps of an urgent nature, would be waiting for me on my return, so I reluctantly declined. I also knew that at this embryonic stage of my tropical career I was very much a tyro, and that what an expert might do in fifteen minutes would probably take me twice as long.

Despite Tim's erratic behaviour and his barely controlled resentment at having to sell his farm, he made sure that his bitterness was not extended towards his workers. Sixteen fat barren cows, which could have been sold to the Kenya Meat Commission, or to the local butcher, for a handsome price, were given to the men to be used as they wished. Half were barbe-cued at intervals over the next month, washed down with innumerable bottles of beer, supplied by Tim. Needless to say for a couple of days after these feasts, in which Tim participated to the full, the standard of work declined somewhat, but as his days on the farm were numbered he couldn't have cared less.

A few days later, during the afternoon surgery, a European man walked in, accompanied by a small, light brown dog. Its tail curved over its back and it had a sharp alert foxy look about it. It appeared to have tender paws and there was a distinct lack of zest in its movements.

'Good afternoon, my name's Baillie, Major Baillie to be exact, and this is Tabu. Tabu's a pure-bred Basenji and he's been lame for a few days. Although not off his food he doesn't seem quite as active as usual. I'd be pleased if you would check him over.'

I knew that Basenjis were African hunting dogs from the Congo and the southern Sudan, peculiar in that they rarely, if ever, barked, an invaluable asset when tracking game through thick forest. I had also read somewhere the 'basenji' was corrupted Congolese Swahili for 'shenzi', meaning uncivilised, third rate, ramshackle or run down. I didn't mention this to the Major, a florid faced individual who looked as though he was used to having his own way. I also knew that 'tabu' meant trouble!

I hoisted Tabu onto the table.

I listened to his heart and lungs with a stethoscope and heard nothing unusual. Palpation of his abdomen likewise brought me no nearer a diagnosis. However, his gums and conjunctiva were paler than expected and some of his pads had small patches of inflammation, tender to the touch, with swelling of the inter-digital web.

A small gong pealed somewhere in the distant recesses of my brain.

I spread a small amount of Tabu's faeces on a glass slide, mixed it with a little water, and examined it with the practice's ancient brass-bound microscope.

Under the low power a mass of debris swept past my vision, rather like the rubbish brought down by a river in spate. Then a worm egg appeared, a neat and tidy oval amid the surrounding detritus. I moved the slide and found several more. These were the eggs of the tropical hookworm.

'Tabu's got hookworm, Major. I'll give him an injection of disophenol which will get rid of the adult worms in his gut. But, as it doesn't kill any migrating larvae he will have to come back in three weeks for a second injection.'

Tabu flinched slightly as I gave him the oily yellow solution beneath the loose skin of his neck.

The lesions on the Basenj's pads were caused by penetration of the hookworm larvae. The adult worm in the intestine lays eggs which are passed in the faeces. Under suitable conditions of temperature and moisture, larvae hatch from these eggs and then infect the host either by direct skin penetration or by ingestion.

The adult worms are very small but are voracious blood suckers. In a full blown infestation, a puppy or an adult dog might well have stools the colour of third grade tomato ketchup pouring out of its rectum.

I asked the Major to ensure that Tabu's kennel was kept as dry as possible at all times, and to have him regularly treated every three or four months.

'And Major, if you get an unpleasant skin irritation with itching and redness, the larvae may well be making a bid to get into you as well! But as you're not their normal host your body will reject them. It's called creeping eruption! Probably won't occur but you never know!'

The Major's beetrooty complexion paled slightly, but, putting on a brave front, he thanked me for my help, and departed, Tabu pussy-footing his way out at his heels.

Three weeks later Tabu returned for his second injection.

He now weighed 40lbs, his paws were healed, and his master's epidermis had remained, thankfully, unblemished.

◎◎◎◎◎◎

Towards the end of only my first week, the fact that I was where I was – namely in the heart of Africa – was emphatically brought home to me by a trio of incidents which suggested that death and disaster struck rather more frequently south of Suez than north of the Isle of Wight.

It was again early afternoon and the surgery was packed with waiting clients when a frantic Asian rushed in.

'My dog is being stung by bees!'

Through the door I could see an alsatian lying in the back of a Peugeot pick-up, flanked by a couple of Africans.

The dog was carried into the surgery on a sack.

It looked moribund.

We lifted it onto the table.

Its body was covered in thousands of bee stings. Its eyes were closed, the eyelids puffy and swollen. The insides of the ears were a forest of stings. The dog's breathing was shallow and laboured, the temperature subnormal. Gums and conjunctiva were cyanosed and dirty blue in colour.

Quickly I injected the once-beautiful alsatian with antihistamine and a massive dose of corticosteroids, but held out little hope of recovery. The toxin of the African bee is extremely potent, causing severe kidney damage which, depending on the number of stings received, often results in the death of the victim. This species of bee is so aggressive that a swarm will frequently pursue an animal or human and sting and sting, until the prey is left unconscious and dying on the ground. In this instance the alsatian was a guard dog. It was chained during the day and only released at night to patrol its master's premises. As a result, when the swarm attacked, it was unable to escape and received what was, in effect, a massive dose of poison by hypodermic injection.

My prognosis proved to be correct. Twenty minutes after being brought in, and half an hour after being stung, the alsatian died.

With much truth it has been said that the bee is one of the most dangerous animals in Africa. In later years I saw many cases of dogs stung by bees and a large proportion of these died. Horses and cattle were also sometimes stung by swarms but because of their much greater size, they usually recovered. The newspapers frequently published horrific accounts of people being stung, either fatally, or sufficiently badly to necessitate lengthy hospitalisation. People were so conscious of their aggressive and attacking nature that the proximity of a swarm or even of a single bee could cause panic. Several car accidents were caused by them. A woman teacher driving near Nakuru overturned her car and fractured her arm as she swerved off the road. From her hospital bed she described her terror of a bee which had entered her car through an open window. An Asian youth died when he drove his vehicle over a precipice into Menengai Crater while trying to evade a swarm. Seconds before he had been quietly cruising along the road which skirts the crater rim. An Israeli construction worker was attacked by a swarm while walking in his garden in Nakuru. He almost died and only recovered after months on a kidney dialysis machine.

So, whenever I was on the roads of East Africa and saw an undulating air-borne carpet, five to ten feet from the ground, approaching at high speed, I would wind up the window of my car faster than the eye could follow, while the vanguard of the swarm smashed itself against the windscreen.

Half an hour later a European policeman came into the surgery.

He was leaving East Africa for Britain and had brought his dog, a hunt terrier, to me for examination, so that, if healthy, a certificate to that effect could be issued to facilitate its departure.

The policeman was in his mid-forties, spruce and sharp in his starched bush-jacket and shorts, but with an almost palpable air of sadness and melancholy hanging about him.

'It's my wife's dog really. Not my kind at all. She doted on the little beggar.'

Then for some reason known only to himself he told me an appalling tale.

He had had a week's leave and with his wife had decided to spend it in Uganda, visiting the Queen Elizabeth and Murchison Falls national parks. They had driven to the former first, staying for a couple of nights at Mweya Safari Lodge on its bluff overlooking the Kazinga Channel and Lake Edward and its stupendous views westward to the dark brooding mountains of the Congo.

Then they drove northwards past the cloud-covered Ruwenzori Mountains to Fort Portal, Masindi and finally to Murchison Falls national park.

The narrow, red road through the park winds across open, rolling grassland dotted with the skeletal remains of trees killed by elephants – elephants in their thousands, for which the park was famous. The road reaches the crest of some low hills and there, flashing and sparkling between high wooded bluffs, runs the Victoria Nile. To the left and downstream the river runs broad and smooth before quietly merging with the vast waters of Lake Albert.

To the right and upstream the river rushes madly through a narrow valley, pouring over rapids and cataracts, past wooded islands and jagged rocks, before squeezing itself through a narrow fissure and over the awful falls, to smash itself on the boulders far below. The volume of water passing over the falls is colossal and to watch it bursting out of its dank and dripping gorge and to be deafened by its unceasing roar is to be numbed, stupefied and hypnotised, until one feels oneself being drawn closer and closer to the never-changing yet always-changing rush of water.

And all the time, in the great pool downstream from the falls, its black waters aswirl with currents and whirlpools, the crocodiles lie watching and waiting for dazed and battered fish and animals that from time to time get swept down from the upper rapids.

The policeman and his wife saw the river glittering in the tropical heat, cool and inviting. They looked upstream and saw the cloud of spray rising and hanging over the great Falls and decided that before crossing the river on the ferry to Paraa Lodge they would drive down and have a picnic.

Just above the Falls there is a flat grassy area where cars can be parked. Along the bank, above the gorge, was a flimsy wooden fence, sagging and mildewed. The thunder of the water filled the air as it crashed over the rocks and into the frightful abyss.

The parking area was empty and they had the Falls to themselves. Often parties of Indians from Masindi and Kampala would come and sit and watch the water as it surged past, as though this savage Nile was a sort of African Ganges. But today the place was deserted.

Above the Falls a bluff commanded a stomach-churning view into the depths of the gorge, seething with spray and foam. A narrow path ran along the top of the bluff.

The policeman's wife stood up.

'Before we go I'm going to nip up there and take a photograph. The view must be fabulous.'

'OK,' the policeman said reluctantly. 'You know I haven't a head for heights. I'll wait in the car. But for Heaven's sake be careful!'

He sat in the car and waited. His wife walked up the path to the top of the bluff. He could see her focusing her camera.

'She'll be down in a minute,' he thought. 'I'll just turn the car while I'm waiting.'

He turned the car and glanced up at the bluff. His wife wasn't there. His heart leapt in his throat.

'She must be just over the brow,' he thought, but he suddenly felt cold in spite of the heat.

Five minutes passed.

He got out of the car and carefully climbed up the bluff and along the path.

His wife had vanished.

He crept to the edge of the gorge and recoiled. A seething cauldron of crashing water and blinding spray met his horrified gaze, terrifying in its intensity and impression of uncontrolled brute power.

The lip of the bluff fell sheer into the falls.

The policeman's wife was never found, her body remained undiscovered. Mesmerised by the falling water she must have slipped with fearful finality. The height and weight of the water would have made death instantaneous, or at least it was hoped so, for only a few hundred yards downstream the crocodiles were still watching and waiting.

I signed the health certificate for the hunt terrier and he and his unhappy owner departed.

As I walked with him to the surgery door, there was the sound of shouting and the pounding of feet in the street outside.

A ragged figure, barefoot and perspiring, came tearing up the street. Close at his heels were several pursuers.

'Mwivi! Mwivi!' they yelled.

'Thief! Thief!'

The desperate wretch dodged from side to side, trying to evade capture. The mob behind him grew with frightening rapidity. Its members seemed to spring up like dragon's teeth. Escape was impossible and the end came with hideous speed.

About thirty yards along the street from the surgery a group of men were unloading batons of timber from a lorry. A large heap lay on the pavement. As the fugitive zigzagged blindly in their direction one of the men picked up a three foot length, and, swinging it over his shoulder like a baseball bat, pole-axed the poor fellow with a fearful blow full square in the centre of his forehead.

The man went down like a stunned bullock and within seconds had vanished from sight, surrounded by a seemingly blood-crazed gang of homicidal sadists who beat, kicked and stamped on his unconscious and, probably, lifeless remains.

A police station-wagon roared round the corner, scattering pedestrians like chaff. Four constables got out as the vehicle screeched to a halt. They forced their way into crowd and stood for a few moments grinning down at the broken shape, bleeding into the gutter, before grabbing him by the ankles and wrists and tossing him into the back of the station-wagon.

They then drove off.

I hoped that their first port of call would be the casualty department of the nearest hospital, but even there, I later learnt, rapid therapy was unlikely to be forthcoming for such as he.

Perusal of the daily news sheets and conversations with residents apprised me that such incidents were by no means rare, and in years to come I was to witness more than one such outrage in Club Lane. Similar ghastly events occurred almost daily somewhere in the republic. A person had only to bellow 'Thief!' in order to have an enthusiastic mob set out in pursuit of some real or imagined miscreant, who, if caught, was likely as not to be beaten, kicked or stoned to death. It seemed not to matter whether what had been purloined was a few shillings, a loaf of bread, a handbag or a goat – the punishment, if caught, was almost invariably the same, as, in a horrific holiday-like atmosphere, 'justice' was meted out.

Well, the Grim Reaper must have enjoyed himself that afternoon.

For several nights thereafter my rest was disturbed by a fearful sequence of nightmares in which, pursued by a mixed rabble of giant bees and *sans-culottes* in approximately equal numbers, I was driven to and over the edge of a seemingly bottomless abyss – but there was a bottom and there the jaws of ravenous crocodiles gaped and snapped, awaiting my arrival.

✳ ✳ ✳ ✳ ✳

The work continued.

Tick-borne diseases were common, and anaplasmosis of cattle, in particular, was often seen. This malady is caused by an organism called *Anaplasma marginale*, a parasite of red blood cells and so-called because it is usually found at or near the margins of the cells.

As it multiplies, it ruptures the cells and so the unfortunate host becomes progressively more and more anaemic, and without treatment, will die. Adult cattle are more susceptible to infection than calves, which in endemic areas display an innate resistance, reinforced by maternal antibodies.

In Kenya, blue ticks – actually slate grey, not azure or turquoise – carry the organism and because they are so common, plunge dips and spray races have been constructed throughout the Highlands. Every week tens of thousands of cattle leap, or are pushed, into oblong vats filled with khaki-coloured fluid, or are driven between rows of nozzles which drench them with pungent, tick-killing liquid.

The incubation period of anaplasmosis is long – 6 to 12 weeks – and because recovered animals maintain their immunity by retaining a few parasites in their blood they, as carrier animals, form the main reservoir of infection. This guarantees survival of the organism.

The symptoms are fairly characteristic – fever, anaemia, jaundice, loss of appetite, weakness, constipation and a loud thumping heart beat.

Treatment consisted of giving a course of oxytetracycline injections and epsom salts if the animal was constipated.

Zebu cattle appear to be as susceptible to infection as those of European origin, but because the former are more resistant to tick infestation they are less commonly infected.

The African name for anaplasmosis is 'digana' and many African cattle owners could diagnose the disease as accurately as trained veterinary personnel.

Occasionally nervous forms of the disease occur, due to involvement of the brain. This causes marked excitement and aggression.

It was my fortune that the second case of anaplasmosis that I saw was so affected.

A call came in asking me to attend to a sick cow on a farm on the edge of the forest above Njoro.

The farm was owned by a Kikuyu co-operative society and I approached it over the usual rocky, rutted track. The patient, a horned, half-bred Ayrshire cow, was sitting in the middle of a dung-covered boma, doing nothing in particular – until I started to climb over the ramshackle wooden stockade in order to inspect her at closer quarters. At this point her head came up and she stared in my direction with more than passing interest. She shook her head and snorted. As I set foot on manure-bestrewn terra firma she was on her feet and coming for me like a fighting bull suddenly released into the ring.

I sprang up the rickety planks with feverish speed, almost debagging myself on a projecting splinter in my haste. I reached the top as bovine skull crashed into woodwork just below me.

Looking down from my precarious perch I watched my patient rampaging round the yard. Every now and then she staggered as she rushed in fury towards the figures of African farm-workers peering into the boma. She appeared to be drunk with rage.

Leading off from one side of the boma was a flimsy wooden cattle crush. It was decided to try and lure the patient into this in order to examine and treat her.

As it was patently impossible to drive her in, she would have to be enticed in, and the most attractive bait was the two legged variety.

Volunteers were called for, and eventually, to the accompaniment of the cheers of his friends, a wiry youth leapt into the arena. The cow eyed him eagerly and, after a moment's hesitation, charged. Quick as a flash, the youth streaked into the crush, horns inches from his straining shanks. Without a pause, he vaulted over the side. Poles were slammed in behind the infuriated beast and she was caught.

Despite the fragile nature of the crush, which appeared to be in imminent danger of collapse, I was able, albeit with some difficulty, to examine her, note the fever, constipation, anaemia, and abnormally loud heart beat, and treat her.

Ten days later, the manager came to the surgery to tell me, to my surprise, that she had recovered.

Another common tick-borne disease with which I was able to familiarise myself early on in Africa was tick fever of dogs.

This protozoal disease is characterised by the extensive breakdown of red blood cells, accompanied by fever, anaemia and sometimes jaundice.

A characteristic pounding pulse, best felt in the femoral artery on the inside of the hind leg, a higher than normal temperature, loss of appetite, an enlarged abdomen due to swelling of the spleen, pale mucous membranes and lethargy are often seen. In very severe cases the dog may actually pass blood-stained urine and then the prognosis is very grave. Or the case may progress to jaundice when the outlook is also often gloomy, and lengthy, careful treatment is needed to pull the patient through.

In order to confirm the diagnosis a drop of blood is taken from the dog's ear. I did this by pricking the inside of the ear with the point of a scalpel blade, making a minute incision. The drop of blood is spread on a glass slide and stained with Giemsa stain. Under the microscope the parasites appear as pear-shaped organisms within the red blood cells, bluish-purple in colour. They usually occur in pairs with their pointed ends close together, and often four or even six parasites may be seen within a single cell.

Using the practice's antediluvian microscope I would laboriously search for parasites. Sometimes it would seem that almost every second cell contained parasites. In other cases, only one or two could be found, but they were enough to make a diagnosis.

The available drugs, phenamidine and berenil, were highly effective, but their use required care, especially in young dogs. It was no good impressing the owner with a spot-on diagnosis and then killing the dog with the treatment.

Nursing and the provision of vitamins and a high protein diet are of paramount importance in speeding the patient towards recovery. In most cases, provided the patient is seen early enough, onset of recovery is evident within thirty six to forty eight hours from the start of treatment.

Following recovery, dogs are normally immune for a period of about eighteen months. This immunity is associated with the continued presence of a few organisms in the blood.

One fact soon became evident. To see an Asian-owned dog with tick fever was almost as rare as sighting snow on the shores of Lake Victoria. This was because these dogs were hardly ever kept as pets. They were there to guard their master's property and, as such, were not entitled to a life of their own. During the day they were, for the most part, confined to insanitary wooden kennels and fed on a diet based mainly on posho or maize meal, enlivened at rare intervals by the odd chapatti or bone. There were exceptions of course. Sikhs, Moslems and Goans tended to feed their dogs better than Hindus who would often impose their own dietary customs on their animals. One apparently high caste Indian woman, whose dog was suffering from diarrhoea, informed me that she would be unable to give her dog meat of any kind for the next month as her religion dictated that during that period no meat of any kind would be allowed on or near the premises. Poor dog!

During the hours of darkness most Asian-owned dogs were released into their owner's compound to protect it against intruders.

On the whole these places were devoid of grass or vegetation, being bare concreted areas, surrounded by high walls surmounted by razor-sharp shards of broken glass. Consequently these dogs encountered no ticks and thus did not contract tick fever. And as they were never taken out for walks their chances of meeting ticks were further reduced to almost zero.

Most Asians, exceptions apart, did not handle their dogs personally. As a result, many of these animals were extremely difficult to handle, with a regrettable tendency to bite whenever they became excited.

African-owned dogs, by contrast, were docile and easy to handle. Like many of their owners they did not have an easy life. However they, again like many Africans, appeared to accept their lot with uncomplaining stoicism, and seemed, with their placid temperament, to be happier and more balanced animals than their hysterical Asian counterparts. Many were thin and undernourished, infested with worms and covered with ticks hanging from their hides like clusters of ripe grapes. As a result many of these dogs were highly susceptible to tick fever. Few, however, were presented for treatment, and if they were, the disease was often so far advanced that heroic efforts were required to effect a cure. Such cases brought little financial gain, but the satisfaction in seeing an animal, which would otherwise have died, returned to its grateful owner was a reward in itself.

Not that such an owner was unwilling to pay what he could. Indeed, the less affluent African client was frequently better at settling his debts than the emergent nouveau riche.

Most Africans with the exception of Moslems such as Somalis and Swahilis, appear to like dogs. Indeed, some tribes are too fond of them for their own good.

The Turkana, who live in the harsh far north-west of Kenya, have the world's highest rate of infestation with the larval hydatid cyst of the tapeworm *Echinococcus*, contracted from their dogs with whom they live literally cheek by jowl.

African-owned dogs are kept as guards or pets and spend much time with the family. Neglect, when it occurs, is often due, not to deliberate cruelty, but to apathy or ignorance. If a stray dog is found injured by the road it is rare indeed for an African to help it. Many will not touch a dog once it has died, or help to bury the body. Dogs are killed daily on the roads of Kenya. Vehicles will steer past the remains. Pedestrians will throw stones at the bloated corpse, but no effort is made to remove it. Mercifully after a few days in the hot sun all that is left is a dark stain on the tarmac, and that soon disappears.

◎◎◎◎◎◎

Dogs owned by Europeans did not conform to any particular temperament, except, perhaps, on occasion, to that of their owners. Although a few were kept as guards, most were family pets and every conceivable breed and inter-breed were seen, from chihuahuas to Great Danes, from poodles to Irish wolfhounds. Hunt terriers, alsatians, labradors, dobermans, and Rhodesian ridgebacks were the commonest breeds.

The one feature many of these dogs did have in common was their names. Africans, Asians and Europeans all tended to give their dogs Swahili names. Simba and Chui, meaning lion and leopard, were probably the commonest. Others of a less complimentary nature were Fupi meaning Shorty, Chafu meaning Dirty and Dudu meaning Insect.

One curious fact was that Asians and Africans frequently gave male names to female dogs and it was not unusual to come across a bitch called Jimmy or Roger.

Some names could be dangerous.

A European farmer living near Konza, south of Nairobi, owned a working labrador retriever called Juno. As his dog retrieved the birds he had shot, or as he walked with her across his broad acres, he would call her name in a loud, affectionate voice. One afternoon the police visited the farm. He was arrested and charged with ridiculing and abusing the name of the President, Mzee Jomo Kenyatta. The farm labourers, hearing him bellowing 'Juno! Heel! Juno!' as he strode over the paddocks, shotgun under his arm, had thought he was calling his dog Jomo. Being unfamiliar with English they had never heard of the name Juno. Neither had the police constables who had come to arrest him. Only after a tremendous struggle, involving the assistance of an expert lawyer, was the case eventually dropped.

Other canine names were related in some way to the animal's background.

Bucket was a much-loved mongrel owned by an English couple.

While living in Maralal, a small town in the land of the Samburu, they had received daily and nightly visitations from a nondescript pi-dog which crept up to their kitchen door in search of scraps.

The husband, despite his soft heart, liked to call a spade a spade.

'Fuck it!' he would shout, as he caught the wretched animal slinking away for the umpteenth time. 'There's that bloody dog again!'

When they finally befriended and adopted the dog, they cudgelled their brains for a suitable name for their new pet. Their solution was an adaptation of the husband's response to the sight of the canine waif. In genteel society the derivation of the name was kept a closely guarded secret.

Barclay looked like an elderly, poor man's labrador, being cream-coloured with a blunt, round head. In fact, he was pure cur.

Originally owned by an Asian he had been abandoned when his owner went 'home' to the UK. He had been left tied to a tree outside a branch of Barclays Bank in Nairobi, and here he had lived for three months, subsisting on rainwater and scraps tossed to him by sympathetic passers-by, until rescued by the Kenya Society for the Protection and Care of Animals, by which time he was a frail tottering bag of bones. He was named Barclay after the bank outside which he had lived for so long.

Adopted by an up-country kennel-owner, who was more dog himself than man, and who fed him on prime steak, he regained weight with amazing rapidity, putting on several pounds weekly, until after a month he was almost rotund.

*****

Across the street from the surgery stood a tall gum tree. The hedge which separated the grounds of the Club from the street made a U-bend round the trunk of the tree, in whose upper branches there roosted at certain times of the year, many hundreds of black kites. At such times great clouds of these birds circled over the town at dusk. Anyone, unknowing or unwise enough to park his vehicle beneath this tree during the late afternoon or evening, when the birds returned from their day's foraging, crops and bellies bulging, would find on their return, bonnet and roof bespattered with their droppings. Even the few yard's walk across the road to the surgery could be fraught with danger as gobbets of avian dung hurtled through the air. The birds' high-pitched wavering calls were a warning to those below, aware of their habits, not to tarry.

The curve of the hedge around the trunk formed a conveniently secluded alcove into which passing pedestrians caught short were wont to enter in order to relieve themselves. This was done, not furtively, as would have been the case in Europe, but in a casual and carefree manner.

In front of the tree a middle-aged woman would often establish herself in order to cook a meal. She was never seen to beg and the source of her food was a mystery. Dressed in rags, she would squat down, unpack her bags, and proceed to light a small fire of twigs upon which she would cook a pot of maize meal, garnished with some indefinable greenery. Oblivious to passers-by, she would complete her meal and depart. She slept in the doorways of shops on the town's main street.

Beggars often came to the surgery to importune for alms. Some were genuine sufferers in that they were afflicted with some physical disability such as blindness, polio, or were deaf and dumb. The problem with giving money to such resident unfortunates was that once given they would regularly return to ask for more until it became almost impossible to get rid of them.

Others were mentally retarded and these would, on occasion, force their way into the surgery, gibbering and shouting. The attire of many of these wretches was often such as to startle the uninitiated. One gent entered clad in nothing but a pair of women's tights and a pair of hob-nailed boots. Another appeared barefoot, dressed, if it could be called that, in only a ragged shirt, and token, tattered underpants. Sympathetic though one might be to their plight, their presence was hardly conducive to the practice of good veterinary medicine, and I had to insist upon their diplomatic ejection.

Another category of beggar was not so easily got rid of. These were the various officials bent upon the collection of money to support projects of a public and personal nature. Some projects were indeed for worthy causes, such as hospitals and schools. Others, for farewell parties and dubious college fees, rather less so. Generally, it was difficult, or unwise, to refuse to contribute.

Sometimes impostors would appear, masquerading as official collectors, armed with imposing notebooks full of the names of people who had contributed to their particular cause.

Late one morning one such individual came to the surgery, stated that he was from the office of the District Commissioner and that he was collecting money for a party to be held for the local District Officer who was moving to another area the very next day. He was smartly dressed, spoke excellent English and I had no reason to disbelieve him.

Time was of the essence he said, the banks had closed, and could he be given cash? He had also run out of receipt books. On being informed that no money could be given without a receipt being issued he looked rather upset and then began using threatening language, insinuating that he had powers to enforce payment, especially from non-citizens such as myself. Reluctantly he agreed to return in the afternoon when he expected to receive his demands. As luck would have it, no sooner had he reappeared than two constables from the Police Dog Section entered the surgery bringing with them an alsatian for treatment. The money-collector looked distinctly apprehensive. On the police being asked if they knew him, he suddenly jumped to his feet, dashed through the door and rocketed up the street, the constables and dog in hot pursuit. A police car was passing. It was flagged down and a few minutes later and half a mile from the surgery the bogus collector was apprehended. He was last seen sitting sandwiched between two burly policemen in the back of the car, on his way to the cells.

Thieves would frequently use the ploy of collecting money for some supposedly worthy cause in order to approach private houses to check out means of breaking and entering.

Even infants barely out of nappies had joined the ranks. Sponsored walks were a popular means of raising money, mainly for schools and churches. How many of the participants were genuine was impossible to gauge and where the money went was equally difficult to determine. In many urban centres one could sometimes hardly walk down the street without being assailed by hordes of school children squeaking 'Sponsa me! Sponsa me!' Sadly, a lot of money sponsored in genuine walks either did not materialise, or cheques bounced.

Then there were the hard-luck merchants. Their stories varied, but lack of money to pay school fees, or being stranded and unable to pay for the bus or train fare home, were common themes, as were the promises to refund the sum involved as speedily as possible.

Christmas was the time when everyone who performed tasks, large or small – gardeners, house-servants, night-watchmen – expected something, preferably money and the more the better, for Siku Kuu (the Big Day) from the Mzungu, the Tajiri or Wealthy One. During the rest of the year they might be Moslems, Animists, Pagans or whatever, but as Christmas approached, their behaviour improved and they all worked that little bit harder. By the time Christmas Day dawned, everyone was an honorary Christian and in expectant mood. And in almost every case, hopes were realised as guilt-laden whites doled out the annual load of goodies and handfuls of red notes to lines of eager recipients.

Sartorial standards among the passers-by on the street outside the surgery were always of interest. Generally utility, not fashion, was the most important feature, although since independence from the British this practical aspect has been clouded by political overtones. Shorts, for instance, seem to be regarded as an undesirable colonial hangover, worn only by neo-imperial, Caucasian remnants and downtrodden blacks who know no better. Policemen sweltering in fatigues and boots on the Indian Ocean coast, or in the northern deserts, probably long for the days of short-sleeved shirts and shorts. Practical tribal garments, such as those worn by the Maasai and Pokot, come in for periodic lambasting, being thought of as being backward and a hindrance to 'progress'. The fact that people like the Maasai and Pokot live in areas where water, let alone facilities such as launderettes and washing machines, are in short supply, and that western clothes worn under such circumstances are not only uncomfortable but unhygienic, appears to mean little to those who make such pronouncements.

Despite the heat, some of the street-strollers wore three-piece suits. Many of the numerous babies strapped to their mothers' backs were wrapped in layers of woollen garments, even to the extent of wearing knitted hats and bootees. Other infants were recognisable only as shapeless humps hidden beneath towels tied round their mothers' chests.

Most men and women wore a variety of European clothes. Only people visiting town from outlying districts appeared in their traditional beads and blankets.

Cast-off European clothes from a bygone era were put to good, if outlandish, use. Giant topees, making the wearer look like a mobile mushroom, occasionally moved along the street, in one instance combined with a swallow-tail coat, shorts and bare feet. Fur coats and gum boots appeared to be not unpopular when obtainable, as were top hats and World War I tin helmets, although these latter items were a dwindling commodity.

The regular but harmless lunatics who passed along the street were not shunned, or regarded with distaste by the African populace as they might have been in Europe or America. Rather they were looked upon as being part of the non-productive arm of the community, a not unenviable role, or were just there, part of the extended African family. One fellow was a metal fetishist, and strode the asphalt, festooned with piston rings and hub caps, ajingle with bicycle chains and cow bells. Another individual, whose larynx had either lost all feeling or was made of cast iron, roamed the streets, stopping at various points to bellow an incomprehensible message at the passing throng, by whom he was totally ignored, before moving on to try elsewhere.

More to be pitied were those individuals with ghastly physical deformities such as those caused by elephantiasis or polio. Many of the victims of the latter disease had limbs so twisted and withered as to be little more than useless and inconvenient appendages. The worst affected shuffled along on their haunches, their stick-like legs bent into contorted attitudes beneath them. One man used stumpy boots on his hands and knees to enable him to crawl along the pavement. Another propelled himself along the street in a little cart. Why they were not killed or injured while crossing the streets, I never understood. Others used makeshift crutches or a cumbersome combination of a crutch and a stick. The lucky ones were those with only one leg affected. Instead of using a crutch most of these used a stout staff with which they propelled themselves along the street with amazing rapidity.

The number of Africans with deformed limbs seemed to be excessive, but polio was still common and it was natural for them to gravitate to the towns where the opportunities for gaining a livelihood were greater then in the rural areas.

Blind people occasionally proceeded down the street in front of the surgery, tapping their way with a stick, or being led by a child. They rarely begged, or, if they did, it was in return for services rendered. The blind man sitting with his back to the wall in front of the post office demonstrated his skill in reading a Braille Bible. A little group of sightless drummers and singers performed on the main street. How much money they were given I do not know. They certainly attracted a large and interested crowd.

The most pathetic victims of poverty were the tiny children of the few women who begged on the streets. There they seemed to spend their entire day, playing, eating and sleeping. At night they slept with their mother in a shop doorway with cardboard or newspaper barriers ineffectually keeping out the cold night winds. And in the morning they appeared again on the hard pavement.

※※※※※

One day, Heather Eames came into the surgery.

Small, dark and attractive, with a mischievous sense of humour, Heather lived in the Solai Valley where her husband Chris owned a large farm on which he grew coffee and maize and milked a herd of Guernsey cows.

Heather was carrying a small box from which emanated a strong, rank odour.

'Good afternoon, Mr Cran,' Heather beamed wickedly. 'I have a small problem here, and I hope you can solve it for me.'

She opened the box. Rummaging around in the chopped-up newspaper at the bottom was a small grey mouse, the source of the smell.

Heather explained that her two children had returned to the farm from Greensteds School near Nakuru for their Christmas holidays with two mice, which they assured her were both female. Sure enough a few days later one of the mice had a litter of eight babies. Twenty one days later the same thing happened again. The other mouse cleaned his whiskers and looked smug and self-satisfied. Now they had eighteen mice and the stench in the house was overpowering. Heather did some research and discovered that mice start breeding at the age of 42 days, that the gestation period is a mere 21 days and that the average litter contains six to ten offspring. She decided that enough was enough and that something had to be done.

88

She explained the situation to the children. The mice either had to go, or the perpetrator of the population, the non-female member of the duo had to be neutered without delay. They chose the latter course of action.

'So here he is. And the best of luck!' She laughed and left.

The tiny patient regarded me with a beady eye, nose twitching as though he found my odour as distasteful as I found his.

To date I had not castrated any animal smaller than a cat.

Restraint and anaesthesia of a male mouse were going to present problems, as difficult as the operation itself. The razor sharp scalpel blade was longer than the patient's hind leg. Complete anaesthesia was essential. Any violent movement by the mouse might result in involuntary amputation. And those organs requiring removal were so small that absolute stillness was mandatory.

I removed the cardboard tube from the centre of a toilet roll, placed it upright on the surgery table and dropped in a pledget of cotton wool soaked in ether. Mousey was then grasped by the root of his tail by the thumb and forefinger of my right hand and lowered headfirst into the tube, which I held steady with my left.

After an initial struggle, relaxation and then anaesthesia occurred within a few minutes. Handing the tail over to Moses, I seized the scalpel and set to work. Fortunately my eyesight was as sharp as the blade and two tiny testicles not much larger then the head of a pin were soon removed. The patient was returned to his box where he rapidly recovered from the effects of the ether.

Heather looked dubious when I showed her the evidence of the operation. However, after a week she reported that the powerful musky smell had gone, and later that the mouse population explosion had come to an abrupt end.

CHAPTER SIX

The Owen-Jones' returned from the coast and, shortly afterwards, I moved to my house at Bahati. This was a cedar-walled, shingle-roofed, bungalow situated at Lavender's Corner, ten miles from Nakuru, in the angle where the road to Bahati branched off from that running on to the Solai Valley. Here the tarmac ended with abrupt and brutal finality.

The house was small but comfortable, and contained all the furniture needed by a bachelor. There was a large living room with a stone fireplace, one bedroom, a bathroom and a small dining room. The kitchen was detached from the house and was reached by stumbling along a short covered walkway, paved with flagstones. Here my cook, an ancient Nyamwezi from Tanzania, pored over his pots and pans in semi-darkness, concocting culinary marvels on a huge blackened stove which he periodically fed with split lengths of firewood.

The windows of the house were so low that they looked as though they had been designed for use by a family of pygmies. The sills were level with my knee-caps. The outsides of the windows were screened with strong weld-mesh to discourage entry by unauthorised persons. The walls were constructed of rough cedar logs. The chinks between the logs were filled with dried mud. In some places the mud had fallen out and daylight could be seen instead. The roof was covered with wooden shingles, many mossy with age. The floor of the living room was made of highly polished wood but that of the bedroom was covered with a curious linoleum-like material, so corrugated that it resembled a choppy sea suddenly frozen by an Antarctic-like drop in temperature.

The house was surrounded by a large garden full of flowers, shrubs and trees and was besprinkled with small lawns. It was tended by two wizened Kikuyu gardeners, and was dominated by a huge pepper tree under which I parked my car each evening. Exotic brightly coloured birds darted among the blooms and bushes. Iridescent sunbirds hovered, sipping nectar. Gaudy starlings strutted on the grass. Weaver birds chattered in the

90

branches of the trees.

Beyond the pepper tree stood a rather dilapidated guest cottage, consisting of a bedroom and a tiny alcove containing a hand basin and a rusty shower.

Water was supplied via antiquated piping from two huge circular tanks behind the back of the house. These were kept filled via more antiquated piping from a nearby rivulet and from rainwater channelled off the roof. At the best of times the water issuing from the taps was of a dusky hue. When it rained it was positively chocolate in colour, and to have a bath under such circumstances, although doubtless beneficial to the complexion in view of the high concentration of mud in the water, was liable to dye the towels an unpleasing shade of walnut. When a few months later I decided to have the tanks drained and cleaned, the bottoms were found to be coated in an eighteen inch layer of reddish brown mud, the result of several years' gradual accumulation.

The lavatory was a primitive affair, which I initially regarded with some trepidation. It was a long-drop, a time-honoured construction consisting of a wooden thunder-box over a twenty-foot deep shaft. It stood in a secluded corner of the garden inside a tiny wooden building hardly bigger than a sentry box, whose hoary timbers, ravaged by termites, appeared to be held in position by the mass of creeping plants which covered them. Used as I was to the modern toilet wherein one could relax with the reading material of one's choice, this mediaeval comfort-station came as a rude surprise and certainly offered no comfort. Indeed, unless one was fortunate enough to possess square-shaped buttocks to conform to the rectangular aperture of this primitive privy, one was unlikely to spend much time inside contemplating the mysteries of the universe. Owing to the lack of illumination, a visit to the long-drop during the hours of darkness was something to be avoided if at all possible. Certain members of the Animal Kingdom normally given a wide berth by most people, such as snakes, spiders or scorpions, could well be lurking in those gloomy corners, waiting to pounce. And if they weren't, the darkness and one's imagination were sufficient to suppose that they were.

Light for the house was supplied by a small diesel generator which was sited inside a small shed about twenty yards behind the water tanks. Each evening, at dusk, I would crank it up. It would snort a few times and then settle down to its monotonous, thumping beat. The bulbs would glow dimly and then brighten. Once the generator had been switched off for the night, one had to rely upon kerosene lamps or candles for illumination. When I first went to Bahati I had to go outside whenever I wished to switch off the generator. I soon got tired of that. Besides, I had heard of those stories of people being attacked and knocked on the head by thugs waiting in the darkness. I could picture the scene – the dimming lights, the

91

slide into blackness, the final asthmatic coughs from the generator, and then the sudden rush by sweaty, strong-smelling bodies.

So I rigged up an ingenious system of wires running from the cut-off lever, through the trees, over the water tanks and through the window weld-mesh to a hook screwed into the cedar wall over the head of my bed. When I wished to douse the lights all I had to do was reach up from my prone position, give the wire a sharp tug, slump back onto the pillows and close my eyes.

The house was home to denizens other than myself.

Chief among these were the rats. Apart from a few non-conformists who dwelt in the house, the majority of these lived in the outside kitchen. During the day they were not much in evidence but at night they emerged from their holes to engage in a nocturnal seek, eat, and destroy mission. My sleep was seriously disturbed by their infernal squeaking and scuttling as they rushed along the kitchen rafters and swarmed over the floor in search of scraps and edible debris.

Owing to my cook's advanced years, his less than perfect eyesight, and the smoky cavern in which he worked, it was inevitable that when he finished for the night some crumbs of food should be left behind.

This proved irresistible to the rats.

Something had to be done.

I bought three large rat traps. As the rats appeared to be of the carnivorous variety, I baited each trap with a small chunk of meat.

After the cook had retired, I balanced the traps on the edge of a beam running under the eaves.

I then went to bed.

I had barely closed my eyes when there was a crash from the kitchen. A few moments later there was another and then another. Grabbing a torch I went to investigate. The three traps had all been sprung and now lay on the floor. Each held a large dead rat.

I reset the traps and returned to bed.

That night sixteen fat rats went to join their ancestors.

The toll on successive nights was not as high, possibly because that element of surprise, so essential in successful hunting, was lacking. It remained at around a dozen a night for about a week and then dropped off.

By the end of two weeks the survivors had got the message, and only on very rare occasions did the odd, bold, marauder venture into the kitchen.

Cockroaches proved considerably more difficult to bring to heel.

Attracted by the debris left by my fumble-fingered domestic, they moved into the kitchen en masse as soon as darkness fell. Inspection of the scene of the crime with a torch would reveal a phalanx of slowly waving antennae as their owners investigated the cause of the disturbance. They made no attempt to bolt for cover but stood their ground. They gave the impression of being somewhat irritated by the presence of the intruder and were only waiting for him to depart in order to resume their interrupted evening meal.

In pidgin Swahili I gave my cook a series of lectures on natural history, entomology and the value of basic hygiene. These were repeated at regular intervals. Although he paid nominal lip service to what I said, it was obvious that he didn't believe a word I said. As a result, the cockroach problem was a continually recurring one and the war of attrition continued until the day I left Bahati.

When it rained, other less friendly creatures made their appearance. Among these were the siafu or safari ants. These ferocious insects had no fixed abode and moved about in long columns, their flanks protected by soldier ants with massive mandibles.

They swarmed over anything, animate and inanimate, which came in their way. Sometimes their numbers were so great they wore a groove in the ground and when they had gone their passage could be marked by narrow, bare tracks through grass and other vegetation. They seemed to tumble along, crawling over each other in their insensate haste to get to wherever they were going. Their normal prey was other insects, but should other animals be unable to move fast enough, they too would be attacked. Small mammals, nestlings, slow-moving reptiles, and any incapacitated animal were frequently found dead or dying and covered with thousands of these savage black ants. Young rabbits in hutches were easy meat, as were goslings and chicks. Larger animals were not immune, especially if they were ill and unable to stand. On several occasions when examining recumbent cattle I was horrified to find swarms of siafu hard at work. Animals which were moribund and unable to sit up suffered most. The ants would enter the nostrils and eyes and their combined numbers were sufficient to destroy these sensitive areas.

As far as humans were concerned, they were seldom more than a painful nuisance and common-sense precautions were usually sufficient to divert their unwelcome attentions. These consisted of stratagems such as placing the legs of one's bed in tins half-filled with paraffin or, when on safari, surrounding the tent with a miniature barricade of wood ash from the camp fire. These ploys were not always fool-proof and from time to time a commando party would find a chink in the defences. The anthropomorphic might suggest that the ants possess a sense of humour as they invariably wait until they have advanced to somewhere between the upper thigh and armpit before letting rip with those fearsome mandibles. As their bites are extremely painful, rapid location of the attackers and their speedy removal are the instinctive reactions by most victims. Any sense of modesty, should the assault take place in mixed company, is generally shed as quickly as the garments covering the area of attack.

The African bee was a frequent visitor to the garden and from time to time swarms of these aggressive insects would make their home within the cedar walls of the house.

One memorable night they met their match.

It had rained intermittently during the previous few days and I had noticed a column of safari ants crossing the lawn outside the front door. A swarm of bees which had taken up residence in the roof appeared to be disturbed by the unsettled weather and whenever I went through the porch I ran the gauntlet of dive-bombing bees.

That night I took the precaution of putting the legs of my bed in tins of paraffin.

Shortly after I had tugged the generator wire a violent thunderstorm broke. To the accompaniment of peals of thunder and flashes of lightning, rain poured down for the next hour.

Suddenly it stopped and all that could be heard was the sound of water dripping off the roof and off the leaves of the trees.

Then I heard a soft rustling sound.

It seemed to be coming from the wooden walls of the bedroom. I strained my ears in an effort to determine what it was. The sinister noise continued so I struck a match and lit the kerosene lamp.

An army of safari ants was pouring through the wall.

There were thousands of them and their numbers were increasing with terrifying speed. The rustling sound I had heard came from their contact with the linoleum floor.

I retreated in some haste to the relative safety of my bed. As I did so there was a buzz by my left ear as an unseen bee shot past me in the semi-darkness. Then another whipped past my right ear. I leapt into bed and pulled the blankets over my head. From within my stifling cocoon I could hear the angry buzzing of individual bees followed by a low-pitched, menacing humming which gradually increased in volume.

It sounded as though the hive was about to break out.

Rising to the surface, I took a quick breath and, in the flickering half-light of the kerosene lamp, surveyed the scene. Bees were zooming hither and thither like miniature fighter planes with kamikaze pilots at the controls. I glanced down at the floor. A mass of ants surrounded each paraffin tin. The looked like a mob of peasants besieging a mediaeval castle, armed with enormous mandibles instead of pitchforks. And equally prepared to shed their lives. Thousands more were hurrying across the corrugated floor to join the siege.

The ominous humming had increased in volume. It sounded like a giant dynamo, out of control and about to explode.

It was time to leave.

Seizing the lamp and my car keys from the bedside table I leapt onto the floor and rushed for the door, simultaneously trying to dodge the bees in the air and the ants underfoot. Inevitably I failed. I was barefoot. There was no point in putting on my shoes. They were all but hidden beneath a seething mass of siafu. By the time I had wrenched open the door and stumbled into the garden I resembled the tourist in Fiji, who, having cast doubt on the claims of the native firewalkers, decided to have a go himself, with lively consequences. Hopping about on the lawn I removed, with some difficulty, several ants from the more intimate parts of my person. I could feel a few moribund bees crawling in my hair, their stings firmly embedded elsewhere in my scalp.

The night air felt deliciously cool after the heated atmosphere inside the house.

The sound of battle raging could be heard from my bedroom.

After keeping a listening brief for about 20 minutes I retired to the Volkswagen where I spent the next couple of hours shivering in ever-decreasing temperatures. Then, fearing the effects of hypothermia, I crept back into the house.

All was quiet.

Opening the door, I peeped into my boudoir. Not a bee nor ant was there to be seen. Scarcely believing my luck, I quickly nipped beneath the covers. An indeterminate sound, rather like a drunk trying to play 'In The Mood' on paper and comb, emanated from the bathroom next door, but, discretion, being, in my opinion, the better part of valour, I stayed put.

I fell into what is generally described as a fitful slumber.

At a time only a little later than my normal hour, I entered the bathroom in order to perform the morning ablutions.

There in the bath lay a huge football of dead and dying bees.

Of the ants there was no sign.

They had come, conquered and left as abruptly as they had appeared.

✂✖✂✖✂

The other inhabitants of the house and garden were positively benign by comparison. Under the eaves small groups of hornets quietly built their mud homes while nearby, borer bees noisily excavated their way into the timbers. In the drains surrounding the house, frogs croaked at night. A colony of fruit bats roosted in a tree in a secluded corner of the garden. Their large eyes and foxy faces swivelled and turned to watch whenever one walked nearby. Even the millipedes, centipedes and stick insects appeared to have beneficial intent. As did the occasionally-seen chameleon and praying mantis, although this view was doubtless not held by the unfortunate insects upon whom they preyed.

The house was rented for fifteen pounds per month from a nearby settler farmer. My employer paid this. I was responsible for paying the servants who came with the house. As a new boy I thought the wages which I was advised to give them on the last day of each month to be somewhat meagre. These were one hundred and fifteen shillings, plus four shillings for posho, or maize meal, for the cook, and 53 shillings for each of the gardeners. These two latter gentlemen were all but retired, but they did keep the garden in good trim. All three had a plot behind the house on which they had each built a thatched hut for themselves and their families and on which they grew maize and vegetables. My own emoluments were not over-generous so I was in no position to be hypercritical.

I bought my groceries in Nakuru at a store on the main street owned by an amiable Greek called John Cardovillis. These I gave to my ancient cook to do with as he would. Considering the primitive facilities at his disposal his culinary offerings were a marvel to behold and even better to eat. No doubt had I a wife with a more sophisticated palate than my own, certain evaluations might well have been raised with regard to variety, presentation and the method by which the food was converted from its raw state to that on the plate.

Such luxuries as a fridge or electric iron were lacking. A curious construction utilising charcoal and wire mesh and operating on the principles of evaporation stood outside the kitchen. This was my refrigerator. By keeping the charcoal wet, the contents, mainly, meat, milk, butter and most importantly, beer, were kept relatively cool.

My cook also attended to my laundry and I often wondered how he imparted the razor-like creases to my shorts. Each evening when I tossed them into the basket they were as crumpled as a screwed-up newspaper.

I decided to investigate.

One Saturday afternoon I went out to the area behind the kitchen where my old Nyamwezi was dealing with the laundry. On the ground stood a charcoal brazier and beside it was an iron, which looked as though it dated from the nineteenth century, which it may well have done. It stood on a small metal grill and, by means of a wooden handle, the top could be opened. This the cook did. Seizing the brazier with his apparently heat-proof hands he poured in a handful of red hot coals. He then proceeded to iron my garments with this antiquated piece of ironmongery to admirable effect. The essential part of the operation was judging the temperature of the charcoal. Too hot and one's clothes acquired a patchy burnt-umber effect, which was perfectly satisfactory if one anticipated being engaged in operations against guerrillas in the Northern Frontier District, but not otherwise. Too cold, and one strode forth clad in garments which resembled crumpled pyjamas. Today, this mode of attire appears to be an acceptable, if avant-garde, fashion. Then, it guaranteed the raising of outraged eyebrows, and the sudden jamming of steamed-up monocles into ex-Indian Army orbits.

One could identify those whose servants plied the antediluvian iron by the tiny charred spots on their clothes, made by the inevitable flying sparks from the charcoal.

Africans who used these irons were extraordinarily reluctant to graduate to electric models, regarding them with nervousness and suspicion. Often they refused point-blank to have anything to do with them, preferring to carry on as they had done in the past. It was best not to force the issue, especially with the older generation. Catastrophe was likely to be the only result.

Watching my cook handle that brazier suggested to me that Africans were even more impervious to heat than my boyhood reading had led me to believe. This opinion was reinforced on many subsequent occasions. The hands of a European are soft. Those of most Africans are like asbestos. They can pick plates out of a heated oven without wincing and carry them to the table without a tremor. If a European tried to do this, the chicken and chips would be all over the kitchen floor, let alone get as far as the dining room.

❋ ❋ ❋ ❋ ❋

I mused upon these and sundry other matters as I lay abed in hospital.

According to the medico I was making satisfactory progress. A month had gone by and I had become accustomed now to lying in the same position, leg up, head down. The poundage of weights on the pulley had been increased slightly. I was becoming quite agile on the monkey bars and as my gluteals shrank in size from disuse so my biceps swelled from constant activity. An incipient bed-sore had been nipped, if that is the correct word, in the bud, by the judicious use of a rubber tyre, which helped to raise the sometimes flagging spirits of the other members of the ward. There is nothing like a bit of embarrassing discomfort to raise a laugh.

One poor fellow in the corner of the ward was suffering from hepatitis. From where I was lying his eyes and skin appeared to be almost green in colour. Because of the damage to his liver he was unable to partake of any alcoholic refreshment.

Which meant more for the rest of us. This included a young chap whose family lived on the shores of Lake Baringo, about 60 miles north of Nakuru, catching wild birds and sending them to zoos in Europe and

America. One day, while strolling along the beach, he had found a cylindrical object lying on the rocks. He picked it up. It was a thunder-flash and it exploded in his face, fortunately doing only superficial damage. Where it had come from no-one knew. Possibly it had been dropped by a fisherman using it to stun fish or scare away hippo.

In the bed opposite lay Hector Vaughan-Ryall, a farmer from Molo.

One warm evening he was driving his pick-up between Mau Summit and Rongai. The window was wound down and his elbow was resting on the door. A lorry came swerving round the corner, its headlights blazing. It missed Hector's vehicle by millimetres but struck his elbow, almost tearing off his arm. The bone was shattered, muscles and ligaments were lacerated and there was blood everywhere. With amazing fortitude he drove himself to hospital in Nakuru. It was pitch dark when he arrived so he blew the horn to summon assistance. Eventually a couple of porters appeared and approached the vehicle. They took one look at Hector and fled into the darkness. So he admitted himself.

The surgeon had done a remarkable job in patching up his arm and told him that, apart from some stiffness of the elbow joint, a full recovery was expected.

The chief nurse, under the formidable Miss Brown, was a tall blonde, Amanda Herring, more commonly known as Sister Samaki – samaki means fish in Swahili. In her early thirties and unmarried, her superficial gaiety disguised an underlying insecurity.

Outside the hospital it looked like the beginning of the Second Flood.

The long rains had started much earlier than usual. Every afternoon the sky would darken menacingly and with a crack of thunder the rain would come hissing down. In a few weeks time the East African Safari Rally would be held over the long Easter weekend. The wet conditions were causing a lot of speculation as to how many cars would finish.

土魚土魚土

In my early weeks in Africa, during the hot dry weather, I was much occupied doing routine work – pregnancy testing cattle in rough wooden crushes under a blazing sun, doing mass vaccinations of stock against Rift Valley Fever, attending to lame horses, treating sick calves, dehorning bulls, creeping like a sweating hunchback into pig sties to examine their occupants, splinting fractures, carrying out post-mortems on fresh and frequently less than fresh carcasses.

In Britain and other so-called developed countries, most vets use shoulder-length disposable gloves when doing rectal examinations in cows, in order to put a barrier between the arm and the dung in the rectum. No such gloves were available here. As a result the arm in use – my left – after spending a lengthy session palpating large numbers of bovine uteri, was stained a displeasing shade of green. This varied from farm to farm, depending on the diet of the cattle and the season of the year. On some establishments my arm would emerge jungle-green during the rains, a peculiar olive-grey when conditions were dry. Whatever the colour, it was the devil's own job to remove, requiring soap, hot water, elbow grease and a lot of time. In an effort to lessen the staining effect and as an aid to lubrication I used to coat my arm with a layer of thick milking grease prior to doing pregnancy tests, but it was even more difficult to remove than the stain.

Dehorning was a strenuous business requiring stamina and strong muscles. After desensitising the horns with local anaesthetic, they were cut off close to the skull with a pair of huge and horrendously heavy shears. These were about five feet long. Although cumbersome, their weight was invaluable, as once they were correctly positioned, closure of their mighty handles effectively and cleanly removed the horns as quickly as cutting paper with a pair of scissors. Bleeding was occasionally a nuisance but could be speedily controlled either by the use of artery forceps or by tying a length of binder twine around the horn stumps to act as a temporary tourniquet.

When there were only a few cattle to be dehorned I did the job with embryotomy wire, a toughened twisted wire normally used to section dead calves within a cow's uterus during exceptionally difficult deliveries. The horns were cut rather like cutting cheese with a wire. Only it wasn't cheese but horn which generally had the consistency of Aberdeen granite. The wire did a smoother, cleaner job than the shears. The heat generated by the sawing action of the wire reduced bleeding to almost zero. The only snag was the effort involved. After dealing with a few pairs of well-matured horns, I was left gasping like an unfit marathon runner, arms quivering like badly set blancmange. Usually I considered it a matter of honour to struggle on to the last bitter cut, puffing like the proverbial grampus, biceps twitching and going light-headed with the strain. The dignity of the Island Race and all that rot.

Now and again however, and especially if I was feeling a trifle fragile after the night before, I would invite one of the African cattle-men to have a go. They were invariably appalled at the effort required. Maasai, especially, had considerable difficulty in completing this exercise. Most of them were accustomed to carrying nothing heavier than a slender spear or a well-balanced club and as a result their upper arms and shoulders would have been a credit to the cover of 'Vogue'. If they had been able to do the job with their legs it would have been a different matter. Their lower limbs were like iron, and, due to continual activity since childhood, they could walk all day and all night without the slightest sign of strain.

The altitude didn't help of course. Being several thousand feet higher than the summit of Ben Nevis caused a strange lethargy to creep over the limbs of certain individuals. A vet dehorning cattle on a farm at 8,000 feet on the slopes of Mt. Kenya, asked a friend newly arrived from Britain to assist. He seized the handles and set to. He got half-way through the first horn before fainting clean away – overcome by the combined effects of effort and altitude.

Carrying out post-mortems on stock, mostly cattle, was a common reason for visiting farms.

I always hoped that, on arrival, I would find a neatly folded, freshly laundered towel, a bucket brimming with clean, hot water and bar of fragrantly scented soap, all made ready for my personal use.

In view of the state of decomposition of many dead animals these items were, in my opinion, essential, if I was not to become a sort of olfactory pariah.

Alas, their availability was the exception rather than the rule. After a while I considered myself fortunate if any sort of water container holding the vital fluid was present.

On farms owned by relatively wealthy Europeans and Africans I felt it was not asking too much to have these meagre perquisites made available. On less productive properties I lowered my sights somewhat. Water was brought in milk churns, multi-welded buckets with jagged, finger-tearing rims, metal karais – bowls normally used for washing clothes, plastic baby baths, and Jerry cans. Where water was in short supply it would sometimes be presented in a container as small as an empty tin can. Knowing just how far the farm women had to walk carrying a heavy drum of water on their backs, I felt that in such cases it was profligate to expend even these few drops on washing my hands.

The colour of the water varied from that of gin to brown Windsor soup, when it often contained an interesting selection of particulate matter.

During my youthful reading of tales of the African bush, the tribesmen were always armed with razor-sharp assegais, carried knives with blades so keen as to make Mr Wilkinson hang his head in shame, and generally kept their weapons so highly polished that to gaze upon them in bright sunlight carried the risk of permanent damage to the eyeballs.

I carried this stirring image with me when I went to Africa.

After my first post-mortem it lay in fragments.

A call came in from an African farm in the Solai Valley. A Friesian cow which had been ailing for several weeks had finally expired.

During this period she had coughed intermittently, had lost weight and had developed an oedematous swelling of her neck and brisket. My boss had seen her and had suspected a foreign body in her chest.

A post mortem was requested, so I rattled out in my VW to discover the cause of death.

As I turned into the paddock, in which lay the carcase of the diseased, it struck me that the number of people awaiting my arrival was somewhat in excess of that needed to assist me while I cut and probed. There must have been at least thirty individuals standing around, squatting on the grass, sitting under bushes, or leaning against trees. The majority seemed to be in possession of containers of various kinds. An air of expectancy hung over the crowd, which turned as one as I got out of the car.

The dead cow lay stiffly on its side.

I walked towards it through ankle-tripping Kikuyu grass. A dense cloud of blue-bottles rose into the air, buzzing noisily in protest. They settled in their thousands on the surrounding bushes and grass stems until they seemed to bend under their weight. They sat there, waiting, glinting green and blue in the sunshine, stirring sluggishly in irritation when disturbed.

Three men, who appeared to be farm-workers, stood beside the carcase. Two had knives in their hands. The third held a panga.

'Naweza toa ngozi,' I asked. (Can you remove the skin?)

They set to work. Starting on the legs they slowly cut their way down to the trunk.

One knife had no handle but was obviously so blunt that there was little risk of the skinner gashing himself. The other was sharp enough, but was only about the length of a pen-knife. The men worked with great care and extremely slowly, trimming off all tags of muscle on the inside of the hide.

I could see that this was going to take forever.

I went back to the car, got my own knife from the boot and sharpened it on my steel. By the time I had returned the men were beginning to remove the skin from the distended abdomen.

I gave my knife to one of the men and asked him to open the abdominal cavity but, under no circumstances to puncture the stomach, which was blown up as hard as a drum.

Slowly he began to cut through the tightly stretched muscle. There was a sudden explosive report accompanied by the loud hiss of escaping gas and the pungent odour of fermented rumen contents. Gobbets of digested greenery shot into the air. The skinner's off-white shirt suddenly looked like a work of modern art with realistic smell thrown in for good measure. Several of the more interested observers, who had been watching from the stalls, retreated with some haste to a safer distance, surreptitiously flicking specks of ordure from their persons.

Eventually the abdomen was opened, the sternum chopped through with a panga, and with much heaving and grunting, the contents of the chest and abdomen drawn out onto the grass.

Retrieving my knife, I set to work.

The main lesions were in the anterior abdomen and chest. Both lungs contained several abscesses. The pericardial sac of the heart was completely obliterated by a mass of yellowish, cheesy pus, which had effectively stopped that vital organ from contracting. As I investigated this with the point of my knife, the blade grated on something metallic. I levered the unseen object to the surface and what appeared to be a three inch nail came into view. There seemed to be something odd about it. I looked at it more closely. The head was that of a nail but the point had been flattened into a wide sharp triangular shape. It suddenly dawned on me that this was a partially-made arrow head.

From its position in the pericardial sac, a narrow track led backwards through the diaphragm into the reticulum, the first stomach, to which it was closely adhesed. Large numbers of abscesses in the liver indicated that this unusual foreign body had introduced infection into that organ before penetrating the diaphragm. Once the point of the arrowhead had entered the muscle of the diaphragm it would be drawn relatively rapidly into the chest during breathing. Because of its ridged, honey-comb like lining, the reticulum is where most foreign bodies swallowed by cattle are trapped, and, if they are sharp, where penetration begins, leading to the condition known as traumatic reticulo-pericarditis.

I was to see many such similar cases, mostly caused by pieces of wire and nails. In one instance I found a length of wire *inside* the left ventricle of a cow's heart. It is amazing what cattle are able to swallow when they put their tiny minds to it. A post-mortem I carried out on a Boran bull revealed a large and totally indigestible leather boot jammed in its stomach.

I showed the arrowhead to the spectators who were suitably impressed and I explained in my rudimentary Swahili why the animal had died. I asked for some water with which to wash my hands and arms. A woman came forward with a small reddish object about the size of a matchbox and a bowl half full of water. As I scrubbed away I stressed that because of the large numbers of abscesses in the carcase and its bloated state from lying in the sun, it was totally unfit for human consumption.

I noticed that several of the interested observers now had knives and pangas in their hands and were advancing in a determined fashion. I repeated my warnings.

I had barely covered the twenty yards to my car before the cow had disappeared beneath a mass of apparently demented human beings. The air rang to the sound of hacking and chopping. Men emerged from the fray clutching half a leg or a great chunk of meat. A child went rushing by carrying a kidney in one hand and a shin bone with the hoof still attached in the other. An old woman tottered through the bushes with an armful of intestines clutched to her withered bosom.

I was appalled.

To these people however, meat was a rare and expensive luxury, something for which, with their monotonous maize meal diets, their appetites craved. Some tribes, notably the Turkana, would do almost anything to obtain meat. They were even known to disinter carcases in order to get their teeth into a piece of flesh. Its state of decomposition seemed not to worry them.

The meat of the animal I had just examined was unlikely to cause much harm. There were many instances on record, however, when people had eaten the meat of animals which had died of poisoning or anthrax. As a result they had become very ill indeed. Deaths were not infrequent. One had to be very sure of one's ground before declaring a carcase fit for human consumption. And even if it was fit to be eaten, it was all too easy for someone with a concurrent malaise to blame it on the meat he had just eaten.

I was amazed that during the violent dismemberment of the cow, no fingers or hands had been lopped off during the scramble for the choicer cuts.

A post-mortem which I carried out on a later occasion indicated that care was always necessary. A steer had died, the hide had been removed, and an axe had been brought with which to chop through the sternum. The axe was owned by a young man, who was asked, before he set to work, whether the head was securely attached to the handle. He asserted that it was. Standing at the head of the animal, which was lying on its back, its legs held by four men, he swung the axe. The head flew off, flashed through the air and struck the thigh of one of the men holding a hind leg. Blood spurted out. I rushed to the car, grabbed a bandage and applied it tightly round his leg. After a few minutes the bleeding eased and I took the man to a nearby dispensary. It could have been much worse. The axe head could have severed his femoral artery or struck his skull.

Thereafter, whenever an axe or panga was used under my supervision, I examined it personally before the cutting began.

CHAPTER SEVEN

Arthur Owen-Jones was a good vet. There was no doubt about that, in spite of his blunt and brutal methods. He had no finesse. Sophisticated techniques were not for him. He did the job in the way he thought best. Sometimes his way was the best, but not always. If someone suggested an alternative method he would listen, and then carry on as before. He never gave intravenous injections to small animals, never used catgut and he spayed bitches with a cigarette hanging precariously from his lower lip. If a fleck of ash dropped into the incision he would laugh and say it was sterile so what did it matter! There was so much money to be made and so much work to do examining cattle on settler-owned farms being sold under the Buy Out Scheme, that he considered it not worth his while keeping up-to-date.

This was all very well from the financial point of view and it suited Owen-Jones. No doubt a hard-hearted accountant would have agreed with him. For a vet relatively newly graduated, it was singularly frustrating not to be able to put into practice those techniques so recently acquired in college.

While he was on holiday at the Coast I had used my employer's surgical instruments, having none of my own. On his return he resumed possession, reducing the stock in my car to almost zero. This proved from time to time to be somewhat embarrassing, and on one occasion it taxed my ingenuity to the utmost.

Late one afternoon a call came in from a place called Likia Farm, to the effect that a cow was stuck calving. Likia Farm lay at an altitude of about 8,000 feet, on the edge of the forest between Njoro and Mau Narok.

I was delegated to go.

I set off, hoping against hope that this was going to be an easy job, with a small live calf lying in anterior presentation inside a large and roomy pelvis, parturition having only just begun and the mother content-

104

edly chewing the cud, just waiting for her offspring to slip out. I knew that this was highly unlikely, but, even in Africa, hope springs eternal in the human breast.

Beyond Njoro the road was unsurfaced murram and as I bumped along the usual dense cloud of dust belched out behind the car. I passed the entrance to Egerton College, originally established to instruct embryo settler farmers in the art and science of agriculture. The road ran straight and level through scattered patches of bush. In the clearings, herds of semi-wild white and grey horses were grazing. They started in alarm as the car passed, long manes and tails streaming in the wind as they galloped off. To the right the forested heights of the Mau escarpment rose blackly into the sky.

The road rose steeply through a forest of alien conifers. Clumps of bamboo grew on overhanging banks. The pine trees ended. Five hundred yards further on, a track led off towards a house on a knoll. With difficulty I deciphered the faded writing on a mossy sign hanging at a crazy angle from a mouldering post. Likia Farm. I glanced at my watch. Five minutes to six. The sun was beginning to sink behind the immense rampart of forest which frowned over the farm.

As I approached the house I could see that it was empty and dilapidated. The windows were broken. The outline of a garden could be faintly discerned. Chickens scratched in the dirt outside the front door.

From a distance, the house appeared to be in good shape, but it was just a sad and hollow shell – all that remained of someone's hopes and dreams and probably a happy home as well. These poignant reminders of a way of life fast coming to an end could be seen all over Kenya. A white house on a hilltop would turn out to be full of chickens. The once manicured lawns of a colonial mansion would be waist-deep in rank vegetation, with goats grazing up to the leaded windows. Stables in which pampered thoroughbreds once munched oats and barley, now housed whole African families.

An Ayrshire cow was standing in a small field about fifty yards from the house.

As I stopped the car I could see two legs protruding from her vulva and from those legs were hanging a pair of ropes. Someone else had apparently been having a go.

A young Kikuyu man, wearing a slightly guilty expression, appeared, followed by two Maasai.

'Jambo! Habari?' I said. 'When did the cow start calving?'

He answered in English.

'She has been calving since two days before yesterday.' He seemed to be almost proud of the fact.

I gulped. This wasn't going to be a five minute job.

I got a rope from the car and made a halter and tied the cow's head to a fence post.

Doffing my shirt I put on a calving overall which I had brought with me from Britain. I noticed with a mite of concern that as I shed my garments the Maasai were busy donning theirs – balaclava helmets and heavy ex-army greatcoats which all but reached their ankles. As night and the temperature fell, the reason for this rapidly became obvious.

After removing the offending ropes, I soaped my left arm and made a manual exploration of the genital tract. Foetal fluids were virtually absent. The calf's head was twisted backwards to the left and held rigidly clamped by the tightly contracted uterus.

The calf was well and truly dead and slightly emphysematous. Try as I might, it was impossible to repel the calf back into the uterus in order to allow correction of the mal-presentation. My eyes bulged in their sockets with the strain.

The correct procedure would have been to section the calf's neck with an embryotome, thereby allowing relatively easy delivery of the calf's body, minus its head, which would be retrieved later. An embryotome consists of two stainless steel tubes through which is threaded a twisted cutting wire. This is passed around that part of the dead calf one wishes to remove. The ends of the wire are fastened to two handles and the sawing done by a third party. The vet guides the instrument and directs the action of his assistant. The stainless steel tubes prevent the wire from cutting the cow's genital passage. The prime object of embryotomy is to reduce the diameter of the foetus, so that it can be extracted through the mother's pelvis with the minimum amount of trauma. All this sounds pretty easy in theory, but in practice a fair degree of strength, stamina and manual dexterity are required. Double-jointed shoulders, elbows and wrists and cast-iron knee caps, in the case of recumbent patients, are also invaluable assets. An additional difficulty in African practice was the problem of explaining to one's untrained assistant just how to manipulate the handles attached to the wire. Many seemed unable to comprehend the procedure involved, and, by the time they did, one's working arm felt as though it had been squeezed through a mangle.

In this particular case, on the chilly heights of the Mau, all of this was academic.

I had no embryotome. Neither had my employer.

Other less ideal methods had to be adopted.

As the calf was less than freshly dead a Caesarian section was inadvisable. In addition I had virtually no instruments. I had with me a small embryotomy knife with a concealed blade and with this I decided to remove both forelegs, in the hope that by so doing there would be created sufficient room to turn the calf's head into the correct position.

Girding my metaphorical loins, I set to work. I placed a calving rope above the fetlock of one leg and asked one of the Maasai to exert light traction. Next I made a circular incision round the leg. Then, holding the embryotomy knife in my palm, I pushed my hand along the leg until it was level with the calf's shoulder. I pressed the blade and drew it backwards through the skin and muscle until it reached the circular incision.

That was the easy part. Now I had to separate the skin and subcutaneous tissue from the underlying muscles and bones and remove the latter in one piece. This had to be done with ones' fingers. With a well decomposed foetus this could be difficult enough. With one from which life had only recently been pronounced extinct, it could be a fearful task, especially where ligaments and tendons were concerned.

It was essential to remove the entire leg including the scapula. If it came off at the shoulder joint then both vet and cow were really in the soup.

So, with aching fingers I broke down the attachments around the joints and shoulder blade and told the Maasai to pull. The leg resisted and then slowly slid out of its skin envelope and fell to the ground. I felt like a Stone Age man who had lost his skinning tool and was obliged to skin his prey with his bare hands.

I repeated the process on the other foreleg and felt a mild sense of achievement.

Surely there would be enough room now.

Applying plenty of soap and water I inserted my left arm as far as the armpit and then a bit further. With great difficulty I managed to put my hand on the calf's nose and attempted to turn the head into the correct position. It wouldn't budge. For the next ten minutes I exerted might and main. It was hopeless. Foetal fluids had long since been expelled and the uterus was now tightly contracted around the calf. All I was doing when trying to push the calf's head into position, was to push the uterus a bit closer to the cow's head.

Lateral deviation of the head is relatively easy to correct in early cases of mal-presentation. The calf is repelled into the uterus and the head is then pushed and pulled into position. The longer the cow has been calving the more difficult does this process become until an embryotomy or, rarely, a Caesarian section is required. The former can only be performed on a dead calf. If the calf is alive there are usually sufficient fluids to allow manual repulsion and correction. Most calves involved in this form of mal-presentation are absolutely or relatively oversized. Not passing easily through the mother's pelvis the calf's head becomes turned slightly to the right or left – most usually towards the mother's right flank. The longer the mal-presentation lasts the harder the cow strains, the further backward the calf's head becomes twisted until a situation arises just like the one confronting me on Likia Farm.

I glanced up at the sky. The shades of night were falling fast, but no youth bearing a banner with a strange device could be espied coming to my rescue.

A decision had to be made. And fast. The calf wasn't going to come out by the normal route. It was now a case of slaughter or Caesar.

I took stock of my meagre collection of instruments. This did not take long, as I had only one scalpel blade, but no handle, one tissue forceps, one artery forceps and one cutting needle. I also had a roll of thin nylon fishing line, cotton wool and methylated spirit.

I asked the young Kikuyu for a razor blade and after a short delay he produced one. With soap and water I produced a thin lather on the cow's left flank and shaved a large rectangular area. This was not an easy procedure due to the patient straining at regular intervals, when I felt as though I was shaving a large hairy drum.

With a 20 ml syringe, I infiltrated local anaesthetic along the line of my proposed incision, which would be about fourteen inches long. Finally I gave the cow an epidural injection to abolish the straining. By raising and lowering the tail, the junction between the sacrum and the first coccygeal vertebra could be felt as a distinct depression. I shaved a square inch of skin, swabbed it with meths and injected 5 ml of anaesthetic into the epidural space. Within a few minutes, evidence of its effect could be seen from the cow's tail, now hanging limp and flaccid, unresponsive to stimuli.

By now it was a little after 7pm and almost dark. The gate into the field was too small to admit my car and it was not possible to move the cow with our limited numbers. One of the Maasai disappeared in search of illumination. He returned with a tilly lamp and a small torch, whose light was so weak that the bulb looked like a small red eye, winking in the gloom.

With a couple of ropes we cast the patient and tied her hind legs below the hocks and her forelegs below the knees. This was not to stop her from kicking but to prevent her from getting up during the operation, with embarrassing results. I laid my instruments on what I hoped was a clean towel and set to work.

I made a vertical incision through the skin. My scalpel blade was a disposable one and hence razor sharp, so the absence of a handle, although a disadvantage, did not inconvenience me too much. I made my way through the various layers of muscle and finally arrived at the peritoneum. Fortunately the cow was in pretty lean condition so I did not have the problem of having to contend with layers of fat. A few small arteries severed en route caused me some momentary anxiety in view of the fact that I had only one artery forceps. I clamped the largest one. The others, I reasoned, from their size, would soon stop bleeding. There was nothing I could do about them anyway.

I pressed on, concentrating grimly in the feeble, flickering light on the task in hand.

A flying beetle, attracted by the glow of the tilly lamp, landed on the shaved area of skin and crawled purposefully towards the incision. I flicked it away with my forefinger. Other insects arrived and made determined efforts to fall, lemming-like, into the abdominal cavity. Some may have succeeded, but my attention was elsewhere.

Inserting my left arm into the abdomen, I located the uterus and identified a hind foot. With considerable difficulty I grasped it and pulled it up towards the outer world. Twice it slipped from my grip and I had to start all over again. I knew that I had to get at least a small part of the uterus up to the incision. The calf was dead and if uterine contents escaped into the abdominal cavity, the cow would certainly contract peritonitis and probably die. Struggling and straining, I finally got a hoof through the lips of the wound and incised the uterine wall with my scalpel blade. There was a hiss of escaping gas and a piece of greenish foetal membrane appeared alongside the hoof. An unsterile operation was suddenly even more so.

'This is a waste of time,' I thought. 'She'll never survive this.'

It seemed as though my assistants thought likewise. I briefly glanced up. Three pairs of eyes regarded me with a mixture of amazement and disbelief.

I seized the hoof and drew it through the incision. I told the young Kikuyu to hold it and pull it vertically upwards while I cut through the uterine muscle, enlarged the opening and withdrew the other hind leg. One of the Maasai came to his assistance, leaving the other to hold the patient's head. Together, with a good deal of grunting and heaving, they extracted the two-legged calf. As they did so, I held fast to the uterus to ensure it did not vanish back into the abdominal cavity.

My relief at seeing the calf emerge was profound, but the job was far from finished.

Next came the lengthy job of stitching the uterus and abdominal wall. I had only fishing line, and pretty thin fishing line at that. Absorbable suture material such as catgut should be used when stitching tissues such as muscle. Certainly not fishing line.

Still, needs must when the devil drives.

Grasping the vital part of the uterus in my left hand, I put in a long single inverted stitch pattern, slipped in a pessary and then put in another layer for good measure.

Now for the abdominal wall.

I re-threaded my needle. As I did so I felt a spot of rain on my bare shoulder.

'That's all we need!' I thought. 'A good downpour to finish us off!'

No wonder the Maasai were wrapped up like Eskimos.

I crouched low over the incision in an attempt to keep the operating field as dry as possible.

The operating field!

I grinned mirthlessly in the dimming light of the tilly lamp. I was glad my professor of surgery wasn't present. Every basic principle in the book seemed to have been broken during the course of this operation.

As the raindrops drummed on my bare back, I feverishly stitched the peritoneum, then each muscle layer separately. It seemed to take forever. In the yellow light of the lantern, it was difficult to see clearly and at one point I started stitching the external abdominal oblique muscle to the internal abdominal oblique.

The torch finally died.

Finally only the skin was left to close. At this point the cow decided to do a bit of straining. As I had no needle holders, I had to use my sole pair of artery forceps, which I had retrieved from its position clamped on the offending blood vessel. I doubled the nylon and stitched the skin in an everted pattern. Even so, on several occasions the nylon broke as the cow's belly rose in the semi-darkness like a giant balloon on the point of rupture.

At last the final stitch was tied and I straightened up, feeling as though I had contracted terminal ankylosis of the spine. I cleaned away the dried blood from the wound and sprayed the area with gentian violet from an aerosol can. After giving her an intramuscular injection of oxytetracycline, we untied the ropes. The cow sat up, and after a few minutes spent in silent contemplation, she rose to her feet and ambled off into the darkness.

With a sense of relief I gathered up my goods and chattels.

At the cost of a great deal of unnecessary effort the job had been done. This somewhat blunted the achievement.

However, some things had been learned. I now knew that it was possible, with sufficient determination and effort, and by not conforming slavishly to accepted ideals, to achieve satisfactory results under the most primitive of conditions, with the barest minimum of instruments and minus skilled assistants.

This knowledge offered me some slight comfort as I slithered down the Mau in a thick drizzle. But I also knew that things would have been much easier if I had had an embryotome and a full bag of surgical instruments.

Twelve days later I returned to inspect my handiwork.

The cow was alive and well, eating heartily, and producing a reasonable amount of milk. There was some slight infection along the suture line.

Hardly surprising under the circumstances. I removed some stitches and inserted some new ones and was able, with some justification, to give an optimistic prognosis. The young Kikuyu and his Maasai henchmen seemed to be mightily pleased and wrung my hands and bade me God-speed as I left the farm. This did not, however, stimulate them into paying promptly for services rendered under shot and fire. Far from it.

Several months later one of the Maasai made the error of walking in front of the surgery. I recognized him, nipped out and steered him inside, where the wrath of Arthur Owen-Jones was unleashed upon his shaven skull.

He paid up quietly.

That Caesarian remains vivid in my memory partly because of the circumstances in which it was carried out and partly because it was my first in Africa. The first of very many. My employer, one of the old school, didn't do Caesars and consequently was suitably impressed. Calvings in Africa are, on the whole, considerably more difficult than in more sophisticated parts of the globe, mainly due to mismanagement, neglect and plain lack of observation. General circumstances, attitudes, and methods of farming are partly responsible, and neither European nor African cattle owners can claim superiority in this regard. Often, by the time it has been decided to call for professional assistance, it is dark, the cow may be unable to stand and be lying in mud or manure, unskilled and unwashed hands and arms have been delving into her uterus, while on the outside an undirected tug of war team of brawny, brainless peasants have succeeded in persuading the calf to shuffle off its mortal coil, probably much to its relief.

When I later acquired an embryotome, I regarded it as my most valuable instrument. Nothing could replace it. Calvings which otherwise would have taken hours of exhausting labour could be accomplished in a fraction of the time.

Embryotomies are only performed when the calf is dead. Should the calf be alive, most of the problems caused by the death of a calf do not arise. The cow has been in labour for a relatively short period of time, foetal fluids are still present, the calf can usually be repelled or rotated with some ease and if necessary a Caesarian section can be carried out with minimal trauma to the cow and a good chance of a live calf to boot.

If the calf has been dead for some time, lubrication – and plenty of it – is essential.

Embryotomy could on occasion be a strenuous exercise, particularly if the patient was recumbent, or if the cow and calf were very large. On these occasions I felt I needed a wet-suit to get right in there to thread the wire round the neck or pelvis, which always seemed to be just out of reach. Somehow or other it was always possible but it was often a close run thing with much loss of perspiration.

Deformed calves, such as the extraordinary shistosomus reflexus monster with its twisted legs, exposed entrails, and bent spine were best dealt with by use of the embryotome. As were other monsters such as bulldog calves, those with hydrocephalus or the hideous cyclops with its one eye glaring in the middle of its forehead.

As these horrors were mostly dead, I had no compunction about sawing them up and the trauma inflicted on the mother was on the whole less than that were I to do a Caesar.

Very occasionally a monster calf would be born alive and survive for a few days. The African workers regarded these creatures with a mixture of fascination, repulsion and fear.

Of the two methods, embryotomy and Caesarian section, the latter undoubtedly made a greater impression on spectators and helpers. During the course of the former, all that could be seem was the daktari, probably on his knees and bedaubed with noxious fluids, manipulating a curious instrument, while one of their mates was obliged to do all of the hard work, sawing himself into a state of exhaustion.

During a Caesar there was plenty to see, there was no strenuous pulling, there was a bit of interesting bleeding, and there was frequently a live calf which was often on its feet by the time the last stitches were inserted. It was all very satisfactory and everyone went away feeling slightly fulfilled. Such was often not the case after an embryotomy. The calf emerged in several pieces, and, if it had been dead for some time, accompanied by a pungent odour and a cloud of flies.

Whatever method was used, some facts were paramount. In all aspects of obstetrical work forethought, common sense, firm decisions and purposeful action were essential in order achieve success.

◎◎◎◎◎◎

I had been in hospital for seven weeks now and felt like part of the fittings. Other patients came and went but I remained, tied to my grotesque meccano set, like a termite queen being fed and fattened by her swarming workers. Not that I was putting on weight. The hospital menu saw to that.

I was also becoming concerned about the mounting medical bills. My monthly salary had been abruptly stopped with my entry into hospital and soon what little I had saved in Kenya was all gone. Although the daily hospital bill was only ninety shillings, by the time I was discharged I had to fork out over four hundred pounds, most of which I had to have sent out from Britain.

One morning I awoke with a pain in my lower back. During the course of the day, the discomfort increased so I casually mentioned it to

Sister Phil Kelly, a no-nonsense Irish colleen, who muttered something about beer and kidneys but said she would telephone the doctor. Mr Thakkar was apparently masked and gowned in the operating theatre of the government hospital, but a message was received advising that I be given some penicillin until he could come and see me. This was done with considerable relish by Sister Kelly who injected the antibiotic into my shrunken gluteals, smiling grimly as she did so. During the course of the evening, I observed with a curious clinical detachment, that I was breathing rather faster then normal and that the pain appeared to be associated with the breathing, an unpleasant rasping sensation, rather like having a piece of sandpaper rubbed against the inside of one's chest. By the time Mr Thakkar appeared, at about 10pm, I was panting like a dog on a hot afternoon. He stuck a thermometer under my tongue and listened to my chest with his stethoscope.

I had a temperature of 103 degrees and pleurisy, the result of my enforced recumbency. More antibiotic was pumped into my protesting backside. Extra pillows were put behind my back. For the next twelve hours I gasped and puffed at a rate I would not have believed possible. Then I began to improve, my rate of breathing slowed down and three days later I was better.

My relief was profound. It is only after a period of illness that one realises that however great one's financial assets, one's greatest asset is good health. As I panted the night away, visions of future mountaineering exploits appeared ludicrous and unreal. With my recovery my spirits soared and I could already see myself cramponing up the Diamond Glacier on Mt. Kenya.

Four months after my arrival in East Africa I had climbed Kilimanjaro. Closing my eyes, every detail of that marvellous trip came back to me.

I had arranged my mountain safari through the Marangu Hotel, a delightful hostelry on the southern slopes of the mountain in Tanzania.

On the Thursday evening before Good Friday, I packed my climbing gear in the Volkswagen and at about 8pm, set off on the long drive to Tanzania. Half-way between Nakuru and Nairobi two uniformed policemen, both carrying rifles, stepped into the road and waved me to a halt. They wanted a lift to the city. Somewhat nervously I watched them force themselves into the little car. Both, however, were very friendly. When I told them that I was on my way to climb Kilimanjaro, they were incredulous. What on earth would anyone want to do that for? They obviously thought I was mad.

I sped through the darkened city and was soon bowling across the Athi Plains. Suddenly I had a rude surprise. The smooth tarmac abruptly ended. For the next 120 miles, as far as Mtito Andei, the road remained unsurfaced.

113

I crossed the Athi River and, with the gravel thundering against the bottom of the car, rattled on towards Ulu. Here and there, in the light of my headlights, a mound of shattered glass indicated where a flying stone had smashed some unfortunate motorist's windscreen. Luckily for me the traffic at that time of night was light, but I hugged the verge whenever an oncoming vehicle approached. Near the Machakos turn-off an entire exhaust system complete with silencers lay on the road. I supposed it had been untimely ripped from its moorings by the horrific vibration, which I feared would loosen the very fillings in my teeth if it continued for very much longer.

Continue it did. Fortunately the Volkswagen's engine was mounted at the rear and its short twin exhaust pipes were almost impossible to dislodge. Now and again I could see the eyes of unseen animals glowing in the bush at the side of the road and twice antelope dashed in front of the car, but I was too occupied concentrating on the state of the highway to be concerned with the identity of nocturnal wildlife.

Beyond Ulu the road descended sharply to the township of Sultan Hamud where the corrugations began. It was like driving on a giant washboard. The experts later told me that if one drove fast enough it was possible to iron out the appalling vibration. I obviously wasn't driving fast enough.

Holding on grimly to the juddering steering wheel, I pelted on past Hunter's Lodge, named after J. A. Hunter, scourge of the savanna and single-handed slayer of a thousand black rhino in the Kibwezi district of Kenya. The Sikh temple at Makindu appeared and then vanished into the darkness. Then the first of the baobab trees loomed up, grotesque and bloated, their enormous trunks gleaming palely in the headlights, their twisted branches resembling gnarled and knotted fingers. With the baobabs came a rise in temperature. The cool highlands had been left far behind.

For the next thirty miles, until Mitito Andei was reached, the road crossed countless luggas (usually dry river beds) and dongas (gullies). The car laboured up the hills, plunged down the other side, ploughed through the stream or dust-wallow at the bottom and then ground up the other side. Thick red dust poured in through the open windows. The heat was stifling and by the time the lights of Mtito Andei appeared at the top of the final hill I was getting a bit desperate.

I could almost hear the car sigh with relief as its tyres bumped onto the tarmac. I certainly did.

Having topped up the tank at an all-night petrol station I pressed on through Tsavo National Park. Thick vegetation, dark and menacing, crowded in on the edge of the road, which, as it was now well after midnight, was deserted. At the famous bridge over the Tsavo River I stopped to obey a call of nature. The air was warm and gentle. A light breeze rustled the leaves of the dom palms on the bank. I looked up at a sky spangled with a million twinkling stars. The river water gurgled musically under the bridge.

It was hard to imagine the reign of terror in 1898 when those notorious lions, the man-eaters of Tsavo, caused a reign of terror among the Indian workers building the railway, picking off their victims almost at will, until they were hunted down and shot by Col. J. H. Patterson. I awoke from my reverie with a start when a shriek like a blast from an off-key trumpet broke the silence. Breaking branches cracked and large bodies pushed through the bush. Elephant. The very word conveyed a sense of massive dignity and restrained power. The herd slowly moved off and the sound of vegetation being beaten to death faded away.

At 4am I reached the township of Voi. Here I turned westwards onto the rocky unsurfaced road to Taveta on the Tanzanian border. For a while the way ran between sisal plantations on the left and the lofty Taita Hills on the right. In the darkness I could see neither. The road dipped steeply down to dry river beds, curved its way along sandy ridges and bored its way through tunnels of bush. A pleasantly smooth section allowed me to slip into top gear, a rare treat.

Suddenly a cheetah leapt onto the road. For a mile it loped along in front of the car, seeming to delight in its grace and strength, remaining always a few yards in front of the bumper, before turning and vanishing into the bush.

It was now 4.30am and I was beginning to become dangerously sleepy, nodding off momentarily and wakening with a start on the wrong side of the road. I strained into the darkness, muscles taut and tense with concentration. It was no good. I drew into the side of the road, turned off the engine, switched off the lights, laid my head on the steering wheel and slept.

I was woken by the sound of birds. A colony of weaver birds was nesting in the branches of the thorn tree under which I had stopped the car and they were objecting to my presence.

The sun was rising and shafts of golden light were piercing a fine mist which lay over the surrounding rolling, tree-dotted plains. I got out of the car to stretch my legs. The air was perfectly still, cool and fresh. Invisible doves cooed in the trees. I glanced upwards towards the west. A vast dome hung in the sky, seemingly supported by a great raft of clouds. On its summit I could see the white of glaciers and snowfields. Kibo, the highest point of Kilimanjaro, dwarfed the nearer and lower peak of Mawenzi, whose jagged ridges and dark gorges looked like a gothic lithograph of an Alpine vista. The mountain was immense, dominating the landscape.

Returning to the car, I drove on towards Taveta through the

southern extension of the western half of Tsavo National Park. During the First World War this area was contested by German troops commanded by the legendary von Lettow-Vorbeck, and British forces drawn mainly from Africa and India. Insignificant hills such as those at Mbuyuni and Salaita on the British side and at Latema Reata on the German side of the border were fought over with considerable loss of life. Empty cartridges and shell casings can still be found, but of the bones of those who fell, there is no sign. The vultures and hyenas have made sure of that.

Antelope and zebra grazed in the distance. Giraffe fastidiously nibbled at the tops of trees. An eland, dewlap flapping, dashed across the road and crashed into the bush.

A flash of light on water indicated where Lake Jipe lurked amid its reed beds at the foot of the North Pare Mountains.

The road crossed and re-crossed the branch railway line from Voi. Greenery appeared amid the desiccation – spiky expanses of sisal. On the top of a conical hill stood a white mansion, formerly owned by Ewart Grogan of Cape-to-Cairo fame and bete noire of the colonial era.

Scattered houses appeared in the distance. The car rumbled over a wooden bridge, spanning a muddy stream, and a few minutes later I was steering a less than direct route down the main street of Taveta, a dishevelled township of a few hundred people. Here, under the mango trees, the early caravans would replenish their supplies before setting out across Maasailand.

A few of the inhabitants were moving slowly about their business. An air of somnolence and lassitude hung over the place, which was obviously well past its sell-by date.

At the Kenyan border post a yawning official flicked through my passport. He seemed to spend an age studying the various customs stamps I had accumulated during my travels in Europe and North Africa. He gave me a long, silent stare and then slowly reached for his rubber stamp. Finding an empty page, he raised the stamp and then with dramatic and sudden force brought it down with a crash onto the virgin parchment. No doubt a psychologist might find something significant in that small display of gratuitous violence. I did not pause to ponder on hidden meanings. Grabbing my passport I jumped into the car and set off towards Tanzania.

The Tanzanian customs post lay a few miles east of the village of Himo. A building hardly larger than a sentry box stood beside the road. A pole weighted at one end with rocks and designed to stop vehicular traffic pointed skywards. The place was deserted. I blew the horn. No one appeared. Apart from the sentry box no other buildings were visible. For ten minutes I waited. The surrounding bush was silent. Kilimanjaro beckoned. I could keep her waiting no longer. I drove on.

At the Marangu Hotel I met my climbing companions, a forester from Malawi, and two agricultural officers from Zambia. They had arrived in Marangu a couple of days previously and looked refreshed, relaxed, and, above all, fit. After my all-night drive I felt like nothing more than a few hours in bed. However, a shave and a lavish breakfast in the small dining room, surrounded by photographs taken on early expeditions to the mountain, went some way towards effecting a semblance of recovery.

The hotel supplied a guide and porters, who carried all of our food and accoutrements for the safari up the mountain. My initial view was that this was a rather effete way in which to tackle a fairly accessible summit. After we had set off however, I decided that there was some merit in the idea after all. It was rather pleasant to stroll along carrying nothing more than a walking stick and a not unbearably heavy rucksack. Besides, the mountain was over 19,000 feet high, employment was being given to local people and with their help, hopefully, we shouldn't get lost.

With my conscience thus suitably salved, I set off to enjoy myself.

From Marangu the track ran through the plantations of the Wachagga, whose groves of bananas, coffee shambas, and fields of maize and cassava lay thick on every hand. Up to the edge of the forest, the slopes were densely populated and intensively cultivated. As we plodded up the path the cheerful inhabitants smiled and shouted greetings as we passed. Children offered us nosegays of flowers. It was all very pleasant. The sun shone. Birds sang. Butterflies fluttered across the track. Little streams tinkled down the valleys.

At about 7,000 feet the cultivation suddenly ended and we entered the forest which almost completely surrounds the mountain. This was my first contact with a tropical rain forest. The vegetation was extraordinarily dense. The initial impression was that of an incredible number of species of trees and plants all engaged in mortal combat for the available space and light. The air was moist but cool because of the altitude, the light dim and green and gloomy. I knew from my reading that elephant, buffalo, and rhino lived in these forests and from time to time I paused to cock my ears in the hope of hearing sound of their passage through the undergrowth. Nothing stirred. I suspected that if I essayed the same path during the hours of darkness I would be stumbling over them round every corner. Birds were equally inconspicuous. I peered into the tangled foliage. Touraco and silvery-cheeked hornbills were reputed to haunt these jungles. A few, small, brown, wren-like birds hopped about among the lower branches. I later saw more hornbills and touracos in the forest remnants near Nakuru than I did in the virgin forests of Kilimanjaro, Mount Kenya and Ruwenzori. Perhaps they were just easier to spot in their dwindling habitat.

We spent the first night in Mandara Hut, formerly named Bismarck Hut after the Iron Chancellor. The original hut was built before the First

World War and lies just below the upper edge of the forest at 8,000 feet.

The following morning we left the forest behind and bore left through an area of giant heather, onto rather bleak moorlands. Their barren aspect was relieved by the remarkable plants which dotted their surface – giant groundsel and lobelia. The former resembled a giant cabbage stuck on top of a thick stalk, six to eight feet high. The latter was a tall, green, feathery phallic column.

Five hours later and 4,000 feet higher, Horombo Hut hove into view. Here the night was spent in temperatures which made me glad I had brought my down-lined sleeping bag all the way from bonnie Scotland. How the porters fared I scarcely dared to think. When they emerged the following morning from wherever they had spent the night, their glossy black complexions had turned a ghostly shade of grey. I was unsure whether this was a consequence of their close proximity to the fire which they had kept burning all night, or to the alpine environment. Whatever the cause I was glad to observe that with the rising of the sun normality was restored. The hut was formerly called Peters' Hut, after the notorious Teutonic explorer, who was such a thorn in the sides of the Brits when they were endeavouring to extend their sphere of influence to Uganda.

There had been frost during the night and the ground was iron-hard as we walked up to the Saddle, which separates the main summit of Kibo from the lesser peak of Mawenzi. I was amazed to see brilliant metallic-green sunbirds flitting among the hoar-covered lobelias. Hopping about among the rocks were mountain chats, small robin-sized birds.

To our right the craggy cockscomb of Mawenzi dominated the skyline. At 16,890 feet it was almost 2,500 feet lower than Kibo. In my eyes, however, of the two, it was by far the more impressive peak. A complex mixture of pinnacles, ridges, gullies, ice-fields and buttresses, it made Kibo by contrast resemble an uninspiring upturned pudding bowl. If it was a duty to ascend the higher peak, it would be a pleasure to return and tackle the lower summit.

The Saddle is a wide, barren, and relatively flat area between Kibo and Mawenzi. It is devoid of surface water and as a result almost without vegetation. It is in effect an alpine desert. All the more strange therefore, that a herd of eland appears to be resident in this hostile environment. How they live, and indeed thrive, on a diet of stunted grass and wiry everlasting flowers is a mystery.

The altitude was now over 14,000 feet and my companions were complaining of headaches and nausea. Initially I thought this was because they were older than me, but later I realised that they were suffering from altitude sickness. Even on the summit I felt nothing. I counted myself as fortunate indeed.

The porters had gone on ahead to Kibo Hut whose aluminium roof could be seen twinkling in the afternoon sun. They were carrying firewood and water as none were available near the hut. Having deposited their loads they would descend to the comparative comfort of Horombo Hut. Had I known how uncomfortable would be the night ahead, I think I might have joined them.

The hut stood at the foot of an appallingly steep slope of scree at an altitude of 15,500 feet. By the time we reached it, the slope and the hut were in shadow and the temperature felt several degrees below freezing. The tin roof rattled in the icy wind. As we approached our night's abode, one of my companions disappeared behind a rock and was noisily sick.

I would prefer not to remember the hideousness of that night but the memory of it refuses to go away. The interior of the hut was dark and dingy, the only illumination being that provided by the guide's oil lantern. The gloom was increased by the smoke from the fire, on which what little food we ate, was cooked. In spite of the fire the temperature steadily fell as the night progressed. Dressed in all the clothes we had and crammed into our sleeping bags, we lay on the hard wooden bunks, teeth chattering and muscles twitching. I was wearing a shirt, three sweaters and an anorak, and was certain I was suffering from hypothermia. The roof seemed to lift with every puff of wind and settle back with a great clang. Sleep was impossible under such conditions.

So it was with resigned relief that we crawled from our sleeping bags at 3am when the guide announced that it was time to make a move. I pulled on my boots, opened the door and stepped out into the darkness. I gasped. It felt as though I had stepped into a giant fridge. The air was icy and it was obvious that movement was essential if such inconveniences as frost-bite and premature rigor mortis were to be avoided. Even in the north of Scotland I had not felt such cold.

The sky was cloudless and sparkled with a myriad of stars. As I felt in no mood to stand pondering the mysteries of the universe, I plodded after the guide whose lamp was to be our guiding light up the scree. For what seemed like several hours we struggled up the dimly visible path, boots crunching on the frozen gravel. Luckily for us our progress was not impeded by snow. Little had fallen during the previous few weeks, the scree was dry and bare, and the ice on the glaciers hard and polished. When Shipton and Tilman climbed the mountain in the early 1930s they had a fearful struggle and just failed to reach the summit after ploughing their way through waist-deep snow.

As we approached Gillman's Point on the crater rim, the sky was beginning to lighten in the east. Slowly the craggy outline of Mawenzi appeared against the paling sky and at last, like a great blood orange, the sun rose above its rocky ramparts. It was an impressive and inspiring sight. At the time however my main interest in the rising of the sun was that therein lay warmth and a return of circulation to chilled limbs and frozen extremities.

Who Gillman was, other than that he was an early member of the Mountain Club of East Africa, I have failed to discover. At 18,640 feet the point named after him is at an impressive altitude, but it is not the summit, which is 700 feet higher. Below I could hear my companions gasping and puffing in the thin air. I waited until they had arrived and then, leaving them with the guide, set off for the summit.

To my right lay the spectacular crater of Kibo, with its extraordinary maze of snowfields, glaciers, seracs and ice towers, 600 feet deep and one and a half miles in diameter. Within it I could see the Inner Cone which rises to within 200 feet of the summit and within which is the Inner or Reuch Crater. Within the latter rises a minor cone called the Ash Cone which in turn contains a central crater called the Ash Pit which is 425 feet deep. The place is a vulcanologist's paradise.

By-passing the Bismarck Towers on the right I walked rapidly along the crater rim, rising gradually over the minor eminences of Hans Meyer and Elveda Points until I reached the top at Uhuru Peak, where a brass plaque on a rock marks the summit, first climbed by the Leipzig geographer Hans Meyer and his guide Ludwig Purtscheller in 1889.

Our guide arrived and after taking the obligatory photos in both stern and nonchalant postures, I retraced my steps. On the way I met my suffering companions who were holding onto each other for support as they clawed their way along the crater rim. Giving them my moral backing, I continued to the point named after the mysterious Gillman, to await their return. The guide, in the best traditions of his profession, turned and accompanied them.

Soon the forester from Malawi appeared, having decided that discretion was the better part of valour. The famous leopard whose desiccated corpse was found on the summit of Kilimanjaro obviously had not turned back in time, and he had no desire to join it. We set off slowly down the scree in blazing sunshine, shedding garments en-route, and before we reached Kibo hut were overtaken by our companions, who informed us that they had eventually reached the summit almost on their hands and knees.

Retrieving our rucksacks from the hut, we made rapid progress down to Horombo Hut, where, as it was as yet only early afternoon, we decided to press on down to Mandara Hut. This exercise was chiefly noteworthy by the simultaneous voiding of a thunderstorm of its contents of hail and water on the route we were following. So, up to our hocks in running water and hailstones, we descended the moorlands.

A dawn departure the following morning and a rapid descent allowed the Marangu Hotel to be reached in time for breakfast.

At the Tanzanian border I found an official on duty. He emerged from his sentry box to express his outrage that I had managed to infiltrate his country without having my passport stamped. My protestations that the place had been deserted on my arrival fell on deaf ears. Finally, after receiving a stern warning as to my future conduct, I was allowed to proceed on my way.

By evening I was back in the salubrious environs of my cedar cottage, girding my loins for further battle with the beasts of the field.

❋ ❋ ❋ ❋ ❋

Three months later I was again moving upwards towards the snowline. Progress on this occasion was less smooth than it had been on Kilimanjaro. This was because I was on the Ruwenzori Mountains in western Uganda where the vegetation, climate, mud and steepness combined to make the ascent of Kibo seem by comparison a leisurely stroll.

I had written to the Mountain Club of Uganda and had been invited to join an expedition to the mountains, primarily with the purpose of extending the Bujuku Hut at 13,000 feet, but also with the prospect of doing some climbing. I jumped at the chance. And so, one evening in June, I had boarded the overnight bus to Kampala and had been transported in moderate comfort to Uganda.

Uganda seemed quite different from Kenya. It was lush and green and fertile. Swamps and rivers abounded. Water was everywhere. The warm humid air oozed fecundity. There seemed to be no end to the banana groves which covered the low rolling hills and which produced the staple diet of the Baganda, who lived in this part of the country. Near Jinja were huge Indian-owned sugar plantations. A little further on, the road crossed the Victoria Nile, as yet still in its infancy, but already an impressive and powerful river, three quarters of a mile wide.

At Makerere University in Kampala I met a well-known zoologist and artist who was going to the mountains in search of the well-nigh legendary Ruwenzori Golden Mole. He had offered to take me there in his ancient Land Rover, together with his African assistant.

Our route initially ran south-west through the swamps bordering Lake Victoria. My companion was an avid collector of all things that flew, hopped, trotted, crawled, slithered or swam. So, when he espied a distant unidentifiable bird minding its own business in a roadside lagoon he slammed on the brakes, whipped out a .22 rifle concealed within the vehicle and, taking a bead on his unsuspecting victim, shot it dead. The bird lay floating on the murky water about fifty yards away. Our African travelling companion was obviously used to such apparently random

121

slaughter of the adjacent bird-life. Without a moment's hesitation he plunged into the stygian depths and, neck deep in the sludge, ploughed his way towards the bobbing corpse.

Victim retrieved, we pressed on.

We passed through Masaka into Ankole district, rolling grassland dotted with thorn trees. Herds of reddish cattle with immensely long horns grazed near the road – the famous Ankole cattle. In the main square of Mbarara, capital of the district, stands a statue of an Ankole cow, an indication of the importance of this animal in the life of the people in this area of Uganda.

We stopped to collect some provisions at an Indian-owned store. Hanging on the wall was a framed photograph of the former royal ruler of the Kingdom of Ankole, Charles Edward Godfrey Gasyonya the Second, the Omugabe of Ankole. No photograph of the president of Uganda, Milton Opolo Obote, who had deposed him, along with the other rulers of the kingdoms of Buganda, Bunyoro and Toro, was visible.

We drove westward to Bushenyi over an indifferent unsurfaced road and then through forested hills supporting a surprisingly dense population. The road gradually rose as we approached the eastern wall of the Western Rift Valley.

Suddenly, as we approached Kichwamba on the edge of the escarpment, a magnificent panorama sprang into view. To our left the land fell steeply away to the dark, sinister sea of the Maramagambo Forest. Beyond could be seen the blue waters of Lake Edward and further still the purple mountains of the Congo. At Kichwamba the road descended steeply to the Kazinga Channel, which connects Lake Edward with the smaller and shallower Lake George. Both lakes lie within the Queen Elizabeth National Park, alive with game of every conceivable variety. To the north, shrouded in cloud and mist, lay the Ruwenzoris.

About half-way between Kichwamba and the town of Fort Portal we turned left up a gravel road. Up this we proceeded for about ten miles, past the chief's headquarters at Bugoye and the settlement of Ibanda, near which was a power station, to the roadhead at Nyakalengija, Here we found the rest of the party, ensconced in a uniport hut, which stood in a clearing close to the Mubuku River.

These were two members of the Mountain Club of Uganda, a Scots volunteer whose main interest was in a walk round the peaks, and an entomologist who wanted to go bug hunting on the upper slopes of the mountains.

The following morning a great gang of Bakonjo porters appeared. Their main task was to carry the equipment needed for the extension to the Bujuku Hut – planks, foam rubber, corrugated iron, nails – but also to carry our food and heavy gear.

The Bakonjo live on the lower slopes of the mountains. They are a short, stocky, sturdy people, cheerful and willing even under the most adverse of circumstances. They are a vital ingredient of any expedition to the Ruwenzoris, without whom failure is almost guaranteed. When they set off carrying their loads by a fibre strap across the forehead it looked like a scene from a book on 19th century exploration in Africa – a long line of porters disappearing into the elephant grass, all carrying long staves and mostly barefoot.

Soon after leaving Nyakalengija we crossed the Ruboni River which flows into the Mubuku from the south. The elephant grass was about ten feet high and effectively cut off all views. It was soon left behind and shortly afterwards the track entered the forest, a dense jungle of huge trees, wild bananas, tree ferns, giant nettles and brambles. Rain had fallen during the night and the path soon degenerated into a quagmire of glutinous mud. Up this we struggled for three and a half thousand feet. At one point the track came close to the Mubuku River, a wide, swift-flowing stream, pouring over boulders and rapids, tearing its way through the forest. The track seemed to make as many descents as ascents, near vertical mud-slides down which we slithered, clinging to adjacent vegetation for support. The Mahoma River was crossed by hopping from boulder to boulder. No-one fell in but there were a few near shaves. The path then rose up an agonizingly steep ridge, covered in bracken, until it finally entered the podocarpus forest in which stood the Nyabitaba hut.

This was a large, two roomed aluminium structure, with a wooden floor and six double tier bunks.

Nearby was a large rock shelter in which the porters spent the night. These rock shelters are a peculiar feature of the Ruwenzori. Found under cliffs and large boulders, their capacity ranges from two to a hundred people. Their degree of comfort varies likewise. Some are better than the huts, possessing an atmosphere all of their own. Others, mere scrapes in the rock, are exposed and only used in emergencies. With judicious planning it is possible to climb in the Ruwenzori, without carrying tents or using the huts, by sleeping in these natural rock shelters.

Nyabitaba has been variously translated as meaning 'mother of tobacco' and 'mother of mud'. The latter, although probably less accurate, is nearer most people's assessment of the place, especially after a Ruwenzori rainstorm. One such storm had fallen just before we arrived and the forest was gently steaming in the afternoon sunshine. Wild rags of cloud were being driven up the slopes of the Portal Peaks and, if one listened carefully, one could hear the Mubuku thundering in its bed.

Nearby in the forest was encamped a wildlife collector from Nairobi and his African assistants, catching birds in mist nets for eventual dispatch to European and American zoos. Their captives appeared to be mostly

123

sunbirds. It was a sad sight to see the little birds hopping about inside their tiny boxes, all the more so in the knowledge that their fellows flitted in freedom through the great forest all around.

The following day the fun really started. The track, after following the ridge for about half a mile, turned sharply to the right and descended steeply to the river. Tall trees wrapped about with a tangle of creepers hung drunkenly over the path, down which we slid over mossy boulders, creeping under half-fallen trees, clambering over fallen bamboos, forcing our way through thickets of brambles, until we emerged into a lovely clearing by the river, full of giant tree-ferns, sunshine and the sound of rushing water.

Here stood a rickety suspension bridge spanning the torrent. It looked as though a strong puff of wind would bring it crashing down. Just upstream the Bujuku River flowed in from the north-west to join the Mubuku. Although there was a good six inches between most of the planks and only one man could safely cross at a time, all the porters made it across, some burdened down with the most awkward and cumbersome of loads. We stopped for an hour to effect some essential repairs to the bridge, tightening the wires, strengthening the uprights and replacing lost planks.

Then it was back into the bamboo and along the obstacle course on the north bank of the Bujuku, fighting our way through a fearful tangle of mimulopsis, (an eyeball-high plant with the consistency of barbed wire) slithering over rocks, climbing over fallen tree trunks, crossing streams, until, near the Nyameluju hut, we entered the giant heather zone. This nightmare world, where every trunk was enveloped in a tumid mossy growth, where waving beards of lichen hung from every branch and twig, where the ground was soft and spongy and oozing with moisture, was like something conceived by Hieronymus Bosch. Not a sound could be heard but the suck and squelch of our boots and ever and anon a muttered curse as someone sank knee deep into Ruwenzori's slimy barrier. The path wound around and twisted among the forty foot high tree-heathers, which far exceeded anything I had seen on Kilimanjaro. Everything was still and quiet. No birds cheeped. No wind blew. A deep silence hung over this enchanted forest. Small ferns grew here and there in the thick mossy carpet, together with coral-pink orchids. When one stopped to listen, one could hear the faint murmur and tinkle of brooks and rivulets, muffled and hushed as they flowed deep below ground-level in a narrow trench of moss.

Suddenly, through a break in the heather, we caught a fleeting glimpse of snow and ice – part of the glaciers of Mount Speke. Then the clouds descended and no more could be seen. But seen they had been and from such exotic surroundings it was a startling sight.

Spurred on by the sight of the Celestial Mountains, we redoubled our efforts, emerged from the giant heather, struggled up two short steep moraines, crossed the Bujuku River and found ourselves on the wrong side of the Bigo bog.

This huge swamp is composed of enormous tussocks up to three feet high. Each giant excrescence is separated from its mate by a glutinous moat of black, cold and apparently bottomless mud. Its botanical name is carex runsorrensis. We called it something else.

The path circumnavigated the bog on the left. At least, muddy footprints could be seen leading in that direction. By the time we reached the Bigo hut on the other side, we had raised the art of tussock jumping to something approaching a science. For all that, certain members of the party looked distinctly piebald by the time we reached terra firma.

The beautifully situated hut afforded us shelter and warmth. A conveniently sited rock shelter nearby did the same for the porters.

Towards evening the clouds cleared and our dramatic situation was revealed. To our north could be seen the southern flanks of Mt. Speke, tier upon tier of forbidding precipices rising to the snowline. The skirts of the mountain were clothed in a seemingly impenetrable tangle of heather forest which looked almost black as the sun set. To our right were the Portal Peaks, no mean mountains, although now dwarfed by their mightier cousins to the west.

In the vicinity of the hut grew stands of lobelia bequaerti, striking plants with a stiff green obelisk eight to nine feet high, based by large purplish-blue rosettes. The species of lobelia is found in the carex swamps at altitudes of between 11,000 and 14,000 feet. They seem to be much favoured by sunbirds, and it was a charming sight to see the lovely little birds hovering and darting among the prehistoric-looking plants in the rays of the dying sun.

In the early hours of the morning I woke with a start.

A piercing scream rent the night air. I sat bolt upright in my sleeping bag, fingers struggling with the zip.

'What the hell was that?' I whispered. I was sure one of the porters was being murdered. Or perhaps he had been attacked by a leopard. The spotted cats were apparently not uncommon in this part of the Ruwenzori.

One of my more experienced companions stirred sleepily.

'It's only a hyrax,' he muttered. 'Go back to sleep!'

The Ruwenzori hyrax is a tail-less, rabbit-sized animal, resembling a giant guinea-pig. It is peculiar in that despite being a race of tree hyrax it spends most of its time among rocks and boulders, feeding on herbs. This it does mainly at night, accompanying itself the while with an ear-splitting cacophony of whistles, croaks and deafening screeches. They live between

10,000 and 13,500 feet in pairs and small groups. Despite their relatively inaccessible habitat, they are much preyed upon by hunters, and when we came to leave the mountains, our Bakonjo porters were weighed down with the skins and meat of the hyrax they had trapped. On one occasion they offered us some hyrax liver. Feeling somewhat guilty but also rather hungry, I tucked in. It was delicious.

The hyrax chorus swelled in volume, rose to a fearsome crescendo, and finally, thankfully, died away. Perhaps they had caught a whiff of a prowling leopard. The silence was delicious and almost at once I fell asleep.

The following morning dawned bright and dry and clear. Incredibly so, considering Ruwenzori's appalling reputation for rain, mist, hail and snow. For the next two weeks the weather remained fine. Cloud formed every day and occasionally it snowed on the glaciers, but that was all. We were amazingly lucky.

Shouldering our rucksacks we moved off in the warm sunshine, wending our way through thickets of huge tree groundsels to the first of the two upper bogs, which to our surprise and delight we found to be virtually dry. The Bujuku river chattered down the valley on our right.

On the open mountainsides grew a chest-high jungle of tough, leafless shrubs called Helichrysum stulmannii, on which grew white everlasting flowers. When the sun shines, the flowers open and it was a pleasant sight as we climbed higher up the valley. When we later came to try and move through this jungle we found it to be at times so dense as to be impenetrable. Its only virtue is that it grows on almost vertical cliff faces. Most of the rock below the snowline in the Ruwenzori is coated with a layer of moss which is liable to peel off in the most alarming fashion, totally without provocation, leaving exposed a slippery, patina of mud. Without the aid of the much maligned Helichrysum, many ascents and descents would be totally impossible.

On our left the north face of Mt. Baker soared upwards for some 2,000 feet. The valley curved gently to the right and as it did so the full glory of the central Ruwenzori was gradually revealed. On the skyline directly above and ahead a line of glittering ice cliffs marked the edge of the Stanley Plateau. The jagged southern peaks of Mt. Stanley – Elena, Savoia, Elizabeth, Philip, Kitasamba, and Nyabubuya – rose starkly above the glaciers. The dark defile of the Scott-Elliot Pass marked the divide between Mt. Stanley and Mt. Baker. To the right the beautiful twin peaks of Alexandra and Margherita, snow and ice and dark rock, the highest summits in the Ruwenzoris, floated at a seemingly impossible height above the Bujuku valley.

Re-crossing the river for the last time, we skirted the muddy shores of Lake Bujuku, a gloomy, shallow expanse of still dark water, passed

Cooking Pot Cave, where our porters would stay, and soon afterwards reached the hut at 13,000 feet.

The Ruwenzoris, by general consensus, identified with Ptolemy's 'Mountains of the Moon', are, unlike most other high East African mountains, of non-volcanic origin, despite the evidence of past volcanic activity in the form of numerous craters around their base in the eastern and southern foothills. The direction of the range is north to south, lies just north of the equator, and is divided by the Uganda-Congo border. Some seventy miles long by thirty miles wide it contains six major snow mountains. These all lie within a convenient diameter of eleven miles in the centre of the range – Mts. Stanley, Speke, Baker, Gessi, Emin, and Luigi di Savoia. The first five are named after eminent 19th century explorers. Mt. Luigi di Savoia is named after the Duke of Abruzzi who led the first successful expedition to the Ruwenzori in 1906. Alexandra and Margherita are named after the consorts of Edward VIII of Great Britain and Umberto the 1st of Italy. The name Ruwenzori is believed to be a corruption of a Lukonjo word ruenzururu meaning hill of rain – an apt description.

The former extensive glaciation is responsible for the immense steep-sided U-shaped valleys which are so characteristic of the range. Most of the present day glaciers are in retreat and others have melted entirely since the beginning of the 20th century. The glaciers are remarkably clean, unlike those in other parts of the world, with the result that the streams which flow from them are clear and carry little silt. The main cause for this absence of detritus is probably the hardness of the rock and the slight temperature variations which cause little rock shattering.

On the peaks and ridges enormous cornices and icicles are common, formed by the deposition of rime by the strong moist winds. These frequently assume the most fantastic shapes, parodying the extraordinary plants in the valleys below.

The area of permanent snow and glaciation is much more extensive than on either Kilimanjaro or Mt. Kenya, both higher than the Ruwenzori. This may be due to the latter's more central continental position and proximity to the equatorial forests of the Congo, providing it with a heavier and more uniform precipitation.

To the south of the mountains lies Lake Edward, to the north-east Lake Albert. Out of the former the Semliki River coils and twists its way northwards through the Virunga National Park in the Congo to the west of the Ruwenzoris before flowing into Lake Albert, which in turn discharges its waters into the Nile. The Ruwenzori's heavy rainfall and cloud cover, together with its huge areas of forest, moss and bog, functioning as a sort of massive sponge, provides this river system, and hence the Nile, with an important source of water, which may arguably be greater than that emanating from the Victoria Nile from the south and east.

The astonishing size, growth, and luxuriance of plant life in the upper Ruwenzori is apparently due to several factors, including the high, day time, ultra-violet intensity peculiar to the tropics and especially at high altitudes, and the freezing temperatures at night. Indeed it has been described as 'summer every day, winter every night'. The perpetual dampness, due to the almost permanent cloud cover, together with the equatorial position of the mountains, encourages slow but continual growth. In the High Andes of tropical South America plants of a very similar appearance are to be found. Botanists refer to the phenomenon as high altitude gigantism and the Ruwenzori is top of the league in Africa.

Because of the nightly frost endured by all plants living above 12,000 feet, many have adapted in order to survive. The thick corky bark and ruffs of dead leaves protect the groundsels from the cold, while some species of lobelia contain a reservoir of water in their leaf rosettes which acts as a heat store to protect the bud.

The Bakonjo living on the lower slopes were of course aware of the presence of snow clad mountains above them. Unfortunately they did not publish their findings, and it was not until Henry Morton Stanley, during the course of the Emin Pasha Relief Expedition in 1888, saw the mountains and their snows that the first reliable information about the Mountains of the Moon was brought back to the outside world. The fact that during the twelve years prior to 1888 several explorers, including Stanley himself, had passed close to the mountains without suspecting their existence will not surprise those who have experienced Ruwenzori weather.

The following eighteen years saw several expeditions in action, a number of which succeeded in penetrating the forest and reaching the glaciers. In 1906 the Duke of the Abruzzi mounted a large-scale expedition including a dozen Europeans and 150 African porters. With characteristic thoroughness the Duke swept the board, climbed all of the major peaks, and with his horde of surveyors, biologists, and geologists exposed the mysteries of the Mountains of the Moon.

Subsequent expeditions, with a few exceptions, were all on a considerably smaller scale. Notable among these were the seven expeditions which Noel Humphreys made between 1926 and 1932, in which, usually accompanied by only one or two companions and a few porters, he explored most of the range, and reached the summits of Alexandra and Margherita for the first time since 1906. Also in 1932 the redoubtable duo of Eric Shipton and H. W. Tilman forced their way up the Bujuku valley and, in appalling weather, camped for a week on the Stanley Plateau before making the third ascent of the highest peaks. In addition they made the first ascent of the north face of Mt. Baker, a route that has yet to be repeated. Later in the same year the massive Belgian Scientific Expedition led by Count Xavier de Grunne approached the mountains from the

Congo and made several important ascents. In 1939 a Polish expedition climbed Margherita by the east ridge.

Since the Second World War numerous parties have thoroughly climbed and explored the Ruwenzori. Despite this, there remain many lovely and remote areas to the north and south of the main peaks which still provide opportunities for real exploration and the chance of climbing little frequented or even virgin summits.

Having established ourselves in the hut, most of the porters were sent back down to Ibanda. We retained four, who settled down at Cooking Pot Cave.

For the first few days we busied ourselves in extending and renovating the hut, using the materials which the Bakonjo had humped up the mountain. During the day it was pleasantly warm, even when the valleys filled with cloud, which they usually did by mid-day. By night the temperature fell to below freezing.

Just above the hut was a small stream from which we collected our water. It emanated from the snout of the Speke Glacier, from which it shot over the cliffs in an impressive waterfall. By day the valley was filled with the sound of falling water. At night when the glacier ice froze the waterfall stopped falling, the stream stopped flowing and the valley fell strangely silent.

A movement in the groundsels and lobelias one morning attracted our attention. As we watched, a small antelope appeared and delicately picked its way among the plants. Its colour was that of a ripe chestnut, a reddish rufous brown with a black blaze on the forehead. It was a black-fronted duiker. Suddenly it became aware that it was being watched and, with a bound, vanished. The species is equipped with elongated hooves to enable it to move with ease over marshy terrain. In view of the conditions prevalent in the upper valleys of the Ruwenzori, these appeared to me to be as essential as snowshoes to a trapper in the Yukon.

The entomologist departed down the valley to where the zoologist was conducting his investigations into the habits of the golden mole, leaving four of us in the hut.

Tired of carpentry, we set off one morning for Mt. Speke, walking up the valley towards the Stuhlmann Pass. The thickets of groundsel were interspersed with clumps of *Lobelia wollastoni*, silvery blue in colour with a fifteen-foot spike. This species of lobelia is found throughout the upper alpine zone, often in areas where there is little vegetation other than black lichens on the rocks.

After half an hour we turned right and scrambled up some singularly unpleasant slabs, coated with mud and moss. After a few hundred feet, things improved and, after climbing up an easy snow and rock gully, we reached a broad ridge.

Although it was still early in the morning, the valley below was beginning to fill with cloud and a strong wind had risen. Snow flurries whipped across the rocks and the few groundsels still clinging to the crevices quickly became plastered with white. Above the boiling mass of cloud, the snows of the Stanley Plateau on the other side of the valley still shone in the rapidly vanishing sunshine. Soon they had disappeared and we were left isolated in a world of white snow and black rocks.

We roped up and continued on up the ridge before turning right onto the glacier. The going was not difficult but visibility was now down to a few yards and it began to snow in earnest.

We had reached the rocks which lie directly below the summit of Vittorio Emanuele peak, the highest point of Mt. Speke, when our Scottish companion was seen to be shaking and shivering uncontrollably.

We moved him out of the wind into some shelter behind a rock. His lips were blue, his speech was slurred and he appeared to be is a state of partial shock. Above our heads the wind howled horizontally over the summit.

We turned and went down.

We had some difficulty negotiating the mossy slabs which were now streaming with water, but once our friend was down on relatively horizontal terrain in the groundsel forest, and, later, in the warmth of the hut, he rapidly recovered.

He did not, however, venture above the snowline again.

The following day, two of us went up Johnston, the most southerly peak of Mt. Speke, an ascent chiefly remarkable by our appalling toils in the near vertical helichrysum jungle which leads up to Trident Col and the South West Ridge. Slabs of rock coated with moss added to our difficulties. At the slightest disturbance great carpets of the stuff would peel off leaving a slimy coating underneath. As a result one's boots would slip off the most apparently secure ledges, and if it were not for the ubiquitous helichrysum, sooner or later we would have come to grief. Our chief rewards for all this effort, before the inevitable cloud and mist obscured everything, were close-up views of the enormous crevasses and seracs of the Speke Glacier, and a more distant prospect of the icy summits of Alexandra and Margherita rising above the yawning void of the Bujuku Valley.

Our next object was Mt. Stanley. So, with two porters, we went up to the Elena Huts which are situated at 14,900 feet at the southern end of the massif close to the foot of the Elena Glacier. In order to reach the huts we went down the valley to Cooking Pot Cave, pussy-footed our way across a swamp and up the well-named Groundsel Gully. From the top of the latter the path continued up scree and beneath overhanging rocks, passing the remains of the Duke of the Abruzzi's Camp 4 at Ridge Camp until the huts were reached. The sun was shining as we climbed and apart from a streamer of cloud blowing from its summit, the whole of Mt. Speke lay revealed to view. Our groping route in cloud up the glacier was at once exposed, and the position of Johnston in relation to Vittorio Emanuele was instantly apparent.

The two Elena huts were small and triangular and, having no bunks, we had to sleep on the wooden floor. However this was infinitely preferable to spending the night in a tent.

The situation was a splendid one. Across the Scott-Elliot Pass, the magnificent west face of Mt. Baker rose to the peaks of Semper and Edward. Above us the Coronation Glacier hung suspended between the rocky molars of Nyabubuya and Kitasamba, while below them the Elena Glacier flowed down from the Stanley Plateau.

Before they descended to the relative comfort of Cooking Pot Cave, the porters ventured onto the glacier. Laughing and shouting, they slipped and slithered on the steep snow-covered ice, throwing snowballs at each other.

The sun was setting as I went to collect some water from a nearby rock pool. The helichrysum flowers were closing up for the night and there was a keen nip in the air. The snows of Mt. Baker were flushed a rosy pink by the dying sun, while the valleys below were filled with great billows of cloud. I felt an extraordinary sense of remoteness. Here we were in the very heart of Africa, in the midst of a range of snow-capped mountains, surrounded by dense, uninhabited tropical jungles. Well are they named the Mountains of the Moon.

Early next morning, cold and stiff, we crawled out of our sleeping bags. After a fairly disgusting breakfast, we walked across the rocks to the snout of the Elena Glacier. Here the three of us strapped on our crampons, roped up, seized our ice-axes and climbed up the glacier onto the Stanley Plateau. The snow was crisp and firm and we made rapid progress. The sun had risen and the morning sky was a lovely, cloudless blue. Passing Savoia and Elena, their rocky crests draped with enormous feathery cornices, we were soon on the gently sloping plateau. The glare of the sun off the vast expanse of white was terrific, and we were glad of our goggles and dark glasses. Mine were of the sort Captain Scott had worn on his way to the South Pole.

Directly ahead of us rose the beautiful twin peaks of Alexandra and Margherita, divided by the Margherita Glacier.

A wonderful panorama surrounded us. To the south we could discern the hazy outline of Lake Edward, while to the west we looked straight down to the forests of the Congo, which seemed to stretch to infinity. Here and there, amid the distant jungle greenery, could be seen the silvery loops of the Semliki River coiling its way northward. And all around rose the summits of the central Ruwenzori.

The good weather did not last long.

As we approached the base of the south-east ridge of Alexandra, by which we hoped to attain the summit, wisps of cloud had begun to drift over the plateau. Within a few minutes the ridge had vanished and we were enveloped in a thick mist.

We started cutting steps in the steep ice leading up to the crest of the ridge. After about half an hour of this we found our way barred by a monstrous growth of huge cross cornices which overhung both sides of the ridge. We ferreted around for a while looking for a way through and moved out onto the steep south-west face in an attempt to find a way round, but in the dense mist we could see nothing.

We decided to descend and try to cross the Margherita Glacier, in an attempt to gain the east ridge of Margherita, in order to try and salvage something from all of our efforts. The mist did not lift and for two hours we floundered like beached whales amid a labyrinth of crevasses, up to our thighs in soft snow. It became obvious that this was a hopeless exercise, so we groped our way back across the Stanley Plateau to the Elena Huts, wishing we were able to take advantage of a pair of skis we had seen there. Apparently some fanatic had taken them up in the early '50s.

As we plodded down the scree towards the Bujuku Valley, a pair of ravens circled overhead, croaking hoarsely as though mocking our puny efforts. They had every reason to do so. I felt like the toad beneath the harrow.

Our appetite for punishment was not yet replete so we decided to make a final attempt on the summit using the Irene Lakes Hut as our base. This spartan bivouac stands on a rocky bluff about 2,000 feet above Bujuku Valley and just below the east ridge of Margherita.

After the customary wrestling match in a near-vertical forest of rotting giant groundsel, we reached this delectable sanctuary and settled down for another night of singular discomfort.

The following morning, shafts of sunlight lit up the icy wall of the Stanley Plateau, while far below the forested flanks of the Portal Peaks sloped steeply downwards into the Western Rift Valley, over which hung a billowy blanket of cloud.

The ridge looked black and ominous, but in the event it proved to be considerably less difficult than it appeared. A scramble up a stony gully brought us to its crest, which alternated between knife-edged rock and overhanging cornices which we were careful to circumvent. After a while our path was abruptly barred by a vertical rock step about 100 feet high. From a distance it looked fairly formidable but close inspection revealed adequate holds and we were soon above it, moving steeply up heavily lichened rocks. The ridge on the right overlooked the steep, North East Margherita Glacier, and at one point I looked straight down into the icy

132

depths of an enormous crevasse.

By the time we reached the snow-covered ridge leading to the summit, the inevitable clouds had built up.

Great banks of huge cornices, draped with icicles, straddled the ridge, but we were able to bypass them without difficulty. The sun shone weakly through the murk.

Directly beneath the summit we entered an extraordinary cave, its roof festooned with thousands of feathery icicles, ranging in length from a few inches to several feet. It looked like the sort of place in which Hans Anderson's Snow Queen might have held court. Then it was round the steep snow slope on the outside of the cave with a dizzy drop below, followed by a short scramble and finally we stood on the summit of Margherita. At 16,763 feet it was the highest point in Uganda and the third highest mountain in Africa.

A few minutes later the mist cleared sufficiently for us to discern the ice and rock of Alexandra across the col dividing the two peaks.

The following day we left the Bujuku Valley to return home via the Scott-Elliot and Freshfield Passes.

Bowed under enormous packs we struggled up Groundsel Gully for the last time. A great cauldron of cloud was boiling along the base of Mt. Baker, although the upper ramparts were clear. Tottering over rocks, cursing the helichrysum, and reviling the groundsel, we slithered for hours through a series of moss-covered tank-traps until we reached the Kitandara Lakes and the beautifully situated hut.

This idyllic spot must be among the loveliest in the whole of the Ruwenzori, the mountains dropping steeply down to the quiet waters of the lake, whose shores are bordered with stands of St. John's Wort, trees up to thirty feet in height and bearing strange, orange, goblet-shaped flowers.

The hut was warm and comfortable, and even had a small stock of paperbacks, which some ardent bibliophile must have installed, perhaps as a result of having been marooned for days, book-less, in one of the huts. Unfortunately the hut was so dark and the illumination so poor I could barely decipher the title pages.

The Freshfield Pass leading to the Mubuku Valley is unpleasantly steep and the only good thing that can be said for it is that, as I struggled up it, I was frequently obliged to stop and tie my metaphorical shoelaces. In so doing I was able to gaze my last on the mystic mountains.

A pleasant, if somewhat noisy, night was spent in the Bujongulo Rock Shelter. A banshee chorus of hyrax screams ensured that sleep, when it finally came, was fitful and intermittent.

From here a series of heathery terraces, bisected by the Mubuku River, led by degrees to a slippery drop down to an overhanging cliff, distinguished by the name Kichuchu. This latter descent was made in the main on the seats of our breeches, from mud slide to greasy rock and back again, aided and abetted by 'thank God' tufts of vegetation. By the time we reached level ground, our nether garments were riven and rent and our persons much bedaubed with mud and other products of the mire.

A swampy stroll brought us once again to the banks of the much-maligned Mubuku River, which was without benefit of bridge. It seemed at this stage fairly superfluous to remove our boots, so we plunged into the knee-deep torrent, and out into dense bamboo jungle. The path, if such it could be called, was fearfully overgrown, and the stems of the bamboo met most inconsiderately at about four feet from the ground. This meant that for hundreds of yards we were obliged to walk bent double. This was bad enough, but to do so with a heavy pack and ice axe on one's back was purgatory. The ice-axe kept on getting entangled in the vegetation and the oaths and curses which rang through the greenwood would have made a navvy blush.

Finally we reached the Nyabitaba Hut and from then on it was literally all down hill. Near the Ruboni River we met the first people on the mountain in almost two weeks – a European priest taking some African boys on a walking tour of the peaks.

The journey home was not without interest.

An overnight train from Kasese took us to Kampala. As the train dragged itself out of the tiny station, a nearby grass fire was attracting hundreds of birds in search of insects flushed out by the flames.

In the middle of the night I was woken by the screech of metal. Peering out of the window I saw that the train was half-way up a long hill and that the wheels were skidding on the rails. With a great gasp and hiss of steam, the train ground to a halt and backed down to the foot of the hill to have another go. Twice more the ancient locomotive hurled itself at the slope and on the final attempt inched its way over the summit. We trundled slowly on through the night to Kampala.

A bus took me across the border at Busia and deposited me at Kisumu on the shores of Lake Victoria. My ice axe was a cause of some concern to passengers and crew. An African boarding the Circle Line carrying a spear might cause a similar stir.

It was by now late afternoon and I was due to resume work the following morning.

So began the most perilous part of the whole trip – a 120 mile taxi ride to Nakuru.

The driver was a jovial Jaluo, excessively so I thought. He seemed to epitomise the happy-go-lucky African, all flashing teeth and rolling eyes. Or perhaps it was because he recognised a sucker when he saw one. He walked with a nautical roll. But then he probably came from a fishing background, and had spent many hours in some fragile craft, far out on the tossing waters of the lake, casting his net upon the heaving billows. At least I hoped so.

In a spirit of bonhomie I sat up front beside my chauffeur.

We set off at a great pace, horn blaring. Pedestrians, goats, chickens and other assorted livestock moved rapidly vergewards as we approached.

Klaxon still blaring imperiously, we howled across the Kano Plains.

There was a sudden crash and forward visibility vanished. The bonnet had sprung up and backwards against the windscreen like a giant sail. Something unidentifiable flew off in a graceful parabola and landed with a splash in a nearby swamp. Careering from side to side we raced to what seemed like imminent destruction.

I had always thought that the Age of Miracles was long since past, but divine intervention must have been working in our favour on this occasion. With a hideous screech of brakes stressed to their limit, we came to a shuddering stop.

The driver's grin had vanished.

So had my mateyness. I retreated to a back seat and remained there for the remainder of the journey.

Bonnet re-secured, we set off again, somewhat more sedately.

About 20 minutes later it began to reain heavily. the driver switched on his wipers.

Nothing hapened, which was not surprising, considering they were sunk without trace beneath the black waters of the roadside swamp, now several miles to our rear. All that was left were the wiper stumps, ineffectually waggling from side to side. For the next half an hour, until the deluge slackened and then stopped, my cabbie frantically cleared a small porthole of visibility on the windscreeen with a sopping rag, held in his right hand. Stopping, which most sensible people would have done, did not come into either of our equations.

Half-way between Kericho and Mau Summit we had a puncture. A balding spare tyre, caked in dried mud, was discovered in the boot, but of jack and wheel-spanner there was no sign. An hour and a half later we succeeded in flagging down a taxi of similar make, going in the opposite direction.

Tyre changed, we pressed on into the gathering darkness.

As we crested the brow of Mau Summit, we ran out of petrol.

There was a long pregnant silence, full of unvoiced thoughts, most of them composed of four letter words.

Fortunately the road from this point was mostly all downhill, and we were able to coast in neutral for several miles, apart from a level section near the turn-off to the township of Molo, where we had to push and shove for about half a mile. From here we cruised down to a petrol station just below the Jolly Farmer Hotel, where a 24-hour service was advertised. After about 24 minutes of shouting and horn blowing, a dishevelled attendant appeared, pulling up his trousers and rubbing the sleep from his eyes.

The midnight hour was tolling as we rumbled up to my cottage at Bahati. I felt lucky to be still alive.

I paid off my coachman and frostily bade him God-speed on his return journey to Kisumu.

I did not offer him a pourboire.

CHAPTER EIGHT

The time had come for me to be cut down from my block and tackle.

The Thomas splint had been removed and the offending limb had been subjected to some mild kneading and pummelling by the resident physiotherapist, a no-nonsense blonde of Viking ancestry, whose forearms and biceps looked strong enough to have rowed Eric the Red and his Norsemen crew single-handed across the Atlantic.

Further sessions of a more strenuous nature had been promised and I looked forward to them with some trepidation.

My nervousness at being engaged in a one-sided all-in wrestling match with this Amazon was tempered with the relief I felt that I would soon be released from my bonds. Confined as I was to my bed and virtually on public display, I seemed to be constantly on the receiving end of the attentions of a variety of females whose motives I could not help but regard with suspicion.

1968 was a Leap Year and sure enough, on February 29th, an offer of marriage emanating from the upper echelons of the nursing corps came my way. As the written proposal was couched in what appeared to be a somewhat jocular vein, I decided to interpret it in that light – a grave error as I later discovered.

On another occasion my bed had been wheeled onto the hospital verandah, so that my pallid countenance might benefit from the sun, which from time to time appeared between the successive thunderstorms.

As I lay there, mind pleasantly blank, a hoarse voice whispered in my ear.

'Have you been saved?'

Startled from my somnolence, I turned to find a small round face, surrounded by a pudding-bowl haircut, surveying me through a pair of spectacles whose glasses were so thick they magnified the orbs behind them to frightening proportions. I quailed, muttering something about general weakness, discomfort, fatigue and the soporific effect of sleeping

137

tablets. Feigning drowsiness, I let my head flop weakly back onto the pillow. Undeterred, her small mustachios bristling, this well-meaning female evangelist let rip for twenty minutes with a fearsome tirade on the evils of sloth, drink and fornication. What this had to do with me was not explained. By the time I was returned to the ward, I was so drained I was obliged to revive my sagging spirits with a double tot of 'Old Gold', a locally concocted whisky, brought in by a public-spirited visitor. Under normal circumstances I wouldn't have touched the stuff with a ten foot barge-pole.

Then there were the frequent visits to the X-ray room to have my femur photographed. So frequent in fact that I began to fear for the effects of the rays on my adjacent gonads. After all I had only two of them. As the plump radiographer fumbled and fiddled in the semi-darkness, visions of lifelong sterility and impotence passed through my mind. Perhaps the woman was a secret man-hater with a devilish mission to surreptitiously sterilise as many of the opposite sex as possible.

So it was that when the surgeon appeared one morning with a pair of pliers in his hand, my overriding thought was that freedom was at hand. The leg was lowered from the pulley, and the corks, on the ends of the pin transfixing the upper part of my tibia, removed. Then, seizing the pin with the pliers, the surgeon whipped it out.

The whole procedure was quite painless.

My leg resembled a withered branch from which the bark had been removed.

With the help of a pair of nurses I swung myself over the edge of the bed and stood on my sound limb. Almost immediately the damaged leg began to swell alarmingly.

Within a few minutes it looked as though it was affected with elephantiasis. With almost equal rapidity its colour changed from a sickly parchment shade, through ugly vermilion to an ominous puce.

I also discovered that I was unable to bend my knee. Three months of traction with my leg in forced extension had tightened the ligaments and tendons. Although the fractures had united satisfactorily there was some over-riding of the bone and I had lost an inch in height.

As a result of these undesirable facts I was obliged to spend the next few weeks in close but, alas, painful, proximity to the Viking physio. Masochism was not my thing and the tortures to which I was subjected, albeit perhaps essential to my long-term well-being, at times made the fracture seem by comparison no more than a bad sprain.

Before I left Scotland for the Dark Continent I would sometimes, in an idle moment, watch an all-in wrestling match on the box. I was particularly struck by the manner in which a certain violent gentleman, named Mick McManus, would frequently try to tear the limbs off his opponents, and what was more, almost succeed in doing so.

Fortunately my blonde opponent bore no physical resemblance to Mick McManus, but I believe she would have given him a run for his money in the ring. She was also vivacious, curvaceous, intelligent and forthright in her views. So much so that at a later stage in my treatment she crossed swords with the surgeon as to when I should start bearing weight on my leg – to such an extent that she threatened to resign. Unfortunately she also had an Australian boyfriend with a penchant for iced beer, who did resemble Mick McManus.

Gradually, with the aid of physiotherapy, parallel bars, crutches, and exercise I began to regain the use of my leg.

On occasion the muscles surrounding the femur were subjected to electrical stimulation from a large black box. How I hated that box. One morning I was wired up to the infernal thing. The operator, a large black woman, switched it on, checked that I was twitching at the correct rate, such that I was unlikely to nod off, and ambled out of the room. Ten minutes of barely-bearable discomfort was about as much as I could take. After thirty minutes I began to get concerned – I felt as though I had been hopping up Everest for the past half hour. My wretched muscles were exhausted, to say nothing of the excruciating sensation pulsing through the electrodes. I was too far from the switch and I was alone in the room. Forty five minutes after turning on the current the woman returned, brushing stray crumbs from the corners of her lips, strolled over to my couch of pain, glanced at her watch, and switched me off. The mixture of relief and fury which I felt in almost equal proportions effectively choked the torrent of well-chosen epithets I was preparing to deliver on her return.

Outside the hospital the rain was still lashing down. The East African Safari Rally was held over the Easter weekend and routed through Kenya, Uganda and Tanzania. It began in mud and ended in mud. Seven contestants finished.

I graduated from wheelchair to armpit crutches to elbow crutches and I could see release in sight.

Since the day I had entered hospital I had received no pay and my financial situation was now fairly grim. The surgeon was beginning to find my frequent requests for early discharge rather irksome. Until now I had managed to settle my hospital bills and pay the aged retainers at Bahati with local funds. Finally these had run into the sands. Until I brought money into the country, creditors would have to wait, but I was especially concerned about my Nyamwezi cook and the aged Kikuyu gardeners.

One Sunday Arthur Owen-Jones' car was stolen from outside the surgery. He had gone there to do some bookwork. Mrs Owen-Jones was driving and had parked the car, a Peugeot 504 station wagon, outside the surgery door. He had gone inside, while she had gone round the corner to an Asian-owned shop, which was open on a Sunday, leaving the ignition keys still hanging in the car. They had apparently followed this routine every Sunday morning and had been observed by members of the omnipresent criminal classes. No sooner had the memsahib turned the corner than a pair of Africans were inside the car starting it up. Hearing the sound of a familiar engine Owen-Jones emerged from the surgery like an enraged rhino, and, despite his bulk, hurled himself onto the bonnet. A wild ride ensued through the streets of the town, with my employer clinging desperately to the windscreen wipers, and endeavouring to kick in the windscreen with his elastic-sided boots. The thieves swerved the car violently from side to side and finally Owen-Jones was propelled into the gutter, where, miraculously, he landed unhurt. The vehicle disappeared at high speed in the general direction of Uganda, and was never seen again.

I was glad to learn that my employer had suffered no physical inconvenience from this experience, but, in view of his lack of concern for my own well-being, I lost no sleep on his behalf over this episode.

During my time in hospital I had received several visits of an ecclesiastical nature from the Scots minister of the local Presbyterian church, which I had erratically attended. He offered to put me up until I found my feet, so to speak. As my own residence was ten miles from town and I was still on crutches and not yet able to drive, I accepted his offer with gratitude. The reverend's mansion on the hill above the town overlooked the lake, and was a positive palace compared to my rustic log cabin.

Finally, after eleven weeks on my back, and a grand total of sixteen weeks in hospital, I was discharged. Funds had arrived from Britain, I had settled my debts, and I was able to depart with a clear conscience.

I was by now quite adroit on the elbow crutches and slid without difficulty into the padre's car. Our first call was to my cedar cottage at Bahati to discover whether four months of moth, rust, termites and general neglect had left anything intact.

The house certainly was in one piece, but the same could hardly be said of my old Nyamwezi cook. As I hopped round the back of the building, he emerged from his hut and, supported by his ancient wife, tottered feebly in my direction.

I was appalled by his appearance. He had always been lean. Now he was thin to the point of emaciation and so weak he could barely stand. It was obvious that he had been ill for weeks.

Lolling in the shade, the two Kikuyu gardeners watched with apparent indifference.

My poor old cook described in a just-audible whisper how he had been taken ill with what seemed like malaria, had been unable to eat for days, and had gradually grown weaker and weaker. His aged spouse had been away at the time, visiting one of their numerous offspring. I was in hospital. He was a Nyamwezi from Tanzania, and, although an African like themselves, the two Kikuyu gardeners regarded him as a foreigner, an outsider, and did nothing to help. He was not of their tribe. Let him die, seemed to be their attitude.

A few more days and he most certainly would have died.

Disgusted, I lambasted the gardeners in my primitive Swahili. They listened in sullen silence.

We helped my venerable major-domo into the car, and conveyed him to the hospital which I had just vacated. There he remained for the next two weeks, before emerging, a frail shadow of his former self, but at least alive, cheerful and pathetically grateful for our help.

⚜⚜⚜⚜⚜

Slowly over the following weeks I regained the use of my leg.

Concerned friends would come to the manse and take me out, as I was as yet unable to drive. They knew that I needed an occasional break from my daily dose of Calvinistic theology and nightly reading of the psalms, beneficial though they were for my spiritual welfare. A brooding portrait of John Knox stared disapprovingly from the otherwise bare walls, as I hopped nimbly out of the house, flesh-pot bound.

I was still on crutches when I attended a Saturday night dance at the Nakuru Athletic Club, at that time the town's principal watering hole as far as the European residents were concerned, although precious few of these could be classified as athletes. The place was packed, and, included among the motley throng were a number of British soldiers, who were training African troops at a barracks just outside the town. The beer and whisky flowed like water. The wooden dance floor trembled beneath the feet of the revellers. The walls reverberated to the crashing beat of the Bongo Boys Band, a sextet of perspiring Africans, whose less than subtle rhythms betrayed their jungle origins.

Propping up the bar and lubricating his tonsils with a cataract of Tusker lager was Mike Hughes, a jovial agricultural contractor. His booming laugh, which not even the uproar on the dance floor could drown, resembled the bray of a startled jackass, and, when the wind was in the right direction, he could be heard with ease at a distance of several hundred yards.

His wife Alex, a flamboyant Polish blonde, swanned round the floor with a succession of partners, while Mike, an avid fisherman, regaled his cronies with tales of the last one to have got away, only pausing for breath to down another beer.

I sat mid-way between bar and dance floor, my crutches lying beside

141

me, in what I assumed to be no-man's land, in a position conveniently close to the source of liquid refreshment and to the scene of the action, where the gyrating couples grappled with each other in the gloom.

It was time for the last dance, announced in a stentorian bellow by the head Bongo Boy.

I noticed that Alex was gliding gracefully around the floor in the arms of a British lance corporal. The African vocalist, microphone almost touching his uvula, eyes closed, crooned a sentimental ditty. Behind me I could hear Mike insisting for the umpteenth time that the Mrs Simpson was still the best trout fly for Kenya.

Suddenly the monologue at my rear stopped and there was the sound of violent movement, as of large bodies being thrust roughly aside. Mike had seen Alex in the arms of the non-com.

I turned my head. Bar stool in hand, eyes blazing and teeth grinding, Mike was heading in the dancers' direction, and I was directly in the line of fire. The crowd parted with amazing rapidity, beer flying in all directions, whisky glasses tumbling to the floor. It was like an action replay of Moses on the Red Sea shore, with people instead of waves in parting mode.

I scrambled after my crutches, visions of further fractures rising unpleasantly to mind.

At the last moment the happy couple, blissfully unaware of the approaching danger, made a sudden, skilful turn in the opposite direction, but Mike, turning with equal speed, moved to head them off at the pass. He brushed past me like a whirlwind. My freshly primed tankard of Whitecap shot off my table and disappeared among the legs of the dancers, gobbets of froth bespattering dresses and trousers in its passage.

Reaching his target, Mike, cast his stool aside, put both hands on the lance corporal's shoulders, and, spinning him around, propelled him into the crowd, where he vanished from sight. Then, his rage suddenly evaporating, he gave Alex a benign smile, and swept her off to the raucous strains of an old-fashioned waltz.

✕✖✕✖✕✖✕

During my convalescence I went with the Scots minister on a short recuperative trip to the Kenya coast. It was thought that the sea might act as a tonic, stimulate healing and generally shorten the recovery period. In the event it turned out that the sea air was the only beneficial feature associated with the trip.

The highlight of the journey was the crossing of the Mtwapa Creek, where the ferry was hauled across the water by a gang of singing, sweating, laughing Africans, led by an enormous fellow producing an incredible volume of noise from a conch horn. The ferry was very small, just large enough to hold two cars and was hauled across the inlet by a long chain.

The road from Mombasa along the coast was unsurfaced and deeply rutted, with numerous stretches of fine sand several inches deep, and by the time we reached our destination we were both exhausted, and to make matters worse, the weather was excessively hot and humid. The house was an extreme form of coast dwelling, built out of concrete, and aptly bore an uncanny resemblance to those abandoned concrete pill-boxes which used to litter the North Sea coastline. No concessions had been made with regard to comfort. Walls, floor and ceiling were all constructed from the same stark material. Water was in short supply and giant millipedes, known locally as Malindi trains, crawled everywhere. The heat and the humidity made sleep difficult, while squadrons of mosquitoes, with their maddening high-pitched whine, clogged the air.

All this was bad enough.

The crowning blow, now revealed, was the fact that the house had been built on top of a stretch of coral cliff. The only access to the beach was via a narrow, near-vertical, crumbling path, difficult enough for one sound in limb, impossible for one hobbling around on crutches.

So all I could do was to admire, from my lofty vantage point, the blue and green ocean, the surf breaking on the distant reef.

I think the sea air did do some good.

❀❧❀❧❀❧❀❧❀

By degrees I returned to the seat of my employment. Initially I was dropped off at the surgery by the Scots minister. While Arthur Owen-Jones went out on calls, I dealt with the small animal clients and farmers coming in for drugs and advice on sick stock.

I was still using elbow crutches, but my honourable employer seemed to regard this as a trifling inconvenience and on several occasions I had the opportunity to tone up my shoulders and forearms during the two mile uphill walk to the house on the hill.

During my absence Nyaga, general dogsbody and message-boy, who kept the surgery clean and ran errands, had become a Seventh Day Adventist. This meant that, as Saturday was now the day of rest and worship, he could no longer perform his earthly duties on that day. This apparently had led to a series of theological confrontations between himself and his employer. Nyaga was firm. His soul was more important than the acquisition of filthy lucre. So he departed to spread the word and sell religious tracts, until his premature demise eighteen months later.

Nyaga had not been replaced and the lay staff now consisted of

143

Vincent Fernandes, the Goan clerk, and Moses, the African assistant.

At last, six months after breaking my leg, I returned to work, wearing a built-up shoe and using a stick.

It was now early August. Owen-Jones, in a spasm of generosity, decreed that I would be paid 50% of my salary for this month, on the grounds that my efficiency was likely to be lessened by my gammy leg. Having received nothing for the past six months, I was in no position to argue.

I bade farewell to the Scots padre and descended from the rarefied heights of suburbia to a rondavel, a round, single-roomed thatched hut I had rented in the town.

I was now, to my considerable relief, driving again, but decided not to return to the cottage at Bahati as Owen-Jones had hinted that he was looking for a house for me in a salubrious part of town. I looked forward to this with keen interest.

The rondavel was a simple dwelling, constructed from whitewashed mud and wattle. It had a roof, but no ceiling. One looked up to the non-rainproof, rural thatch. Here I dwelt for fourteen months. The place was owned by a retired hospital matron. I seemed to be pursued by members of the medical fraternity. The important thing was that the rent was just affordable. At times I thought the old lady should be paying *me* to be staying there.

My faithful old Nyamwezi cook, weakened by his all-but-terminal illness, had retired from active service. His replacement, a small, shifty, middle-aged Kikuyu, lasted for three weeks before he also had to be retired from my service. He spent most of his time, at my expense, brewing changaa, a native spirit, whose effects could be lethal. This foul concoction, which to the uninitiated tasted like a draught of equal parts of prussic acid, hemlock and weed killer, made meths, by comparison seem like a glass of shandy. My new man appeared to be an addict, lurching about the room in a state of inebriation and denial. One night he vanished, arrested during a police raid on a drinking den, bubbling with illegal stills. It seemed that my cook was the head brewer. I decided that his talents could be put to better use elsewhere, outwith my menage.

His replacement was an improvement, though at times I found this difficult to believe. On one occasion, I discovered that the contents of a bottle of gin, from which one tot had been removed, had mysteriously vanished. I had been given the bottle by a client, sampled it, found it not to my taste, and had put it away in a cupboard. When confronted by the evidence – or lack of it – the cook solemnly declared that the fluid must have evaporated. A bonus point for quick thinking, I thought.

Unlike at my Bahati residence, the kitchen wherein the cook prepared my meals was not connected to the rondavel by a covered walkway. The result was that during the dry season his culinary offerings not infrequently arrived seasoned with a fine peppering of gritty dust, while during wet weather nothing reached the table at the temperature at which it had departed, and its degree of sogginess depended on whether the cook was in an early or advanced state of inebriation at the time.

My hut had no running water and a jug of water for washing purposes would appear outside my door at 6.30 each morning. Furniture was scant – a table, a couple of chairs, a bookcase and a settee behind which stood my bed – not luxurious by European standards but much better than that of most of the Kenyan population.

There was no phone, but then I expected to be moving to a more august establishment in the near future.

I started to go out on calls. Provided I was not required to spend too much time on my knees, I managed well. Soon I discarded my stick and later the built-up shoe.

✳ ✳ ✳ ✳ ✳

I hadn't been out of hospital for long when Owen-Jones and his wife went to Nairobi for several days, leaving me in command. They had business there which required their joint presence. Its nature was not divulged.

Soon after I had started working again, I had noticed a stranger in the surgery. He appeared on a number of occasions but he was not introduced and I assumed that he was a friend or acquaintance of the Owen-Jones'. When I asked him his business he would turn the conversation to trivial topics.

About a month after I had emerged from the comfortable confines of the Presbyterian manse, Mr Owen-Jones informed me that, having done the work of two men for the past six months, he was in a state of mental and physical exhaustion, in dire need of a break, and intended taking three weeks rest and recreation at the Coast.

I made the appropriate noises, extended my sympathies, and hoped that he would enjoy a relaxing holiday, and return refreshed and re-invigorated, ready to resume command.

With his spouse and labrador dogs, he departed.

The following three weeks went by in a blur of activity. The date of the Owen-Jones' return came and went, but I was far too busy to notice it. I had noticed, however, that a number of surgical instruments, and other items of equipment had unaccountably vanished.

It might have been my imagination, but there seemed to be a substantial increase in work following my employer's departure. Although he was efficient and decisive, his manner was frequently brusque and off-hand and this did not endear him to many clients. Whatever the cause, I was kept busy from early morning until well after dark every day.

145

Another week went by and there was still no sign of my employer and his wife – or their dogs.

Then, about ten days after the date of their anticipated return, an invoice arrived by post from an aircraft engineering firm based at Wilson Airport on the outskirts of Nairobi. It was addressed to Mr A. Owen-Jones, charging him for sending a mechanic to the town of Tabora in central Tanzania to repair the starter motor of a light aircraft – a twin-engined Commanche.

This struck me as decidedly odd.

That evening I fished out my map of East Africa and found that Tabora was a very long way indeed from the sun-drenched beaches of Kenya's Indian Ocean coast. I had no doubt that Tabora was just as sun-drenched, but it did not strike me as the sort of place in which one would want to spend a holiday. It appeared to be in the middle of nowhere and, from my readings of Stanley and Livingstone, sited in a waste of endless scrub.

Over the next few days and weeks further information from a variety of sources filtered in my direction.

It appeared that while I was languishing in hospital, my employer was quietly disposing of his various assets. Buyers were found for car, house and kennels. It was all done so cleverly that no-one, except his cook, Opondo, who was either sworn to secrecy, or paid to keep quiet, had an inkling that anything was afoot. An aeroplane was bought and a pilot hired. This was the mysterious stranger I had seen in the surgery. Then, after filling the plane with goodies, such as Persian carpets, they took off into the wide blue yonder, heading south towards the Zambezi and Rhodesia, which at that time was under the control of Ian Smith and his UDI government.

Meanwhile the dogs and bulky, heavy items were dispatched across the borders by road. A smokescreen of confusing information about buying a new house in Nakuru, which was too small to contain all the furniture from the house at Lanet and which therefore had to be put into store in Nairobi, served to obscure the exodus.

It was a moonlight flit on a grand scale, carried out in broad daylight, and one could not help admiring the skill and planning that had gone into its execution.

Part of the reason for the unannounced departure became apparent when a demand notice arrived from the Income Tax Department. Couched in its usual unambiguous language and stiffened by a number of dire penalties, it required that the sum of sixty thousand Kenya shillings be paid immediately. The money had been outstanding for a long time and the hour of reckoning had arrived.

So, when the plane landed at Tabora to refuel and was unable to take off, the passengers and pilot must have felt more than a twinge of anxiety, especially in view of the fact that the plane had been flown out of Kenya without completing the required formalities.

In 1968 one couldn't leave the country without first obtaining an Income Tax Clearance Certificate. I am sure that the perspiration undoubtedly shed by the fugitive trio as they anxiously awaited the arrival of the mechanic was not all due to the torrid heat of Tabora.

Rumours about the further progress of the flight drifted up from the south. One had it that the pilot made a navigational error and had been forced to land in Mozambique, then ruled by the Portuguese. All three travellers, so said the rumour, were put in the cells and fed on maize meal, beans and water, before being released and allowed to proceed on their way. I found it difficult to imagine Owen-Jones accepting this fare with much enthusiasm, but was certain it must have done wonders for his figure.

Several months later it was rumoured that Mrs Owen-Jones had been seen in Nairobi. The authorities had approached her on the matter of the unpaid income tax, when she trumped their card by revealing that she wasn't Mrs Owen-Jones at all, and although she had lived with the man, had never been married to him.

Owen-Jones was not a pilot and had hoped to sell the plane for a tidy sum when he arrived in Rhodesia. Unfortunately he had failed to obtain a Certificate of Airworthiness when buying the aircraft, and for years the plane sat on the tarmac at Salisbury airport gathering dust and bird droppings.

Initially it seemed that Rhodesia was an ideal place for a man of Owen-Jones' temperament and inclinations. The country had a white government and even under UDI the economy flourished. Then the bush war, like an insidious cancer, crept over the land. Everyone, white and black, felt its effect. Owen-Jones, living in Umtali on the Mozambique border, had mortar bombs dropping into his garden. Finally Rhodesia became Zimbabwe. The war for independence was succeeded by civil strife, tribalism, and a lack of concern for the rights of the individual. Over all loomed the ugly spectre of Marxism.

Perhaps the grass in Rhodesia wasn't so green after all.

Meanwhile I appeared to be up the creek without a paddle.

With only half a month's pay in the bank, out of which I had to pay for my food and rent, it wouldn't take much to have me classified as a Distressed British Subject. I scrutinised my bank statement with fierce concentration. There wasn't enough to pay for a pedal cycle let alone a car or the other essential items required to run a veterinary practice.

My late employer's accountants approached me with the glad tidings that the Volkswagen which I had been driving, and which belonged to Owen-Jones would have to be sold to settle some of his outstanding debts.

The future did not look bright.

CHAPTER NINE

As I drove the soon-to-be-sold Volkswagen at ever-increasing speeds over the rutted roads of the Rift Valley, I wondered what to do. Preoccupied with the present problem and keen to get the most out of the old jalopy before we parted company, I shoved the accelerator closer to the floor than was wise in view of the shocking state of the roads. This did not help the car, but it did help me. As I rocketed from farm to farm, my serotonin levels surged to unprecedented heights.

I made an appointment to see the manager of one of the main banks in town.

He was a cadaverous Scotsman, with a graveyard sense of humour. Seated behind a vast mahogany desk he spent most of the interview rubbing his large, mottled, hands together, flicking imaginary specks of dust from the cuffs of his jacket, and peering disapprovingly in my direction.

I put my problem to him, and broached the subject of a loan.

'And what security can you offer, Mr Cran?' he inquired in his sing-song Lowland Scots accent.

A pertinent point.

I said that in view of the amount of work I was doing it should not take me long to repay a loan sufficient to cover the cost of buying a car and a stock of drugs and equipment.

'And what would happen if you had another accident with one of your patients?' He bared a set of piebald dentures in a hideous caricature of a grin.

I smiled mirthlessly back.

He then went into interminable detail to explain why, in his opinion of course, I was an unacceptable risk. I owned no property, no vehicle, or other assets which could be repossessed should I default on a loan. I had been in the country for a relatively short time and I was, in his personal view of course, an inexperienced greenhorn, in other words, a raw liability.

The answer was a resounding no.

Only later did I learn that the manager had been a close chum of my late departed employer.

But the word had spread among the banking fraternity. The damage had been done, and all the other banks I approached turned me down flat.

Help was at hand, however, in the form of the farming community of the Rift Valley.

A group of about forty farmers, European settlers, but at least one African cabinet minister, decided in their collective wisdom that my services were of sufficient value to warrant my retention.

So a syndicate was formed. Each farmer contributed a sum of money to a common pool. The total was sufficient to purchase a new car, a Peugeot 204 saloon, install a phone in my rondavel, buy sufficient drugs and equipment to get things going, and pay the first month's salary for the staff, including me.

I was in business!

In place of Nyaga, the Seventh Day Adventist, Opondo, the Owen-Jones' ex-cook, was recruited to act as bottle-washer and general dogsbody, mainly in view of his apparent honesty, and good nature. Age was certainly not in his favour. He must have been well over 65, which in African terms meant that he was as old as Methusalah.

In Mrs Strickland I was fortunate to find an efficient secretary to tide me over my embryonic period. Brisk and attractive in a savage sort of way, like Boadicea in tweeds, she brooked no nonsense from staff or clients.

Although initially it seemed that there were many similarities between veterinary practice in Britain and Kenya, as time passed it became apparent there were as many differences.

The range of diseases was very much wider. Virtually all those which occurred in Europe were to be found here, in addition to a veritable host of tropical ailments. Many of the latter were transmitted by insects. Ticks, tsetse flies, midges, and mosquitoes were the main culprits. In order to fend off diseases carried by ticks, most cattle in the Highlands had to be dipped or sprayed once or twice a week, at considerable cost to the farmer, both from the purchase of the appropriate chemicals, and the loss of milk and weight as reluctant cattle were driven through hissing spray races or goaded into plunge dips.

Cattle had to be vaccinated – against Rinderpest, Rift Valley Fever, and Foot and Mouth disease, which if unchecked could wreak havoc in unprotected herds.

Horses had to be vaccinated against African Horse Sickness. Pigs had to prevented from coming into contact with warthogs and bushpigs, carriers of deadly African Swine Fever.

Sheep were not spared. Afflicted from within by cohorts of intestinal parasites, at risk from the viruses of Bluetongue and Nairobi Sheep Disease, they could, and did, die by the hundreds.

Large areas of the country were deficient in minerals, which if not supplied in the form of mixtures or blocks, resulted in stock failing to thrive.

In some parts of the district predators – lion, hyena, and leopard – took their toll.

As the four-legged carnivores followed their natural instincts, so did those on two legs, rustling cattle, stealing wire fencing and setting snares which caught wild and domestic animals with equal indiscrimination. As a result night watchmen had to be employed on a large scale. Armed with spears, shotguns, and bows and arrows, they patrolled farms, and, when they weren't snoring beside their camp fires, guarded flocks and herds.

These threats obliged animals to be herded into protected enclosures at night, depriving them of grazing and their owners of profit. And a daily count had to be made to ensure that none had been stolen, eaten, fallen over a cliff or been drowned in a swamp.

Heavy rain could turn unsurfaced roads into quagmires. Vehicles became stuck in mud, and milk sent to the creamery often arrived looking like rejected yogurt.

Violent hailstorms, accompanied by fierce, strong winds could kill small stock such as sheep and goats, destroy tea plantations, and batter ten foot high stands of maize to the ground.

And drought could reduce prime, fat cattle to listless, apathetic skeletons, which died beneath brassy skies, or succumbed at the onset of the first heavy rains.

If this was not enough, periodic infestations of a caterpillar called army worm would arrive to devour pastures until little was left but bare earth. For the wheat farmer the low, constant, murmuring chatter which heralded the arrival of flocks of the red-billed quelea, was a sound to chill the blood. A species of weaver bird, they sometimes congregated in flocks numbering hundreds of thousands. They were the avian equivalent of the locust. When disturbed from the trees in which they roosted they would fly off in huge, undulating swarms. So co-ordinated were their movements, they appeared to act as a single organism and not as a flock of individual birds.

In outlying areas, properties adjacent to forest or bush would be invaded by unwelcome visitors. Elephant would walk undeterred through fences, leaving a tangle of wire and smashed posts in their wake. They would break pipes, damage water troughs, and terrify farm workers. Acres of maize might be eaten or flattened in one night. Buffalo, bushpigs and porcupines loved to feast in fields of wheat. In some places baboons had multiplied to plague proportions. Bold and arrogant, they strutted through the paddocks, plundering as they went. The rearguard males would maul or kill dogs, or lure them over cliffs, scrambling nimbly aside as their pursuers fell to their deaths.

The farmers all appeared to experience problems with their labour, who seemed to be forever falling sick, running foul of the law, pilfering or watering the milk, or turning up for work under the influence of alcohol. And lack of spare parts for vehicles and machinery was a common theme.

There was an extraordinary diversity of farming systems in the area I now covered – huge ranches, tiny peasant plots, well-watered dairy farms with lush paddocks, thorny scrubby patches of semi-jungle, all dictated by altitude and rainfall.

The clientele resembled a miniature U.N., although in the main without the rancour and bigotry which so typifies that blighted body. In the surgery, blanket-clad Maasai rubbed shoulders with turbaned Sikhs, khaki-clad settlers sat down beside Hindus and Muslims, wealthy African businessmen chatted with chic, young hausfraus bringing their pets in for vaccination. Kikuyu and Kalenjin, Gujarati and Punjabi, together with Swahili, were often heard more frequently than English.

The Europeans came from almost every country east of the Hebrides and west of the Urals. Although the majority was of British stock, there was a substantial leavening of other nationalities. Stolid Swedish missionaries and earnest Finnish road builders contrasted with volatile Italian farmers and exuberant Greek sisal estate owners. From east of the former Iron Curtain came Poles, and Yugoslav construction workers. There was a large Dutch community in the town, composed of aid personnel and their wives, while in the surrounding area were several Danish farmers. Like their compatriot Karen Blixen, many possessed curious foibles, which made them stand out, even in a community noted for its eccentrics. Reserved Irish priests competed with extrovert American Baptists for the souls of the uncommitted. Contingents of clannish, reclusive Israelis, engaged in the construction of roads, shopped en masse in the town. For official and other purposes the Americans and Israelis were classified as Europeans, which did not always please them.

This, then was the technicoloured background to my work. A far cry from the monochrome of Aberdeenshire.

❋ ❦ ❋ ❦ ❋

East Coast Fever is endemic in the highlands of Kenya. This devastating disease is caused by a protozoan parasite and carried by the brown ear tick.

Corridor Disease, a symptomless disease of buffalo, is very similar and both cause oedema of the lungs – the wretched animal dies of asphyxia

– literally drowning in its own fluids.

In 1968 there were no curative drugs, and even now, fifty years after the disease was first identified, there is no commercial vaccine.

One morning a message came in from a dairy farm in the Solai Valley asking me to investigate an outbreak of disease in the calves. None of the adults was sick.

Feeling brisk and efficient in the new Peugeot 204, I sped along the tarmac which extended for ten miles out of town. On the left the land sloped steeply into the lava-filled bowl of Menengai Crater, a craggy wasteland with steam jets rising ominously into the still air.

Eight miles beyond the end of the tarmac I eased my car into the rocky enclosure which passed as a farmyard.

Almost before I had opened the door a squad of infants had materialised, as if out of nowhere. They regarded me with such glee and curiosity of expression that I began to wonder if I had perhaps put my shorts on back to front, or had grown some hideous deformity in the night. A thin-faced Boran woman regarded me impassively from the doorway of her hut, a sombre contrast to the melee of excited urchins gambolling around me.

'Jambo, mzungu! Jambo, mzungu! Habari yako?' (Hello, European! Hello European! How are you?)

The arrival of the farm manager, a friendly flop-eared Tugen, called Kiptanui, sent the children flying in all directions, laughing and giggling.

He led me into the calf-house where the inmates were kept in individual pens.

Kiptanui spoke good English.

'So, Kiptanui, what's the trouble?'

'These small calves, now several have died. They cough and then they die. And more are sick, even now. Breathing fast, very fast. And they refuse to eat their hay.'

'OK. Let's listen to their lungs first.'

I stuck my stethoscope against the chest of a calf. It sounded terrible, a horrible, gasping, wheezing noise with a ghastly gurgle in the background. I inserted a thermometer into the rectum. 106 degrees. I whistled. I noticed a swelling at the angle of the calf's jaw. The parotid gland was enlarged.

'Look, Kiptanui, the lymph gland here is swollen. And here as well.' I checked the glands in front of the shoulder.

The other calves were the same.

'This must be East Coast Fever.'

'But, daktari, these calves have never been outside since they were born. They have never even grazed grass.'

Yet it had to be ECF.

I thought.

What about the hay, then? I grabbed a handful and pulled it apart.

Nothing! Dammit! I seized another handful and searched more carefully. After a few minutes I found a tick. And then another, and another. All brown ear ticks.

'Kiptanui, where did this hay come from?'

'From the shores of Lake Nakuru, daktari.'

At that time Lake Nakuru was not a national park, only a bird sanctuary. I knew that buffalo living in the forests around the lake came out at night to graze on the grassy flats near the shore. This grass had been cut to make hay and the buffalo, I knew, were frequent carriers of tick-borne disease. This had to be it.

'You must remove all this hay and burn it. I'll give these sick calves a shot of oxytetracycline but I'm afraid most will die. Get fresh hay, and you must look through it very, very carefully for ticks. OK.'

'Yes, daktari.'

I took some blood and gland smears and confirmed the diagnosis back in the surgery. A few more calves died and then the outbreak came to an end.

All the farms bordering Lake Nakuru were at risk. There was no perimeter fence, as there is now, to prevent buffalo wandering at will.

On the southern and eastern shores of the lake, Robin and Liza Long ran their large ranch, rearing Boran beef cattle, Ayrshire milking cows and thoroughbred racehorses. They lived in a massive, sprawling, colonial mansion built on a bluff overlooking the lake. Articulate, intelligent, hospitable and charming, they ran one of the most efficient farming enterprises in the Rift Valley. Numerous problems had to be overcome before this state had been attained. Their property lay in an area notorious for its mineral deficiencies, so much so that the wasting disease, which affected cattle reared there, was known as 'Nakuruitis'. Cattle failed to thrive, were listless, anaemic and were susceptible to disease. It was discovered that this was due to a deficiency of cobalt in the soil. Supplementation of this element in the diet worked like a miracle and allowed cattle to be sent for slaughter fourteen months earlier than was previously possible.

No sooner had one problem been solved than others appeared, to torment the latter-day pioneers.

The beef cattle grazed the open eastern plains, the dairy cattle the wooded pastures to the south of the lake. Here the narrow Nderit River trickled through swamps and groves of fever trees, to merge with the alkaline waters of the lake at a point much favoured by flocks of pelicans. The river was dark brown, thick with mud, but fresh, if such a word can be applied to water which resembled oxtail soup. And therein lay its attraction to the buffalo which lurked in the dense thickets and patches of bush.

One day a telephone call summoned me to the estate. Reception was appalling and I could barely hear what was being said. The tiny, high-pitched, gender-less voice at the other end sounded as though it was competing with an artillery bombardment, with a thunderstorm raging in the background. I bellowed in response. There was an abrupt silence, as though the caller had been the recipient of a well-aimed round. The operator seemingly was also deceased, as repeated diallings went unheeded.

I knew where the call had come from, but no idea what it was about.

As I sped along the dirt road to the ranch, leaving the town behind, my irritation eased. The road was well maintained and ran across open, breezy plains towards the cross-roads at the hamlet of Elementaita, where there was a police station, a few hovels, and an Indian-owned store. The place always reminded me of the collection of ruinous shacks in the film *Shane*, where Jack Palance has his final shoot-out with Alan Ladd, in the mud and the blood and the beer, which was about all that was on offer in Elementaita.

To the left of the road was the blue-blooded estancia of Lord Delamere. The no less vast empire of the Longs covered the right horizon. Scattered groups of Thomson's gazelle nibbled the grass. In the distance a lone secretary bird stalked moodily along, head bent, crest tossing in the wind, searching for snakes and rodents. An augur buzzard swooped over the road to land lightly in a small tree. A long-tailed widow bird, accompanied by a small contingent of dowdy females, flew jerkily a few feet over the waving grass. His startling red and buff shoulders contrasted violently with the rest of his jet-black plumage.

Robin Long, customary cigarette drooping from nicotine-stained fingers, met me at the house.

'Hello, Hugh, old boy, thanks so much for coming.' Robin was ever courteous, even in the face of imminent crisis. 'Pop into the Merc. and let's drive down to the cattle. Six of the Ayrshires are sick, bloody sick.'

We drove down a steep track into the acacia forest. Vervet monkeys skipped through the branches. A troop of baboons moved slowly and insolently off the road. A family of warthogs rushed off through the undergrowth, tails stiffly erect. In the distance I could see a number of waterbuck grazing beneath the trees. A rufous bushbuck slipped like a wraith into the shadows and vanished.

The affected cattle were standing near a movable milking bail, listless and depressed. As I walked towards them, one coughed convulsively several times. I stood watching them. All were breathing heavily. One had diarrhoea. The eyes of another two were a milky blue colour. All their coats were dry and their hollow flanks indicated that they had not eaten for some time.

Things looked bad, very bad.

I turned to a Maasai herdsman and asked him in Swahili to put the cattle into the bail.

All had fevers of up to 106 degrees. All had enlarged lymph glands. The ones in front of the shoulder were almost as big as coconuts.

'The herdsmen tell me they have seen buffalo grazing in one of the paddocks,' said Robin.

'Well, that's it then,' I replied. 'This must be Corridor Disease, and with no effective treatment available, the outlook is grim.'

I spoke more truly than I thought possible.

As we were walking back to the car, a Maasai stripling came panting across the grass.

'Ngombe ingine likwisha kufa!' Another cow has just finished dying!'

The youth got into the car to show us where the animal had expired. With him came a not unpleasant smell of smoke, sweat and cow's urine, but when Robin wound down his window, I deemed that a whiff of oxygen would improve the bouquet, and raised my questing nostrils to the passing breeze.

In the far corner of a fifty acre paddock we espied a small group of men. Creeping through the knee-high grass, expecting at any moment to crash into an unseen antbear hole or crack the sump on a boulder, Robin drove in their direction.

Beneath an acacia tree lay a fine, fat Ayrshire cow. In front of its nose was a small pile of froth.

Two of the Maasai squatting beside the carcase were carrying simis (swords) in leather scabbards and they were razor sharp. In short order they removed hide and innards and laid the latter neatly on the grass.

As they did so a torrent of fluid and froth poured from the severed windpipe. Both lungs were heavy and waterlogged. I cut into them and out flowed a tidal wave of watery blood and foam. I hefted the lungs. They contained so much fluid that I felt I was holding two bags filled with water.

This was Corridor Disease.

I told Robin that he must immediately start dipping his cattle twice weekly. He must clip the long hair at the ends of the tails, where ticks frequently attached, and apply pyrethrum grease inside the ears, another favourite nestling place. And he must move the cattle well away from areas frequented by buffalo.

A boffin-based suggestion that massive doses of antibiotics injected into the abdominal cavity might be efficacious, proved to be yet another pipe-dream. During the next four weeks, 150 cattle died. Carcases littered the plains and woodlands. The jackals, vultures and hyenas dined richly. As did some of the workers.

To me and the owners it was a depressing disaster, an occurrence all too common in Africa, difficult to prevent, and difficult to control once it happened.

Finally the deaths stopped, twice weekly dipping was maintained, the buffalo were either shot or driven into the forests of the Mau Escarpment and the cattle were kept away from the acacia woodlands.

Fortunately for the Longs, they had other enterprises to fall back on. Their large numbers of thoroughbred racehorses and thousands of beef cattle kept them afloat.

Such, alas, was not the case with the African sans-culottes living on the other side of the lake.

Here, too many people lived on too many plots carved out of the desiccated remains of a former sisal estate. They had no electricity, no piped water, no sewage system. Their water came from the muddy Njoro River, a narrow stream which ran between high, near-vertical banks from the forests of the Mau to the alkaline waters of the lake. Cattle waded into the turbid water to slake their thirst, dunging and urinating as they did so. Nearby, women would be filling drums with water, which they would then hump on their backs to their huts. Upstream, a group of naked boys might be playing in the water, laughing and splashing. In the dry season the river dwindled to a trickle until it ceased entirely. Then the only water available had to be taken from stagnant pools, hissing with insect life, and breeding grounds for mosquitoes.

This scarcity of water had dire effects on the control of tick-borne disease, including Corridor Disease and East Coast Fever.

For all of the hundreds of tiny plots, there was only one communal dip, the original one of the former sisal estate. Being a communal dip it was controlled by a committee. As a result no-one was prepared to take responsibility for it, to replenish it with chemicals, to repair the leaking roof, to take samples for testing, to pump it out when required. So the dip was always under-strength, the ticks were not killed, tick resistance developed and the area around the dip became a place for cattle to pick up fresh ticks and new infections. Many farmers believed that the large numbers of waterbuck living in the woodlands around the lake played a part in infecting their cattle, and many years later this was found to be true.

As most of the farmers owned only a few cattle, when disease struck the blow was severe indeed.

I made innumerable visits at all hours of the day and night to diagnose and treat. I would talk myself hoarse exhorting people not to send their animals to the communal dip. Buy, borrow or steal a hand-pump and spray the cattle on your own shamba, I would beg.

Garnering my modest fees was another matter altogether. By British standards the sums involved were laughable, considering the time involved and the wear and tear on my car. The tracks were either axle-deep in dust, or a series of giant mud wallows, separated by islands of drier land towards which I gunned the vehicle in a great shower of ochre-coloured water, hoping that no hidden chasms lay beneath the soupy surface.

Often when I did arrive at my destination it was to find that the patient was over the hills and far away, together with the owner. Running both to earth could be equally difficult and infuriating. Sending an invoice requesting payment to a communal post office box number shared by several hundred peasants, most of whom were illiterate, was a fruitless and frustrating exercise. Cash in hand was what was required and most people appreciated this. Most Africans appeared to prefer to pay a modest sum for a prompt and efficient service, than rely upon a free state-run organisation devoid of drugs and equipment, run by unmotivated personnel who might, or might not, turn up when requested to do so.

I was the only practising vet within a hundred mile radius: I felt that the African farmer needed all the help he could get and made strenuous efforts to ensure my fees did not deter the poorest from seeking help when they wanted it.

If at that time western science had failed to find a cure for these diseases it was at least trying to extend the frontiers of knowledge. Its influence was positive, and relatively benign and beneficial.

The same could not be said of some local methods of treatment.

Granted that the animal would die anyway, the barbaric business of hastening the wretched beast to greener pastures in the most unpleasant manner possible drove me wild with rage.

One afternoon I was asked to examine some cattle owned by an African lawyer. He was an Abaluyha by tribe, from western Kenya, and highly educated. He owned a small farm on the edge of Menengai Crater and he lived in a large house, previously occupied by a European.

As I drove up to the house, I saw four or five cattle lying on the lawn at the back of the building. Beside them stood the lawyer.

Above the cattle there appeared to be a red mist, which quivered and trembled in the sunshine. I stared at it, wondering what it was.

As I got closer I saw that the lawyer had a knife in his hand, and that the cattle had no ears. They had just been cut off by the educated savage who stood beside them.

Blood spouted from severed arteries, filling the air with a crimson miasma. The animals' backs were thickly clotted with gore.

I saw red, figuratively, as well as literally. I was so enraged I could barely speak.

Restraining the urge to wrest the knife from his hand and remove his own ears, I asked the lawyer as politely as I could under the circumstances just what the devil he was playing at.

'Now don't get upset, old boy. It's just an old Abaluyha custom. Pay no attention! It helps to draw out the poison!'

His accent was pure Oxford. By comparison my own was rude and rustic. The tirade which fell upon his unsevered ears was equally rude.

As for paying no attention, this was a difficult task with the air full of fountains of blood, and with the lawyer's malignant presence at my elbow.

Needless to say the cattle shuffled off their collective mortal coils at an even faster rate than I would have believed possible. All were dead by the following day.

Many years later when curative drugs were available, similar treatments were still being meted out to affected cattle.

An African farmer asked me to examine and treat two of his animals, which he suspected of having East Coast Fever.

Indeed they did, and they stood forlornly in a crudely fenced compound, coughing and gasping for breath. Their coats stood on end, their eyes streamed moisture, their lymph glands were swollen, and both had fevers.

As they were being driven into a crush, of which Heath Robinson would have been proud, I noticed that the smaller of the two had had the hair over its superficial lymph glands shaved off. In the centre of each shaved area was large puncture.

A lengthy question and answer session followed.

The farmer had been using the services of a local witch doctor. During the previous month eight other cattle had shown symptoms of disease, and had received a visitation from the medicine man, who had inserted red hot wires into their lymph glands. This process was not appreciated by the patients, who manifested their displeasure by dying in rapid succession.

Finally it dawned upon the farmer that perhaps the witch doctor wasn't doing a very good job of curing his cattle.

At the last moment he asked me to visit, and presented one skewered and one unskewered patient. I treated both with parvaquone and oxytetracycline and to the amazement of the farmer and to my gratification, both recovered.

Chapter Ten

Although the British buy-out scheme continued to inexorably engulf those farms owned by citizens originating from the Sceptred Isle, the majority of large estates were still in the hands of Europeans. Plough disc signs marked the entrance to their properties. Dirt tracks wound away, over plains or hills, until they reached the distant farmhouse.

Some of these were basic mud and wattle thatched cottages, devoid of expected conveniences such as electricity and flush toilets. Others were overblown mansions of stone and marble, surrounded by acres of manicured lawns, tended by droves of gardeners. Within their imposing walls, swarms of befezzed servants rushed around, ministering to the needs of the bwana and memsahib. Most were somewhere in between.

One thing the vast majority of owners had in common was their hospitality.

I used to arrive on farms and ranches at all hours of the day and night. No matter. Whatever the hour, almost without exception, I would be invited in for a cup of tea, or a drink, or a meal. Often, due to pressure of work, I had to refuse. But, when I had the time, there was nothing more pleasant than indulging in the delightful custom of having breakfast on a cool colonial verandah, especially if it followed a long strenuous calving, or several hours examining cattle for sale to Uganda or Tanzania. Late breakfasts were the rule, after the farmer had done his early morning chores.

Most verandahs overlooked a shady oasis of greenery, to which were attracted all manner of birds: metallic-blue starlings, yellow and black weaver birds, tiny blue and red finches, black and white shrikes and clouds of doves and pigeons. Swallows and martins frequently nested under the eaves and would swoop over the breakfast table as they returned to feed their nestlings.

If I was called out at night it was rare not to be asked in for a drink or dinner. I would phone my rondavel to ascertain from my major domo

159

whether any calls had come in. If they had, I would present my apologies and proceed on my way. If not, I would settle down with a sigh of relief and gladly partake of whatever was offered.

The meal might be served at a beautifully polished table, eaten with silver cutlery and presented by soft-footed, impeccably mannered servants. David Fielden's board fell into this welcome category. With his wife, he gentleman-farmed at Subukia, and a dinner in their genteel company was a gustatory experience to be treasured and fondly remembered when later I picked at unidentifiable fragments presented by my own steward. David had a herd of Guernsey cows, and his wife kept a few thoroughbred horses. The cows were as tame as lapdogs, were milked by hand in the paddocks without any form of restraint, and when I was asked to carry out pregnancy examinations, this is where it was done, al fresco. A single herdsman would croon softly to the animal, while the bespectacled headman, an imposing African of vast bulk and majestic mien, would intone details of its often-depressing reproductive history from an enormous ledger, whose weight would have disjointed the arms of a lesser man. My heart would sink as, with impassive countenance, he would blandly inform me that the cow up whose rectum my left arm was inserted, had been served no less than twenty times without conceiving.

At the other end of the culinary spectrum was Tommy Pearson, an ebullient bachelor, who haphazardly farmed near Rongai. Wet or dry, getting to Tommy's place was an adventure, the road an obstacle course, guaranteed to hospitalise any vehicle reckless enough to set wheel upon it. Half way along it was a bridge, hanging drunkenly over a stream. Several planks were missing and the entire structure sloped steeply from left to right. If the weather was dry I approached at speed in the hope of clearing it before it collapsed. If it was wet and the planks greasy I crept across in first gear to the sound of the creaking and groaning of its rotting timbers, wondering how I would return. Just before Tommy's house was another stream over which there was no bridge, and depending on the weather this might, or might not, be fordable.

The approaches to his farm virtually ensured Tommy's immunity to visitations from undesirables such as travelling salesmen and income tax inspectors.

The house was spartan, the garden a riot of weeds, the kitchen a noisome and smoky dungeon. Of liquor such as Whitecap and Tusker there was never any lack, but one had to imbibe with care. The way back was beset with perils.

Tommy's cook was his pride and joy.

'Splendid fellow!' Tommy would boom, pouring another ale over his tonsils.

'He's deaf and dumb, you see. Works like a slave, never knows when

160

to stop, and can't answer back! And he can cook!'

Indeed he could. And if the food he slapped before us with a flourish and an inarticulate roar might have caused David Fielden's lip to curl ever so slightly, it was good enough for me after a hard day's work.

On the chilly heights of the Molo Downs lay the farm of Alan and Shirley Douglas-Dufresne. Even at mid-day, with the sun shining, the air was fresh and breezy. It was, after all, 9,000 feet above sea level. Their farm was at the end of the road. Beyond stretched tangled forest, inhabited by bushbuck, monkeys, elephants and the tribal hunter-gatherer Dorobo people.

⚜⚜⚜⚜⚜

Oats, wheat, barley, Hampshire sheep, and Galloway cattle all thrived in the rarefied atmosphere.

During the wet season these upland farmers might be unable to leave their properties for days or weeks on end, even using four wheel drive vehicles.

The Douglas-Dufresne's house was an extraordinary structure.

It was very large and roomy. Indeed one might say that it had only one room.

The house was thatched with a thick, solid mat which overhung the eaves to such an extent that one had to bend double in order to enter the front door. Once inside, the first impression was one of space. The main reason for this was the absence of ceiling. The house was a giant rondavel. The rooms – dining room, bedrooms, lounge, bathroom – had walls, but no ceilings, so that anyone of above average height could, without much difficulty, see into almost every room in the house. Privacy apparently did not rank highly in the Douglas-Dufresne's list of priorities when they were building their house.

A generator supplied electricity. Tanks collected rainwater.

For many settler-farmers, meals were often moveable feasts. Breakfast was usually eaten late, after the farmer had been out and attended to stock and machinery. The former was often the prerogative of the farmer's wife, especially where dairy cattle were concerned. The husband dealt with the tractors, ploughs and crops, while the wife looked after the cows, calves the milk.

As far as irregularity of meals was concerned, the palm had to be handed to Jasper Evans of Kampi-ya-Moto. Perhaps irregularity is not the right word. They weren't irregular – just several hours later than the norm. Lunch usually appeared between four and five in the afternoon, dinner between ten and eleven at night. When I accepted one of Jasper's pressing

161

invitations to stay for a meal, I needed plenty of time in hand.

They were always friendly, informal affairs. A pack of dogs, mainly labradors and dachshunds, trooped into the dining room as well, as though they owned the place. They sat around, staring fixedly at each mouthful as it was forked or spooned between the lips, gradually creeping closer and closer, until a pleading head was placed, uninvited, on one's lap.

In the centre of the table stood a large circular wooden tray, set upon a spindle, which allowed it to revolve. Upon this was laden a dense mass of jars, mostly unlabelled, of various jams, chutney, piccalilli, marmalade, butter, salt, pepper, Marmite, mayonnaise, and a bewildering array of condiments. Beside each place at table stood a brass finger bowl.

Jasper's artistic, long-suffering and easy-going wife, Jill, presided benignly over the archaic scene, while their ancient cook protracted the event by the extreme slowness of his movements. He resembled an aged tortoise set upon its hind legs. Between courses he disappeared for such an inordinate length of time that I often wondered if he had perhaps expired in the kitchen, and was even now communing with his ancestors. Then the door would creak open and he would shuffle in, a gentle smile upon his ebony features.

After the meal, mandatory post-prandial drinks would be imbibed in the living room, a place of glorious and comfortable disorder. Pictures lined the walls. One side of the room was filled with an enormous bookcase crammed with volumes on every conceivable subject. Framed photographs stood upon tables, competing with piles of yellowing magazines. Dogs sprawled upon the floor. Animal skins lay upon the backs of sofas. Saddles lay heaped in corners. If it was evening, a log fire would be crackling in the grate. Finally, after several false starts, I would depart, quite bemused by the combination of good company, splendid hospitality and too much gin.

When Jasper and Jill sold their Kampi-ya-Moto farm, and moved to a ranch at Rumuruti, they took with them their own personal blend of domesticity, unique gypsy lifestyle and open-house atmosphere to the plains of Laikipia.

✗✗✗✗✗

Night visits to farms and ranches allowed me to catch sight of animals and birds which only became active after dark. Red-eyed nightjars would flutter up out of the dust at the last moment, before the car wheels ran them over. An owl might be seen gliding in the light of the headlamps. A mongoose might scuttle across the road or a pair of jackals might casually lope in front of the car for a few hundred yards before vanishing into the bush. On the Elementaita plains, spring hares, small rodents resembling miniature kangaroos, bounded across the grasslands. On rare occasions

I caught a glimpse of an African civet disappearing into the vegetation beside the road.

The later it was and the more remote the location, the more I was likely to see. The early hours of the morning were best, preferably on an unfrequented dirt track. My senses were not at their most acute at this time, especially if I had been roused from my couch after a hard day's work to attend to what in many cases required the marshalling of all my mental and physical faculties. Life, I felt, and especially mine, was at its lowest ebb. Other lives, however, were at their most active, and, if I was fortunate enough to see them, then I at once felt more alert, brisk and ready to tackle the job that lay ahead. It was curious, like a sort of ocular pep pill, an optical amphetamine. Perhaps it was the sight of that purposeful life, undisturbed except by the lights of my car, which stimulated and buoyed me up.

The leopard, which I saw one night in the old railway cutting, near Eburru, was a case in point. For a second it stood surprised, glaring at the headlamps as they approached. Then, with a soundless snarl, it leapt in one bound up the rocks at the side of the road, and was gone. It all happened so quickly that, for a moment, I wondered if I had imagined the whole thing. But I knew I hadn't, and my immediate change of mood confirmed that knowledge.

The aardvark, or antbear, is an almost entirely nocturnal beast, and is most active during the darkest nights as it searches for ants and termites. As a consequence it was seldom seen by accountants or bank managers, unless they stumbled upon one when returning home late at night from some rural party, when they probably thought the animal was the result of too many pink gins. Its massive body and immense tubular snout made it a worthy inhabitant of an alcohol-fuelled nightmare. My nocturnal forays permitted me to see aardvarks on many occasions. Once, on a farm track near Rongai, composed almost exclusively of rocks and holes in equal proportions, I came across a female of the species, shuffling along, with an infant close behind, following her white-tipped tail, which seemed to gleam like a strip of phosphorescent paint in the darkness. Daylight or bright light made them almost blind. On the steep winding road which connected the Solai and Subukia valleys, I met aardvarks several times. Dazzled by the headlights, they would weave backwards and forwards, until almost touched by the bumper. I would stop the car, and after a few moments they would move off into the darkness. Occasionally I met them in the most unlikely places. One I saw was perambulating down the tarmac on the outskirts of Nakuru, and another was galumphing across the polo ground at Gilgil by the light of a full moon.

Porcupines and serval cats were other elusive creatures of the night which occasionally swam into my orbit. The former always reminded me of a rather irritated North American Indian, with its rattling quills and crest of bristles on its head and neck. The slender, long-legged serval, with its small aristocratic head put me in mind of a ballerina, with its graceful movements and delicate demeanour.

Driving at night in Africa was always a bit of an adventure. Once I had left the main roads, where pedestrians staggered about regardless of the density of traffic and where I ran the continual risk of running into unlit lorries or tractors, or being mown down by buses being driven on the wrong side of the road, I never knew what I might see, or what might happen. As roads became surfaced and as the population increased like dragon's teeth, this sense of adventure diminished, but some of the spice always remained.

✱ ✱ ✱ ✱ ✱

Mrs Strickland's temporary stewardship as vet's secretary came to an end, and her place was filled by Sophie Sinclair-Smith.

Sophie was young, blonde, attractive, bubbly and very, very vivacious. She seemed to be constantly on the point of bursting out of her skin with vitality. Her sense of humour was highly developed, and her unrestrained laugh could be heard piercing the hubbub of the most raucous party. In her recent past she had been both a racing car driver and a mannequin, probably at the same time. Her husband, Peter, was a major in the British Army. Most of his time appeared to be spent suffering the slings and arrows of outrageous fortune in the Northern Frontier District, advising his equals and underlings in the Kenya Army on the finer points of soldiering. Their two children spent most of their time in the care of an ayah.

Sophie's parents lived in the Persian Gulf on the island of Bahrain. As did Peter's parents.

Sophie's father was married to Peter's mother, so in effect Sophie and Peter were stepsister and stepbrother as well as man and wife.

I was never very good at maths and algebra at school, and when I contemplated the marital ramifications of this relationship my mind would go blank. I never discovered whether the coming together of Dad and Mum had taken place before or after that of their offspring.

Sophie's extraordinary joie de vivre, general gusto and wild enthusiasm took Nakuru by storm. Unfortunately it also took her own marriage by storm and it finally foundered under the strain of life in the fast track.

In the meantime, for a while at least, she was Nakuru's very own Blonde Bombshell.

I was never very sure just how efficient she was at coping with the accounts and book-keeping, being a relative tyro myself in such matters.

Of one thing I was sure. She was good for business.

On returning to the surgery from visiting farms, I often had difficulty in forcing myself through the crowd of farmers blocking the entrance. They were predominantly male, and ostensibly there to pay bills, buy drugs and seek advice. On a couple of occasions the crush was so great I was obliged to slip in through the back door. Farmers who hitherto had always sent their cheques by post, now found it necessary to settle their accounts in person.

Sophie also found it convenient to entertain her female friends with coffee and biscuits in the morning and tea in the afternoon. Very nice, I thought.

Virtually the whole of the animal-owning population of the central Rift Valley, it seemed, plus many others, from further afield, or with no connections at all with the animal kingdom, passed through the surgery portals.

When dealing with the public, the front man or woman performs a vital role. Sophie played the part to perfection.

Her Swahili was pretty patchy, but in times of need she could always call upon Vincent Fernandes, my Goan clerk, for help. And her generous, warm-hearted, open nature made it relatively easy for her to deal with the growing number of African clients.

Some of these were pretty unsophisticated fellows.

One afternoon an African farmer came into the surgery.

He seemed to be in a rather irritable frame of mind.

'Hey, daktari!' He jabbed a knobbly finger in my direction. 'Those pessaries you sold me. They are no good!'

A few days previously he had bought some Cooper's uterine pessaries. His cow had recently calved, her foetal membranes had not been expelled and he wanted some medicine. Pessaries play little part in the expulsion of foetal membranes, but they do assist in preventing infection. So he was sold the requisite number, formidable-looking bombs, three inches long, coloured a dark, ominous purple.

'Now, the foetal membranes, they are still hanging, and her waste, it has gone purple!'

Behind me, Sophie gave a barely suppressed snort. With some difficulty I restrained my mirth and gave him a quick course in basic anatomy and advised him of a more suitable orifice.

※ ⚘ ※ ⚘ ※

With frightening rapidity the work built up.

With maddening regularity I would be woken by the shrill of the telephone. It was a rare and treasured treat if breakfast was consumed without interruption. Mid-day meals soon became a thing of the distant past. At best they consisted of a sandwich hastily wolfed down in the surgery. Following the afternoon session with small animals, my assistant Moses and I would set off to complete the calls which had come in since morning. This often took till long after dark. The area I covered was large, and getting larger, the roads, with few exceptions, unsurfaced.

Night calls and ruptured meals were common. The most verbose clients seemed to always choose the hour of the evening repast as the most suitable time to impart their problems by telephone. The result was that what might initially have been acceptable fare was rendered null and void by the passage of time and declining temperatures.

My cook's limited store of patience was strained to its limits by my irregular hours. Frequently I would not get home until late evening, by which time whatever he had been cooking looked limp and tired, if not burnt and blackened. But I had to give him his due. No matter what the hour, he was always ready and waiting, if not exactly willing, when I returned.

The snag about late hours was that the sun always rose the following day, with all that it might bring.

Night is the time when the vast majority of mares give birth to their foals. This apparently inconsiderate behaviour hearkens back to prehistoric times when wild horses roamed the plains of the world. Mother and offspring were at their most susceptible at, and shortly after, birth, from predators, such as cave bears and sabre-toothed tigers. Horses are large animals and the cover of night offers mares and their newly born young the best protection available. By dawn the foal is on its feet and able to run beside its mother in the herd.

With gritted teeth I pondered upon this miracle of nature one night after having received a phone call from Mrs Rowena Hunter-Smart, to the effect that a foaling mare was in difficulties on her farm on the far shore of Lake Naivasha, some sixty miles from Nakuru. It was a few minutes before midnight, I had been fast asleep, and now I lay in the darkness, hoping that, by some superhuman effort of willpower on my part, the foal would be summarily expelled from its mother's womb. After having been promptly informed of this happy outcome by Mrs Hunter-Smart, I would close my eyes with a heartfelt sigh of relief, sink back on my pillows, and allow the tide of sleep to gently wash over me.

I waited for ten minutes.

Nothing happened.

It never did.

Although the incidence of problems at birth in mares is low compared with other species, I knew that when they were in difficulty delivering their foals, they really were in difficulty. Strength, ingenuity, patience and purposeful action were required to effect a successful outcome – all attributes in singularly short supply in the early hours of the morning.

Once foaling starts, the entire process is usually completed within thirty minutes. Expulsion of the foal is accompanied by powerful contractions. These can be so violent that it is impossible to maintain an arm within the birth canal. Repulsion and correction of the mal-positioned foetus in such circumstances becomes a herculean task, not helped by the fact that the mare is usually recumbent during this stage of labour. At such times, with his working arm being crushed between foal and maternal pelvis, with his muscles being strained to their uttermost limits, with his knee caps groaning under his own weight, and with other parts of his anatomy in uncomfortable proximity to the mare's hindquarters, the luckless vet may be justified in feeling that his lot is not a happy one.

The great length of the neck and legs of the foal means that when any of these is wrongly positioned, its correction can be a major task, especially when coupled with the violence of the expulsive process, and the unpredictable nature of the equine temperament. If the foal is dead then the embryotome can be invaluable. If it is alive then surgery is an option. But once foaling starts, the foetal membranes quickly separate from the uterus, so a prolonged, difficult foaling is unlikely to yield a live offspring.

With these happy thoughts in mind, I retrieved my discarded garments from the laundry basket, donned them, and set forth into the night.

The sky was clear, the Naivasha road dry, with potholes few in number. I made rapid progress. To my right, Lake Elementaita lay sleeping beneath the stars. With the exception of the occasional bus and lorry, the road was empty. Many of these few vehicles possessed the barest minimum of lights necessary for progress during the hours of darkness. Some had no rear lights, others only one headlight, on occasion none at all. How the driver saw where he was going was a continual cause of wonder to me. No matter how deserted the road might appear, one had to be constantly on one's guard lest one ram the rear end of an unlit lorry or mistake a bus with only one headlight for an approaching motor cycle.

Broken down vehicles were an ever-present hazard. These were usually parked to best advantage on the brows of hills, on blind corners or on the inside of bends. The first indication that one might be approaching such a vehicle was usually a litter of branches or other vegetation strewn on the road, as an alternative to warning triangles. As a variation on a theme, rocks were sometimes used as a substitute for leafy fronds, and it could be disconcerting to round a corner at speed and find a hundred-weight block of granite in the middle of the road.

Sometimes broken-down lorries and buses would remain immobilised on the same spot for days on end, while major repairs were carried out. It was not uncommon to see an entire engine lying on the road, while a crew of mechanics tinkered with its innards. As time passed, a small encampment would grow up around it, until the engine appeared to take on the role of an iron idol, surrounded by a fumble-fingered congregation of oily acolytes.

I sped through Gilgil, narrowly missing an inebriated reveller emerging from the shadowy recesses of the Kurungu Holiday Inn.

Twenty minutes later, I left the tarmac for my semi-circular tour of Lake Naivasha. The dirt road was in good condition, having been recently graded. I rocketed through Maasai Gorge and tore down towards the lake shore. The knobbly heights of Eburru rose lumpily on my right, black against the starlit sky.

A long stretch followed where the road was overhung with huge fever trees. The occasional section of ankle deep dust did little to impede my progress. I hurtled round a long sweeping stretch, where thickets of leleshwa sloped up to crags overlooking a sinister-looking crater lake.

Suddenly a huge black shape reared up in my headlights. With force almost sufficient to propel my foot through the floorboards, I stamped on the brake.

In a great cloud of dust and flying gravel the car slid to a stop.

'Shee—it!' I gasped.

As the dust settled I saw a rather surprised-looking hippo peering at me through the murk, from only a few feet away. His small pink eyes squinted in my direction, blinded by the lights. Then, with an irritated snort, he threw up his enormous head, and plunged into the adjacent vegetation and vanished.

Proceeding on my way I was soon at my destination and inspecting my patient.

She lay on her right side, a big, black thoroughbred mare, outside a row of thatch and wattle stables. As my car headlights swept over her, she sat up briefly, flopped down and strained. As she did so, her abdomen swelled like a giant balloon, and notwithstanding her supine position, all four legs rose stiffly into the air with the effort.

'Good grief,' I thought.

From her vulva a lonely leg protruded.

Trying hard not to imagine what horrors lay within the mare's reproductive tract, I opened the car door and stepped out.

From the nearby shadows emerged a motley collection of individuals, clad for the most part in black, ankle-length greatcoats, balaclava helmets and wellington boots, from which toes and heels protruded. In the midst of this ragged brigade was the owner, a well set up European matron, a thoroughbred herself I surmised, judging by her patrician appearance.

Bidding her good morning, I doffed my shirt and donned my overalls.

A chill lake breeze caressed my naked shoulders.

'Mr Cran, I'm Rowena Hunter-Smart. I'm so terribly sorry for dragging you all this way at this time of night, but this is my very best mare, my very best, and she started foaling at 11pm and as soon as I saw that she was in trouble I phoned you right away. She's foaled three times before with no bother, and now look at her. Look at her! Please save her! Do you think she will be all right? She won't die will she?'

My limited, in other words, non-existent, experience in foaling mares, did not allow me to give a categorical answer to her questions, so I mouthed a few placatory remarks.

'Of course, of course. We'll sort her out, don't you worry!'

But already, in addition to the frigid zephyrs from the lake, the wintry breeze of anxiety was playing around the brow of my expectations.

'Perhaps it's warmer closer to the ground,' I thought as I dropped to my knees.

The mare's ample hind quarters acted as an effective windbreak, and it was almost cosy down there. After I had inserted a well-lubricated arm into the vagina I felt even warmer – too warm.

The foal was dead, and its head was jammed in a flexed position under the front of the mare's pelvis. One leg was lying normally. The other I could not feel. Either it was retained within the uterus, or the foal had only three legs. I suspected the former.

I conveyed my findings to Mrs Hunter-Smart, who was hovering somewhere above and behind me. They were received in silence.

Theoretically, it seemed a simple idea to repel the head of the foal forwards into the abdomen of the mare and then flip it up into the normal position. After this I would slip an arm down the foal's flank and retrieve the lost limb, and Bob's yer uncle!

Fat chance.

It was impossible. As soon as I exerted any pressure on the top of the foal's head, the expulsive efforts of the mare increased to such an extent that there was a serious risk of prolapse of the bowel. I had seen this happen once during a foaling carried out by my late-departed employer, and the mare had died.

With Mrs Hunter-Smart breathing like a Puffing Billy down the back of my neck, this was something to be avoided at all costs.

After about ten minutes of unproductive effort by obstetrician and patient, during which it rapidly became apparent that exhaustion of both and risk to the life of the latter – and possibly of the former as well – were likely to be the only outcomes, I removed my aching arm and rose to my feet.

Since the departure of Arthur Owen-Jones I had acquired an embryotome. I now retrieved it from the car. It consisted of two adjacent stainless steel tubes through which a cutting wire was threaded. The wire was looped around that part of the dead foetus one wanted to section.

With it I proposed to remove the foal's head.

The task of choosing the most intelligent of my helpers to assist in the operation of the instrument was a difficult one. I knew that the head syce was likely to be well advanced in years, full of grey hairs and native wisdom, but unlikely to be willing to readily adapt to the manipulation of a surgical instrument, however simple.

So, hoping that I had made the right choice, I selected a young, brawny fellow with a sharp look about him. Decision making was not helped by it being now 2am, with a distinct lack of illumination, apart from the stars, a waning moon, and my car headlights, and that most of the individuals gathered around were as dark as the night itself.

Back on my knees again, I unthreaded the embryotome, tied a small metal weight to the free end of the cutting wire, and handed the twin tubes to my assistant, who grasped them with as much confidence as he might a pair of poisonous snakes.

The mare still strained with might and main, grunting with the effort, her belly rising and falling in the darkness like some grotesque bellows. Occasionally she kicked out backwards, but, in her prone position, could do little harm. Now and again she would sit up and look at me with an exhausted and resigned look, as if to say: 'For Heaven's sake! Do whatever you have to do, but do it quickly and let's get it over and done with!'

My own sentiments entirely.

The plan was to thread the cutting wire around the foal's neck, and then saw through it. As easy as that!

I always used my left arm for obstetrical work, and now it was to be put to the test. As my hand, grasping the weighted wire, approached the point where the foal's head was bent under its mother's pelvis, the mare, as though to demonstrate her superior strength, let rip with a contraction, which, had the foal been lying normally, would have propelled it ex utero for several feet. As it was, the main recipient of this unproductive effort was my unfortunate left arm, ground between the upper millstone of the foal's head the lower of the mare's pelvis.

Bending my head in silent supplication, I slowly forced my hand into the angle between the foal's neck and lower jaw. My muscles ached and my joints creaked with the strain. Very, very gradually, progress was made. Then I found, like the monkey with its paw full of grain inside a gourd, that I was unable to withdraw my hand unless I unclenched my fist. When I did this and pulled out my hand, the weight and the wire came out as well. Finally I pushed it through with my fingertips, gasping hoarsely with the effort.

Retrieving the weight from the opposite side of the foal's neck was an exhausting and frustrating business. At full stretch of my arm I could just touch it with the tip of one finger. As the mare was lying on her right side, and I was using my left arm, my proximity to Mother Earth was very close indeed. My contortions would have been amusing had the situation not been so serious.

I knew that if the foal's head was not removed, and soon, the mare would die. There was no question about performing a heroic last-ditch Caesarian section. That would be guaranteed to kill the patient in a fairly unpleasant and protracted manner.

But I possessed a certain tenacity and wiry strength, doubtless derived from my Pictish ancestors. Exerting myself to the limit, I finally grasped the elusive weight and wire, and drew it though.

My relief was profound.

Using a long metal rod designed for the purpose, I pulled the wire through the vacant tube, tied it to metal handle and handed the embryotome, primed for use, to my assistant.

Instructing him to hold both handles I gently inserted the embryotome into the mare's vagina and pushed it forwards until its end rested on top of the foal's head. The metal tubes would prevent the mare from being cut once the procedure started.

Taking a firm hold of the embryotome I told my recruit to take up the slack and start sawing.

Nothing happened.

I looked behind me.

The fellow was leaning backwards, pulling both handles together. This was not going get us very far, so I told him that he must pull with one hand and then the other. Try doing that when your command of Swahili is First Primer, it's pitch dark and you are lying grunting on the ground with both arms inside a hulking great mare, who resents every move you are making.

The penny dropped, he began sawing with long, smooth rapid strokes and in a trice the foal's neck was severed.

I withdrew the embryotome, re-inserted my arm and, after a struggle, removed the head. I tossed it onto the ground. There was a collective intake of breath as the knot of helpers took a sudden step backwards.

Their retreat did not last long. Within a few seconds they were breathing down the back of my neck, wondering what my next move would be.

This was to find and extract the missing foreleg. Now that the foal's head had been removed, my task, although not easy, was considerably simplified. The mare had stopped straining and there was room for my arm, which I passed down the foal's neck and flank. At first I could feel no foreleg at all, even at full stretch. I removed my arm, applied a soft rope to the other leg, instructed two men to pull it, and tried again. As they did so, the blade of the scapula of the missing leg moved under my fingers, and, with a tremendous effort, I was able to move my hand down and grip the humerus and bring it a few inches closer.

Using another rope I threaded it around the lost leg, pulled the noose taut, and asked one of my attendant myrmidons to pull. This he did, and by degrees, I was able to slip the noose down the leg until it was below the knee. This was then brought up to the rim of the mare's pelvis. I pushed the noose down the foal's leg until it was below the fetlock and pulled it tight. I then repelled the knee upwards and backwards into the uterus. Further pulling brought the leg up into the normal position, while I guarded the hoof with my cupped hand lest it damage the uterus or vagina.

When the leg finally appeared through the vulva I felt like cheering. I imagined the mare felt the same.

A final pull by my helpers, a last squeeze by the mare, and the foal was out, to be followed a few seconds later by the great slithery jellyfish of the placenta.

I slipped an antibiotic pessary into the uterus, and gave her an injection of penicillin, and an antihistamine to ward off laminitis, a painful inflammation of the hooves, which can follow difficult foalings if proper precautions are not taken.

The mare still lay on her side, breathing heavily, exhausted. By the time I had returned my tackle to the car she was sitting up, ears pricked, looking around at the circle of syces.

The aristocratic Rowena Hunter-Smart re-emerged from the shadows.

'Oh, Mr Cran! Thank you so, so much. She has been saved! Saved! Wonderful! How much do I owe you? Here, have a nip of this. You must be absolutely perished!'

She produced a mammoth sized hip flask, from which she poured me a huge tot of whisky.

I suddenly realised that it was now three o'clock in the morning and decidedly chilly. I tossed the lot back in one swallow.

'Ye Gods! Thanks for that!' I gasped, barely able to speak.

As the fiery fluid rushed in a molten stream to my stomach, the mare scrambled to her feet, shook herself and bent her head to a bucket of water. I felt a warm glow of satisfaction which wasn't entirely due to the whisky.

'Well, that's a fine sight, now,' I said to Mrs Hunter-Smart. 'You keep an eye on her and phone me if you're worried about her. But she should be OK.'

Bidding farewell to her and to the grooms, I subsided gratefully into the car, started the engine, put on the heater, and set off on the long journey home.

As I drove along the lake shore a large building loomed up among the fever trees. My headlights flashed over it, giving me time to observe that it was a fully fledged Elizabethan mansion, complete with thatched roof, whitewashed walls, leaded windows, black external beams, and all the other architectural peculiarities which typify that era. So this was the domain of the regal Mrs Hunter-Smart. 'Zowie! I thought. 'Delusions of grandeur or just plain grandeur?'

I carried out a mental post-mortem of the foaling I had just done, sifting and weighing the details of the case and trying to decide whether it might have been better handled. Perhaps giving a narcotic, such as chloral hydrate by injection, might have helped to control the straining. But then the mare might have had trouble getting up afterwards. What about an epidural? Would it have caused panic as the hindquarters would have been desensitized? Hell! Why beat the case to death? Each case was different. The mare was fine, up and OK. What more do you want?

I must have driven a dozen miles without paying any conscious attention to the road. Lack of sleep and preoccupation with the case led to a state of mind and body in which I was able to drive the car, change gear, and turn corners and avoid obstacles without any recollection of having done so.

I came to with a start.

A group of large dark shadows was crossing the road.

I slowed sown and stopped. A herd of buffalo was coming down off the Eburru Hills to my left and moving towards the swamps surrounding the lake. For five minutes I sat and waited while the herd ambled across the road – cows, calves, half-grown youngsters, with a few bulls bringing up the rear. By the light of the headlamps they looked huge and menacing.

When the last straggler has disappeared into the darkness I set off once again.

A mile further on I crossed a small bridge which spanned a stream, fringed by hanging vegetation.

On the other side stood an enormous buffalo.

His hide was caked with wet mud. It was larded thickly upon his shoulders and hindquarters. Even his head was covered in mud and his black eyes glared angrily in my direction through a mask of glistening ooze. I had disturbed him during the high point of his wallow in the stream and he was displeased.

From where I was sitting he seemed to be about ten feet high. He raised his muzzle in the ominous way that buffaloes do and advanced a few steps in my direction. I slipped into reverse gear in preparation for retreat. He shook his head and flapped his great ears. His horns, sprouting from the huge boss in the centre of his forehead, looked as sharp as rapiers. I could imagine them gouging their way into the radiator and ripping through the paper-thin bodywork of my fragile car.

Then he threw up his head, wheeled round and with a clumsy, rocking gait, galloped across the road and vanished.

Breathing a sigh of relief I moved rapidly through the gears, floor-boarded my right foot and was soon moving at high speed down the rocky road that led to Nakuru and bed.

Something resembling a four-legged Centurion tank erupted from my left and charged across my bows. I had no time to brake and missed it by a centimetre.

There had been another bull buffalo waiting in the darkness.

One Monday morning I arrived at the surgery to find a group of sobbing, wailing women clustered round the door.

Opondo, the odd job man, was dead.

The previous Saturday evening he had felt unwell and had been conveyed to the main hospital in the town. There he had been examined by a doctor. No diagnosis had been made. He was given some aspirins and sent home.

At three am on Sunday morning he collapsed and died. Quick and painless, or at least I hoped so, a massive cancer of the oesophagus had seen him off.

'Aieee! Aieee! Aieee!' The women howled and clutched their heads and beat their sagging bosoms. They surged to and fro, screeching and moaning. The noise was beginning to give me a headache.

Opondo had been a Jaluo and according to the customs of the tribe the body had to be taken back to the ancestral homelands around Lake Victoria for burial. The women had come to collect whatever emoluments were owing so that they could pay for the construction of a coffin and the hire of a vehicle for the long journey down to the steamy lowlands of Nyanza.

I paid them their dues and they eventually departed. The wailing died away.

The cost of such funerals can reduce a relatively poor family to beggary, but such is the strength of tradition that the full ceremony with all the trimmings is seldom flouted.

A few weeks later I felt as though I might be soon to follow Opondo across the River Styx.

One evening, after I had written up the invoices for the day, I retired to bed feeling unaccountably fevered and flushed. In the early hours of the morning I awoke to find myself soaked in sweat, shivering and shaking, like someone adrift on an ice-floe in his underwear, feeling like a limp, dank rag. For several more nights this irritating scenario was repeated. I was excessively busy so, although I felt that death was nigh, I struggled on. I took my temperature and discovered that each evening it rose to 103 or 104 degrees, and each morning it returned to normal.

Finally after about ten days of this nonsense I repaired to my medico, the irascible Irishman, Dr Satchwell, who had admitted me to hospital when I had broken my leg.

'Aha, so it's you again, is it? And what brings you here? Come along, now, spit it out!'

Satch did not believe in mollycoddling his patients with sweet talk.

'Well, each night, in the early hours actually, I get the shakes and the sweats. I have a fever and have zero energy – none at all in fact.'

'Is that so now. Well, let's just see how high it is, shall we?'

So saying, he stuck a thermometer under my tongue.

'Hah! Normal! Dead normal! Maybe you've got brucellosis. I'll write you a note. Take it to the General Hospital and they'll check your blood.'

As this was the same establishment wherein the unfortunate Opondo had been advised to take aspirins only hours before his demise from cancer, my faith in the ability of the staff to diagnose something as obscure as brucellosis was not of a high order.

The sample was reported as being negative and the symptoms continued unabated.

Not long afterwards I was invited to dinner by Ron and Helen Shanks, on the coffee and dairy farm they managed at Bahati. I was sitting on the porch in the gloaming, nursing a tankard of Tusker, which Ron had thrust upon me. I did not feel in the mood for beer.

'Are you all right, Hugh?' asked Helen, who was a very experienced nurse 'You look a bit piano to me.'

As she spoke the shakes started. 'We-e-e-ell, nnoo..., noo...' I stuttered between chattering teeth.

'Here, shove that in yer gob and shut up.' She pushed a thermometer into my mouth.

'104.8!' Helen whistled. 'You've got malaria. No doubt about it. Got just the stuff for you right here.'

She came back with four yellow Nivaquine tablets. 'Knock those back and in forty eight hours you'll be right as rain!'

And I was.

I was astonished that neither the doctor nor the hospital had diagnosed the disease, which is one of the most common in the tropics.

Shortly afterwards an African gentleman, who described himself as the head paediatrician of the main government hospital in the town, came into the surgery. He had with him a thin, undersized puppy aged about five months.

Its coat was dry and harsh, its ribs stood out like a row of railings, its spine resembled an Alpine ridge and it stood on the table with its head hanging as though it lacked the energy to even lie down.

'This puppy, Daktari, has got bloody diarrhoea,' said the paediatrician. 'It's changing its teeth, and when it swallows them, they're lacerating its intestines. So, I want you to remove the rest of them.'

'Blimmin' 'eck! Whatever next?' I thought, but said nothing

The pup's gums, instead of being a nice healthy pink, were almost white. Anaemia was obviously far advanced. I inserted a thermometer into its rectum. It came out covered in dark red blood, mixed with mucous. I examined a little under the microscope. As I squinted down the brass tube a great mass of hookworm eggs drifted across my gaze. They looked like logs floating down a Canadian river.

'Your pup's infested with hookworms. It's bad, very bad. Kids also get hookworms, as you know.' Well, I hoped he knew. 'Have a look down the microscope and see for yourself.'

I weighed the wretched creature, gave it an injection of Disophenol and asked that it be returned in three weeks time. I gave the doctor a course of vitamin and mineral tablets.

'And you must give your pup a high protein diet and that means raw meat, liver, milk and eggs. If you don't it may well die. It may die anyway.'

The paediatrician seemed to accept what I said but I could see that the myth about the swallowed teeth died hard. I thanked my lucky stars that I was out of nappies.

CHAPTER ELEVEN

It very soon became apparent that the Peugeot 204 car I was driving was neither sufficiently robust nor powerful enough for the job it was expected to do. After a relatively short period of giving of its all on the highways and byways of the Rift Valley and beyond, ominous cracks began to appear in a number of vital body areas. Gravity alone appeared to be holding the roof in place. I became accustomed to the rhythmic clonking of worn and leaking shock absorbers as I moved as fast as I dared over roads more suitable for the ox wagon than the combustion engine on wheels.

Potholes were bad enough, especially those in broken-up tarmac roads. The car would fall into these with a sickening crash to the accompaniment of oaths and expletives. The juddering and shaking caused by the ubiquitous corrugations made me fear that at any moment the engine might be torn from its mountings.

The area I covered was vast, with farms and ranches up to a hundred miles from base. When I had work to do on these far-flung properties I had to get there fast and get back fast in order to deal with whatever work had come in during my absence. I could not afford to cruise gently through the countryside, leisurely admiring the passing scene, bird spotting, or taking note of quaint native customs.

Percival Russet-Williams, whom I had yet to meet, was an Anglicised Welshman, of reputed uncertain temperament, and one of the last white farmers in the Ol Arabel valley, near Rumuruti, about 65 miles from Nakuru. He phoned to say that his daughter Megan's pony had sustained a long tear in the lower part of a hind leg, following a close encounter with a stretch of barbed wire. Could I come? As soon as possible.

Apart from two short stretches of tarmac between Nakuru and Dundori at 8,000 feet, on the eastern wall of the Rift Valley, and between the hamlet of Ol Joro Orok and the town of Thomson's Falls, the road was unsurfaced.

It had been raining for the past month and when I left Nakuru at half past three in the afternoon the sky over the eastern hills was an unpleasant purple-grape colour. By the time I had reached the dukas (small shops selling basic essentials) at Dundori, the rain was sheeting down.

For another mile the road, still tarmac, snaked upwards through dripping woods. Then the tarmac abruptly ended at a wooden barrier. Rising steeply ahead was the dirt highway to Ol Joro Orok. Its surface resembled a badly ploughed field. It had been raining hard up here for some time. The deeply rutted road was a waste of dark red mud. Rivulets coursed down it. On either side lay a deep ditch, down which rushed an angry flood.

I stopped and looked. All the alternative routes were unsurfaced and likely to be just as bad. I had no wish to spend the night stuck in a ditch. Why didn't I just turn back and phone Percy to tell him that the road was impassable.

'Very sorry, Percy. No go, I'm afraid. Did my best, but the whole area is under water and mud. Just got out by the skin of my teeth. Heaven knows what damage I've done to my car.'

Oh, what the hell!

The barrier was unattended and up. Dropping into second gear, I left the safety of the tarmac for the perils of mud and morass.

On wet, muddy, slippery roads you should not drive so fast that a skid will result in an ignominious slither into the nearest ditch, wherein which you are likely to languish long, until dragged or pushed out, accompanied by the pungent whiff of your burnt-out clutch. Neither should you go so slowly, that vital momentum and grip are lost. A happy medium is the theoretical rule, by employing a judicious blend of second and third gears and gentle pressure on the throttle.

All very well, until you come to steep, greasy hills, such as the one I now faced.

The ditches on either side yawned hungrily. Trying hard to ignore them, I roared up the hill in low gear. I knew that any hesitation could be disastrous. I struck a slippery patch and the car shot sideways, the rear end had a will all of its own, a strategically placed boulder loomed up, I hit it, my foot was knocked off the throttle, and I bounced back into the middle of the road, more or less back on track.

A new obstacle loomed up. Ruts. I shot up, wheels on either side of the mud-filled furrow, teetering along like an elephant on ice. By some latter day miracle I managed to avoid falling into its glutinous, thigh-deep depths.

With whitened knuckles, and dry mouth, I reached the top. Just over the summit a bus was slewed across the road. A gang of drenched and bedraggled passengers was endeavouring to push it back into the centre. As I slowed down, the driver depressed the throttle, and slowly and majestically the inappropriately named 'Desert Dueler' slid off the crown of the road and crashed with ponderous finality into the ditch.

His misfortune was my gain, and I slid past, hoping that a similar fate did not await me round the next bend.

Under favourable conditions there was a splendid view from this point, over the Rift Valley, down to the lake and the extinct volcano of Menengai. Today it was totally obscured by lashing rain and driving cloud and my preoccupation with the state of the road precluded any glances to either right or left.

I battled on, plunging in and out of innumerable potholes, ploughing through axle deep stretches of sticky ochre-coloured goo, constantly changing gear, windscreen wipers working overtime in an effort to clear away the rain and the sheets of mud and water thrown up with each fresh semi-immersion. From time to time, when cleaving through an especially sticky section, forward vision was totally blocked by curtains of semi-liquid mud layering the windscreen.

Matatus and lorries stuck in the ditch were now a common sight, their mud-bespattered crews labouring heroically in the monsoon conditions to extricate them from the mire.

I pelted on.

At one time I found myself moving sideways at high speed down a hill, where the camber of the road resembled the back of a beached whale.

Finally I reached terra firma in the shape of the short section of tarmac between Ol Joro Orok and Thomson's Falls.

By the time I had reached the latter township, named after the Scottish explorer, Joseph Thomson, the skies had cleared and the bone dry conditions on the road to Rumuruti indicated that the rains, which had been falling further south, had yet to arrive. From here on, I rattled, crashed and bumped my way over a non-stop succession of iron-hard ruts, potholes and corrugations, trailing a dense plume of dust behind me.

Half way up the Ol Arabel valley, without warning, the car stopped. The unholy blend of mud and dust had been too much.

My knowledge of the inner workings of my car was sketchy at best. As I stood, bonnet up, peering without hope or knowledge at the mud-encrusted engine, a pick up truck drew up alongside.

'Jambo, sahib! Problem?' Two Indians stepped out onto the road.

'Well, er yes. Blimmin' car's stopped. Jerked a few times, and then stopped. And now it won't start.'

They were from Rumuruti, where they had a hardware store, selling everything from nuts and bolts to leaf springs for lorries.

'OK, let's look see.' They fiddled around for a few minutes, adjusting this and that, until they seemed satisfied.

'OK, sahib, fire her up!' The car started at once. The points needed adjusting, that was all, but without their help I would still have been there, peering helplessly at the muddied engine.

'Where are you going, sahib?'

'To Russet-Williams' place.'

They looked at each other, but said nothing.

Thanking them profusely, I continued on my way.

Ndofu Farm, P. Russet-Williams: so read the signboard. At long last. I roared past it, up a lumpy track and towards a group of stables. It was 6pm. Pretty good going I thought. Not bad, not bad at all.

Percival Russet-Williams seemed to think otherwise.

Clad in baggy jodhpurs, riding boots and a red shirt, which matched his florid complexion, he stood glaring in my direction, like a sun-burnt turkey, thrashing his boots with a springy riding crop.

'Where the Dickens have you been? I've been waiting for you for hours! Bloody hours, I tell you. Megan is beside herself with worry. That pony is her pride and joy.'

He peered aggressively as I got out of the car.

'You're new, aren't you? Where's old what's-his-name? You've got to be better than him! Had the kiss of death, he had! Always killing off my horses!'

'Great! This is really great!' I thought. 'Better not call him Percy, that would really get his goat!'

With a start I realised that there was a slight female figure standing in the shadows behind my testy interlocutor.

Presumably this was Megan.

Her father ignored my proffered hand of peace.

'Follow me!' he barked.

We did as we were told and a syce led out an irritable Welsh pony onto a patch of grass. It tried to bite the syce. 'Takes after his owner!' I thought.

The pony had a long, jagged tear on the inside of his right hind leg, below the hock, about a foot long and an inch wide.

'Happened last night,' said Russet-Williams, 'Bloody syce was drunk as usual. Drinking pombe instead of doing his job, which is what he was supposed to be doing, looking after the horses!' His voice rose to a scream as he stared, pop-eyed, at the syce, who quailed and shrank backwards.

'OK then, let's have a look at the damage,' I said, hoping to cool things down a bit. It was difficult enough dealing with the patient, without having the owner running riot as well. I ran my hand along the pony's back and down his leg. The pony shivered but stood still. Perhaps he wasn't like her owner after all. The skin had retracted away from the wound and I knew that trying to stitch a wound like this was a waste of time. Even if I was able to get the edges of the wound together, which was highly unlikely, the stitches would never hold and would tear out after a few days.

'Stitching is not going to work here, believe me. What we have to do is to clean the wound, remove all the dirt, apply a dressing and a firm bandage and then keep on changing it until it's healed.'

'You mean to tell me that I've paid for you to come all this way just to be told to apply first aid?' Russet-Williams was not pleased. I did not point out that so far I had not been paid anything.

'This will work, I assure you, so let's get on with it before it's too dark to see what we're doing.'

'Well, you get on with it! I'm going in for a much needed drink! Ye Gods! Ye Gods!' He stormed off.

'Right, then. I'll give him a sedative first,' I said to Megan. 'A small dose of acetylpromazine, I think.' So saying, I injected the drug into the jugular and got some bandages and dressings from the car while it was taking effect. The pony's head drooped and his hindquarters swayed.

'Right. Megan, can you hold her head and speak to him, tell him everything is going to be fine. Syce, come and support his rear end and make sure I don't get kicked in the teeth. OK?'

The pony stood quietly while I swabbed the wound, removing as much dirt and hair as possible, dried it, applied a tulle dressing and a roll of cotton wool, and finished off with a firm layer of bandage from the hock to the hoof. A turn of adhesive tape top and bottom held everything snugly in place. A shot of tetanus antitoxin and another of penicillin and I was done.

'OK Megan, that's it. Now I saw that you were watching what I was doing . In two days' time I want you to remove the bandage and apply another, just like I did there and do this every three or four days and phone me to describe what you see – all right?'

She nodded shyly.

'It will heal slowly but we don't want any proud flesh to grow from the wound, so it must be kept covered by a firm bandage until it has healed.'

I gave her a supply of bandages and other essentials and turned to go.

'Sorry about my dad,' she said. 'He's under a lot of pressure. Mum's in hospital, the farm has been sold and we're off to Australia in six months' time.'

It was dark when once again I passed through Thomson's Falls. Not wishing to take the risk of being benighted on the appalling Dundori track, I decided to investigate the road back to Nakuru via Subukia. This included a descent of the precipitous Subukia escarpment, something not to be contemplated should the surface be slippery. Heavy rain frequently brought boulders of considerable size cascading down onto the road from the heights above to further stimulate the flow of adrenaline, should one be rash enough to attempt the route during inclement weather.

To my amazement and relief, precipitation had been light. Apart from the irregularity of the road surface there was little to interrupt my progress. A greasy stretch on the climb out of the valley afforded me a few moments of excitement, but otherwise the journey was incident-free.

I had arrived home in one piece, but from the anvil's chorus emanating from the various segments of my luckless steed, separation of its body into several pieces was imminent.

Not long after, I was driving slowly along a track, upon which no self-respecting goat or yak would have set hoof, when I had the misfortune to strike with considerable force a cunningly-concealed boulder, whose presence I had failed to notice. The impact took place somewhere in the region of the gear box, rendering reverse gear null and void. This was not a great inconvenience. The traffic in Nakuru was not such as to demand a great deal of precision reverse parking, or accurate three-point-turns à la Highway Code. However, coupled with the general deterioration in the vehicle's body and suspension, it seemed like another nail driven into it's already-assembled coffin.

The decision to sell and buy another vehicle was not long in coming.

One morning a call came from Soysambu, Lord Delamere's ranch which bounded Lake Elementaita. One of the stud stallions had colic, and would I come as soon as possible.

Most cases of equine colic can be regarded as potential gastro-intestinal time-bombs, and early and effective defusing is an essential prerequisite in order to prevent a rapid deterioration in the patient's condition.

Horses, despite their size, are extraordinarily susceptible to shock and pain. What might make a cow merely grunt and hunch its back will make a horse pour with sweat, throw itself on the ground, writhe in agony and generally behave so violently that emergency action is needed to avert catastrophe. Not all cases take this course, but until the animal has been examined, it is impossible to know if one will be dealing with a simple case of indigestion, or a strangulation of the small intestine, with death as the probable outcome.

Bearing all this in mind, I made sure that I had all the appropriate drugs in the car and left the surgery at high speed. As I pulled away, Moses, with his customary expertise, made a skilful, mobile entry into the left-hand seat.

At Lanet I turned onto the road to Elementaita.

The road ran straight and true towards the distant hills, before turning onto the ranch, just before the conglomeration of shacks which constituted Elementaita.

I depressed the accelerator pedal and reached a speed which seemed to iron out the customary cacophony of rattles and bangs rising from the tortured chassis. Thus diverted, my thoughts turned to my distant patient. My imagination painted a picture of a frenzied equine threshing around in acutest agony, nostrils flared, eyes rolling. I extended my right knee. I glanced in the mirror. A great wake of dust boiled out behind the car. A bit more throttle and I was almost airborne.

There was a sudden, ear-splitting crash, followed by a succession of lesser concussions. The car lurched to the right and, as I applied the brakes, I observed, with some alarm, that an ominous mound of metal had appeared on the bonnet. With each bang the mound grew larger. It looked like an embryo volcano about to blow its top. There was something beneath trying to get out.

I ground to a ragged halt and opened the bonnet in order to pin-point the damage.

It was immediately apparent. The right front shock absorber mounting had burst free from its moorings. Every irregularity in the road surface resulted in violent contact between the top of the runaway shock absorber and the nether surface of the bonnet. Hence the rising mound of metal.

'Damn! Damn! Damn and blast!' I said. 'That's what happens when you hit a pothole at speed.' Moses nodded sympathetically.

Now forward motion was reduced to a painful crawl, little more than walking pace. Anything faster produced the most appalling clatter from the bows.

After snailing along for what seemed like hours, we finally crept into the stable yard at Soysambu.

I fully expected to find the stallion lying stiff and stark upon what passed as the local greensward.

An ancient syce shuffled over to the car.

I inquired in Swahili, 'Where is the sick horse?'

He cleared his throat and expectorated reflectively into the dust.

'Iko huko,' he pointed with his chin towards a distant paddock.

'We waited for you and when you didn't come, we gave him three bottles of Tusker and now he has finished getting better.'

Indeed he was. I walked to where a large chestnut stallion was grazing on the wiry, yellow grass. He was easily caught. Pulse, heart rate, mucous membranes, abdominal sounds, all were normal. He must have had spasmodic colic, which is usually transient and self limiting, which is not to say that the beer did not help. I could have done with some myself. The source of the pain is disruption of the blood supply to a localized section of small intestine. This is extremely painful. The affected bowel becomes distended, while the unaffected segments become excessively active. This juxtaposition of sections of gut with differing levels of activity could well be the mechanism causing such abdominal catastrophes as torsion, displacement and intussusception. The cause of the disrupted blood supply is believed to be due to a hypersensitivity response to the migrating larvae of the parasitic worm Strongylus vulgaris, resulting in a local intravascular coagulation or vasoconstriction. Why the worm should choose to migrate within the walls of the cranial mesenteric artery of all places was beyond my comprehension.

'Good bye, old man,' I said to the syce. 'Good bye, daktari. Sorry about your car.'

When I had the car examined it was found that, in addition to the broken shock absorber mounting, three of the four bolts holding the engine in place had sheared. The mechanic was a Kamba and his canine teeth had been filed to needle-sharp points. His eyes widened in disbelief. 'Kumbe! Behold! The engine was held in by one bolt alone. Aiee! You are one lucky mzungu!' I agreed.

The car was rapidly traded in for a Peugeot 404, a larger, stronger and more powerful machine. I asked that it be reinforced and strengthened in those vital areas which experience had revealed were likely to wilt under the strain of perpetuum mobile on the Kenyan roads.

✕✖✕✖✕✖✕

Opondo's position was filled by Bernard Mwai, a middle-aged, thickset Kikuyu of limited initiative and modest intelligence, but possessing two rare and precious assets – honesty and a willingness to work. During the Mau Mau Emergency he had taken part in a daring and much publicised raid on the police station at Naivasha. For this misdemeanour he had been detained for a time by the colonial authorities in one of Her Majesty's re-education centres.

Having read about some of the more blood curdling aspects of the whole ghastly and unnecessary episode I was glad to observe that he appeared to harbour no trace of anti-European feeling.

The work proceeded at a furious pace. The extent of the practice increased to an alarming degree. My monthly mileage increased until the yearly total averaged 60,000 miles. Clients brought their small animals – dogs and cats – from as far afield as Maseno, Kisumu, Kitale, Kericho and Eldoret. Sometimes, even from Uganda.

To a degree, this apparent enthusiasm for my services was flattering. It had its drawbacks, however. I became shackled to the wheel of work, unable to escape. I was expected to be always on hand, ready to leap into action when the call came, day or night. Sundays as a day of rest and relaxation in the pursuit of healthy interests diminished, dwindled, and finally vanished into a distant, seemingly idle past. Mornings were spent doing farm visits. The early afternoon was taken up with the examination and treatment of animals brought to the surgery. These were mostly dogs and cats, but included snakes, monkeys, wild birds, sheep, goats, bats, fish and assorted rarities such as hyrax and mongoose. Operations were also carried out at this time. When the last client and patient had been attended to we would set out to complete those farm visits which had been phoned in since the beginning of the afternoon surgery. On the equator it grows dark between 6.30-7pm every day throughout the year. There was no time to waste in such frivolous pursuits as the imbibing of a cup of tea. No sir. The swiftly descending tropical night frequently found me on the road with, in the words of Robert Frost, 'promises to keep, and miles to go before I sleep'. On return to the surgery there might be another operation to do, such as the pinning of a broken bone.

Then it was home, with a stomach which felt no larger than a shrivelled walnut, hoping that the next inevitable phone call would be an invitation to a dinner and drinks party, or a request for advice, and not a summons to venture forth into the outer darkness to stitch up a lacerated equine or calve a long-recumbent cow.

When I was a student I had spent a few weeks in southern Spain, during one summer vacation, helping to build a school in a mountain village near Ronda, north of Gibraltar. There I had observed that the natives kept watch on the passage of the sun across the firmament with keen and practiced eyes. When it reached its zenith they vanished with astonishing speed into their dwellings. The siesta was observed with an almost religious fervour. When they emerged, sluggish and torpid with sleep, their footsteps frequently directed them, not back to the fields they had so speedily vacated, but into the nearest tavern.

In Kenya, no account ever appeared to be taken of the sun. Work went on as usual, no matter what the temperature. Perhaps it had been different before the arrival of the work-obsessed Brits. Even when it was hot enough to fry an egg on the pavement, no concession was ever made to the vertical avalanche of ultra violet light smiting the skulls of toiling mortals, including my own. After a while I became accustomed to working in an impossibly wide range of daily temperatures, from the refreshing chill of early morning to the stifling heat of mid afternoon, when drawing a breath of overheated air was an unpleasant effort. On the heights of Molo and Mau Narok I had seen barefoot Africans skirting ice-covered puddles, while in the fields the grass sparkled with frost. A few hours later I would be soporific and sluggish and looking forward to the cool of late afternoon.

Driving for long distances in the sun after a spell of hard labour often made me dangerously drowsy, especially on the rare stretches of smooth tarmac. In the late afternoon I would struggle to keep awake, eyes drooping. Spasmodic buttock clenching and furious blinking gave me only a temporary respite. With a start I would wake up to discover that I had covered fifty yards while fast asleep. At night I would see imaginary hyenas crossing the road in front of the car. I would jam on the brakes, to find nothing there, just a long headlamp-lit tunnel bounded by blackness through which I moved as though in a trance.

No matter how late I got home, I always liked to have a bath before retiring. In view of some of the tasks which came my way, choice did not really come into it, if I wished to live with myself, let alone do business with the public. This had certain drawbacks, and on a number of occasions, after an exhausting day, the ravelled sleeve of care had been knitted up before I was aware of it and my head would suddenly slip beneath the murky surface. Because of my penchant for reading in the bath, several books did not benefit from these immersions.

I had read somewhere that a good, solid meal diverted a considerable volume of blood from the brain to the gastro-intestinal tract, in order to cope with the beef, curry, sausages or whatever had just been ingested. I assumed that the converse was true and that there was nothing like an empty stomach for keeping one on one's mental toes. Although I had plenty of opportunities for testing this hypothesis, I cannot vouch for the results. Friends were constantly telling me that my irregular eating habits were bound to end in ulcers, both gastric and duodenal, colitis and other horrific ailments. Although a number of medical unpleasantries, mainly of a tropical nature, came my way, digestive disturbances were not among them.

Despite the appallingly long hours, insufficient sleep and distorted feeding pattern, coupled with the occasional bouts of physical and mental fatigue, it always surprised me how restored and invigorated I felt after a couple of nights of undisturbed slumber. It still does.

♠♠♠♠♠

'Dr Cran, sir, this is Bhola phoning from Maralal. My manager at Rumuruti has just told me that he has a cow on my ranch there, which has prolapsed her uterus. She is one of my best cows, sir, and they say she calved yesterday, but I cannot vouch for that. She is a very good cow. I know it is Saturday afternoon, sir, but I would be most grateful if you could go and treat her.
There will be someone waiting for you at the junction to Nanyuki: Salim, my Somali headman.'

Saddiq Bhola was a quietly-spoken Pakistani, an entrepreneur who ran his business from Maralal, where he owned a garage and construction business.

Prolapse of the uterus in cows, after giving birth, is a dramatic condition, which if treated promptly and efficiently, yields satisfactory results to the patient, owner and vet and, in Africa, to the spectators. The condition is unmistakable. If the cow is recumbent, the uterus may be spread out on the ground behind her, covered, if one is lucky, by the undetached foetal membranes. If one is less lucky, and the environs are not freshly mown turf, the organ may be turgid, congested and covered in dung, dirt and flies, or mutilated beyond repair by dogs.

If the animal is standing, the everted uterus can hang down almost as far as the hocks. To the uninitiated it presents a horrific sight, and many a farmer has slaughtered a cow, in the mistaken belief that it cannot be treated. Replacement looks about as easy as forcing a camel through the eye of the proverbial needle.

The weather was dry and the road surface surprisingly good. Two hours saw me emerging from the confines of the Rumuruti Forest and bearing down on the township, which consisted of a police post, a small prison housing local miscreants and surrounded by barbed wire, a line of dukas, an airstrip and the club, built in 1924, standing rather aloofly half a mile away, by itself, in the shade of a knot of tall gum trees, presumably a safe distance from the plebs in the village.

As I slowed down a tall, skeletal Somali flagged me to a halt. This was my contact.

'Salaam, Salim,' I said.

'Salaam, effendi,' replied Salim.

In the shade of some nearby shacks, a group of Turkanas squatted comfortably in the dust, backs against the woodwork, out of the glare of the sun. Under an acacia a couple of bodies slumbered away the afternoon heat. I saw the Somali glance at them, envy in his eyes.

In more sophisticated parts of the world it is usual practice to advise the farmer to cover or wrap the prolapse with a large towel or sheet until the arrival of the vet. I usually asked that clean sacks or banana leaves be used for the purpose. Then I asked that a rectangular pit about three feet long and about two feet deep be dug next to the patient. This request usually ensured that there were sufficient men at hand to render assistance when required.

On arrival I would give a bottle of calcium borogluconate intravenously. It helped to tone up the uterine muscle. I then tied the cow's legs together with two separate ropes, washed the uterus with the cleanest water available and then, supporting the massive organ in my arms, had the front end of the cow lowered gently into the pit. Gravity was now on my side and it was a relatively easy matter to feed the uterus back into the abdominal cavity, although sometimes it was like trying to shove an enormous jellyfish down a rabbit hole.

The size of the pit was critical. If it was too long, the cow's pelvis was liable to slip over the edge, dragging the uterus with it. Then there could be the most fearful struggle dragging the cow out, once the job was completed, especially if insufficient men were present.

If the ground was too hard to allow excavation, or if labour was in short supply, I might give an epidural anaesthetic, just enough to stop the cow from straining but not enough to make her lie down. If she was already recumbent I would have to make do with whatever slope there was and get on with it. In one instance I found the patient lying on a rocky hillside, which was covered in cactus and thorn trees. The only available help consisted of a woman, whose actions were so slow I wondered if she was retarded, and an adolescent whose left leg was encased in plaster of paris from ankle to hip.

'OK Salim, point me in the right direction.'

'You just forrow the road to Nanyuki and then you tun reft after five miles onto Bhora's fam.'

'OK, ret's – solly – let's go!'

The first part of the track to the farm resembled a dry water course, with cricket ball sized boulders as the bed rock. The heat was intense. A chorus of crickets and cicadas mocked us from the thorny bush. There was a change in the nature of the soil and the track became two deep trenches, with a ridge so high it threatened to tear the car's exhaust pipe from its moorings. Delicate manipulation of the steering wheel was necessary to avoid this eventuality.

'Bad road, effendi,' said Salim.

'I'll say,' I grunted through gritted teeth.

After some miles of this torture, at Salim's behest I left the track and lurched across a rutted plain towards a distant group of huts.

Beside them stood, or, rather, leaned, a circular cattle boma, its timbers standing at every angle other then the vertical. The surface of the boma was ankle-deep in fine dust. On the far side stood a Boran cow, her engorged and congested uterus hanging down as far as her hocks. Even at this distance I could hear and see the cloud of flies swarming over her. As I stood there with my shirt clinging damply to my back, I bleakly took note of the encrustation of dung and dirt covering the uterus. No ten minute job this, I thought.

The huts, which resembled see-through wigwams, appeared to be deserted.

Then, from the interior of one of these architectural travesties, tottered an ancient Turkana woman, her rheumy eyes blinking in the fierce sunlight.

Salim spoke to her in Swahili. No response. He tried Somali. I tried

188

English. It seemed she only understood Turkana. Fair enough, I thought.

In the distance I could hear the tinkling of goat bells. The pleasant cacophony grew louder until the flock of eager nibblers hove into view, followed by a young Turkana girl.

Like her aged fellow tribeswoman her linguistic knowledge was limited to her mother tongue.

Nearby stood a huge stone water tank.

'Well,' I said, 'At least we've got plenty of water.'

I walked across, climbed up the steps of its outer wall and stared down.

It was completely dry.

A lizard scuttled across the stonework and vanished with a flick of its tail into a crevice.

'Salim! I will need some water. Can you get some?'

'I will try, effendi, but this is a poor place, and it is very dry.'

'Yes, I can see that, but do your best – jaribu tuu, OK.'

After a while he came back with a couple of tins which had formerly contained the universally-used cooking fat, Kimbo. Now they contained about a litre of water, which had probably been earmarked for the old lady's afternoon tea.

I had read somewhere that the application of fine sugar to the exposed uterus encouraged it to grow smaller, presumably from the process of osmosis. The very thought of asking for sugar in a place like this was laughable.

We tied the cow's head to one of the more upright posts. Then, using obstetrical lubricant, which had thankfully succeeded milking grease, I set to work, the sun beating on my bare back.

I had already given her calcium borogluconate, but I decided against an epidural. With the little water I had it would be difficult enough to remove the encrusted dirt. If she went down into the dust of the boma, it would be a total impossibility.

Skeletal Salim held the cow's tail, while the female members of my crew braced her flanks from either side. Their mounds of blue necklaces glinted dully in the afternoon sun. Their heads, shaven at the sides, and crowned by a top knot of strands of hair, were turned in my direction. Beads of sweat dotted their foreheads. Their eyes, the sclera yellowed from repeated bouts of malaria, seemed indifferent to either my exertions or to the sufferings of the cow. But I knew that if I was obliged to live as they did, a stoical, fatalistic outlook on life would become a necessity to my survival. They were the toughest of the tough.

I lifted the mass of the uterus, and, supporting it from below with my left arm, and bracing it with my chest, removed as much of the encrusted debris as possible with my right. I poured on some lubricant. Great clouds of flies rose and fell with each movement. With both arms fully occupied there was little I could do about them except to twitch my shoulders like Jamie Foxx playing Ray Charles in the film 'Ray'. Without music.

Having removed as much of the dirt as the available H_2O allowed, I attempted to return the wayward uterus to its normal anatomical position, starting with those portions closest to the vulva. The everted mass was heavy and I couldn't wait to get it back where it belonged. My arms ached with the strain of holding it. As I manipulated another potion forwards and it vanished from sight, I consoled myself with the thought that my task could only get lighter.

Inch by inch the gigantic, engorged, slippery organ grew smaller as I encouraged it to return from whence it came. I was almost there but I was growing tired with the effort of holding up what seemed like a hundred-weight of solid tripe, and with keeping my fist bunched for fear of perforating the organ. There wasn't much left to go. The cow began to strain. The perspiration started from my brow as I fought against her. The flies buzzed louder and bit harder. The cow gave an almighty heave and the whole organ burst forth like a warthog erupting from its burrow, slithering through my helpless arms and back down to its original position.

'Ah, pole,' murmured Salim. (Oh, sorry).

The Turkana women said nothing. At least they didn't laugh.

Back to square one. I applied some more lubricant and began again. I felt like Sisyphus rolling his huge stone ceaselessly uphill.

The sun felt hotter. I felt desperate. I felt weak, but there was no question of giving up. That was not on my agenda.

I closed my eyes, opened them and began again.

Lifted and kneaded and propelled and pummelled and pressed and finally, finally, bracing my chest against the cow's hindquarters, the last of the uterus disappeared from the light of day.

My relief was profound, but my task was not yet finished, as it was vital to ensure that complete inversion had taken place. This I did by clenching my fist and slowly straightening my arm and pushing it forward up to the armpit. I stood up, and my attendant cloud of flies rose with frustrated irritation, buzzing with annoyance.

One of the women grunted. Whether this was to express her appreciation for what I hoped was a job well done, or merely to clear her throat I was unable to ascertain. Salim looked as though he was about to faint.

Using the final few drops of water I re-soaped my arm and slipped a pessary into the uterus. Then, using an instrument resembling an enormous needle with an eye at the tip, I inserted two eversion sutures in the vulva. Soft wide material is essential to prevent any cutting of the tissues. I used a bandage. I gave her an antibiotic and a shot of multivitamins and my job was done.

As I returned to the car to divest myself of overalls and boots, I could feel the intermingled layers of uterine discharge, obstetrical lubricant, blood and unidentifiable colouring matter, which lay thick upon my arms and chest, congealing into a horny carapace. Within a few minutes I felt as if I was coated in Super Glue. I bent an experimental elbow and my armour plating cracked. I tried to prise it off, but it was stuck fast to the hairs below. Hot water and soap were the only answer. Here there was soap, but of water, neither hot nor cold. I debated with myself the niceties of donning a shirt under such dubious circumstances and, with commendable speed, decided that, as night and declining temperatures were in the offing, there was little to be gained by playing the hard man. I put on my shirt.

The cow, meanwhile, had been released. Having found a convenient opening in the side of the boma, she was now ambling across the plain, pausing every now and again to inspect and sample some desiccated tuft of interesting vegetation.

Feeling like a mediaeval knight whose armour had been doused in some horrid cocktail thrown from the battlements of an enemy castle, I eased myself gingerly into my car. Within the close confines of the vehicle I at once became rather aware of myself. A ripe and penetrating odour filled the air and assailed the nostrils.

Although to my mind the aroma was singularly disgusting, it sent the flies wild with delight. Several hundred of them swarmed into the car after me and proceeded to devote their exclusive attention to my person.

Salim was standing at a respectful and sensible distance, up-wind and out of fly range.

'Salim, my friend, can you remove those stitches in the vulva after four days?'

Salim looked as though he would rather not.

'OK effendi. Safari njema!' (Have a good journey!) Did he smile?

I departed.

I theorised that if I moved at a reasonable clip with all the windows wound down, the cool, passing breeze would suck out my uninvited passengers. So much for theory. The road from the point where I left the cow to the start of the tarmac at Thomson's Falls was such that it was impossible to attain that critical speed which would allow removal of the flies without also destroying the car. So I crawled along in the gathering dusk, in constant danger of driving off the side of the road as I waged battle with my tormentors.

One learns by one's mistakes and omissions. Thereafter I always carried a can of powerful insect killer wherever I went.

Once on the tarmac I was able to speed up, and this, together with the increase in altitude and dropping temperatures, dealt a body blow to the majority of my fellow travellers.

191

No such blow was dealt to my all embracing bouquet, alas, and I completed the remainder of the journey to Nakuru with the windows still firmly wound down.

🐜🐚🐜🐚🐜

'Daktari! Daktari! (Doctor!) – I really did like being called doctor – 'Doctor! Can you come? A mare has given birth and its uterus has come out – all of it!'

'Not again! This is too much!'

It was dusk. Further inquiries revealed that a Somali cross pony on a farm about 15 miles away, near the hamlet of Elburgon, had been found lying on her side in an open field with a complete prolapse of her uterus. A large dead foal had been discovered some distance away.

The owner was away on business in Nairobi, and the head syce was calling in a panic.

Prolapse in the mare is rare and considering the sensitivity of the horse to pain and its susceptibility to shock, I would have expected a rapid sideways shuffle to greener pastures.

By the time I arrived at the farm it was dark and very temperate. The place was at over 7,000 feet.

As I drove into the field to which I had been directed, a few warning spots of rain spattered against the windscreen. In the western firmament, blacker even than the night sky, I could see the thunderclouds of a monstrous storm, building up over the distant hills. Soundless lightning flickered briefly, like the occasional gleam of the embers of a fire behind the bars of a grate. Thunder was grumbling in an ominous, threatening way, like an irritated giant muttering under his breath.

The car headlights picked out a small group of shadowy figures. I bumped my way across to them.

As I got out of the car, the first chill gusts of the approaching storm swept over the field.

The head syce was tall, lean, bespectacled and very black.

'Jambo, habari gani?' I asked. (Greetings! How is the news?)

'Mzuri sana, bwana. (The news is good, sir)' he replied.

It did not look too good to me.

Lying on a muddy bank was a grey pony mare. Close by was a shallow ditch from which she had been extracted. Her uterus, spread out on the ground behind her, was covered in dirt, earth, leaves and grass.

'Oh my holy aunt!' I thought.

I placed my hand on the mare's skin. It was icy cold.

I shook down the mercury in my thermometer as far as it would

192

go and inserted it into her rectum. After two minutes I took it out. The mercury hadn't moved.

With no recorded temperature the mare was clinically dead.

'Well, that's that then,' I thought. 'She'll be completely dead pretty soon.'

However, as the mare was still breathing, she wasn't totally dead. So, in the sure knowledge that she had little hope of recovery, I set about replacing the uterus. An academic exercise. Educationally instructive, but academic none the less. Ho hum.

I had just removed my shirt and donned an unpleasantly cold protective apron when the owner, Watford Pickering, arrived on the scene.

Watford was wearing a deerstalker hat, a multi-pocketed waistcoat, corduroy trousers and green wellington boots: his city attire, as he had just come from Nairobi. A slender, jerky, hyperactive individual, he always peppered his speech with expressions such as 'now, look', 'good, good', and 'I see'. He caused me much irritation by always carrying around a little green notebook into which he jotted down the details of all my treatments and drug dosages, so that he could 'have a go' himself should a similar case arise in the future. I was glad to see that he was notebook-less.

'Hello, Watford,' I said. 'We've got a bit of a problem here, but we'll give it a go, although I'm not hopeful.'

'I see.'

'The mare's got a uterine prolapse and it must have happened some time ago. She's in shock and extremely cold.'

'Now look. I went to Nairobi this morning, but before I did I asked the syce about this mare. She was due to foal, you see. The syce said she couldn't be found anywhere. I was a bit worried as we had an inch and a half of rain last night. If fact the road to Njoro was almost impassable, the mud was so bad.'

'Well, she must have foaled last night during the storm, prolaped everything, and in the general struggle in the rain and the mud and the darkness, slipped and got wedged in that ditch over there. No wonder she's cold. It's a miracle she's still alive.'

And another storm was fast approaching.

If the mare was to be saved and I was not to succumb to hypothermia there was no time to be lost.

Under the light of the car headlamps I examined the uterus. It appeared to be undamaged. I knelt down, lifted it and placed it on a clean sack, which Watford fortuitously had in his car. Then I washed off the accumulated debris with warm water.

I felt a surge of gratitude towards the person who had, unasked, provided hot water prior to my arrival. The mare, if she had any feeling left, must have felt the same. In most cases, when called to a farm to deal with an obstetrical problem, hot water was the exception rather than the rule, and on cold nights the warmest part of my anatomy was my arm inside my unfortunate patient.

I could feel Watford peering over my shoulder, breathing on the back of my neck. 'Now what are you going to do, Hugh? What's that thing hanging there?'

'That, Watford, is the placenta or afterbirth and I going to try and remove it before trying to shove everything back inside.'

'Good, good. Look here. Can I have a go?'

'No, you bloody well can't! I'm not having you push your clumsy mitt through the uterine wall. Bring that bucket a bit closer.'

The placenta was still attached to a small area. I removed it without difficulty and without Watford's help. Next I poured obstetrical lubricant over the uterus and proceeded to replace it. To my surprise I found this was relatively easy, certainly much more so than the same procedure in the cow.

'Well, that wasn't too hard, was it?' said Watford.

'No indeed,' I agreed. 'Cows are perhaps more difficult because the uterus is covered with knobbly carbuncles like Brussel sprouts, which get in the way.'

I could read Watford's mind. This wasn't so difficult. Next time one of his animals had a prolapse he would have a go first, and if he failed, would call me. Great.

Within a few minutes the offending organ had been returned to the inner darkness from whence it came, while in the outer darkness I made haste to complete the exercise before the arrival of the approaching storm. The vulva was now revealed to be grossly contused and swollen. After inserting a pessary, I put in two sutures.

During the whole procedure, apart from the occasional groan and sigh, the mare made no reaction at all to my various manipulations. I began to wonder if all my labours were in vain.

'OK Watford, I'm going to give her an antibiotic, a shot of oxytocin to make her uterus contract, an injection of antihistamine to ward off laminitis and some multivitamins to try and rally her sinking energy reserves.'

I could see Watford's fingers rummaging around in his pocket for a pencil to record all of this, but it was too late. I wasn't in the mood for repeating my self.

'OK. Good. Good.'

I straightened up. Suddenly it felt unpleasantly cold. All the African workers were clad in ankle-length great-coats. Watford was now wearing a hideous, hairy sweater which almost reached his knees.

We propped the mare up on her brisket. To my astonishment she began nibbling at a little hay, brought to her by the syces. Then she drank some water.

My hopes began to rise.

The mare was unable to stand.

'Watford. Can you get a tarpaulin and a few bales of hay, please?'

Watford roared off, and was back in no time. We covered the mare with straw up to her ears and then spread the tarpaulin on top so that only her nose protruded.

'OK Watford. That's it. I'll come back in the morning. Fingers crossed!'

'Thanks, Hugh. Drive carefully!'

As I left, the heavens, which so far had held their fire, opened up with a vengeance. My hopes for a recovery began to fall, and by the time I had reached the tarmac, having ploughed through several mud wallows and almost slithered into the ditch, I had abandoned them altogether.

The following morning, more out of a sense of duty than anything else, I resignedly drove out to the farm.

As I bumped slowly across the field towards the tarpaulin-covered mound, I fully expected to find a stiffening corpse stretched beneath it, glazed eyes staring sightlessly into infinity.

Approaching the tarpaulin I detected movement beneath it.

I pulled it back and, as I did so, the mare sat up and then, after a tremendous effort, struggled to her feet.

An oilskinned-clad syce materialised from beneath a nearby tree, where he had probably spent the night in peaceful slumber. Together we assisted the mare to totter stiffly to a stable about half a mile away.

Just as we got there, Watford appeared.

'Ah, there you are, Hugh. Wondered where on earth you'd got to. I've been up for hours. Well, she looks all right. She obviously wasn't as bad as you thought she was, what? Now what were those drugs you gave her last night?'

He pulled his green notebook from his pocket.

'As soon as she comes into season I want the stallion to cover her. Damned pity that foal of hers died – hey, are you all right? You're looking a bit pale?'

Behind us the mare was tucking into a breakfast of bran and hay, washed down with draughts of clean, fresh water.

'Oh yes, Watford, fine, fine, just had a bit of a late night, you know.'

'Ah, yes, yes. Quite. Quite. OK, I'll leave you to it then. Just ask the syce for anything you want.'

He hurried away. Must have got the vibes, I thought. Arrogant pustule.

I repeated the antibiotic injection and returned the following day to remove the stitches. By now the mare had a normal, healthy appetite. The vulval swelling quietly regressed and within a few days her stiffness had gone.

I was impressed.

The horse, certainly the pony, could be a much tougher animal than is generally given credit for.

* * * * *

Meanwhile in the country at large, disturbing rumours were on everyone's lips of a return to the bestial practices of the days of Mau Mau, of large numbers of people travelling at night to Gatundu, the President's home, to swear loyalty to the House of Mumbi – the female founder of the Kikuyu tribe – of people being forcibly dragged from their homes and beaten up for refusing to participate in 'oathing' ceremonies.

Then in October 1969 President Jomo Kenyatta visited Kisumu to open a Russian-funded hospital. While there, stones were thrown. The presidential bodyguard opened fire, killing at least twenty people and wounding a hundred others.

The result was a general tightening up of security and the immediate installation of police and army roadblocks at various strategic points.

With the passage of time, these became permanent features of the Kenyan road system, a daily irritant to the law-abiding motorist.

Shortly after the Kisumu catastrophe however, it could be disconcerting to be stopped at one of these roadblocks, especially at night. Metal spikes barred the traveller's progress. Identification would be demanded by armed gendarmerie, whose attitude ranged from bluff bonhomie to sullen truculence and surly suspicion. I would be ordered to get out of the car and open the boot. This invariably evoked cries of consternation as its contents were revealed: drugs, bottles, ropes, knives, instruments. Further proof of identity would be demanded, more explanations required. In the ditch a few feet away, soldiers crouched over machine guns glared aggressively at me. Finally, after an interminable delay, I would be allowed to carry on my way

'You may proceed.'

'Thank you, officer!'

After a while things settled down to an uneasy calm. The surface was smooth, but unseen currents and eddies swirled and boiled in the hidden depths.

CHAPTER TWELVE

A man with a high-pitched pneumatic drill was hard at work, boring his way through the foundations of the Eiffel Tower. Spread-eagled on my back, wrists and ankles shackled to steel ring bolts set into concrete at a point equidistant from each of the iron legs of the Gallic monstrosity, I stared upwards at the mass of metal towering above me. It resembled a foreshortened spider's web, constructed in Meccano by some demented French arachnid. Any second now it was going to collapse and crush me beneath a mass of twisted girders. The drill took on a higher and more insistent note.

I awoke with a gasp, damp with perspiration. The phone, a few inches from my right ear, reverberated through the darkness. Its hideous clangour smote my tympanic membranes until they quivered in protest.

Still semi-paralysed from sleep and my experiences on the banks of the Seine, I clumsily tore the phone from its cradle and clapped it to my ear.

'Harisingh Gujabhai here, sah'b,' said an Indian voice. 'Dog, Raja, he is womiting too much and motions are welly fluid. He is too sick. Can you treat him? I am much wollied he vill not surwive if ve vait.'

I glanced at my watch: ten minutes past five in the morning.

As I dressed I wondered how Mr Gujabhai had discovered that his dog was ill at such an excessively early hour. In view of the fact that most Asian-owned dogs were kept to guard their master's property, it was unlikely that this specimen had been curled up on Gujabhai's bed. Perhaps the man was an insomniac or a fanatically early riser, and while engaged in his early morning gargling session had noticed that his dog was unwell.

I arrived at the surgery a few minutes later. Mr Gujabhai, middle-aged, with a head and hair-cut resembling that of a Prussian general, was waiting on the pavement outside. He was clad in striped pyjamas and his blue-grey feet were thrust into a pair of lace-less shoes. A bleary-eyed African, whose feet were thrust into no shoes at all, stood beside him, holding a heavy chain, at the end of which was attached a large alsatian

197

dog, whose general demeanour struck me as being markedly anti-social.

As I opened the surgery door, it bared its teeth and lunged in my direction. Mr Gujabhai stepped nimbly backwards. The African handler was fortunately familiar with his charge and stood his ground, keeping the dog on a tight chain, rather like a salmon fisher playing a heavy fish on a light line.

The first ten minutes of the examination were spent applying a tape muzzle to the dog's snapping jaws. During this procedure Mr Gujabhai led his troops from the rear, advising and exhorting from a safe vantage point. Once the situation was secure he moved in to perorate on the merits of herbal remedies used in the treatment of diseased canines on the Indian sub-continent.

'We are using garlic and chilli peppers for many problems and result is most marvellous, I am telling you.'

'I am sure you are right, Mr Gujabhai. Now what are you feeding Raja on?'

'Well, we are giving him chapattis, a little dal, soup and maize meal. Meat we are never giving. We are not finding this necessary for essential diet.'

While Mr Gujabhai droned on I examined Raja carefully. I checked blood and faeces under the microscope. The latter was loose but I saw nothing of significance. His temperature was normal.

'Mr Gujabhai, I don't think that chapattis and dal are the best basis for a well-balanced diet. The dog is primarily a carnivore and appreciates meat. I know that garlic and chilli peppers are essential ingredients in many oriental dishes, but they really cannot be considered to be vital weapons in the modern canine therapeutic armoury.'

Mr Gujabhai inhaled sharply. I had prodded a sensitive nerve.

'Oh, sah'b, sah'b, meat we cannot have in household. We are all welly strict Hindus. Meat we are never eating.'

'Well, feed him outside, then. I am convinced that Raj's trouble is caused by dietary imbalance and you must give him some protein: chicken, lamb, mutton, if you can't give him beef. OK?'

'OK, sah'b, I will try. But don't you think that a pinch of garlic might help?'

His African myrmidon gazed blankly into the middle distance, rocking gently on his large bare feet, eyes vacant.

'Give him garlic, but give him meat as well!'

I injected Raja with an anti-emetic and an antibiotic and we went our separate ways.

I drove back to my rondavel, gently grinding my teeth as I navigated my way around the potholes.

My watch informed me that it was still only a quarter to six. Time for another forty five minutes in the sack.

As soon as I opened the bedroom door I sensed something was wrong. I glanced around the room. Then my eyes fell on the bed.

It had been stripped bare!

Sheets, pillows, blankets – all had gone.

The curtains over one of the windows were moving slightly. I rushed across and tore then open. The burglar-proof wire mesh was intact, but one window was half open. I had forgotten to close it when I went out to attend to the sick dog.

And there on the window sill was the fresh imprint of two large bare feet.

I had been polefished!

Polefishing is an art, which has been developed, modified and refined by certain members of the African criminal classes. It is principally used when entry to a building is prevented by the presence of burglar-proof mesh, bars, or metal grills. The thief is in possession of a long pole, at the end of which is a hook. He inserts this through any convenient opening into the room of his choice, and proceeds to withdraw whatever he fancies and which is within his extended reach. People with bars on their windows frequently leave them open at night, especially when it is hot. Polefishers have developed their devilish skills to such a degree that they can go about their business without disturbing their slumbering victims. Should the sleeper awaken to find his trousers in mid-air and fast vanishing before his outraged eyes, he may be discouraged from seizing the pole whereon they are suspended by the row of razor blades inserted along its length.

❈❙❈❙❈❙❈❙❈

Disasters seem to occur in Africa with a regularity rarely observed in more temperate parts of the globe.

Small scale tragedies, which take place in every corner of the continent on a daily basis, go, for the most part, quite unnoticed by the mass of the populace. Occurrences, which would merit a paragraph on page three of the 'Daily Telegraph', and probably make the front page of the 'Express', if they were to occur in Britain, are here rarely considered to be newsworthy, even if they were reported. If they are printed, it is often days or weeks after the event has taken place. Stabbings, spearings, bludgeonings, shootings, the consumption of women and children by crocodiles, deaths from poisoning and snake-bite are usually lumped together in one unparsed paragraph, like corpses thrown into a mass grave.

Catastrophes of greater magnitude also occur with frightening frequency.

Buses collide, fall over cliffs, or tumble into rivers, with horrific loss of life. Canoes full of non-swimming occupants slip below the waters of Lake Victoria. Cholera, enteritis, measles, dysentery, AIDS and tuberculosis, claim their toll. In the under-policed northern areas, banditry takes many lives. When the Turkana, Merille or Pokot go on the warpath, they abide by no rules except their own. The object of the exercise is to make off with as much of the opposition's livestock as possible, and at the same time, to dent the opposing tribe's breeding potential by killing as many women and children as they can. There is no such thing as a gentleman's agreement to spare the young and the defenceless. Far from it, and hundreds are killed in some raids. The acquisition of firearms has exacerbated the situation, and AK47s are now more common then spears.

In the animal world in Africa, disasters of equally-depressing proportions litter the landscape, supplying sudden bounties of carrion for the vultures, hyenas, stunned stock-owners and two legged scavengers, who pop up like dragon's teeth whenever calamity strikes.

One morning I received a call asking me to go to an African-owned farm at the northern end of the Subukia valley.

The quickest route was to drive down the parallel Solai valley and then to cross over a low ridge, rocky and covered in thorn trees. The road was a narrow track, cut through bush, which encroached menacingly on both sides. Above, to the east, hills rose sharply, merging into the Rift Valley escarpment. The occasional homestead of a Tugen peasant farmer could be seen clinging, limpet like, to their steep slopes.

Rain had fallen during the night, and, as I approached the flats surrounding Lake Solai, I observed, with a degree of personal interest, that the usual ribbon of fine, choking dust, snaking its way through the acacia jungle, had been transformed into something resembling a black, treacly anaconda.

The area was thinly populated, car pushers in short supply. I sat up straighter, dropped into second gear, gave my adrenaline pump a boost, and shot into the morass.

I bounced, bucked and kangarooed my way down the valley. I roared through mud wallows, fountains of thick reddish water cascading over the car, windscreen wipers working overtime, until I was peering at the road ahead through an ochre-coloured porthole. On more than one occasion, as I madly pumped the stalk on the sheering wheel, which activated the washer, forward visibility was totally obscured by sheets of liquid mud, and when it had partially cleared I found myself heading for the ditch. The compulsion to step on the brake was almost irresistible. To have done do would have guaranteed a lengthy sojourn in the mire.

A short, rocky section led down to the greensward bordering shallow Lake Solai. I was perturbed to find that the lake had risen to such an extent that a four hundred yard long stretch of road was covered with water.

I stopped the car and took stock. I donned wellington boots and waded into the flood. To my relief it was only six inches deep and the bottom was firm and sandy.

I drove slowly across in first gear. A high speed approach, accompanied by a spectacular bow wave, usually has only one ending: a flooded and stalled engine.

The rest of the road, although greasy, caused no problems, and twenty minutes later I was in lower Subukia, gazing on the scene of a bovine disaster.

Also doing some gazing was a motley mob of locals, including a large knot of tough-looking Turkanas, hunkered down beneath a thorn tree.

I saw what they were looking at. In a corner of a field, beside a track leading off the Subukia road, 25 cattle lay dead. The field was bounded by a wire fence. The carcases lay, either touching the wire, or touching each other. There was no sign of a struggle. They looked as though they had all been simultaneously struck down by a bolt from the blue.

I walked into the field, which sloped slightly towards the north. The grass was long and wiry and flattened. Here and there a gobbet of yellowish foam nestled in depressions in the ground. Debris and detritus were piled up around the fence posts. Wet mud steamed in the sun.

'Jambo, daktari!' A spokesman for the group came forward and we shook hands, first the palm and then the thumb. 'This is very bad luck.'

He was tall and lean and very black, with a neck like a stalk of asparagus. His head wobbled when he spoke.

'Ndio, sana,' I said. (Yes, very).

This was a serious understatement.

Asparagus-neck told me that a storm of monumental ferocity had broken during the night. Accompanied by thunder and lightning, the rain had poured down, until the whole area was submerged beneath strongly-flowing water. A herdsman, guarding the cattle against stock thieves, described how the herd, driven by the lashing rain, had drifted through the bush, until brought up short by the wire fence. Along this they had meandered. Finally they congregated in the corner of the field, with a wire fence on two sides.

There they stood, hunched in the darkness, heads down, tails to the wind, up to their fetlocks in rushing water, the rain hissing down and crowded against the wire.

There was a lurid flash of lightning, which lit up the scene, as though by searchlight. Simultaneously there was an ear splitting crash of thunder. According to the watching herdsman, the wire fence took on a life all of its own, leaping around like a demented, white-hot snake. He shivered dramatically with the remembrance.

There was a great thump and a mighty splash as cattle dropped where they stood. The smell of singed hair filled the air. The atmosphere was pervaded by an unpleasant tingling sensation. The herdsman turned on his heels in terror and fled into the darkness.

As I walked among the carcases, I glanced at the waiting and still-gathering tribesmen. An air of tense expectation hung heavy on the crowd.

They were meat-hungry. A daily diet of posho and beans must result in a constant craving for a thick, juicy steak. The cattle were owned, not by any individual, but by the group co-operative which owned the farm. There was no sense of personal loss. They were awaiting a decision – my decision – on whether the meat was fit for human consumption

I examined the carcases. They were all prime Boran steers.

Everything pointed towards death by lightning strike.

Close inspection revealed areas of singeing of the hair of several animals, taking the form of straight and branching lines. I vaguely remembered having read in a textbook about there being capillary congestion beneath the singe marks. In order to prove the point I decided to have one of the steers skinned.

The flaying of carcases in Africa is invariably a tedious business. Knives are rarely sharp or in sufficient supply. They often lack handles, or are broken or rusty. Sometimes the only bladed instrument is a panga, more suitable for chopping firewood than the skilful removal of a cowhide from its erstwhile owner. There was nothing more irritating then to stand and watch while a couple of fumble-fingered yokels sawed their way through the skin with a knife blade resembling half of an old pair of scissors, and then with infinite slowness, proceed to remove the hide, square centimetre by square centimetre. Invariably during this process, despite the bluntness of their cutting tools, one or other of these gents would manage to force his blade through the hide, ruining a large area.

To have to stand and watch this pantomime, knowing that equally pressing engagements awaited my attention, was calculated to raise my blood pressure, promote ulceration of my stomach, and generally shorten my allotted span on Planet Earth.

In order to avoid such undesirable side effects I had purchased a large wooden-handled knife, which I kept honed to razor sharpness. The blade was protected by a sheath made from the hide of an enormous Santa Gertrudis bull, on which I had carried out a post-mortem. He had been called Lazarus, as he had miraculously recovered from a series of life-threatening ailments. Finally he had succumbed to an inhalation pneumonia when he was drenched, while suffering from ephemeral fever. His throat muscles were paralysed and he was unable to swallow. So he died.

By the time I returned to the steer, the animal was lying on its back and was being supported fore and aft by a gang of tattered tribesmen, whose interest in the proceedings I judged to be somewhat less scientific than my own. A couple of lads with simis had already started to remove the hide from the legs.

I peeled back the skin of the chest and examined an area where the hair had been singed. The capillaries in the subcutaneous tissue were congested and appeared to form a curious arboreal design. I opened the thorax and abdomen. Apart from some congestion of the lungs, spleen and liver, everything looked normal.

'OK, that's it then,' I said.

Asparagus-neck was at my side.

'Well, my friend, it's lightning strike, as we all know, and in my opinion the meat is fit for human consumption. After all, in other parts of the world, animals, such as pigs, are stunned by an electric shock at slaughter, so maybe this is God's way here.'

Asparagus-neck smiled gently and nodded.

'Yes, indeed, daktari.'

Anticipating that my decision would be popular with the salivating spectators, and not wishing to be personally incorporated into the butchery and mayhem that would inevitably follow, I chose a vantage point a little distance away from the nearest dead steer to make my announcement.

There was a roar of approval, the crowd rose as one man, and in an instant, the carcases were surrounded by a tidal wave of people in whose minds was only one thought: *meat*.

Knives flashed, axes chopped, pangas slashed, men laughed, men quarrelled, women giggled, women bickered. Pi-dogs skulked on the edge of the crowd, darting in to seize a morsel when the opportunity presented itself, and rushing off yelping when they were kicked away.

The sun shone bright and strong. The ridges of the nearby Marmanet Escarpment stood out sharp and clear in the rain-washed air. A dove cooed contentedly in a thorn tree close by.

Despite the warmth of the sun, a sudden shiver ran down my back. I turned and walked back to my car. I got in, and drove quickly back up the track towards Nakuru.

><><><

Donald Thomas farmed near Njoro, about fifteen miles from Nakuru. Here he milked one of the best Jersey herds in the Rift Valley.

Donald was a Kenya citizen, with a degree in agriculture. He had decided that the time had come to sell up and enter fresh fields.

Accordingly he had applied for, and was appointed to, a post in the Faculty of Agriculture at the University of Nairobi, teaching the subject for which he had been trained.

Donald was a first-rate farmer, one of the best. He rarely lost an animal and his milk and butterfat yields were among the highest in the country. There was a constant demand for his stock. He kept a firm hand on the helm and like the good Quaker that he was, believed in the ethics of hard work and social responsibility. Unlike some other farmers, who took advantage of the relatively inexpensive labour force to employ a manager, who did the bulk of the work while they joined the Muthaiga crowd at the races, or fished for marlin off Malindi, Donald made the decisions and delegated little to his workers.

This was an excellent system while he was on the farm, rather less so when he wasn't.

Although negotiations to sell were well under way when the time came for Donald to start his new job, no money had as yet exchanged hands.

Donald was in a quandary.

If he did not go he would lose his new position. And leaving his unsold farm to the tender mercies of his unsupervised employees was something he did not even like to contemplate.

Finally Donald departed for the big city, leaving the farm in the charge of his headman, with strict instructions to contact him should anything go wrong. This worthy's main duties, as far as I could gather, up to the time of his employer's disappearance over the horizon in the direction of Nairobi, were the jotting down of the daily milk yields as they were weighed and poured from bucket to churn, together with general supervision of the dairy and rearing of the calves. An earnest well-meaning fellow, he had worked for Donald for many years, and regarded his words as pearls of wisdom handed down from on high. He kept his addiction to his daily dram well hidden from his employer.

Late one afternoon I was hard at work in the surgery, dealing with the daily flood of portable members of the animal kingdom and their respective owners.

The telephone rang.

The tide was on the ebb so I was able to answer it personally. Besides, through the door, I could hear the vivacious Sophie engaged in a spirited cut and thrust with a client who had apparently failed to pay his bill, and from the sound of his mumbled responses it sounded as though Sophie was doing most of the cutting and thrusting. Having a personal stake in the encounter, I had no wish to queer her pitch.

The caller was Donald's headman.

He sounded desperate.

'Daktari! Daktari! Can you come, please! Many cattle have died! Many! They started dying at one o'clock and the total is now 31!'

I glanced at my watch. 4.30pm.

He paused to draw breath. I could hear him panting, like an overweight, unfit runner.

His voice rose, until I feared it might reach the point where it would only be audible to my last canine patient. Gasping and panting, he sobbed out the remainder of his tale.

'They've died of bloat. I've tried to phone Mr Thomas many, many times, but I can't get through. The line is so bad.'

I didn't wait to hear the rest of his appalling epic. Slamming the phone down, I grabbed a gallon container of bloat mixture, and ran out to the car. I checked to make sure that I had a couple of trocars and plenty of cannulas in the glove box, started the engine, and departed at high speed.

Fifteen minutes later I roared into the farm yard, braked and skidded to a halt in a cloud of dust.

The place looked as though it had been hit by a bomb.

Dead cattle lay everywhere. The majority were lying on their backs, abdomens grossly distended, legs pointing stiffly up to the sky.

A solitary animal stood amid the carnage, supported on both sides by several men. Its legs were spread wide apart as though unable to support its own weight. Its tongue protruded obscenely from its foam-flecked mouth, like a large piece of steak. Its eyes bore a strained expression and its flanks heaved with the effort of drawing air into lungs compressed and squeezed by its enormously distended rumen. As I looked, it staggered as though about to collapse.

Seizing a scalpel and the largest trocar and cannula I possessed, I rushed across to the stricken cow. I made an inch long incision through the skin in her upper left flank and shoved the trocar and cannula in one movement through the muscles and into the rumen. As I removed the needle-pointed trocar from the cannula I stepped smartly to one side while still maintaining my grip on the cannula.

There was an explosive hiss as the pent up gases of fermentation trapped in the rumen blasted their way through the tube. The cow rapidly deflated. Her distressed breathing eased and her eyes lost their look of desperation.

'Bring me some binder twine,' I barked, as froth and foam began to bubble through the tube, which moved as the rumen musculature contracted.

I secured the cannula in position by threading the twine through the holes in its base and then around the cow's abdomen. I injected several ounces of bloat mixture through the tube into the rumen. This mixture, of which I always kept a large stock in the surgery, was composed of paraffin oil, turpentine, creosote, soap powder and water. A primitive concoction, but effective.

One cow having been saved, I turned and gazed around me.

'Hells bells!' I thought.

The scene was one of utter devastation. Thirty four prime milking cows lay stark and stiff in the dust. The unbloated members of the herd hung apprehensively on the perimeter of the yard as though expecting at any minute to meet the same fate as their mates.

Turning to the headman, I inquired, as politely as it was possible for me to do under the circumstances, what exactly he had been doing during the past four hours.

He looked at me nervously, avoiding my eyes, swallowed and stammered through his story.

At ten in the morning, the herd had been driven into a field of columbus grass, the grazing lush and succulent after the rain which had fallen during the previous weeks. An hour or so later some of the younger cows appeared to be in some discomfort, showing the first signs of bloat. They had stopped grazing and their left flanks were distended.

Unsure what to do, the headman went to the house and attempted to contact Donald Thomas in Nairobi by telephone. This proved to be a futile exercise. First he had to contact the operator manning the Njoro exchange. This took about twenty minutes. This worthy then tried to phone Nairobi. Long periods of silence were punctuated by clicks, buzzes, and humming noises, enlivened by the odd burst of random conversation on another line. Finally a last click and the rest was silence as the line went dead.

The headman returned to the field to take stock of the situation, no doubt hoping that a miracle had taken place in his absence. It had not. One or two more animals were now also mildly bloated. Those initially affected seemed, to his criterion, to be no worse. So, leaving the herd under the eagle gaze of a one-eyed Turkana herdsman, he departed to attend to more pressing business.

He returned about mid afternoon, full of posho and pombe, (cooked maize and local beer) mind blessedly free from concern about pastoral problems. Sauntering into the yard, a song upon his lips, he was met with a sight which brought him to his senses with brutal rapidity.

Eight Jersey cows, young matrons full of prime milk, lay dead, bloated with the gases of fermentation. The remainder of the herd milled around. Of these, twenty were severely bloated, their rumens blown up until they protruded vastly on both left and right flanks.

For the next couple of hours the headman and his myrmidons rushed around like a pack of headless chickens, full of sound and fury, expending much energy and accomplishing nothing. Cows dropped down on every side, but so conditioned had they become to acting under instruction, that they were incapable of taking even the most basic of initiatives. Even the simplest of treatments, such as drenching with lamp paraffin, or forcing the animals into a gallop, were ignored.

Instead of phoning for me, fifteen miles away, the headman exercised his time in trying to contact Donald Thomas, who was one hundred and twenty miles from the farm. When he finally did so, he was given an earful of un-Quaker like advice and told to phone me at once. This he succeeded in doing at four thirty in the afternoon, by which time thirty three of Donald's best breeding stock were deceased. Number thirty four expired as I risked life and limb on the road between Nakuru and Njoro.

I knew that my words would fall on deaf ears, but I had to go through the motions. So I gave the headman a brief and basic run-down on the causes, mechanics, prevention and treatment of bloat. As the headman swayed gently to and fro, under the influence of whatever he had imbibed over his extended lunch break, I wondered just how much of what I had said he had assimilated.

I did not have long to wonder.

Two days later he put what remained of the herd back into the field of columbus grass and four more cows died of bloat.

*****

As any Agatha Christie fan knows, hydrocyanic, or prussic, acid is an extremely potent poison. It kills by depriving cells of oxygen. A sort of chemical suffocation.

A variety of plants, especially during the early stages of rapid growth, contain the precursors of prussic acid. Wilting, or a check to normal growth, by, for example, drought or frost, tends to increase the amount of free acid in the plant.

Such knowledge was, I have to admit, far from my mind when I received a call to attend to a sick Friesian cow at Avondale Farm in the upper Subukia valley.

When I arrived, I saw my patient plunging through a field of ten foot high napier grass. I approached with some caution. She was staggering from side to side and was having great difficulty in breathing. Every now and again she was gripped by a violent muscular spasm, which almost threw her to the ground. Her tail twitched, she was salivating and there was bright red blood oozing from one nostril.

Certain aspects of this bizarre behaviour resembled that of a cow with hypo magnesemia, or 'staggers', which I had often seen during the autumn in North East Scotland, when the icy winds straight off the Russian steppes swept over the land, chilling livestock, and me, to the bone. As far as I knew this condition was unheard of in Kenya.

Whatever it was, death was nigh unless I did the right thing – fast.

'Moses, my friend, do we have any hypo in the car?'

'Aaaaaah. I think so. Let me look.'

Whenever I asked Moses whether we had this or that in the car or in the surgery he invariably prefaced his answer with 'aaaaaah'. Mildly irritating, but quirkily amusing.

Hypo, or, to be precisely pedantic, sodium thiosulphate, was used in the developing of black and white photos, a throwback to the halcyon days of the flash bulb and the box brownie. It is also used to treat animals poisoned by arsenic, another Agatha Christie stand-by.

I knew that this wasn't arsenic poisoning, but I was sure that it was poisoning of some kind. So, in desperation, and for want of any other purposeful action, I resolved to try the hypo.

Deciding this was a case of do or die, I poured a large handful of the colourless, transparent crystals into a bottle and topped up with sterile water, and attached a flutter valve for intravenous infusion.

The patient by now had been cornered in a dense thicket of napier grass. Although standing, she looked as though she might collapse at any second.

Moses seized her by the nose and I injected the solution of concentrated hypo into her jugular vein. I removed the needle and stood back to watch the effect, fully expecting sudden and dramatic death. On the contrary, the results were gratifying. After a few minutes her respiratory distress eased, the muscle twitching stopped and the general restlessness lessened. So, for good measure, I gave her another handful of hypo by mouth and departed, feeling rather pleased with myself, but still clueless as to what condition I had been treating.

That evening, after I had finished writing up the day's invoices, I broke out my meagre collection of textbooks and deduced that I had been treating a case of prussic acid poisoning. I also discovered that the recommended treatment was the intravenous injection of a mixture of hypo and sodium nitrite. Pretty good, I thought. I did a quick calculation and found that I had given the cow about ten times the advised dose. Not quite so good.

Next day I made sure that both items were installed in my car – a large bag of hypo crystals and a small tin of one gram sodium nitrite tablets. The latter were labelled 'anti-rust' tablets, something which I viewed with initial concern. The chemist who supplied them, a lean Caledonian, whose physical appearance gave rise to the belief that he was too mean to eat more than one meal a day, assured me that they were perfectly safe for the use for which I intended them.

'Take it or leave it, laddie. Besides, ye hiv'nae any choice. That's all there is.'

Many months went by before I saw another case of prussic acid poisoning.

Then, one Sunday morning, long before the first self-respecting lark had left the nest, the phone rang.

I groaned.

'Cran, is that you?' I wondered who else the caller thought it might be. 'This is Captain Barclay. Look here, I've got a bit of a problem. One of my best cows, just milked three and a half gallons, dropped down stone dead. Backed out of the milking bail, walked a few yards, gave a bit of a twitch and a grunt, and down she went, bit like a fellow I saw once cop a Boche bullet on the front.'

Captain Hugh Barclay was an original soldier-settler, who had come to Kenya after serving with some distinction in the Great War. Bluff and hearty, he ran a large herd of Friesians on his farm, Crater Estates, at Menengai.

'She's dead, and others look as though they might soon join her – can you come out and treat them? Now?'

I glanced at the alarm clock beside my bed. Six fifteen. I supposed I should have counted myself as fortunate. Some masochistic farmers milked their cows in the middle of the night, as early as 4am, apparently in order to get first in line in the milk delivery queue. Not my idea of fun.

The exhaust pipe of my car had developed a major leak and as I roared out of town I hoped that the gendarmerie were not up and about, ready to apprehend me on a joint charge of breaching the peace and breaking the speed limit.

The good captain was waiting, mustachios a-bristle.

'Stout fellow, Cran. Sorry to disturb you on the Sabbath, but the need is urgent. Just look at those cows over there, will ye? They look as though they've got St. Vitus's dance the way they're twitching and jerking.'

The milking bail stood at the edge of a field of young clover. The dead cow lay about twenty yards away. About a dozen others were milling around. One was staggering blindly in no particular direction, gasping for air. Another stood rooted to the spot, mouth open, eyes protruding.

'What the dickens is it? Is it poisoning, or what?'

'It looks like prussic acid poisoning to me, and we're going to have to be quick to save them. By rights we should give them an iv injection but by the time we've done that to one or two, the rest will have died, so the best plan is to give them all the antidote by subcutaneous injection.'

'OK, you're the expert. Let's get on with it!'

I had computed that three anti-rust tablets and a small handful of hypo dissolved in 30mls of sterile water would treat one cow. One 400ml milk fever bottle would contain enough antidote to treat thirteen animals.

With Captain Barclay bellowing at his troops, it took no time to treat the affected cows.

'Kiplangat! Arap Soy! Ruto! Shika ngombe! Come on! Come on! Futa socksi yako bloody juu!' (Get hold of those cows! Pull your bloody socks up!)

I shoved in the solution as fast as I could and, *mirabile dictu*, within about half an hour, things were on the mend.

'Now, just to make doubly sure we don't get any relapses while I'm at church, let's give them a handful of hypo by mouth.'

'That sounds like a good idea,' smiled Captain Barclay.

So we drenched them. Finally I made up another bottle of the injectable antidote and left it behind so that should any more animals be affected, they could be treated promptly, by the farm staff.

Not long after this episode, I was halfway through an afternoon surgery, applying a plastercast to the fractured metacarpus of a collie bitch, when I heard some clients enter the reception room, and sit down.

These appeared to be three European women.

A spirited wide-ranging conversation ensued, fragments of which drifted in my direction through the closed door. One female possessed a penetrating high-pitched voice. I was glad the door was closed. Their subject-matter was diverse, touching on such motley items as a well-known stallion's disgraceful lack of libido, the amount of sugar their respective cooks had filched during the past week, the fearful delay at the cemetery the other day, when it was discovered too late that the deceased was too long to fit into his coffin, and declining standards in general – even at the Club, my dear!

My task, as I waited for the plaster cast to dry, of necessity took some time.

There seemed to be a hiatus in the conversation. Suddenly the shrill voice of the main speaker rang forth, shattering the welcome silence.

'He's taking a frightfully long time in there, isn't he? I wouldn't be at all surprised if he's not stretched out fast asleep on the operating table!'

Peals of laughter greeted this sally.

I considered this witticism for a moment. I decided that my best course of action would be to tousle my hair, open the door and stumble forth, stifling a yawn and screwing up my eyes against the unwelcome light of day. But, before I had time to put my riposte into effect, the product of Alexander Graham Bell's genius gave tongue.

'Hello, Hugh Cran here, can I help you?'

'I sincerely hope so. My name is Kamau. I am the manager of Gicheha Farm, owned by Mzee.'

Mzee, the Old Man, was His Excellency, the President, Jomo Kenyatta, the Most Important Man in the Country.

My pulse quickened.

'Yes, Mr Kamau, and what appears to be the problem?'

Visions of death, disaster, and deportation rose grimly to mind.

'Well, we have about a hundred of our best Friesians grazing in this big field of young sorghum.'

'I see.' I knew what he was going to say next.

'Well, in the past hour seven cows have died, and there are many, many others sick. You are coming right away, isn't it?'

Despite the worrying grammatical inexactitude I knew that this was not a question, but a demand, and one requiring immediate action. This sounded like yet another, and this time massive, case of prussic acid poisoning. And on the President's farm. Great! From my recent readings I now knew that young sorghum was the plant par excellence for the production of the stuff. Agatha would have been proud of my detective work.

The collie's cast was now hard and dry. The garrulous ladies had only come in for a chat with Angela and to get some hookworm tablets for their dogs, so their wants were speedily satisfied.

I gave a hoarse shout to Moses to bring several bottles of sterile water, a couple of kilos of hypo and all the anti-rust tablets he could lay his hands on.

'Start making up the antidote, Moses. Our necks will be on the block if we – correction, I – mess this one up.'

On the long downhill stretch to Rongai I touched a 100 mph. In the left seat Moses was imperturbably pouring in tablets and crystals and shaking up solutions as the trusty Peugeot, gravity on its side, rocketed down the hill. His faith in my driving ability was rather touching. He never, even at the highest speeds, or on the worst tracks it was possible for man to have constructed for vehicular use, turned a hair. Often he would quietly nod off as overloaded buses and matatus, emblazoned with such mystic slogans as 'Careless Whispers', 'Japanese Worrier' and 'First Violin', hurtled towards us on the wrong side of the road. Now *we* were howling down the hill on the wrong side of the road.

I roared up to the farm gate and screeched to a halt in a cloud of dust and gravel.

As I did so, a posse of heavily armed members of the dreaded General Service Unit, paramilitary police, dressed in camouflage uniform, heavy boots and red berets and carrying light machine guns, rushed out of the sentry boxes flanking the gate.

Their demeanour was not friendly.

'Weh, mzungu! Wat are you doing here? Eh, do you not know that this is a restricted area? This is the President's farm.'

'Yes, I *know* that, officer. The farm manager, Mr Kamau, has phoned about some sick cattle. It's urgent!'

'You wait here while I radio him. Who are you? Get out and open the boot!'

I did so, wondering how many cattle might die while all this was going on.

A few interminable minutes later, I was allowed entry.

'Ploceed!'

Mr Kamau was short, stout and looked as though he liked to smile a lot.

He was not smiling now.

His job and, maybe his freedom, were on the line.

We drove at breakneck speed to the scene of the crime.

Chaos was the name of the game.

The affected cattle were all in one huge field. Dozens of animals were milling around, staggering, twitching, jerking, salivating, falling down or threshing on the ground. The dead lay discreetly and conveniently in one distant corner.

The total number of cattle needing treatment was 65.

'Ye blimmin' Gods!' I thought.

For the next hour we worked like demons. Fortunately Mzee had a very large number of workers on his payroll, plus others who were not on his payroll, in the form of convicts from Nakuru prison, detailed to labour on the presidential estates. So treatment proceeded apace, the cattle were seized and held for my examination and attention, fresh bottles of antidote were being continually made up by my trusty assistant, until finally, in a lather composed of equal parts of sweat and dust, the task was completed.

'Thank you, daktari,' wheezed Kamau, exhausted by all the running and catching in the hot sun. 'Now what.'

'We wait and watch. Any that don't seem to be recovering, we re-inject. I left Nakuru in such a hurry I'm running out of antidote, so when I leave, if there are any more cases, phone me at once, OK? And get the cattle out of this field! Mara moja! Now!'

I gave the guards a cheery wave as I drove back through the presidential gates. They gave me a hesitant salute. I wondered if I would get any more reward than that for my efforts.

Mzee was lucky. He had lost only seven cattle. Prussic acid poisoning can be devastating, but at least it does have an antidote, and rapid treatment is effective.

Other poisons are not so cooperative in their response, and no matter what you did or how long you persisted, the depressing outcome was always the same – death – and the Grim Reaper had scored again.

My heart always fell whenever I had to deal with copper poisoning. The stuff came as a blue powder, which was made up into a solution and sprayed onto coffee bushes to control fungal diseases. If cattle got access to either the powder, or the solution, their fate was invariably sealed. They were found either dead, moribund, or afflicted by a bizarre, bluish diarrhoea. The antidotes mentioned in the textbooks were unavailable, and probably useless anyway, and empirical treatment was a mere sop to one's conscience. Any animal that did survive did so, in spite of, and not because of, treatment. Less severely-affected animals often developed liver failure and jaundice and died. So, copper poisoning was not something to uplift the spirit and put a spring into one's step.

Neither was salt poisoning, although recovery did occur from time to time.

Periodically, cattle salt would disappear from the market. The salt was normally fed ad lib, or in combination with other minerals. When it did become available, sometimes after a period of months, I would have to deal with a rash of cases of poisoning, as unsuspecting farmers fed unlimited quantities to the deprived animals. Severe gastro-enteritis and profuse diarrhoea due to the irritating effects of the concentrated salt were bad enough, but frequently there was involvement of the central nervous system, with blindness, staggering, collapse and death within a few hours. The less severely affected cattle responded satisfactorily to the provision of small volumes of water supplied at frequent intervals.

Curiously, plant poisoning per se was not common, and normally only occurred after prolonged periods of drought, when stock, desperate for anything to eat, sampled plants they would not normally have touched.

For many years arsenic was used in cattle dips to control ticks. It was effective, but was highly poisonous and had little residual effect, and gradually fell into disuse as other more effective compounds became available. Cattle are highly susceptible to arsenic. The main organ affected is the gastro-intestinal tract, with ultra-severe inflammation, and the loss of huge volumes of fluid in the form of watery, foetid, diarrhoea, mixed with mucous and shreds of gut lining. Very nasty. The acuteness of the damage, and because there is frequently a delay of between 25 and 50 hours between ingestion of arsenic and the appearance of symptoms, means that the response to treatment is poor. In acute outbreaks the mortality can reach 100%, and so the consumption of arsenic by large numbers of cattle sets the scene for yet another bovine catastrophe.

To make matters even worse arsenic is indestructible. Once it is in the soil, unless physically removed, it is there forever.

Angus Mottram-Smythe was a pseudo-Scot. He liked to think of himself as a fully fledged member of the Scottish diaspora, entitled to wear the kilt, sporran and associated accoutrements, and pontificate on the merits of Burns and Sir Walter Scott. His links were tenuous indeed.

A distant cousin of his maternal grandmother had been a fishmonger in Arbroath, and from this faint connection Mottram-Smythe had woven a rich tapestry of myth and legend, far removed from his mundane roots in the Isle of Wight.

Not for the first time I was struck by how many double barrelled surnames contained the rather plebeian name Smith (or the pretentious Smythe). Add another name and a hyphen and, with attention to superior diction, a member of the proletariat could easily upgrade himself several social rungs.

Mottram-Smythe was tall, slightly stooped, and possessed an impressive nose which he used rather like a schoolmaster's pointer to impose his superior knowledge on those he considered to be his inferiors, which was most of humanity, including myself.

M-S, as he liked to call himself, was the manager of Nyati Estate in the green and pleasant Solai Valley.

I was on the premises, pregnancy testing the herd of Guernsey cows, when M-S came into the dairy.

'Hello, Hugh, when you've finished doing that, can you look at a couple of cows? We've been losing a few from scours recently. I think they've probably got liver fluke or worms.'

M-S gave his knowledgeable laugh, and skipped nimbly aside as a jet of dung shot by my arm and spattered onto the floor.

'Fine. How many have you lost?'

I struggled to palpate the large cow, teetering on the edge of her stall.

'Oh, I would say – at a rough guess – about 25.'

'Whaaaaat?'

I almost lost my footing on the greasy flagstones.

'Yes. Anyway, I'll see you outside when you've finished.'

M-S strolled out of the dairy.

In the ramshackle crush, a forlorn group of cows stood waiting my attention. Heads hung low, eyes were sunken, flanks were hollow and tails were soaked with rank diarrhoea.

M-S was inspecting his cuticles as I clumped up in wellington boots and apron.

'Well, when did all this start?'

'Hmm. I would say, let me think, about a month ago – no, more like six weeks.'

'Have you been treating them?'

'I'll say we have! Dosed 'em for worms and fluke, stabbed 'em with just about every antibiotic known to man, drenched 'em with sulphonamides, even given 'em charcoal and kaolin. No damn difference.'

I hoped that M-S would not say 'em again.

214

'I see. So we must look for a cause other the parasites and infection, I think.'

'Really? What do you have in mind?'

'Well, it could be Johne's Disease, but I doubt it. More likely to be poisoning of some kind.'

'Poisoning? What sort of poisoning?'

'Could be arsenic. Arsenic causes catastrophic gastroenteritis and death – just like you've been experiencing.'

'But my dear fellow, where would they have got it from? Tell me that. 'Eh?'

'First of all we need a diagnosis. These animals are going to die very soon, so we might as well sacrifice one now and send some samples of liver, kidney and stomach contents to the labs at Kabete.'

M-S's nose twitched convulsively.

'It might not die. Can't we treat it? It might survive.'

Maybe he had more Scots blood than I thought.

'Well, you've already lost 25 animals. Better lose one more and find out what's causing this, than hope for a miracle which isn't going to happen. I'll give the others some hypo.'

M-S looked excessively doubtful.

'Very well, get on with it then! Let me know when you get an answer.'

He picked his way carefully through the cow-pats and disappeared.

The dosed animals all died, in short order. M-S was not impressed.

The lab report came back a week later, positive for arsenic. In the meantime another 20 animals had died.

I returned to the farm, determined to find the source of the poison.

I searched high and low: in the feed troughs, the barns, the water troughs; nothing.

'What about the dip?' I thought. In the distant past arsenic might have been used there. Could that be it?

I dug up samples of soil, ripped up hanks of grass, scraped shavings from the fence posts, and sent them to the lab. All were positive for arsenic.

The dip was surrounded by long, lush, succulent grass. When the cattle emerged from the dip they stood in a fenced passageway to drain – and push their heads through the wire and pull at the sweet, green grass, their roots buried in arsenic-laced soil. The last time arsenic had been used in the dip had been 18 years previously.

Although Mottram-Smythe seemed impressed by my detective work, trying to get him to take action was another matter altogether. That widespread ennui, which hangs like an invisible and all-penetrating miasma over so many aspects of tropical life, had not failed to leave its mark on our Man from the Isle of Wight. Mottram became Manana and, forever after, I knew him as Manana-Smythe.

Persuading him to remove the cattle from the holding pens immediately after dipping, to cut the long grass adjacent to the fenced passageway and to cover the dangerous areas of soil, was a labour that made those of Hercules seem minor by comparison. It wasn't as though he would be out there in the mid-day sun himself, personally digging and delving. All he had to do was to issue the orders to his droves of perspiring minions. Only when the death rate approached the upper 80s did he finally gird his sluggish loins and follow my advice. The deaths stopped. The total carnage was 90 animals.

Peter Pring owned a farm in the Subukia Valley. With his family he lived in some splendour in a colonial mansion, designed and built by Sir Phillip Mitchell, who had intended to use it as a retirement home, following the completion of his tenure of office as Governor of Kenya in 1952. The unacceptable face of nationalism, in the form of Mau Mau, dented those aspirations.

Peter Pring's cattle were Ayrshires, fat and sleek and fair of aspect, brimming over with milk and the apple of their owner's eye.

Of the herdsmen assigned to keep watch over the cattle was one Somali, far removed from the blighted deserts of his northern native heath. He was, like other members of his tribe and faith, although poor and devoid of material wealth, proud, highly-strung and easily slighted.

One day he decided that insult had been directed at his personage and lineage and plotted revenge. The reason for his action was never discovered. A sharp word, or a reproof before workers of lesser tribes, might have stirred his hot blood to anger. Cattle began to sicken and die. Analysis of the cattle food revealed large quantities of arsenic. Treatment was, in the dead-pan terms so favoured by the writers of textbooks, generally unavailing. In other words, useless – and seventy five animals died.

Of the Somali herdsman there was no sign. As soon as the seeds of his noxious handiwork had begun to sprout, he had silently struck camp and vanished, never to be seen again.

Gareth Jones, the manager of Fisi Farm, was luckier.

He had taken delivery of several 40-gallon drums, containing arsenical weed killer. Gareth read the directions on the outside of the drums with care. Included in the small print was a statement to the effect that after use, the drums could be converted into water troughs for use by cattle, provided that they were first thoroughly washed out. As 40-gallon drums and water troughs were expensive, this was an unexpected bonus.

After the weeds had been bombarded with the contents of the drums, Gareth had them bisected and scoured out. He then had them placed in a large field, containing a herd of Friesian heifers

Within a very few days 15 of the heifers had acute arsenical poisoning, while other members of the herd, less severely affected, exhibited those symptoms so graphically described in toxicology textbooks, namely pipe-stem and projectile diarrhoea.

Gareth's temper could never, even at best, have been described as moderate. He was not one to fume quietly, grinding his molars. He would explode suddenly and violently, like an erupting volcano, a stream of oaths cascading from his quivering lips. The luckless recipients of his rage, usually his African workers, would quail and bend beneath the blast, standing silently, while the white bwana ranted and raved. These storms of anger soon passed, but for a while their effect was magical. Metaphorical socks would be pulled up, and backs would be bent, as everyone worked feverishly, lest he find himself singled out by Gareth for a verbal flogging.

The milk yield would rise and petty pilfering would cease. The results of these outbursts were by no means permanent, but as Gareth vented his spleen on a fairly regular basis, it was a pretty good second best.

On this occasion the manufacturers of the weed killer were the target of Gareth's wrath. Twelve prime heifers had died. Others would take many months to recover, their innards severely damaged. The loss was considerable.

As Gareth hove over the horizon, roaring like an irate hippo, the weed men whipped out their cheque books and signed for a sum to cover the cost of the dead animals, and then some more.

The sight of Gareth, features purpling with self righteous fury, eyes bulging, drove their pens with frantic haste across the virgin parchment.

CHAPTER THIRTEEN

I was vaguely aware that there were other diseases, besides malaria, which afflicted those members of the human race rash enough to reside in the tropics. Like most people I gave the matter little thought. I hoped that I would be spared the more unpleasant maladies, which from time to time were detailed in the local press, when they eliminated their victims in more than usual numbers.

One Friday I felt a curious lethargy stealing over my limbs. This I attributed to the fact that it was a Friday, often the busiest day of the week. And this particular week had been one crammed with both emergency and routine work, including the examination of large numbers of cattle for sale to Tanzania and Uganda.

That evening I retired early.

As I gingerly nibbled a piece of toast at breakfast the following morning, Nick du Toit phoned from his farm at Naivasha. Nick was of Afrikaner stock.

'Hi, Hugh, this is Nick here. Look, one of my Sahiwal cows has got a prolapse. She's pregnant, and, Christ, man, the thing is twice as big as a rugger ball, as hard as iron, covered with flies, and caked with dung and dried mud. She's one of my best cows too. Heaven knows how you're going to get it back inside her. It's been out a while, as my phone's dead and I had to drive miles to get to one which works. How soon can you get here?'

Nick's South African accent was strong and thick.

Nick was a big man, broad and beefy, with a neck which merged imperceptibly into his massive, close-cropped head. He wore short shorts, revealing muscles I never knew existed, and calf length leather boots.

As I stepped from my car an hour later, I felt the sun to be excessively warm as its rays smote my forehead.

The patient, a large belligerent cow, with a semi-spherical mass, caked with dried dung, swinging below her vulva, was held by the neck in a metal milking bail in the middle of a large field, which sloped down to the papyrus-fringed margins of the lake. On the other side of the water, the shapely shoulders of Mount Longonot were revealed to perfection against a cloudless sky. As I gazed at this lovely landscape I was rudely brought back to earth by a hoarse grunt and the sight of the Sahiwal's back being bent into a semi-circle, as she strained in what I fervently hoped was a futile effort to expel the contents of her abdominal cavity through her terminal orifices.

As I stripped for action I felt a spasm of faintness and nausea, accompanied by a wave of clammy perspiration on my forehead.

Nick must have noticed something.

'Hey, man, Hugh, are you all right? You look a bit pale about the chops.'

'Yes, sure, sure. I'm OK. Touch of malaria perhaps.'

I gave the cow an epidural anaesthetic to abolish the worst of her propulsive excesses. The prolapse resembled one of those obscene medicine balls, with which sadistic physical education teachers are wont to torment their charges. It was as solid as lead, and in my dubious state, felt as heavy.

The desiccating effects of the equatorial sun had dried and evaporated its surface until it resembled a wrinkled, abandoned, overgrown vegetable marrow. Having washed and removed as much of the dung glued to its surface as I could, I began the tedious process of returning the prolapse from whence it came. The mass had to be lifted until it was level with the vulva, in order to ease its impeded circulation. Then it had to be manipulated through the lips of the vulva. The word manipulation suggests delicate and precise movements until the object of the exercise is attained. The replacement of a grossly congested and contused bovine cervical prolapse had nothing delicate about it. It can be done, and one is always surprised when it is done, but a good deal of kneading and pummelling are required before the task is completed. Now I knew why master bakers had massive forearms and shoulders. It was all that bashing away at the dough.

As I was not a master baker I decided to try other means to lessen the diameter of the grotesque mass I was unwillingly cradling in my arms.

'Nick, can you get me some sugar, please?'

Nick's sandy brows lifted a fraction. Perhaps he thought I was suffering from a sugar low.

'Hey, Ole Tipis, man.' He addressed one of the herdsmen in attendance, one of a number of non-participating observers. 'Na weza lete sukari? Chop, chop!' (Can you bring some sugar?)

Ole Tipis hitched up his skirts and dashed off in the direction of his hut. He returned with a bag of what looked like badly sifted gravel. This was the local sugar, a grey granular substance, with which I was familiar, as I was wont to add a teaspoonful of the same to my morning cup of chai. If I was lucky I would find and filter out the odd nuggets of foreign body before they entered my cup. If not, they would eventually beach themselves with a horrid crunch between my teeth. I would console myself with the thought that this coarse material was dietetically superior to the refined rubbish which western man daily poured down his throat. Certainly my cook thought so, for he regularly purloined pounds of the stuff from my larder.

With a liberal hand I sprinkled the sugar over the prolapse. There was a sharp intake of breath from the observers at this wanton profligacy. I waited impatiently for the Laws of Osmosis to come to my aid. This they did, but not to the extent to which I had hoped. A fair amount of the oedematous fluid trapped within the prolapse did indeed rise to the surface, but my hopes that this would reduce its size to that of a small, malleable grapefruit were dashed. By the time I had pummelled the mass to the size and shape of a deformed football, and forced it back and out of sight, much time had passed and much perspiration had been shed.

'Shit, man, Hugh, you're sweating like a pig,' said Nick, ever the one for the delicate turn of phrase.

As I inserted a series of sutures I decided that my feeble state dictated a gentle amble home, followed by an afternoon in the hammock.

As I gathered my implements together, a ragged barefoot youth panted up and thrust a folded piece of paper into my hand. On it was scrawled a message from the farm clerk requesting me to go to a farm near Gilgil to trim a bull's hooves. I thanked the tattered postman and muttered something unprintable about the phone always working when you didn't want it to, and vice versa.

'Tot siens, Hugh, take it easy, now!' Nick waved a meaty paw as I drove away. 'And thanks, man!'

The farm was called Ol Bolodi, a Maasai name, and the owner was an ancient aristocratic buffer, with the most colossal upper crust accent. Kind and thoughtful though he was to plebs such as myself, I didn't expect to see him out in the afternoon sun, hauling away on the ropes. He was probably lolling back in his rattan chair, shouting for another pink gin before tiffin.

The dusty track wound its way through thickets of grey leleshwa bushes, now almost colourless in the blinding light as the sun approached its zenith. A small group of zebra standing motionless in a clearing shuddered and shimmied in the heat haze. A ponderous eland moved off in slow motion. The heat inside the car was terrific and it was not possible to go fast enough to generate a cooling draught. Some sadistic road builder had constructed a series of near vertical drainage ridges, inserted diagonally across the track, and by the time I reached the farm buildings I felt as though my temperature had risen by several degrees.

'Surely it's not that hot?' I thought.

As I got out of the car I noticed a purple mark, about the size of a pea, on my leg, but such was my spaced-out feeling that I paid it no attention.

The bull, a Hereford, was a huge, curly headed fellow, with a bright copper ring in his nose. After persuading him to enter a double strength bull yoke, a gang of cattle men hauled up a leg by means of a rope flung over an overhead beam. As they did so they chanted the local landlubber's equivalent of the sea-shanty, as sung by mariners of yore as they hoisted sails to the yardarm. Under other circumstances I would have been enchanted by this touching musical rendition.

The bull had bovine ingrown toenails and because of the recent dry weather his hooves were as hard as pressed steel. Initially I seemed to make as little impression with my hoof cutters as I would with a toothpick on a block of Aberdeen granite. Gradually, however, the outer defences crumbled and I made slow, if strenuous, progress, until Curly's massive hooves were shaped into something approximating the norm. This was not achieved without discomfort suffered by both parties: the bull by having his legs winched into abnormal and uncomfortable angles, and me from the stooping and head lowering necessary to carry out this crude chiropody, which had the effect of increasing my already-raised intracranial pressure, until I felt that at any moment my skull might explode with a loud and unpleasant report.

As I retired from the fray and bumped slowly down the track I observed with detached interest how the volcanic cones on the flanks of Mt. Eburru danced crazily in the superheated air. Further on, the crater called Delamere's nose overlooking Lake Elementaita, assumed grotesque proportions until it resembled a cloning of the snouts of the late Jimmy Durante and Charles de Gaulle.

Saturday afternoon found me reclining on my couch like a dyspeptic Turkish pasha sending smoke signals up to the Almighty, asking for no further calls that day. The purple blemish on my nether limb had increased in size, my torso was now bespeckled with an unpleasing rash, and the waves of nausea which periodically assailed me seemed to be more on the flow than the ebb. Feeling the approach of a neap tide, I rose in some haste in order to reach the basin beneath my bed. As I did so, the thatched roof of the rondavel began to whirl round in a fast and furious fandango and I almost fell to the floor.

Dr Satchwell, the Irish medico, who had attended to me during the fractured femur episode, lived nearby and I decided to phone him, if only to confirm my own provisional diagnosis. Judging by the shortness of his

221

response to my queries, I appeared to have disturbed him during his post prandial siesta.

'And let me tell ye, young fella, I'll be the judge o' what's wrong with ye. Bloody vets. Always diagnosing themselves! I'll be round shortly.'

Half an hour later the choleric Irishman entered my humble dwelling. Leaning heavily on his walking stick, he glared at my recumbent form. Whipping a thermometer from the pocket of his tweed jacket, he thrust it under my tongue. I hoped it had been sterilized. As he pulled down my lower eyelids, the better to observe my mucous membranes, I was afforded a frightening close-up of his large proboscis, which varied in colour from mauve through several shades of purple to violet and puce, and was patterned with a sinuous network of veins which resembled the branching tributaries of some mighty tropical river. The result of a lifetime's dedication to Guinness and Irish whiskey. Satch retrieved his thermometer, glanced at it, and, in the manner of most doctors, shoved it back into his pocket with a non-informative grunt. I did not tell him that I had already, with my previously sterilized veterinary thermometer, taken my temperature, and knew that it was five degrees above normal.

I pointed out the tell-tale blotch on my leg. Satchwell's eyes gleamed with delight. He drew nigh and peered closely at the site with all the enthusiasm of a forty niner stumbling across a nugget of gold in a pile of discarded pay dirt.

'Sure, it's tick typhus you've got and it's into hospital ye must go.'

I felt gratified that my presumptive diagnosis had been confirmed by the local expert. The mark on my leg was where I had been bitten by an infected tick carrying the organism responsible for the disease. I felt less gratified to be thus summarily dispatched to the infirmary while still capable of standing on my own two feet. To prove the point, I essayed a casual stroll across the rondavel and almost fell down again.

'You do that again and ye'll founder yer heart, ye eedjit,' said Satch.

'OK, OK, I've got the message,' I said.

My arrival at the hospital resembled the welcome given on the return on the Prodigal Son. Even Miss Brown was there and unbent so far as to allow the faintest glimmer of a smile to crack – ever so briefly – her armour plated features.

I had underestimated the gravity of my condition and for the next ten days I was almost glad to be in hospital, in spite of the insipid food, the lumpy bed and the constant disturbances by the night nurses and the antisocial activities of the nearby trains. I was unsure whether my condition was being improved or worsened by the medicinal compounds with which I was dosed, morning, noon and night. Shortly after the start of the treatment I went into a sudden and dramatic decline. For 24-hours I was unaware of my surroundings. An ominous placard was hung on the door of my room, barring all visitors. Then the treatment was changed and thereafter I made rapid progress towards recovery.

Light relief was provided one memorable afternoon during one of Satchwell's regular visits. He arrived accompanied by Miss Brown, who stood, grim-visaged, at the foot of the bed while he carried out his examination. This done, he turned to take his leave. As he did do, he espied a large cockroach crawling up the wall. It had probably just dined on a morsel of the desiccated sponge pudding, which had formed the latter part of my mid-day meal, and was now returning to complete its digestive processes in peace and quiet behind the chest of drawers, which stood in the corner of the room. Its feelers waved gently to and fro as it ambled up the wall. Satchwell's hunting instincts were immediately aroused. Before he could be stopped and before the cockroach could be alerted to the approaching danger, the good doctor had seized his walking stick, and crushed the wretched insect against the pristine paint.

It would be a gross understatement to say that Miss Brown was displeased. As she gazed incredulously at the brown mess sticking to the wall, her features slowly turned white with fury. I slid a little further down the bed. Satch gave a rather sheepish smile, as if to indicate that he didn't know what had possessed him to eliminate the cockroach in such a crude fashion, all the while waiting for the inevitable storm to break. For a full ten minutes it raged around his hoary head. Then he grinned, gave me a wink and limped out.

A few days later I was discharged, but advised not to over-exert myself and if possible to take a week's break at the Coast, so that there would be no risk of damage to my heart. I decided to follow this advice, although by now I was beginning to wonder if a prerequisite for a visit to the Coast was a sojourn in the Nakuru War Memorial Hospital.

Roy Richards, a roly poly butcher friend, offered me the use of his house at Kilifi, about 35 miles north of Mombasa, together with the services of his resident cook. I accepted with alacrity.

I made a staggered departure towards the Indian Ocean.

Prior to my entry into hospital, my car had been experiencing radiator and fan belt problems, so I decided it would be wise to have these attended to before I left. Accordingly I asked Stewards, the Peugeot agency in Nakuru, to rectify the situation and left the vehicle with them on the day before my departure.

The following morning I collected the car and set off, a song on my lips. About ten miles beyond Naivasha I heard a noise like a metallic woodpecker tapping its way through the forequarters of the vehicle. Hurriedly stopping, I raised the bonnet. A quick inspection revealed that the fan had been put on back to front and as a result it was doing its best to eat its way through the radiator. How it was possible to put a fan on back to front was beyond my comprehension, but Africa is daily littered with such examples of perverted genius, which are accepted without comment by the native inhabitants; with incredulous fury by newly-arrived expatriates; and with dumb resignation by long-term settlers.

I did a temporary repair and closed the bonnet. A rapid U-turn had the assembled goat boys and passing hewers of wood and carriers of water scuttling nimbly towards the verge.

Back at Stewards I surrendered the car to the tender mercies of the Kamba foreman. I gave him a curt description of my findings and requested a speedy correction.

He bared his teeth in a huge grin.

'Ndiyo, bwana, tafanya mara moja!' (Yes, sir, it will be done right away!) I had been in Africa long enough to know what mara moja meant and it wasn't what my Swahili/English dictionary said it meant. I did not press the point, as it would probably have resulted in the job taking twice as long. When the foreman laughed so jovially at my modest request, I took note of the fact that his canines were filed to needle-sharp points. In my book only cannibals and vampires had teeth like that and I had no wish to irritate either.

About an hour later I left town for the second time and on this occasion the journey was trouble-free. I enlivened the coastward drive with a brief foray into Tsavo National Park to examine the elephant, rhino, buffalo and other variegated wildlife at close quarters. Several days spent relaxing beneath the coconut palms, quaffing tankards of Whitecap lager, interspersed with soothing bathes in the almost too-warm ocean, served to speed me towards recovery.

✼✼✼✼✼

I entertained fond hopes that on my return from the languid delights of the palm-fringed strand, I would be able to ease myself gently and surreptitiously into full harness. I was speedily disabused on this point. News of my imminent return had preceded me from tropic shore to breezy highlands. Word of mouth, rumour, conjecture, hearsay, the latter day bush telegraph served to project items of interest over hundreds of miles with amazing rapidity.

The fact that for every mile of distance covered the news item departed markedly in detail from the original truth did not lessen the interest engendered by these transmitted gems. Deviation and hyperbole served to fan the flames of imagination. In my case, the exception proved the rule and my return had been accurately reported.

The drive from the coast had taken eight hours. I had made a late start, reluctant to leave the soporific seaboard and it was dark by the time I parked outside my rondavel. As I opened the car door, feeling as though I was suffering from terminal gluteal gangrene, the first sound that struck my ears was that of the telephone.

I staggered inside. My factotum, Njoroge, was on duty, moving some dust around, presumably in an effort to give the impression that he had not spared himself during my absence to keep things spick and span. The cobwebs, complete with occupants, with which the eaves were festooned, were a mute, but eloquent, denial of his deceptive efforts.

The phone stopped, just as I stretched out a hand to pick it up. I breathed a sigh of relief. A few minutes later, as I was unpacking my suitcase, it rang again. This time I was not so lucky.

It was the manager of Kiratu Progressive Farm. I groaned. Bitter experience had taught me that whenever the word 'progressive' or 'modern' was included in a farm's title the chances were that the conditions thereon were likely to be primeval.

'Harro, daktari, harro, can you hear me? Harro! Harro! Are you there? We are having our cow here, endeavouring to have child since two days. The cow, he now cannot stand. We have been trying to assist as you were not available, being, we were told, on safari.'

'Mmm,' I thought. 'Some safari. Sounds like a bit of blame transference.'

'OK,' I said, 'What else can you tell me?'

'The calf has no front legs as they came off when we pulled, so it is dead. You are coming very soon?'

'Great,' I thought. 'Here we go again!'

Not for the first time was I to be presented with a parturient animal in dire straits, at all hours of the day and night, often due to the absence of owner or farm manager. Feelings of self-righteous wrath, which helped neither wretched patient nor blood pressure, would rise unbidden to the surface, when I received such messages.

'Nyathuna Farm: cow stuck calving – pulled calf – now broken in two.'

'Peter Kihara: cow, chap thinks it's due to calve, its insides seem to be coming out.'

'Muriuri Kimani: midnight – cow stuck calving for five days.'

On one memorable occasion I was called to calve a cow, which had been neglected for so long that I was able to inform the herdsman, who was guiding me across the large paddock in which it lay, that his charge was already dead. When he asked me how I knew, when I had not even examined the animal, I drew his attention to a vulture sitting on her corpse. It flew off, looking rather peeved, as we drew near.

But back to my current challenge: as the present cow had been in her predicament for at least two days, I felt that a few more minutes would make little difference to the outcome, while fortification of the inner man might tip the scales in her favour. Strength, patience and perseverance were essential ingredients to the successful outcome of the average Kenyan calving, and these were unlikely to be present when one felt faint with hunger and thirst, when one's stomach had contracted to the size of a marble from disuse, and one felt irritable to boot. Accordingly, I requested Njeroge to pull up his non-existent socks and boil an egg and make a cup of tea.

Having thus followed the dictates of the ads which at one time exhorted the British public to 'go to work on an egg' – until cholesterol reared its ugly head – I drove to the surgery. There I loaded my drugs and instruments into my car and set off.

As I did so, a light rain began to fall. To my dismay this rapidly increased in intensity until the wipers were barely able to cope with the deluge battering the windscreen. The farm lay about ten miles to the south west, a short distance for the average crow, but one that took an inordinate time for earth-bound mortals. The initial part of the route lay through a succession of noisome alleys, where furtive figures could be glimpsed, peering suspiciously from the interiors of dimly lit, open-doored, window-less, wooden shacks. An open drain, transected at irregular intervals by inflowing tributaries, split the track into two unequal parts. Progress, as a result, was somewhat jerky. The bed of the drain, normally a series of foetid, black pools, was now filled to capacity with a frothy, foaming torrent, upon whose tossing surface all manner of interesting debris was being borne towards the distant lake.

Having cleared the suburbs, the track wound its way through a belt of rural slums, which encircled the town like an impoverished and besieging army. Many of the properties were surrounded by a high fence made of irregular lengths of wooden off-cuts. Normally one's passage through this zone would be enlivened by the barking pursuit of the car by a relay of pi-dogs. The pelting rain effectively dampened their ardour.

I bumped and slithered down to a plank bridge spanning the Njoro River at a point where cattle drank and people drew their water. The approaches to the bridge, which was tilted at a slight angle and was innocent of hand rail, were unpleasantly glutinous and much churned by bovine hooves and human feet.

I crept cautiously across, dank fingers gripping the steering wheel, and ground to an ignominious halt in a mud wallow at the foot of a steep hill on the other side.

'Hell's Bells!' I muttered. 'Now take it easy, easy. One false move and you'll be spending the night in that ditch.'

Gently accelerating forwards and backwards, I rocked the car onto slightly firmer ground. Then, trying hard to ignore the ditches yawning hungrily on either hand, to the smell of roasting clutch and the whine of spinning wheels, I crept with agonising slowness to the top of the hill.

From here the way lay through the blighted remnants of a large sisal estate being broken up into small-holdings. I counted myself as fortunate in having been to the farm before. It was difficult enough to find during the hours of daylight, when every twist and turn in the track looked the same and no man seemed to know his neighbour's name. During the hours of darkness it was all-but impossible.

Finally I reached my destination and splashed my way into the deserted farmyard. The rain had eased slightly, but of human or animal life there was no sign. I blew the horn. Time passed. I was beginning to wonder if I had come to the wrong farm. Or, still suffering from the after-effects of the journey from the coast, I had imagined the phone call. Suddenly a face pressed itself against my window.

I jumped. It was the night guard. Clad in a moth-eaten black great-coat, the lower half of which he had hitched up to protect it from the omnipresent mire, he resembled a rather swarthy French poilu returning to his trench after a raid across the wire.

I rolled down my window.

'Wapi ngombe nashinda kusaa?' (Where's the cow stuck calving?)

Without taking his hands out of his pockets the guard pointed with his chin.

'Iko huko.' (She's over there.)

Depending on the emphasis laid on the word 'huko' it was usually possible to form a rough estimate of the distance from the speaker of the object under discussion. In this case I was fairly sure that the cow was not close at hand.

I asked the guard to jump in and show me where she was.

He clambered in, together with several pounds of clotted mud, which he spread around the front of the car. Over his shoulder he was carrying a tightly strung bow, while in his left hand he held a sheaf of arrows, the heads of which bore barbs of such a fearsome appearance that their extraction would have required major surgery. Sticking out of his right pocket was the handle of his rungu or club. He drew it out in order to seat himself more comfortably.

The head of this medieval weapon consisted of a single, enormous steel nut, of the type used to hold tractor wheels in place. I felt that my companion was suitably armed to have fought in the ranks behind the standard of the Black Prince, equally equipped for long distance combat and close quarter grappling.

After a circuitous guided tour of the farm, at the end of which I no more knew where I was than if I had attempted to thread my way blind-folded through Hampton Court Maze, we stopped beside a clump of trees. I could see a fire flickering in the darkness. The night-guard produced a pocket torch and switched it on. It produced a light of which the average glow worm would have been ashamed. Stumbling and slipping, I followed him towards the fire, beside which I could see a recumbent bovine form. As I drew closer I realised that the fire was surrounded by other recumbent forms, human in outline. Our arrival stimulated a number of these to rise. One prone figure, however, continued to slumber on for a further half an hour, head so close to the ashes that I feared for cerebral hyperthermia and expected at any minute the spontaneous combustion of the owner's hair.

I asked which of the worthies present was the manager.

'He hasn't come back from town since he went there to phone for you,' someone piped up in reedy Swahili, across the darkness. The voice seemed to find this a source of considerable amusement. In the flickering firelight I caught a glimpse of outsized incisors as a face split into an ear-to-ear grin. In my imagination I saw the manager propping up the bar of some urban tavern, lubricating his palate with a torrent of local firewater, the cow conveniently forgotten.

Trying to ignore the still-falling rain, I stripped for action.

Having always found it easier to deliver cows when they were standing, I wanted to know whether this patient was lying down because she was too idle to get up or whether the force employed by the yokels sufficient to rip off the calf's forelegs had crushed the all-important obturator nerves, and rendered the hind legs paralysed.

I asked the owner of the outsized incisors to step forwards.

'Uma mkia yake!' I ordered. (Bite her tail!)

The cow's tail was not in a sterile state and he indicated some reluctance to comply with my modest request. Eventually, goaded by the ribald comments of his mates, he selected what appeared to be a relatively clean section, bent and bit. To my relief the cow reacted by scrambling hastily to her feet.

I put a rope on her head and tied her to the nearest tree.

Lubricating my left arm, I inserted it with some difficulty through the swollen vulva. Lubrication was certainly necessary. The genital tract was so dry it felt as though it was coated with sand. Voicing my thoughts about inept management and poor herdsmanship, I poured a substantial volume of lubricant into the vagina and set to work.

The two-legged calf was well on the road to decomposition. Its hair was coming off, it was distended with gas and it stank to high heaven, with a smell which I knew would linger on my person for days. As the calf was minus its fore legs, it was essential to locate its head. I was glad that this at least had been left attached to the trunk. At full stretch of my arm I found it turned back along its flank. I could just touch an ear with my forefinger. By trying a little harder I managed to extend my reach by another couple of inches and got the aforesaid digit into an eye-socket.

I withdrew my arm and produced my eye hooks, two stainless steel hooks attached to soft ropes. Cupping one in my hand, I introduced it into the vagina and inched my way towards my goal. At the critical moment, just as I was about to slip the needle-sharp hook over the rim of the orbit, the cow made a unilateral decision and sat down. As I was up to my shoulder inside her I had little choice but to descend to Mother Earth with her, coming to rest in a supplicatory position behind her.

The ground was moist and, with the rain pattering through the trees, so was I. It was time for action. A supreme effort, a twist, a crack of joints strained to their limits and the hook was in. A tug and it was firmly anchored in the bone of the skull. I repeated the performance on the other eye, pulling the head a few inches closer by means of the rope attached to hook number one.

I requested the night-guard to surrender his rungu (club), to which I attached the two ropes. I gave the rungu to two men, re-inserted my arm, and told them to pull. As they did so, the calf's head came within reach. It felt abnormally large. Not without difficulty, I passed my hand over the top of its skull. This was surmounted by a huge dome. Hair was absent and there was a wide gap in the centre where the bones of the cranium had failed to meet.

It was a case of hydrocephalus.

'Thank you very much!'

While the men pulled, I manipulated the head until it was facing the outside world. In the absence of both forelegs this task was relatively straightforward. The next question was whether the head would navigate the perilous passage of the maternal pelvis. Although very big, the large aperture at the top of the skull gave grounds for hope that the cranium would be compressed as it was moved along. If the entire skull had been solid bone it would have been necessary to reduce its diameter by bisecting it with embryotomy wire, a difficult and strenuous task.

Pouring in some more lubricant I instructed the two men to continue pulling, but to pull carefully.

This seemingly simple command seemed to stimulate the two unseen sons of the soil at my back into a melee of purposeless activity, jerking and twitching at the ropes.

'Simama! Simama! Stop! Stop!' I roared. Visions of the head being ripped off rose unpleasantly before my eyes.

'Look, if you tear that head off, we're going to be here all blimmin' night trying to get the rest out, OK? Now only pull when I say so. All right, let's start again.'

They took heed and slowly the head inched its way through the pelvis and vagina. The swollen vulva slowed things up for a while and I thought I might have to do an episiotomy incision, which in the presence of a decomposed calf would almost certainly get infected.

The head, large as a football, slowly emerged, the skin white and devoid of hair. There was a sharp intake of breath followed by the sounds of mass expectoration as the men expressed their disgust. Slowly the neck and then the front part of the chest appeared, shedding hair and smell in equal proportions. The hair and skin were dry. The skull, where the eye hooks were inserted, began to part at the seams. I looped a calving rope around the chest behind the point from which the two forelegs had been so untimely ripped.

We carried on.

Infinitely slowly the chest crept into view, although, because the light from the dying fire was so dim, it was hard to see what little movement there was. But, despite the lack of illumination, it was becoming rapidly and depressingly apparent to me that the rear half of the calf was not going to come out still attached to the front half. As if to emphasize the point the lower thoracic vertebrae began to part company with their neighbours-a bit like watching a cliffhanger when the threads of the rope holding a suspended climber begin to snap and unravel, to the sounds of gasps and small, sharp cries from the audience. If I had had the energy I would also have been making small, sharp cries to accompany my gasps of exhaustion.

I called a halt to the proceedings to re-assess the situation. With an effort I stood up and straightened my aching back. I staggered to the car and dug out a large sharp knife. With this I cut the calf in half at the level of the lower ribs and removed the abdominal organs. As I did so I sensed an atmosphere of resignation descend like a lowering cloud upon my companions as I carried out this seemingly senseless action.

It was embryotomy time and as I prepared for the last act of what I fervently hoped the attendant critics would not classify as an unmitigated tragedy, I could feel unseen eyes boring into my person.

I handed the embryotome to the nearest man, sank to my knees and bent to my task. I threaded a weight, to which I had attached the embryotomy wire, over the back of the bisected calf until I reached its tail. I pushed it a bit further and withdrew my ravaged arm. Now it was necessary to retrieve the wire from below the calf's pelvis and draw it backwards so that it could be cut in half. At full stretch I could feel nothing but decomposed calf. I went in again over the calf's back and managed to shove the weight a few more centimetres into the unknown. It was enough. With an out stretched finger I could just touch it. Flopping in the mire like a Weddel seal making its way across the Antarctic ice towards the open sea, I managed to hook my overworked digit around the elusive weight and draw it out.

My relief was profound as I pulled the wire through the embryotome, attached it to its handle and gave both handles to my shadowy assistant. I pushed the end of the embryotome hard up against the calf's truncated spine, made sure that the wire was lying snug up against its tail and told my recruit to take the strain and start sawing. To my surprise and relief he performed like a hero, sawing smoothly with long, smooth strokes.

'Mzuri sana, rafiki', I croaked. (Thanks a ton, mate)

Too often a weak and jerky action results in the wire becoming jammed in the bone, or worse, breaking, ending in tears and a back-breaking action relay. But now there was no hitch, and there were no tears, only the occasional grunt from my auxiliary as he shifted position as the wire moved through spine and pelvis.

The job was soon done and the calf's pelvis was now in two pieces. I pushed one half forward into the uterus, and, despite the foetal legs being bloated with the gases of decomposition, their separate removal was an almost leisurely and relaxing affair compared with what had gone before. Calf hairs were super-glued to my arms and the stench was enough to knock out Samson, but these were minor irritants now that it was all over, bar the shouting.

I washed as best I could in a bucket of murky water, checked the uterus for damage, and finding that it was intact, slipped in a pessary and gave her an injection of oxytocin to contract it down. The placenta was still attached but it would separate later. Finally I gave her antibiotic and vitamins.

Someone had thrown some more wood on the fire and the scene, apart from the disjointed remains of the calf lying scattered on the grass, was rather more cheerful than when I arrived. A furtive pi-dog had crept in from the darkness and was nibbling nervously at one of the bloated hind legs. In contrast to the tense mood which had prevailed during the extraction of the calf, the air was now filled with a cacophony of laughter, chatter, jokes and shouts of merriment.

I noticed that the rain had stopped. I also noticed that the manager had failed to make an appearance.

'Might be stuck in the mud,' I mused. 'More likely drunk and disorderly in some bawdy house.'

The cow was still recumbent. I could see my acquaintance with the flashing grinders throwing back his head in a gargantuan guffaw as he discussed some of the finer points of the late obstetrical procedure with one of his cronies. He saw me looking in his direction and tried, unsuccessfully, to merge into the darkness. He looked decidedly mutinous as I approached, doubtless as a result of having seen the condition of the calf as it emerged. I pointed out that the cow's tail had been held well to one side throughout, but he was not convinced. As we debated the matter the cow settled the argument by considerately rising to her feet and strolling off without a backward glance.

I gathered up my ropes and instruments and, together with the night watchman, whose torch had by now expired, groped my way through the dripping greenwood to my car. In other parts of the world, such as Merry England or Bonny Scotland, after the successful completion of such a calving, one might expect to have one's hand wrung by the squire or laird, or even invited to partake of a cup of mulled wine or a dram by the cosy inglenook. I knew by now that things were different in Africa, and that if I expected to depart from the scene of the action with the huzzahs of the grateful peasantry ringing in my ears I would be sorely disappointed. They were by now probably bedding themselves down in their huts, having melted away as soon as the cow regained her feet.

I was reluctant to hazard the route by which I had approached the farm in case I slipped irretrievably into one of the deepening sloughs. The watchman described an alternative exit, which I decided to follow. This ran westwards, parallel to the river for several miles, before finally crossing it and meeting the road to Njoro. Apart from the occasional stretch of water covering the track it was almost too good to be true and half an hour later I was back home, steeped in an aroma which could have been cut with a scalpel, and wondering what were my chances of being paid, but thankful to be back on dry land and not spending the night stuck in the mud.

As I switched out the light a little later and composed myself for sleep the sound of drumming and singing started up nearby. It was loud and rhythmic. Initially I found it rather attractive and, thinking that the performance would be relatively short – it was after all 1am – hoped it would set me in the mood for slumber with its repetitive beat. At 3am the drummers and songsters were still hard at it. Every now and again there would be a short break, which I fervently hoped signified the end of their activities, but these were obviously only breaks for rest or refreshment, because after each pause the participants set to with renewed frenzy. The finer points of the various renditions were obviously passing me by. It all sounded the same to me.

The approach of dawn appeared to have a similar effect upon the assembled minstrels and choristers as it did upon the nocturnal affairs of Count Dracula.

As the first glimmer of light appeared in the eastern sky there was a sudden diminution in volume from drums, whose skins must have been rendered paper thin from hours of relentless pounding. Larynxes strained to their limits faltered hoarsely to a croaking pianissimo.

Finally there was a blessed silence as the members of the infernal glee club presumably fled the scene to their various abodes.

But by this time it was too late for sleep. After an endless night I was exhausted and it was time to get up.

⁂

The number of settler-owned farms continued to decline as their owners took advantage of the British buy-out scheme. It was a depressing business, participating in the end of a way of life, the unwanted termination of decades of endeavour, trial and error, failure and success. It struck hard at many farmers to see their flourishing farms, their acres of coffee and wheat, their sleek cattle and fat sheep, handed over, for whatever price they were offered. The vast majority accepted their lot gracefully. The wind of change was far too strong for a few white farmers, however progressive, to resist.

Despite the taxing circumstances the tradition of settler hospitality continued unabated, and I seemed to be wined and dined after every job I did.

All the cattle in each herd had to be identified by ear tagging, all the cows and heifers had to be pregnancy tested. Their ages had to be checked, their teeth, eyes and udders examined. Any blemishes or signs of ill health had to be observed and recorded. Should there be any suspicion that the herd was infected with a breeding disease, such as vibriosis, trichomoniasis or brucellosis, I would have to take samples and the sale might be delayed for several frustrating months until the situation was rectified.

After the sale was over, the farmer would depart to his chosen destination. The elderly might retire to the Coast to have their declining years shortened by heat, humidity, boredom and alcohol. Others returned to the English shires, from whence they sprang. Many younger farmers left to start a new life in Australia, New Zealand, South Africa or Rhodesia. A handful of bold spirits found themselves pioneering in the wilds of Brazil and Bolivia. Very few of the younger men returned to Britain, a country which some regarded as having left them in the lurch, having encouraged them to settle in Kenya after the war, and then, less than twenty years later, sold them down the river. Few had genuine cause for complaint. Most had had a marvellous life farming in a part of the world where extremes of climate were rare, where labour was plentiful and cheap, the hard pioneering work had already been done and profits were assured – and at the end of the day, payment was made in sterling.

L.E.Goddard, who farmed at Rongai, was an exception to the general settler rule. Whenever I saw him I was reminded of Scrooge, in *A Christmas Carol*, by Charles Dickens. Unfortunately, in Mr Goddard's case no Ghost of Christmas Past, Present or Future had appeared to persuade him to correct his miserly ways. L. E. Goddard was thin-lipped, stoop-shouldered and narrow-gutted. He resembled an undersized, spent salmon, beached at the end of its final run upstream. He looked mean and he was mean.

To my dismay I received at short notice a request to examine Mr Goddard's herd, so that he could sell his cattle through the British buy-out scheme. It was hinted that the matter was urgent. There were 350 animals, all Friesians, including 80 heifers. The farm was 18 miles from Nakuru.

The dairy in which the milking cows were to be examined was a rude structure, which offered no concessions to hygiene nor to the comfort of the cows or the workers, who performed their tasks squatting upon makeshift stools or blocks of wood. The floor was made from rough-hewn stone and the roof was a patchwork of corrugated iron sheets, supported by cedar posts. Eight cows could be milked simultaneously.

Opening off one end of the dairy was a gloomy annex. Within was a table, shiny and slippery with grease, at which sat a clerk, recording milk yields in a grubby and much-thumbed ledger. Suspended from the roof was a hook and a spring balance. Here each cow's morning and evening yield was weighed, after which it was poured into a churn, in the neck of which was a square of cheese cloth, supposedly designed to filter out the larger particulate matter. In one corner of this horrid cell was a stone trough, sunk into the floor and filled with murky water, there to chill the evening's output until it could be sent the following morning to the milk factory in Nakuru.

I was extremely busy and because of the so-called urgency of the summons I was frequently obliged to visit the farm in the late afternoon, breaking off work with the onset of darkness. Mr Goddard seemed to regard this as a delaying tactic specifically designed to delay the sale of his farm, and regarded me with mounting suspicion.

As the cattle were known to the milkers and herdsmen by name only, I was obliged to ear tag the lot. At one shilling per head this did not please Mr Goddard, whose furtive figure, shaped like a mobile question mark, I could espy from time to time watching the proceedings from behind the locked gates of his nearby garden. My explanation that the party funding the whole exercise was unlikely to view favourably a certificate in which cows were only identified by names such as 'Baragoi', 'Tumbo' and 'Kenya Bus', was received by Mr Goddard with a snort through pinched nostrils and a muttered remark that it was merely a ploy to extract more money.

The rapport which the African milkers had with their cattle on this and other farms was fascinating to watch. They knew all the animals by sight and by name. They had only to call a cow by her name and she would amble through the waiting herd and obediently insert her head into the yoke, start munching her ration of food in the manger and stand quietly to be milked.

On occasion an especially apt name would be found for a particular animal. Bob Simpson, who farmed in Bahati, had the misfortune to possess a partial hare-lip. During a routine visit to a farm in the Solai Valley I observed a bull calf with a similar affliction. Inquiry revealed that the calf was called Robert.

Mr Goddard's dairy, I soon discovered, was not designed for the rapid or detailed examination of his cattle. In front of each yoke was a box-like contraption, constructed of aged, corrugated iron, which effectively screened the cow's head on three sides. Into this structure was deposited a ration of chopped maize. As part of my examination required a close scrutiny of every animal's eyes and teeth, the handicap of having to surmount these obstacles in order to separate the occupant from her evening meal and raise her head for inspection prolonged the whole procedure considerably.

This stimulated Mr Goddard to fresh bouts of irritation, which he later condensed into a summarised form and communicated to me in writing. My discovery that his heifers were infected with vibriosis caused his cup of hemlock to brim over and to conclude that I was conducting a personal vendetta to deprive him of a fair and honest price for his stock.

As the pregnancy rate in the heifers was unacceptably low and in their present state of infection they were deemed unacceptable for purchase I advised Mr Goddard on corrective action. This entailed removal of the bull responsible and calling the Artificial Insemination Service when heifers were seen to be on heat. The time scale required for significant improvement would be at least three months.

Mr Goddard went puce with rage.

I continued with my examination of the remainder of the herd, visiting the farm whenever I had a spare hour in the afternoon. As I did so, I assembled a detailed report of impressive proportions, copies of which were later presented to owner and buyer. The baleful aura, spread by the presence of Mr Goddard, seen or unseen, cast a pall over each visit.

Of the infected heifers only twenty percent were pregnant at the beginning of their period using artificial insemination. Four months later this percentage had risen to eighty, with a corresponding increase in their value and acceptability.

Mr Goddard received this information without comment or thanks.

Two months later, loyal British citizen that he was, he departed to settle in South Africa.

Six months later he had a heart attack and dropped down dead.

CHAPTER FOURTEEN

David Hayton-Hayward was in a panic, and on the phone.

Tall, well-fleshed and bespectacled, he was a pleasant, easy-going dairy farmer living on the outskirts of Nakuru. His laid-back nature extended to the settling of bills. He seemed to take the view that such matters were the province of tradesmen and the lower orders. When reminded of his indebtedness he would merely smile benignly, and by adroitly turning the conversation to such unrelated matters as the rocketing cost of school fees and the plummeting value of pigs and sheep, make me feel a first class heel for having mentioned the subject at all.

David was seriously stressed.

'Hugh, old fruit, it's Mildred. She's just been bitten on the nose by a puff adder.'

I reminded myself that Mildred was a dog and not his wife.

'Mildred's my Great Dane bitch, as you know. She's only six months old and I don't want to lose her! I was out having a quiet post-luncheon stroll on the farm, when she turned aside into a patch of dead grass and started barking at something on the ground. Then she leapt backwards with a yelp and there was this bloody great puff adder, which slithered off into the bush, but I caught up with it and bashed its brains out with my walking stick. Happened only five minutes ago, and already she's beginning to swell up.'

'OK, David' – I almost said 'old fruit' – but stopped myself just in time –'just get here as fast as you can.'

The puff adder has the rather unsporting habit of lying camouflaged and immobile until its prey arrives within striking distance of its haemotoxic venom, which causes severe local tissue damage, massive swelling and destruction of the area bitten and, without treatment, an unpleasant demise.

Fortunately I had been in the surgery when David had phoned and he arrived, panting, some ten minutes later. Although such a short time had elapsed since his dog had been bitten, already there was a large, painful, oedematous swelling extending from the bridge of her nose down to her upper lip.

With their splendid Teutonic efficiency, the German firm Behringwerke had developed an anti-snakebite serum, effective against all the major venomous snakes of East and Central Africa. In my fridge were a few vials of this invaluable lifesaver, still available at a price which the average animal owner could afford without risking bankruptcy.

Because anti-snakebite serum is of equine origin, as are many vaccines administered to human infants, there is always a risk of allergic or anaphylactic reactions when it is given to people bitten by snakes. This risk is remote in animals and a full dose can be confidently given immediately by the intravenous route.

Each vial contained 10ml. I opened two vials, filled a 20ml syringe, and slowly injected the serum into the cephalic vein on the Great Dane's forearm. I followed this by an intra-muscular injection of a corticosteroid, methylprednisolone, to counteract the shock that frequently accompanies snakebite, to minimise the tissue destruction and to reduce the painful swelling.

'Now, David, Just to make sure things don't get infected, I am going to give Mildred a shot of long-acting penicillin.'

'Right.' David's eyes goggled apprehensively behind his lenses as I turned my attention to the site of the bite, carefully shaving the area to expose the fang marks, from which dark blood was oozing. I scrubbed them with an antiseptic solution and applied an antibiotic spray.

'When you get her home, David, soak a cloth in ice cold water and apply it to the ridge of her nose – that should help to slow the absorption of the poison. Don't worry: when anti-serum is given intravenously as soon after the bite as this, recovery is virtually guaranteed.'

A few days later David phoned to say that the swelling was almost gone and that Mildred was eating and behaving normally.

With any bite by a poisonous snake, without treatment, the prognosis generally worsens with the passage of time. Even so, I was constantly amazed by the ability of animals to recover, albeit assisted by the powers of modern science.

The sluggish puff adder was responsible for the vast majority of cases. The more active cobras and mambas tended to take avoiding action whenever animals larger than their normal prey were in the vicinity. The exception was naja nigricollis, the dreaded spitting cobra.

The majority of puff adder bites were on the head, nose or lips, and to a lesser extent on the forelegs. The swellings varied greatly in size, but dogs were frequently presented with heads so enlarged that their eyes were invisible, their lips up to two inches thick, with a great dewlap of oedema hanging below their jaws.

Despite their horrendous appearance the anti-serum was so effective that very few of these dogs died, and then only in cases of gross neglect.

The virulence of puff adder venom was vividly demonstrated in a canine survivor, resident at the Djinn Palace, a pseudo-Moorish mini-chateau on the south shore of Lake Naivasha, a former nerve centre of the Happy Valley set. The dog, an alsatian, had been bitten on the cheek some four days before I was summoned to render assistance. Treatment was given. The patient survived. The muscles of the cheek did not. As the swelling subsided, the affected tissue began to separate and slough, and, as the dead muscle and skin fell away, the bones and teeth of the jaw were exposed, a most unpleasant sight. The dog appeared to be little inconvenienced by this loss and ate with surprising vigour. Slowly, healing took place. Infinitely slowly, scar tissue and new skin crept like an advancing tide over the open bone, to be followed later by rear guard parties of isolated colonies of hair, whose subsequent growth and spread eventually resulted in a most satisfactory cosmetic appearance.

Horses and cattle were less frequently bitten, but, when they were, the results were often spectacular. The former, especially, reacted violently to puff adder venom. While grazing, a horse might have the misfortune to disturb a snake and be bitten on the nose or lip. The resultant swelling was often so large and grotesque that the wretched animal's head resembled that of a hippopotamus: square, solid and shapeless. The bitten horse usually had great difficulty in breathing. Its lips were so distended and painful that eating was impossible. Blood-stained fluid trickled from the nostrils. When first confronted by such a scenario my heart sank as I observed this pathetic caricature of a once handsome animal, wondering how on earth it was possible to ease the obvious distress, let alone effect a recovery and trying to decide how soon it would die. The cost of anti-snake bite serum, and the number of vials required, prohibited its use except in extremely valuable animals. So I used corticosteroids, antibiotics and antihistamines, with gratifying results. Horses did not die. Although they endured several days of physical purgatory until the swellings subsided and their pain eased, they made remarkable recoveries.

Months might go by without a single case of snake bite being brought to my attention. Then I might see several cases in the course of a single week, especially after a spell of heavy rain preceded by a period of drought, when snakes were flushed from their places of refuge in holes, beneath logs or under stones.

The other snake, whose anti-social activities are notorious, is the spitting cobra. The fine jet of venom, which it is able to direct from a distance of several feet at the face of an approaching man or animal, is capable of causing blindness, or at the very least, extreme ocular discomfort. Although this long-distance ejection of poison through the fangs is really a defence mechanism, this is of little comfort to the unfortunate victim, who is probably rolling around in agony. The most effective remedy is to immediately wash out the eyes with water or milk. When neither of these are at hand, extreme measures are occasionally employed, such as urinating into the patient's eyes, a form of treatment which has led many East African residents to regard being spat at by a spitting cobra with more than usual trepidation.

The majority of animals presented for my attention had not benefited from any of these treatments and in many cases a lengthy course of therapy was required in order to effect a cure. The odd animal remained permanently blinded.

As did the occasional human.

One morning an elderly European farmer went out to examine his coffee bushes. He was arthritic and short of sight. As he hobbled between the dark green rows, his attention was caught by a movement in the lower branches of one of the bushes. He bent down and peered into the shadows to see what it was. As he did so, a spitting cobra, coiled there, spat at him, scoring a direct hit in both eyes, which were unprotected by spectacles. He reeled backwards with a cry of agony. Unable to see, he staggered drunkenly through the bushes, yelling with pain. His workers, on observing this alarming sight, thought that he had gone mad, and, instead of going to his assistance, took to their heels. By the time that the old man had collapsed and the cause of his delirium had been discovered, it was too late. His eyes had been permanently damaged and he was blind.

Others were luckier.

Rusty Drum did wear spectacles.

The kitchen of his farmhouse at Kampi ya Moto was an ill-lit and unsavoury chamber, which in the evening was filled with smoke from the wood stove upon which his aged cook struggled manfully to prepare his master's dinner. Stacked against one wall of this colonial cookhouse was a pile of firewood, or kuni, as it was universally referred to in Swahili. Directly opposite the kuni was a door leading into the house, where, after the day's work Rusty liked to relax with a tumbler of whisky before the arrival of his dinner.

One evening Rusty was feeling more than usually peckish and not a little irritated by the non-arrival of his food.

After having fussed and fumed for several minutes, he banged his glass down on the table and strode off to the kitchen to investigate the cause of the delay.

He entered the kitchen with some force and considerable noise.

This precipitate action caused a number of things to happen.

The ancient major domo, who was crouched in a foetal position over the stove, started violently, upsetting the bwana's soup, which cascaded onto the firewood so laboriously kindled, thereby effectively delaying even more the long-awaited repast. And a spitting cobra, concealed in the pile of kuni, alarmed and threatened by Rusty's sudden entry, reacted by sending two bursts of venom at his eyes, which were fortunately protected by his specs.

Rusty retreated rapidly in search of his shotgun.

The cook, meanwhile, was frantically doing his best to bore his way through the kitchen wall, Rusty having slammed the door shut behind him as he went out.

The snake had disappeared into the kuni by the time Rusty had returned with his Purdey's cocked, but he knew that it was there and he was prepared to wait all night if necessary in order to kill it. The house, certainly the kitchen, would be virtually uninhabitable while it remained on the premises.

Rusty and the cook waited in an almost palpable silence. After about twenty minutes, during which the only sounds were the thudding of the electricity generator nearby and the last sighs of the soup-swamped embers, the snake's head, tongue flickering, cautiously emerged from a chink in the stack of kuni.

Rusty waited until a few more inches were in view and then squeezed the trigger of his double barrelled shotgun.

Within the close confines of the thick walled kitchen the blast of the gun was deafening. The snake's head disintegrated. Its body slithered onto the floor, where it writhed and twisted in aimless contortions. Rusty lowered his shotgun. Then his eye fell on his aborted dinner, the extinguished stove and his cook, standing in the far corner of the kitchen like a non-survivor of the last days of Pompeii. He drew an extra deep breath, counted slowly up to ten, uttered an unprintable expletive, broke open his gun, removed the spent and unspent cartridges, turned on his heel and marched back into the house for another glass of Glenfiddich.

◎◎◎◎◎◎

After two year's residence in my rondavel, I moved to a slightly more salubrious and conformist dwelling in the shape of a two bed-roomed bungalow. This was not occasioned by any personal dissatisfaction I felt with my primitive one-roomed shack, but with the fact that I had persuaded my mother to come to Kenya for a holiday and I decided that more spacious living quarters were required to accommodate her, together with such little luxuries as an indoor toilet, bath and kitchen, running water, ceilings etc.

Locums were as scarce a commodity in Kenya as hen's teeth. Eventually I managed to obtain the services of a Norwegian veterinary officer, who agreed to deal with emergency cases on a part-time basis. This was less than satisfactory, but he served, like the boy with his finger in the Dutch dike, to stem the tide until I returned.

The East African Community was a functioning entity, and border crossings were accomplished with an ease and lack of formality which would astound today's harassed, ulcerated traveller. Lodges produced value for astonishingly little money and the game parks were full of the animals so soon to be decimated by the poachers and the nabobs who controlled them. Uganda was a green and pleasant land. Idi Amin had yet to rise like a cannibalistic Kraken from the stygian ooze of his native swamps.

So for three weeks I conducted my aging parent on an exhaustive and exhausting tour of the highlights of East Africa. Amboseli, the Serengeti, the Masai Mara Game Reserve, Tsavo National Park and Treetops were all graced by our presence. In Uganda a circular route brought us via Kampala to the Murchison Falls and Queen Elizabeth National Parks. Our departure from the latter coincided with fifteen hours of continuous heavy rain. The road ran up the wall of the western branch of the Rift Valley to Kichwamba and thence through forested country via Bushenyi to Mbarara, where we joined the main road to Masaka and Kampala.

Unfortunately the road between Kichwamba and Mbarara had recently had its epidermis ripped off by an Israeli construction company prior to its conversion into a deluxe tarmacadam highway. The soft underbelly of the road lay revealed, rendered even softer by hours of torrential rain. For seventy miles this embryo autobahn snaked through hilly, wooded, farming country, slashing through dramatic cuttings, soaring over dense forest with near vertical drops to right and left, coiling its way down the sides of steep valleys. The surface was ankle deep in dark red mud and the edges ended abruptly over drops I didn't want to look at. The adjacent Maramagambo Forest was shrouded in mist. My interest in the passing scene was continually being distracted by the overturned lorries, the buses stuck fast in the ditches, and the vehicles which had failed to negotiate the next bend and had shot off the road entirely. Travelling down the road sideways under a spray of red ochre concentrated my mind to the exclusion of everything except my immediate surroundings.

Although my own field of vision was necessarily restricted to the road ahead, I had hoped that my mother might have been able to keep me apprised of the nature of the adjacent countryside and its exotic inhabitants.

I shot a quick glance in her direction.

Her eyes were closed and her lips were moving, Whether this was in silent prayer for safe delivery or a mute tirade at the driver, the rain and

241

the road makers, I neglected to ask. Her eyes remained closed for the next two hours.

Twenty miles beyond Kichwamba I desperately inquired of a gang of youths, who were pushing us up a hill, how much farther it was to Mbarara.

'Hapana mbale' (Not far!) they laughed, with that thoughtless optimism, which makes the average African such a pleasant fellow to deal with: that same thoughtless optimism, whose combination with the lofty and ill-conceived plans of the western expert has made Africa the grave-yard of so much foreign aid.

After another fifty miles of wondering how long we might have to spend in the next ditch, we finally rolled into Mbarara, the car covered from headlights to rear bumper in a representative soil sample from the foundations of the new road.

Treetops was a minor disappointment in that, as the shades of night descended upon the waterhole and the surrounding forest, so did a dense mist.

It is the custom in that establishment for sleeping guests to be woken when one of the larger denizens emerges from the woods to quaff its thirst at the pool.

It was therefore with some excitement that we scrambled from our bunks when aroused by an eagle-eyed flunkey battering on our respective doors.

In frantic haste we tumbled down the narrow stairs, expecting at the very least to feast our eyes on a herd of buffalo, a rhino or even a bongo.

All we saw through a curtain of mist were the baggy knees, wrinkled shanks and flat feet of a solitary elephant. It stood in what we assumed was morose discomfort in the mud at the edge of the pool. Occasionally the tip of its trunk appeared in the murk. Of its head, tusks, body and tail we caught not a glimpse.

A final few days spent at the Coast south of Mombasa rounded off the odyssey. There the atmosphere was rather clearer than that at Treetops, although, when, from time to time an overweight and underclad German or Italian sun worshipper swung into our ken, we wished it were less so.

❦❦❦❦❦

More farms were sold. In most cases this was a relatively rapid procedure. In some instances disputes arose over the value of stock, crops, land or machinery. Re-valuations then had to be done until a price agreeable to all parties was arrived at.

The vast majority of farmers relinquished their property without too much fuss. A few British farmers decided not to sell. Others had become Kenya citizens, while others of Greek, Danish or Italian nationality carried on farming amid a rising tide of peasant small holdings. There were instances where pressure, official or unofficial, was brought to bear, and, by making his life unbearable, the owner would cave in, sell and leave. The farmer might be attacked when he went out of his house to switch off the generator before going to bed. The occasional cow would be hamstrung. The culprits were rarely found. A farmer might wake up in the morning to find that his farm had been invaded during the night, with tractors ploughing up his fields, and gangs of women camped around his house. Recourse to the authorities was seldom satisfactory and most recipients of this sort of treatment eventually sold up and left.

For a while most newly-acquired farms remained intact entities, carried along by an ongoing momentum. Some, however, were rapidly divided into small subsistence units, to the sound of the felling of trees, the burning of bush and the erection of barbed wire fences.

Between Njoro and Mau Narok lay the extensive estate formerly owned by the Prettejohn family. For three or four years after its purchase by a co-operative society, it remained as it had done for the past decade. The property continued to be ranched and cropped in the relaxed, laid-back manner so assiduously cultivated by the previous owners. The tracts of forest and bush remained untouched and their wild inhabitants unmolested, except by the occasional wandering Ndorobo tribesman. The streams remained undammed and the grass in the glades grew tall and lush. Here grazed scores of semi-wild horses. Mostly grey or white, their manes and tails long and ragged, they were of Arab stock. Due to a lack of infusion of outside blood, several showed evidence of inbreeding, mostly in the form of deformed hooves. The majority, however, were of good conformation and made a splendid sight as they galloped through the forest clearings, manes and tails streaming in the wind.

In the face of the burgeoning population this happy state of affairs could not last long. The farm was surveyed and divided into hundreds of pocket handkerchief sized plots. The crack of axes, the crash of falling timber, and the whine of power saws replaced the sylvan silence formerly broken only by the bark of a bushbuck or the twittering of birds. As I passed up and down the road to Mau Narok I saw the area of exposed land growing with alarming speed, peppered with a rash of huts and tin roofed shacks.

The horses grew more and more nervous as their living space diminished. Then the new settlers, mostly Kikuyus, hired a gang of Maasai to eliminate them. Their weapons were mostly spears, bows and arrows and pangas. Horses were shot with arrows, hamstrung with pangas and speared to death.

Fortunately there were those who were prepared to expend time, trouble and money in order to capture and remove those horses which had escaped the slaughter. These included the Anti Stock Theft Unit at Gilgil, various ranchers and neighbouring farmers.

So the committee of directors which ran the fragmented farm was approached and permission was given for the removal of the remaining horses.

A large wooden stockade was built and a posse of men drove as many horses as were available inside. From here most allowed themselves to be persuaded to enter lorries backed up to a ramp. A few animals panicked and broke their way through or leapt over the side of the stockade.

The animals thus removed were transferred to secure horse-proof enclosures. They were, however, basically wild mustangs, untouched by human hand, and, in the light of their recent experiences, terrified of homo sapiens in any shape, colour or form.

At this point I was called in to render assistance.

Approximately half of the captured horses were stallions. Some of these were large, mature animals with thick, arched necks. Others were young, skittish colts. The rest were fillies, mares and foals.

One group of horses was at Gilgil, another was at Elementaita, while the third was at Njoro.

I advised that all the horses be kept confined, be fed well on lucerne, oats and bran, and, above all, be treated gently until physical handling was possible. Unfortunately there was no Monty Roberts among the syces assigned to this task, and so the process took several weeks. At the end of this period it was possible to handle and halter the mares, foals and fillies with a minimum of risk to life and limb.

The stallions and colts were a rather different matter.

It was decided that these should be castrated and haltered at the same time. Unfortunately, although by now approachable, they were far too wild to tolerate any form of physical restraint and any attempt would have resulted in an unacceptably high syce and horse wastage. In the Australian outback or on the South American pampas, the risks might have been justified and the horses expendable. With the tyro horse handlers I had at my command, I decided that a little more finesse was required if mass hospitalisation was to be avoided.

To this end I purchased a dart gun, a gas-powered pistol of American manufacture and design. It was powered by a small carbon dioxide cylinder and the barrel held the appropriate size of light alloy syringe. This was filled with the requisite immobilising drug, while a nosepiece incorporating a needle was screwed into the business end. At the other end was a recessed rubber plunger into which fitted a cartridge-type detonator. When the syringe hit the animal the impact exploded the tiny detonator, propelling the plunger forwards and injecting the syringe contents in a fraction of a second.

Thus armed, I was ready to do business.

The most suitable immobilising drug, which also conferred a period of anaesthesia of sufficient depth to enable me to do the job, was etorphine. This was available commercially under the trade name Immobilon, and it also contained the tranquiliser Acetylpromazine. The effects of Etorphine could be conveniently reversed by the antidote diprenorphine, marketed as Revivon. When given by intravenous injection it dramatically reversed the effects of etorphine in about ninety seconds.

Etorphine, originally known by its number-99 in the M series of compounds, was first developed for the chemical immobilisation of large African herbivores, in particular, elephant, rhino, giraffe, zebra and wildebeest, and as such proved to be outstandingly successful. It is a derivative of morphine, but is several thousand times more potent, and its use demands a modicum of care and common sense. An accidental needle prick and you are on your way to joining your ancestors.

I had used the drug on several occasions when gelding more tractable colts, and was well aware of its dangers and limitations: the profound respiratory depression, when I sometimes wondered whether the horse was dead or alive; the sweating; the loud rapid heart beat and raised blood pressure; the lack of muscular relaxation; and the frequent muscular tremors. A formidable list indeed, and one which caused much hypertension and controversy amongst the equine arm of the veterinary profession. In my view these disadvantages were outweighed by the drug's advantages: its rapidity of action; the excellent analgesia; its reversibility; and by the fact that it could be given by intramuscular injection – something not possessed by any of the other injectable anaesthetic agents available. All the others had to be given intravenously, which was out of the question in the present situation.

At Njoro about twenty horses had been gathered on Montello Ltd, a large farm owned by one of the ubiquitous Italian counts. The manager was Frank Roos, an Afrikaner, who, in independent Kenya, still retained his South African passport. Short, barrel-chested, his bald head and bare legs burnt mahogany by the sun, he was a walking example of an iron hand inside a velvet glove. His pleasant, good humoured manner belied the firmness of his character and under his direction the farm ran like clockwork.

After about a month's residence on the farm the first group of colts and stallions was judged to be ready to receive my attention.

I arrived late one afternoon, armed with dart pistol, Immobilon, Revivon, scalpel and emasculator. Usually I preferred to castrate colts in the early morning, before the sun became too hot and so that there was plenty of time during the day for any untoward effects to be seen and attended to. An excess of work on this occasion meant that I had to come when I was able.

My unsuspecting patients were grazing quietly in a large field.

Frank Roos was on hand.

'Good afternoon, Mr Cran.' Frank was always very formal and polite. 'You may be performing before an audience!' His dark eyes twinkled.

'Really?'

'Yes, it's milking time.'

Close by was the dairy, separated from the field by a dirt track. The cows were being driven into the yard over the rockery and through the swamp, which guard the entrances to most Kenyan dairies. Scores of women and children, and numerous men were waiting for their evening milk ration, all carrying a variety of containers, ranging from tin cans to beer bottles. The arrival of a mzungu resulted in a collective pricking of ears and within a few minutes a sizeable crowd had gathered along the fence line to watch the daktari in action.

While assistant Moses laid out the requisite ropes and instruments, I assembled and filled the dart syringe, screwed on a one and a half inch needle, and slipped it in into the barrel of the pistol. I filled a hand-held syringe with the antidote and was ready for my first mustang.

I had chosen a large, well developed grey, which, judging by his dished face, had a fair volume of Arab blood coursing through his veins. If the size of the organs I was about to remove was anything to go by, he must have been responsible in no small degree for the dramatic increase in the wild horse population.

I cocked the pistol and slipped on the safety catch.

'Mr Roos, would you please ask everyone to stand well behind me. A few drops of this stuff can kill and I don't want to have any more blood on my hands than necessary.'

Frank barked a few words in Swahili and, looking suitably impressed, syces and camp-followers all withdrew to a respectful distance.

Walking slowly, I carefully approached the stallion from the rear, stopped when ten yards away, slipped off the safety catch, aimed and fired the syringe into his ample rump. He gave a little leap, kicked his heels in the air, dislodging the syringe and then resumed his grazing as though nothing had happened.

For the next few minutes he continued to crop the greensward, until I began to wonder if the syringe had discharged its contents. The growing mob of onlookers watched impassively.

Then the stallion stopped grazing, raised his head and, with a glazed expression in his eyes, began to goose step in slow motion, like an inebriated Prussian soldier on parade. Twice he stumbled to his knees and then he collapsed onto his side.

There was a burst of cheering from the crowd as the stallion went down.

I had briefed one of the syces to restrain the animal's head by kneeling on its neck as soon as it descended to earth. This he did with commendable speed. I followed more leisurely, waiting for the drug to exert its full effect.

I covered the horse's eyes with a towel to protect them from sun, dust and flies. Next I gave a prophylactic injection of antibiotic and a shot of tetanus antitoxin, and, slipping a soft cotton rope round the upper hind fetlock, gave it to a syce to hold out of my way.

The testicles of young colts can sometimes be difficult to locate. With this fellow there was no such difficulty. They were the size of coconuts. After swabbing the skin with methylated spirits I made what the textbooks call a bold incision and set to work. After withdrawing the first gonad I cut and clamped the spermatic cord with my emasculator, giving the instrument to Moses to hold while I ligated the blood vessels with strong catgut, an essential precaution when castrating colts anaesthetised with a drug which raises the blood pressure. Trying to stop profuse haemorrhage from a twitchy, fully conscious, recently castrated colt can be the stuff of a vet's nightmares.

Within a few minutes the stallion had been converted into a gelding, the rope had been removed from his leg and a halter put on his head, and I was ready to administer the antidote. This I gave by intravenous injection into the jugular vein.

I stood back to observe its effect.

Preoccupied as I was with the job in hand, I had failed to observe that the host of onlookers had surreptitiously crept through the wire fence and had tiptoed to within a few feet of the unconscious horse, the better to watch the surgeon in action.

By the time I noticed them, it was too late.

The horse suddenly raised his head and, then, with a convulsive leap, was on his feet, bounding across the paddock like a demented kangaroo.

There was a communal scream from the uninvited guests as, with one accord, they turned and fled, bursting their way back through the fence, like a herd of maddened wildebeest. Women and children scrabbled helplessly on the ground, borne down by an unseeing and uncaring tide of men-folk, who trampled over them like a herd of stampeding elephants.

Miraculously, no-one was hurt as the horse, confronted by what appeared to be an advancing Zulu impi, had shied violently to one side and thundered off in the opposite direction.

By the time the excitement had subsided, the horse was standing quietly in the far corner of the paddock, minding his own business.

Frank Roos was bent over, shaking with laughter.

'Man, Mr Cran, that was the funniest thing I've seen in years! I would never have thought that cutting colts could be such fun!'

Everyone seemed to think the same and a great roar of mirth ran through the crowd.

In the years to come I darted scores of horses and castrated hundreds of colts using Immobilon and reversed their anaesthesia with Revivon, but I always made sure they were pointing away from any spectators, official or unofficial.

Meanwhile I dealt with the rest of the mustangs on Montello, performing before a markedly thinner audience. The seats in the stalls, I observed, were vacant.

Of the three hundred feral horses roaming the forests between Njoro and Mau Narok only a few score were captured. The rest scattered. Most of these met untimely ends.

Many years later I was to encounter the last of these wild horses, and their descendents, in bizarre and alarming circumstances in the olive forest overlooking the western shore of Lake Nakuru.

* * * * *

On Saturday mornings I held a surgery for small animals between 11am and 1pm. Sometimes I actually finished at 1pm but this was about as rare as sighting a walrus off Mombasa. When the last client did finally depart I would phone my cook to find out if any calls had been made to the house and to advise him that I would be along soon. This procedure frequently took some time, despite the fact that an outside telephone bell had been installed directly above the kitchen door. This was because my cook was an extraordinarily sound sleeper.

I lived in the hope that while I was toiling with thermometer, forceps and scalpel, he would be similarly toiling at his pots and pans, preparing tiffin for the sahib.

Unfortunately for my stomach, Saturday lunch was an immovable feast, and when the latter had been prepared, the former was seldom present. This was partly because my cook was of a stubborn disposition and a man of rigid habits, who refused to be swayed by trifles such as canine fractures, bovine births or equine colics, with which I might be embroiled. Lunch, if eaten at all, should be eaten at 1pm and if I failed to appear, it was just too bad.

One Saturday I phoned home as usual.

Answer came there none.

I laid the phone down and allowed it to ring while I cleared up the surgery. Five minutes later it had still not been answered.

I decided to investigate.

Perhaps poor old Njoroge had dropped down in the midst of his duties, felled by a massive heart attack, or been overwhelmed by gas from a leaking cylinder, or been slashed by a gang of panga-wielding thugs and was even now desperately trying to drag his poor, grievously wounded body towards the ringing telephone as his life's blood drained away.

The possibilities were endless.

Allowing the phone to continue ringing, I closed the surgery door and drove home.

As I passed through the gates and onto the very short drive leading to the closely juxtaposed front and back doors, I could hear the outside telephone bell sounding shrilly in the hot, still air. The latter door, leading into the kitchen, was open and I could see a pot on the stove. Judging by the fumes issuing from it, whatever was within was on the point of incineration. On the microscopic lawn outside the back door lay a prone figure, spread-eagled upon its back, mouth open, eyes closed, limbs relaxed.

It was my cook.

The phone continued its noisy clangour, but the figure did not move.

I inched the car closer for ease of observation.

My steward's chest rose and fell in that gentle rhythm indicative of well-established slumber.

My fears for his safety had been ill founded.

I crept a few feet closer and gave the horn a sharp, peremptory blast.

Njoroge, eyes still closed, jack-knifed into a sitting position.

After a few seconds in what appeared to be a yoga-like trance, he opened his eyes, heaved himself to his feet, gave a rather irritated glance in my direction and strolled unhurriedly into the kitchen, there to administer the last rites to the morbid remains of my lunch.

I knew that to remonstrate with Njoroge at this moment would be akin to sticking a needle into a grizzly bear, newly-emerged from hibernation: a procedure unproductive to both parties.

The more subtle, delayed approach, such as putting my sugar supplies under lock and key, or asking for the only slightly dirty lounge curtains to be washed, omitting any reference to the recent momentary lapse, was a more satisfactory admonishment.

On those rare Saturdays, when I did arrive home in time to ingest an unburnt offering, the onset of my digestive processes seemed to act as a catalyst for whatever animal emergency, near or far, was about to happen. If a call failed to come in during the act of mastication, then it was only waiting until I had collapsed into an arm chair, boots off and beer in hand.

As far as the animal was concerned, an emergency was a serious matter, as indeed it was for me. The majority of owners thought likewise, and did their best for both parties by contacting me as soon as the adverse state of affairs was brought to their attention. Even so, due to various circumstances, such as non-working or non-existent telephones, distances of up to a hundred miles to be covered in either direction by vet or owner, awful roads, and the widespread myopia on the part of those assigned to observe and report on animals under their care, many cases were in dire straits when I was called upon to strain my various nerves and sinews on their behalf. Emergencies, such as poisonings, equine colics, snake bite, and foalings, were serious enough when attended to immediately. When treatment was delayed by hours or even days, the margin between death on the one hand and recovery on the other narrowed to the veterinary equivalent of one of the ridges of the Matterhorn, where success could be only attained by skill, constant vigilance and strenuous effort. An unforeseen complication or a pre-existing condition could bring all to naught, with the patient a lifeless lump and the luckless vet tasting the bitter bile of defeat and disappointment and possibly the opprobrium of a disgruntled owner.

It was bad enough when delays in obtaining treatment were due to natural causes. When they were due to the inattention or neglect of owners I tended to get more than a little irritated. A common cri de coeur was 'I've just got back from safari!' This would often occur on a Sunday evening well after dark. Although the sick animal might well have been spotted by herdsmen or grooms, their lowly status frequently prevented them from having access to their owner's telephone, which was in many cases locked, ostensibly to prevent its being misused during the latter's absence at near or distant fleshpots.

Another excuse, commonly employed during cases of neglected calvings, was the statement that 'we thought she would calve by herself, so we waited a bit longer'. This bland utterance was in the main made during the hours of darkness, with the wretched patient unable to rise, the calf dead and bloated inside her and with a freezing wind or icy rain further reducing her chances of survival. It was at such times that I occasionally wondered about my own chances of survival.

Worst of all was an emergency caused by an owner 'having a go' himself, using the drugs so easily obtained without prescription from pharmacies. With his minimal knowledge, stabbing blindly in the dark, he would treat the animal and hope for the best. Sometimes it worked. When it didn't, I would be called upon to resurrect the unfortunate patient. Or a farmer might attempt to calve one of his own cows, and fail, causing irreparable damage to mother and calf, and then call me in to salvage the wreck.

When a farmer, rancher or other animal owner lived beyond telephonic communication or veterinary assistance, he had no choice but to treat his own animals. Where he resided where such facilities were available, he had little excuse, no matter how poor he might be. There was nothing to prevent anyone from treating his own stock, of whatever species, but when such arrogance failed to produce the desired results it struck me as the height of impertinence to drag a professional from his bed to bail out the amateur botcher.

I would have preferred to have had nothing to do with such cases, but the plight of the maltreated animals left me with no choice but to restrain my wrath.

'Do your utmost and charge double', became my mantra.

Michael Stroud did not regard himself as a lay healer.

An ex-Guards officer, he was tall and good looking, seemingly a prerequisite for entry into that august establishment, together with the essential private income. Michael spoke impeccable English in a cultured upper class accent, but, despite having spent the best part of two decades in Kenya, his knowledge of Swahili was less than impeccable, being virtually limited to 'jambo' and 'kwa heri' (hello and good-bye), and such abominations as 'steward, please bringi pinki gini kubwa for memsahib'.

On the shores of Lake Baringo, 65 miles from Nakuru, Michael and his equally tall and equally good looking wife, Joanna, owned and ran a private lodge. There they catered to the demanding tastes of an exclusive clientele, drawn from the upper echelons of European and American society. On their spacious verandah, well-heeled New Yorkers and English aristocrats would of an evening lower their spacious backsides into comfortable armchairs. There, drink in hand and attentive waiter at elbow, they would listen to the nightly grunt of surfacing hippos, the croak of bullfrogs and unseen cicadas trilling beneath the manicured lawns, while bats hawked for insects in the warm, velvet dusk. A few steps away, a swimming pool awaited their immersion, should they find the ambient temperature too high for their liking, the altitude being only three thousand feet. The crocodiles, which lurked in the lake shallows, acted as an effective deterrent to the incursion of visiting bathers. Occasionally a posse of dancers from the local Njemps tribe would appear on the lawns. This small tribe is an offshoot of the Maasai, with similar customs and accoutrements and hence of considerable interest to even the most jaded globe-trotter.

Many of the tourists who enjoyed the amenities at Michael's lodge were flown in by light aircraft, thus avoiding the long, car-breaking journey over the rocky road from Nakuru.

One Saturday, as I was preparing to close the surgery, mentally girding my palate for whatever Njoroge might choose to place before me, Michael's patrician form suddenly loomed in the doorway, his brow furrowed with anxiety.

'Good afternoon Mr Cran,' he said, 'I wonder if you can help me? I've just flown in from Baringo. As you know, there are no phones there and our radio is out of action. Our ridgeback, Ruby, has been trying to have pups since last night without success. Joanna is in Nairobi and I'm meeting her there this evening. Can I fly you to Baringo to do whatever is necessary?'

I glanced at my watch. It was almost two o'clock. Secretary and staff had long since departed to their respective repose or recreation.

'Certainly,' I answered. 'Just give me a few minutes to put whatever I think I might need into my bag and to phone my cook to advise him that I'll be a bit late for lunch.'

For once Njoroge was awake and, at the seventh ring, lifted the receiver. As I imparted my news he gave a croak like a constipated raven and said no more. Whether this signified displeasure at my non-appearance or sympathy with the plight of one of man's best friends, I could not ascertain.

Nakuru's airstrip was at Lanet, six miles to the south west. Michael's plane, a low winged, single-engined Piper, stood on the grass outside the small, trim building of the Nakuru Aero Club.

After doing a methodical inspection of the various parts of the outside of the plane and after examining the engine, Michael climbed onto the right wing and lowered himself into the left hand seat. I followed with my surgical bag, wondering how, in the event of a crash, with his passenger rendered unconscious, the pilot could get himself out of the cockpit, there being no left door.

After studying the mass of dials on the instrument panel for several minutes, the while muttering what I hoped wasn't an incantation to the Almighty for delivery from the perils of the heights, my companion fiddled with a succession of knobs and finally turned a key. There was a roar as the engine burst into life, the propeller vanished in a blur of light and the plane rocked in the slipstream. Michael switched on the radio, spoke a few unintelligible words into a microphone, turned the controls to left and right, then backwards and forwards, stamped on left and right rudder and finally we were bumping gently over the grass to the end of the airstrip.

Michael brought the plane to a halt and turned into wind. An increase in power, more checking of the dials, more checking of the controls. Flaps were lowered, harnesses were tightened, door and window handles closed. A final scrutiny of the instruments and we taxied onto the runway. Without hesitation Michael pushed the throttle fully in and we were away.

As we rumbled with ever-increasing speed down the grass strip, small unidentifiable birds deferred to our greater size by launching themselves skywards with all the velocity at their command. As I peered over the instrument panel I could see a much larger member of the feathered tribe standing in the middle of the runway, about a couple of hundred yards from the sharp end of the aeroplane. My pilot companion appeared to be oblivious of its presence, and the bird seemed to have more important things on its mind than imminent extinction. It was either preening itself or scratching its ear. When we were about fifty yards from impact it awoke from its reverie and, with a worthy turn of speed, cleared our bows with a few feet to spare.

Visions of the flight ending in a cloud of feathers before it had even begun rapidly faded as the rumbling of the wheels ceased and we left the ground and skimmed over the end of the runway. Michael raised the flaps, spoke another few unintelligible words into the mike and turned the plane northwards in the direction of Lake Baringo.

As we climbed away from Mother Earth, the mid-afternoon heat spiralling up from the ground below caused the plane to rock violently in the rising turbulence. After a few stomach-churning minutes we reached calmer air. Michael levelled off, reduced power to cruising speed and appeared to doze off.

Below us lay the crater of Menengai. A stream of solidified lava cut a wide swathe through the rocky, bush-covered floor before being brought up short by the crater wall. To our right rose the wooded heights of Dundori and Bahati, forming at this point the eastern wall of the Rift Valley. As we passed over the neat fields and dark green coffee plantations of the Solai Valley, I studied the ground below, identifying the farms I had come to know so well. To our left now, the vast, light green, Greek-owned sisal estates stretched away until they merged into the bush, that, from this height, looked grey and featureless.

Staring over the high instrument panel, I caught a glimpse of water – the flat, swampy expanse of Lake Solai. Beyond, the land rose abruptly to rocky, thorn covered hills.

The plane droned on, seemingly motionless in a slowly moving landscape. I looked down at the craggy, inhospitable hills. Here and there a cluster of huts cowered in a clearing, surrounded by a sea of encroaching bush. Down there people and animals were seeking refuge and shade, away from the hostile sun. Up here at eight and a half thousand feet, the air was fresh and cool. I studied the dials: altimeter, air speed indicator, rev. counter, compass, artificial horizon, vertical speed indicator. This, I thought, is the way to travel. No dust, no heat, no arriving sweaty and exhausted at one's destination after hairsbreadth escapes from death or mutilation on the highways and byways, tyres and nerves shredded, shock

253

absorbers and composure stretched to their limits. This, by contrast, was a mental exercise, with just the bare minimum of physical input. Perfect. Apart from the odd interjection on the radio, there was no outside interference. The pilot was indeed master of his ship, and, if the hostile earth below was anything to go by, master of his destiny as well.

My daydream was rudely interrupted as the plane, without warning, dropped with sickening force, accompanied by a snoring roar from the engine. We were passing over an escarpment. Below lay the long, narrow, alkaline Lake Bogoria, formerly called Lake Hannington after the unfortunate bishop, murdered in October 1885 on the orders of the Kabaka of Uganda, the bloodthirsty Mwanga. As the plane bucked its way through the turbulence I wondered where we could land if the engine failed. To the east, steep mountains rose from the water's edge. To the west there was nothing except an uninterrupted expanse of thorn and rock. I could perceive no sign of life anywhere.

We crossed the northern end of the lake and then, through the haze, Lake Baringo came into view, islands dimly visible on its brownish surface. A river wriggled below us, banks dark green with trees clustered at the water's edge.

Michael reduced power and we began a gradual descent.

As we approached the lake, the ground below became more and more devoid of vegetation until it was little more than a pancake of bare, brown earth, relieved only by the occasional stunted tree and thorn-enclosed homestead.

'Now,' I thought, 'if the engine stops, we have a chance of survival!'

Above the roar of the engine Michael shouted something about goats and soil erosion.

I could see no sign of an airstrip.

We continued our descent.

The superheated air rising from the baking earth below caused the plane to buck violently. In the distance, by the water's edge, I caught a glimpse of buildings. On our left stood a long rampart of black volcanic cliffs. On our right was the lake. Presumably the airstrip lay somewhere in-between.

Michael reduced more power and lowered the flaps.

As he did so, a dark shape plummeted vertically from the sky directly in our path. It was a vulture. Michael, his hand on the throttle as we descended, immediately applied full power, banked sharply and raised the nose. The bird flashed by a few feet away.

Our bumpy, straight-in approach to the unseen airstrip had been rudely interrupted and by the time Michael had sorted things out and got the plane on an even keel we were too high to make a safe landing and had to go round again for another attempt.

As we climbed away I looked down. There, below us, was the airstrip, a long bare stretch of gravel, upon whose desiccated surface a flock of goats, in the company of a herdsman, was apparently finding nourishment. The wire fence surrounding the airstrip seemingly had been no deterrent to their desire to sample a fresh pasture of pulverised rock.

We turned and flew directly towards the black, volcanic precipice. Violent contact looked inevitable and imminent. As the cracks and crevices grew nearer with frightening rapidity I envisioned myself nesting unpleasantly on one of the upper ledges.

We cleared the crags by about twenty feet, proving once again how distorted one's vision of forthcoming events can become under the stress of anticipation.

Thorn trees and boulders flashed beneath us as we roared along the cliff top. The airstrip had vanished once again. As we banked onto base leg it re-appeared, a ridiculously thin, brown thread in a carpet of bush.

Once again Michael reduced power and lowered the flaps as we turned onto finals. As we descended and approached the boundary fence, I could see that the herdsman and his goats were still pottering about in the middle of the airstrip, totally oblivious to approaching disaster. At a hundred yards and fifty feet above the gravel not a head had been turned in our direction. At fifty yards and twenty feet from the deck there was still no movement from goats or goatherd. Michael added some power and we skimmed over their heads and landed with a thump on what was left of the runway.

As we taxied slowly to the end of the airstrip I became aware that the air temperature had risen somewhat since our departure from Nakuru. Lake Baringo lies at little more than 3,000 feet above sea level. As I stepped out of the plane a blast of hot, dusty air swirled around me. A red dust devil, a hundred feet high, marched rapidly though the bush to the distant water's edge, where it abruptly vanished.

A Land Rover approached.

We got in and were driven in moderate discomfort to the lodge, around whose entrance a number of languid figures sat or slumbered in the shade. As we drew near a few of these figures sprang to their feet, rude artefacts clasped in their hands. When they realised that we were not a hoped-for truckful of gullible tourists, fat with dollars and deutschmarks, they returned with rather less vigour to their places of rest.

The lodge, stone built and surrounded by green lawns, tall trees and flowering shrubs, was an oasis of coolness amid the heat and glare of the mid afternoon bush. Little birds, bold and unafraid, hopped along the walls of the verandah in search of tit bits. Soft-footed waiters padded to and fro. The lake waters glittered through the trees a hundred yards away.

With an effort I reminded myself that I was here to do a job of work, to attend to a patient, that I wasn't on holiday.

Ridgeback Ruby lay, torpid and distended, in her basket in Michael's office. As we entered, she briefly wagged her tail. The effort seemed to exhaust her. She lay panting on her side. She was young, three years old and this was her first litter.

I knelt to examine her. Her grossly enlarged abdomen was tense and resistant to palpation. Conjunctival mucous membranes were, I was relieved to observe, a healthy salmon pink. I felt her pulse. It was faster than normal, but strong. Temperature was slightly elevated.

'OK, Ruby, let's see what we can feel.'

I washed my hands and carefully inserted a finger into Ruby's vagina. She strained and grunted.

'Well, Michael, there's a big pup here and I can just, just touch the tip of its nose. Can't tell if it's dead or alive. No movement. Still, it might be alive. I could try forceps, but with this degree of distension there's a serious risk of damaging the uterus.'

'So what's the problem? Why won't they come out?'

'Looks like uterine inertia. She must have a mass of pups in here and the wall of the womb is stretched to such an extent it's unable to contract in a purposeful manner and expel its occupants.'

'And what can you do?'

'Well, her pelvis is wide enough for them to come out, so I'll give her an injection of oxytocin. If the uterine muscle is receptive it will contract and things should start moving. If not, then an operation may be necessary.'

I gave Ruby ten units by intra-muscular injection. She didn't move as the needle sank into her hind leg.

Crossing metaphorical digits, I followed Michael onto the cool verandah, where, a few moments later, cushioned in a large armchair, I was presented with a brimming tankard of ice-cold passion fruit juice by an exquisitely mannered waiter. Beyond the restful lawns the lake shimmered and sparkled in the afternoon sunshine. Lumpy, brown islands broke the distant surface. A fisherman slowly paddled a primitive log canoe through the choppy inshore waves. A heron, still as a statue, stood motionless in the shallows.

I was roused from my observations of the distant scene by a message that Ruby had delivered one pup. By the time we reached the delivery room another pup had emerged. Both were dead.

Ruby took no interest in what was happening at her nether end. Eyes closed, she lay like a bloated dolphin, stranded on a mud bank with the tide fast receding.

Anther thirty minutes on the verandah enabled me to identify several birds not new to science and to down another pint of passion fruit juice.

Back in the obstetrical ward the puppy count remained stubbornly at two. I gave Ruby another shot of oxytocin and returned to my bird watching. By now I was awash with passion fruit juice and desperate for something with a bit more body, but with iron resolve I bit the bullet of abstinence. Michael and I glanced simultaneously at our watches.

'Mike, if Ruby hasn't obliged after another twenty minutes then it will have to be a Caesar-OK?'

'OK.'

The twenty minutes passed. Ruby did not oblige.

We drove back to the airstrip with the patient lying limply in the back of the Land Rover.

During the return flight I shared the narrow back seat with Ruby and my new found fascination with the mysteries of flight was perforce diverted to the mysteries of thwarted canine parturition.

I had read somewhere that gravid female members of homo sapiens, wishing to precipitate childbirth, would have themselves taken for an automobile ride over a rough road, and I wondered if a bumpy flight and a hard landing might have a similar effect on the canine species. I was unable to discover if this might be possible as the late afternoon air was now as smooth as silk and Michael landed as lightly as the proverbial thistledown.

We drove to the surgery, where we decanted Ruby into one of the kennels.

Michael glanced at his Rolex.

'Good Lord!' he said 'Look at the time! I'm due at the Muthaiga Club in an hour's time. I must fly!' He gave a restrained aristocratic laugh. 'I leave everything in your capable hands, old boy. Do whatever you think best and I'll phone you tomorrow evening. Many thanks.'

And with that he was gone, leaving me holding the baby, or rather babies, which were unfortunately still inside Ruby, and probably dead to boot.

I made Ruby a comfortable couch with a couple of clean gunny bags. Further drugs were obviously a waste of time, so I returned home to consider my next move over a spot of sustenance.

My main problem was lack of assistance, skilled or otherwise. It was now dark and it was Saturday night. Njoroge had already drunk deeply at the well, if his swaying gait was anything to go by, and would be a positive danger, to both beast and man. To attempt to find the modest home of the faithful Moses in unlit African suburbia would, I knew, be a futile task. Besides, there was no reason why he should be at home awaiting my summons for help.

As I sat there, cogitating, there came a sudden, loud knock at the door.

There on the step stood Tom Dixon.

Tom had been born and bred in India. A life-long bachelor, he lived with his brother Pat, who was also an old India hand. After taking a degree at Trinity College, Dublin, Tom returned to India where, until the early fifties, he worked in the Public Works Department. The two brothers, together with their widowed sister, May, then moved to Kenya. Tom was now in his mid-sixties, tall, mild of manner and passionately devoted to dogs, whether his own or the strays he fed daily at the Nakuru Golf Club.

'Hello, Tom,' I said. 'How are you? Come on in. How can I help you?'

'It's Scruffy,' Tom answered, gesturing towards a hairy face peering from his dilapidated, blue Ford Zodiac, which stood in the drive. 'He came in a few minutes ago, with blood spouting from his hind leg. Must have cut a blood vessel or something. I've tied it up with a handkerchief to stop the bleeding, but it needs a bit more than that. Can you fix him up?'

As I surveyed Tom, standing in the doorway, I decided that here was the answer to my problem. Here was my assistant! After attending to Scruffy, Tom, I reasoned, would be only too glad to help, especially as I was turning out to deal with his own dog on a Saturday evening.

I followed Tom to the surgery, where we unloaded Scruffy and carried him inside. The less-than-clean handkerchief, tied round his left hind leg above the hock, was soaked in bright red blood.

Scruffy, a nondescript mongrel with big shaggy eyebrows, stood rather apprehensively on the table while I prepared some instruments. When these were ready I removed the bandage. A jet of blood leapt out and struck me in the right eye. Frantically blinking, I seized Scruffy's leg and applied pressure above the inch long wound, from which the blood was spurting. Reaching behind me, I grabbed a bandage off a shelf, tore it open and tied it tightly round the leg to act as a tourniquet. The bleeding stopped and I inspected the wound more closely. The pipe-like ends of a large artery were severed half way across the gash.

After I had shaved and swabbed the adjacent skin, I injected some local anaesthetic into the subcutaneous tissue. I applied a pair of artery forceps to the ends of the severed blood vessels, before opening a packet of catgut with which to tie them off.

As I pulled out a length of suture material, I glanced up at Tom. The surgery walls were painted in what had been once a tasteful shade of lilac green. The passage of time had not been kind and what had once been a gentle spring-like colour was now positively autumnal. Tom's normally ruddy complexion had taken on a similar hue, so much so, that his greyish-green countenance almost merged into the background. Beads of sweat stood out on his forehead. He swallowed, swayed and almost fell.

258

'Hold on Tom!' I called. 'Sit down on this chair.'

Tom sank down and closed his eyes.

Fortunately he was still holding on to Scruffy's neck. As fast as I could I tied off the offending artery, released the tourniquet, stitched the subcutaneous tissue and put in a few skin sutures. I quickly applied a bandage and gave an injection of antibiotic.

'OK, Tom,' I said. 'It's all over.'

Tom warily opened his eyes and rose gingerly to his feet. My hopes for using him as my assistant were fading fast.

I coughed.

'Tom, I wonder if you would mind giving me a hand with an operation?'

Tom looked as though collapse was nigh.

'Well, perhaps you could just hold a dog's leg while I give her an anaesthetic. Please?'

A long pause and Tom nodded mutely.

I extracted Ruby, still puppyless, from her kennel, weighed her, and carried her through to the surgery where I laid her on the table. I filled a syringe with sodium pentobarbitone and clipped the hair over her right foreleg. I then cleaned the area with spirit.

'Right, Tom, can you press your thumb into the crook of Ruby's elbow, like so. The cephalic vein will appear – at least I hope it will – and then I will slide the needle into it.'

Tom did as requested, then closed his eyes and turned away.

The vein appeared and I inserted the needle.

'OK Tom, you're doing great. Now, just raise your thumb, but still support her elbow. I've got to trickle this stuff in very slowly. Ruby's very toxic and weak and I'm sure the pups are all dead. Too much will shove her over the edge. This is not the ideal anaesthetic for this sort of job, but I haven't got a gas machine so needs must when the Devil drives and he's been doing that today!'

After I had given Ruby about a third of the computed dose for her bodyweight she was virtually out cold. I turned her over onto her side, very slowly gave her a bit more and then stopped. She was breathing steadily and slowly. Her membranes were a pale pink. I pinched her toes. No reaction. Her abdomen swelled out like a balloon about to burst.

'One last thing, Tom. Can we just lift her onto the operating table?'

Tom rolled his eyes and wearily nodded assent.

I quickly pulled out the table and we hoisted Ruby onto it, laid her on her back and tied her legs down to the four corners.

'Thanks, Tom,' I said. 'That was a great help.' I meant it.

Tom took one final look at Ruby, lying there, ready for the knife, and, taking Scruffy with him, bolted into the night.

Once again I was left alone.

I pulled out Ruby's tongue and gave her some atropine sulphate to control the flow of saliva. Next I began boiling up the instruments needed for a Caesarian section. Then I soaped and shaved Ruby's vast abdomen, scrubbed it with spirit and draped the area of incision.

As I laid out the forceps, scissors, clamps and suture materials, the silence of the evening was broken by the sound of music. I cocked an attentive ear. Whoever or whatever was giving tongue out there, it certainly wasn't Julie Andrews. The mounting crescendo was more akin to the howling of inebriated wolves, accompanied by an orchestra of tom toms and maracas.

About a hundred yards from the surgery stood The Curried Whelk, an eatery of overblown pretensions which, on a hoarding three feet high and twenty feet wide, proclaimed itself to be the Classic Restaurant of the Rift. This hyperbolic statement did not mean that The Curried Whelk was on a par with the Savoy or the Ritz. It merely meant that its competitors in the culinary stakes were so far behind, their major menu offerings being roasted meat and mealie cobs, that anything else, especially if presented on tables with real tablecloths, cutlery and glasses, would attract the frustrated gastronomes of the Rift Valley like a ripened carcase luring vultures out of an empty sky.

The floor above the restaurant also came under the aegis of The Curried Whelk's proprietor. On Saturday nights the digestion, to say nothing of the eardrums of the diners below, was put to considerable strain as the rafters and ceiling above them creaked and groaned to the poundings of a gyrating horde of revellers, stomping to the strains of a deafening discotheque.

Tonight was Saturday night.

The oath which rose unbidden to my lips was not stifled.

As Chuck Berry bellowed out 'Roll Over Beethoven', 'Little Queenie' and other classics of the era of Rock 'n' Roll, the skin and midline were incised and the abdomen opened. Abba came next and as 'Waterloo' and 'Nina Pretty Ballerina' split the night air I gently eased the tense and distended womb through the incision. With a scalpel I cut into the body of the uterus, taking care to avoid a number of large blood vessels. The hind legs of a large, dead pup appeared. I gently extracted it, together with its pancake-shaped, bottle-green, foetal membranes. I began to milk the pups in the left uterine horn down to the incision I had made. As I did so, that deathless ditty from the genius of Little Richard, 'Great Balls Of Fire', emerging as it did from the odious Whelk at a volume sufficient to rend the walls of Jericho, did nothing to improve my powers of concentration. One after the other, I slowly inched three more dead pups down the uterine horn and carefully withdrew them.

To the strains of Rod Stewart's 'Hot Legs', I turned my attention to the right horn. This contained four pups from which life had long since departed. A thorough inspection of the uterus and abdominal cavity revealed no further inmates, so I closed the incision with two rows of inversion stitches of fine catgut.

I repaired the peritoneal and muscle layers with strong catgut, using an eversion pattern to close the peritoneal cavity.

As I started to close the skin, The Curried Whelk's offering of musical culture rose to full fortissimo. Ruby stirred. Whether this was due to a lightening of the anaesthesia or to an unconscious rejection of the choice of the unseen disc-jockey was impossible to ascertain. I suspected the latter.

Speedily I inserted the remaining stitches, untied Ruby's pinioned limbs and laid her on her side. I inspected her tongue and conjunctival mucous membranes and was relieved to find that they were still pink. I touched her eyelids and there was a satisfactory reflex blink. Filling a syringe, I gave her an intra-muscular injection of oxytocin, to induce involution of the uterus and expulsion of unwanted debris. Finally I gave her an injection of long-acting penicillin.

As I carried Ruby to the kennel room, there was a sudden, unnatural silence. The only sound was the singing in my ears. I laid her gently on a clean sack, made sure her tongue was well out of her mouth, and glanced at my watch. It was midnight and the party was over.

As I weaved my way home, through a horde of laughing, shouting, staggering and gesticulating merry-makers, many the worse for wine, who were pouring down the middle of the street, I reflected that now at least Ruby should recover from the effects of the operation and the anaesthetic in peace and quiet.

She did, and never looked back.

Chapter Fifteen

Before I left the Sceptred Isle for black Africa I imagined, like many others before me, who had never set foot south of the Sahara, that the place was positively shoulder to shoulder with wild animals. It was impossible to move without tripping over them. Pythons hung looped from every branch. Every thicket held a pride of lions. The plains were dark with herds of migrating antelope and zebra, while at night the yapping of jackals and the cackling of hyenas made sleep impossible.

Although outside the game reserves and national parks such, alas, was no longer the case, the influence of wild animals on my job, both directly and indirectly, was infinitely greater than was the case in Britain, where I was lucky to meet anything more exciting than the odd orphaned owl or road-killed rabbit.

Many diseases in Africa had wild animals as their reservoirs. African Swine Fever lurked in warthogs, Ondiriitis in bushbuck, Corridor Disease in buffalo, Malignant Catarrhal Fever in wildebeest.

Orphaned wild animals were popular as pets and from time to time they would need my attention.

The population of wild creatures in the area was much larger than was evident at first sight. By natural instinct or by force of circumstance most were nocturnal and only at night did they become active. Hippo would emerge from lakes to graze, and buffalo materialise, mud-caked and malignant, from the swamps wherein they had wallowed during the heat of the day. Leopard would yawn and stretch and silently descend from rock or tree to begin the quest for food.

Close encounters at night with hippo, buffalo or leopard were likely – if one survived – to be memorable.

Even during the day the unexpected could happen.

Many of the tea estates in the Kericho area, sixty miles to the west, were bordered by natural forest, from which they had originally been carved. The forest was home to numerous wild animals, which, for the most part, lived unseen, secretive lives within its shadowy depths.

All the white estate managers and technicians owned dogs, mostly labradors and pointers, which had been trained to retrieve the ducks their masters shot in the paddy fields on the plains edging Lake Victoria. The time had now passed when one could order one's bearer into some armpit deep swamp to flounder after a mortally wounded bird.

The tea people had the reputation of regarding themselves as being rather a cut above the rest of humanity. Living as they did in large, luxurious mansions, frequently sited, as though for strategic purposes, on the summits of hills, surrounded by vast estates of exquisitely manicured tea bushes, in which hordes of small serf-like figures – the pluckers – could be seen toiling beneath the noon-day sun, this was not altogether surprising. With the dark, tangled mass of the forest to the east and the vast, intricate network of Kipsigis homesteads to the west, some planters in the middle probably regarded themselves as the modern equivalent of the medieval baron, ruling their fiefdoms with a strong but benevolent hand, distributing largesse to those in need, succouring the sick and, by their knowledge and expertise, making a substantial contribution to the economy of the state.

David Taylor managed the tea factory on an estate called Chomogondy. David was large and ebullient, full of bonhomie, good humour and up-country hospitality, which I had savoured on several occasions. A favourite finale to an evening was for David to persuade me – not a difficult task – to knock back a couple of 'Rusty Nails', a pleasing potion combining a substantial slug of malt whisky and Drambuie. His effervescent wife, Anne, was a singularly attractive blonde, slender and possessed of a roguish eye and a bubbling laugh, which sounded like a sudden peal of bells. She was fond of horses, dogs and men, not necessarily in that order. She looked after a small herd of dairy cattle, supervised a piggery and a weaving enterprise in which African women workers, using little more than looms and spinning wheels, turned raw wool into rugs, which often incorporated motifs which looked as though they might have been designed by Salvador Dali on an off day. They sold well.

The Taylors had four dogs – two hunt terriers and two labradors, one of which was a yellow dog, called Spike.

Early one Saturday morning, before breakfast, David took the dogs for a walk along a grassy bank through the tea plantation. The forest was not far away.

The dogs ran around, sniffing, cocking legs, rooting and generally enjoying the sun and the crisp morning air.

Spike disappeared into the tea.

For a few minutes there was silence, broken only by the echoing calls of a pair of augur buzzards, circling and wheeling in the immaculate blue sky.

A sudden cacophony of yelping, squealing, snorting and grunting made David throw down the Sportsman cigarette, whose soothing fumes he had been gently inhaling, and run, with surprising turn of speed, in the direction of the sound. As he burst his way through the tea he caught a glimpse of a large rufous-coloured body with a white dorsal mane and short sharp tusks.

It was a bush pig.

Spike had vanished. David shouted and whistled for several minutes, before turning for home to organise a search party. As he did so, Spike appeared from beneath a tea bush.

He was a pathetic sight. His smooth yellow coat was daubed with blood. A great gash split his left haunch and as he moved the white of exposed femur could be glimpsed through a welter of blood and torn muscles. Another wound had rent his right shoulder. Worse by far was the damage done to his face. Both mandibles had been broken. Unable to close his mouth, his lower jaw hung down, while a mixture of saliva and blood drooled onto his chest.

Hurriedly swallowing his own saliva, David picked up Spike and hastened home as fast as possible.

When David phoned the surgery – mobiles had yet to be invented – I was a hundred miles away, shivering on the chilly heights of Mau Narok, dealing with a Hereford bull suffering from High Altitude Disease. Imported from England six months previously, he had developed massive oedema of the brisket, general weakness, diarrhoea and marked distension of both jugular veins. His breathing was laboured and he was reluctant to move. The cause was congestive heart failure due to the altitude – 9,400 feet.

I turned to the farmer, a middle-aged Yorkshireman, called Josiah Thornton,

'I'm sorry, Mr Thornton, but if you don't get him downhill, and fast, he's going to die. His heart's going to pack up at any moment. He can't take the height and lack of oxygen up here.'

'Can't ye try drugs or summat? To tide 'im over like, 'til he gets used to it? Wot about it, lad?'

'Well, they might help a bit, but they won't cure him. I tell you, if he doesn't get down to a lower altitude he'll be dead meat and no good for eating either.'

'OK, lad, I'll phone Pat Sessions at Elementaita and see if he'll take him for a while.'

He nodded his massive, grizzled head. His vast abdomen was encircled by a broad leather belt supporting ancient moleskin trousers. His feet were thrust into huge, hob-nailed boots. He seemed impervious to the biting wind sweeping across the open fields. As I cowered behind the slight shelter afforded by the cattle crush, a scantily clad Maasai herdsman wandered past, clad in little more than a blanket and a pair of sandals, fashioned from a discarded tyre.

'Soba,' I greeted him. 'Eba,' he answered. 'Dagunyo,' I said. 'Igo,' came the reply. 'Sere.' 'Aya sere.'

My teeth were chattering. His sleek brown skin shone, not a goose pimple in sight.

'You're getting soft, lad,' I thought, as I got into the car and switched on the heater, and bumped down the rocky road to Njoro and Nakuru. 'Time you toughened up. This is equatorial Africa, you know, not blimmin Spitsbergen.' All very well, perhaps, but I still recalled, with a shudder, one early morning at Molo, the sight of barefoot Africans walking over frozen ruts and through ice-covered puddles.

As I descended, my thoughts turned pleasantly to the wedding to which I had been invited that afternoon. One of Guy and Marie Heath's daughters was to be married to a young fellow from Nanyuki. Guy farmed at Solai and had been with the Eighth Army in North Africa. He held strong views on those officers who had been in the British army and had elected to become Kenya citizens. 'Bloody traitors!' he would fulminate, blue eyes popping as he poured another gin. 'Wore the uniform, took the King's shilling, Quisling turncoats! The swine should be flogged and sent to the Tower!'

The reception was to be held in the club, just across the road from the surgery. Most convenient. A marquee had been erected to give shade to the throng of guests, eager to toast the health of bride and groom. Shade was vital on these occasions. Alcohol and tropic sun was not a good mixture, at least not for those luckless enough to be required to deliver speeches.

As I approached the surgery I glanced at my watch. It was just after noon. Time enough to deal with whatever patients were waiting, nip home for a quick bite, change into something respectable and get to the church before the arrival of the major participants.

I hadn't calculated on Spike, however.

Together with half a dozen other patients, fortunately less seriously afflicted, he was waiting in the surgery for my return from Mau Narok. An African driver had brought him from Kericho.

I examined him and knew at once that general anaesthesia and pinning and wiring of the broken bones were necessary in order to rectify the damage. I scribbled a note to David, gave it to the driver and asked him to return on Monday to collect Spike.

I asked Moses to prepare the instruments for the operation while I attended to the other patients.

A slender Asian youth brought in an emaciated alsatian puppy which was infested with hookworms. Next came a young African from western

Kenya with two dogs which he wanted to take to Uganda to sell. Both required rabies vaccinations and a certificate of good health. They passed muster and I proceeded to the next patient. This was a lamb with tetanus, brought in by an aged, grey-bearded Kikuyu, ragged and barefoot. The lamb, stiff as a board, unable even to twitch its ears, rolled its eyes in fear as I examined it. There was little I could do except to give it a massive intravenous dose of crystalline penicillin and hope for the best. The old man hobbled out carrying his pathetic woolly bundle, which probably meant more to him than most people could imagine. As he went out, in came a be-tweeded English woman, followed by a diminutive 'dog toto' (children were sometimes paid to look after the dogs of wealthy owners), leading a large and very lame Great Dane. An ominous painful swelling of his lower right leg suggested the possibility of an osteosarcoma, a bone tumour to which these unnaturally large, ungainly dogs are prone. I advised that an X-ray examination be done as soon as possible and I tried to explain as carefully and as gently as I could, what the prospects would be should the X-ray reveal what I suspected. She listened attentively though her eyes glistened with moisture, and agreed to take her dear dog to the War Memorial Hospital on Monday, where the admirable Miss Brown, as fond of the canine species as she appeared to be averse to the majority of the human race, was always gratifyingly co-operative.

I glanced at my watch again. Good grief! Twenty minutes past one and I still had Spike to deal with.

There was still a small knot of blanketed Maasai clogging up the doorway, only one of whom required attention. I singled him out, a tall, lop-eared fellow with a knitted cap on his head. He sensed that I was in no mood for the protracted verbal fencing normally required to winkle out a straightforward request – in this case, advice on worming sheep and the remedy thereof. I gave both, received in return a couple of well-oiled bank-notes, extracted from somewhere in the region of his right armpit, firmly closed the door and turned at last to the long-suffering Spike.

We carried him into the operating room and laid him on the table. I gave him an anaesthetic and set to work. Both lower mandibles had transverse compound fractures and the central symphysis was split. For the next hour and a half I reconstructed the shattered bones, inserting longitudinal and transverse stainless steel pins. Finally, I wired the lower canine teeth together and stitched the torn gums. I put corks over the sharp ends of the pins to prevent food and debris becoming lodged on them. To my eyes Spike now looked quite respectable, although one client who saw him later, when I was changing the corks, remarked that he resembled a porcupine's backside.

I turned to the wounds on his shoulder and hind leg. The latter wound was about nine inches long, very deep and the muscles were badly torn by

266

the bush pig's tusks. As I painstakingly shaved the adjacent skin, taking care that no hairs fell into the wound, I reflected that doctors cobbling together hacked up human patients were at least spared this part of the procedure. Apart from the odd hairy Ainu, most members of the human race were basically hairless, or covered in nothing that would deflect more than a few strokes of the average razor blade. By contrast some breeds of dogs, cattle, and pigs in particular, were covered in a pelage so coarse that several blades were required to shave a few square inches.

As I inserted the final stitches Spike moved his head. The anaesthetic was lightening. We carried him into the recovery room and laid him on a blanket.

It was half past three. There was still time to go home, get smartened up and get to the reception in time for the speeches and toasts, that section of the proceedings regarded by the plebeian portion of the guest list as considerably more important than the earlier ceremony in church.

As I carried my instrument bag to the car the telephone rang.

I stiffened, sorely tempted to feign temporary deafness and move rapidly to where the clashing of beer mugs and voices raised in inebriated conversation would effectively drown the loudest telephone bell.

I hesitated and then turned back.

'Jambo, daktari!' An African voice boomed in my right ear. 'Habari yako?' (How are you?)

The preliminaries over, he explained that he was head groom to Horace Catchpole of Naivasha: 'Mimi Sammy, syce ya bwana Catchpole'.

There had been a sudden rainstorm, the horses had rushed wildly round the paddock, as is their wont on such occasions, and one had torn itself badly on the barbed wire fence. Not for the first time I cursed barbed wire and horse owners who used it to enclose their fields.

'How bad?' I asked.

'Very bad. The skin is badly torn and bleeding profusely.' His description in basic up-country Swahili of the damage done was alarmingly vivid.

Where was the tear, was my next question.

'A hind leg, high up and on the inside,' Sammy's staccato Swahili had an ominous Shakespearean ring to it.

Great, I thought. There's nothing I like better than stitching up horses' hind legs on Saturday afternoons, bent double, my head in an equine groin with the prospects of having my brains dashed out at any second by a flailing hoof. Marvellous for stimulating the adrenal glands.

'Okay, I'm coming. By the way, where's Mr Wallington?'

'He's gone with his wife to a big wedding in Nakuru.'

The diminishing numbers of wild animals were subjected to constant harassment by the rural population. Zebra and antelope were the chief sufferers. Shot at with cruelly barbed arrows, throttled with wire snares, it was a wonder any survived at all. As populations of game became encircled by ever increasing numbers of settlements, the pressure on them grew. Small herds of impala or zebra would find themselves stranded on a farm or ranch where the owner regarded them with favour. If they tried to leave, their chances of survival were slim. Sometimes a single individual would appear out of nowhere on a farm far removed from the nearest wildlife area. On a farm at Bahati a solitary zebra lived for many years, grazing with the cattle, coming into the dairy at milking time and showing no alarm at the close proximity of people or vehicles. The surrounding area was densely populated and intensively farmed. The zebra knew that it was safe where it was. So it stayed.

On Kima Farm at Rongai dwelt a small herd of zebra. The farm was owned by Mike Butler, known locally as the Rongai Bull, on account of his massive frame, curly head and winning ways with the girls.

One day Mike came into the surgery.

'Good afternoon, Hugh' – Mike was always polite – almost formal. 'You know that group of zebra on the farm? Well, some bastard has shot an arrow into the big stallion. Got him in the chest. He seems all right, eating OK, but sooner or later things are going to go bad. Can you come out one day and remove it? Come late afternoon and we can have a couple of ales after our labours.'

So one afternoon I crossed the Molo River and turned up the track to Mike's farm. I was relieved that the weather was dry. In the wet it became little more than a steep, slippery gully wherein one ran the constant risk of temporary or permanent lodgement. Now it was merely dusty and bouldery.

I had brought my dart pistol, projectile syringes and a vial of Large Animal Immobilon and Revivon. The dose required to knock down a zebra is considerably less than that needed for a horse of similar weight. This has the advantage that the smallest available syringe can be used.

I met Mike in the farmyard, where he was attending to a disabled tractor.

'Hello, Mike, got a patient there, I see!'

Mike laughed. 'Yes, nothing serious though. Just changing the oil filter and doing a bit of greasing. I'll just clean myself up and be with you in a tick.' He wiped his perspiring forehead with the back of his hand, spreading some more oil over himself.

While I waited I prepared a 2ml syringe and screwed on a 3cm barbed needle. Mike returned, driving a well-bashed Toyota Land Cruiser pick-up. I put my surgical bag in the back and climbed in, pistol in hand.

The zebra were in a field at the upper end of the farm – four mares, two yearlings, a foal and the perforated stallion. Mike drove slowly into the field. As we approached, the zebra stopped grazing, raised their heads and stared in our direction, then turned and trotted off. Mike stopped the Toyota. The zebra stopped and looked back. We moved off again. The zebra did the same, reached a fence, wriggled beneath a loose wire and vanished into the surrounding bush.

After crashing around in the bush for about twenty minutes we located our prey about half a mile away and began to herd them slowly back towards the field. Zebra, if chased and subjected to undue stress, exertion, fear or excitement, are susceptible to acute metabolic acidosis and myopathy, which can be fatal. A short intensive chase over a mile or so is more dangerous than a longer, less intensive one. The resultant profound drop in blood pH values leads to cardiac dysfunction, pulmonary oedema and death within thirty minutes to twelve hours. Less severe manifestations can occur, mainly stiffness and skeletal muscle spasm. In some animals death can occur several months after capture, apparently from kidney failure. Originally it was thought that capture myopathy, or overstraining disease, as it is sometimes called, was due to exhaustion and overstraining of muscles and vital organs. The acute phase of the condition can be remedied by the prompt intravenous infusion of sodium bicarbonate.

So we drove gently through the thickets of thorn and leleshwa, with the zebra drifting before us, sometimes visible, sometimes not. Eventually the fence line came in sight. The zebra began moving along it, searching for a way through. We drew closer, and as we did so, the striped horses began to panic. I cocked the pistol and put on the safety catch. One animal pushed its head beneath the wire. In a trice it had loosened it sufficiently to be able to wriggle underneath. The others began to follow. Mike put his foot hard down and the Land Cruiser burst its way through the bush. I slipped off the safety catch and as the stallion squirmed under the wire, hindquarters in the air, I took aim and shot the projectile syringe into his ample rump.

He kicked his heels in the air, trying to dislodge what must have felt like another arrowhead, and galloped off to disappear behind a distant clump of thorn trees. We made a wide circle and as we approached the point where he had vanished, we saw the stallion rise and then stumble and fall into the knee-high grass. Five minutes had elapsed since he had been darted. We stopped. Mike turned off the engine and we waited for another five minutes before moving slowly towards the spot where the zebra had gone down.

We found him lying quietly in a hollow surrounded by grey rocks and tall, yellow grass. He was breathing slowly. Now and again a leg would give a slight quiver.

I jumped down, retrieved my bag from the back of the Toyota and laid out a few instruments. I filled a syringe with the antidote Revivon, ready to be given as soon as I was finished. First I removed the projectile syringe, nicking the skin with a scalpel to ease out the barbed needle.

Next I turned to the arrowhead sticking out of the stallion's chest. I shaved a few square centimetres around the entry hole and disinfected the skin. I made a small incision and gave the projecting metal neck a gentle tug. Nothing happened. I enlarged the cut the tried again. Still it refused to budge.

'Problems?' asked Mike, at my elbow.

'Yes, the damned thing won't come out. I'm going to have to make what my old surgical professor called a bold incision, to get the arrowhead out before the stallion starts to come round. Here we go.'

So saying, I plied my scalpel with some vigour, and spread the wound edges with tissue forceps, the better to see what I was doing. At last I could see the reason for the impasse. In addition to the arrowhead being fanged with rows of long, needle-sharp, reverse-pointing barbs, it had, in the course of its trajectory, struck a rib and been bent backwards from the neck, at an angle of 145 degrees. No wonder it was reluctant to move. After some manipulation it finally emerged, an unpleasant-looking object, black and dripping with blood.

I cleaned the two wounds, minor and major, filled both with antibiotic cream, and inserted a few catgut stitches in the latter, leaving a small opening for drainage. A syringeful of penicillin and streptomycin injected into the hind quarters came next, followed immediately afterwards by an intrajugular shot of Revivon.

'OK, Mike, lets see what happens next.'

We retired to a convenient distance and awaited developments. After a minute or so the zebra's breathing deepened and quickened. For a few seconds more he lay quietly. Then his eyes snapped open and he sat up on his chest. He lowered his head and nibbled at a few blades of grass. Suddenly, with a convulsive movement, he leapt to his feet, a surprised look on his handsome face, and trotted off towards his wives and offspring, who had been watching the proceedings from the cover of a clump of leleshwa a few hundred yards away.

'Hey, that was impressive,' said Mike. 'Come on. Let's go back to the house for a snort. That was a good job well done!'

I hoped so.

As we trundled down the rutted track, the sun was sinking below the Molo Hills behind us. The enormously elongated shadow of the Land Cruiser preceded us, veering from side to side as we turned, extending and contracting as we rose over bumps and descended into potholes. At our backs Mt. Londiani and Kilombe Hill stood in shadow, forested summits

270

black against a rosy sky. The plains of the Rift Valley below us were spotlighted with the remaining shafts of sunlight. Details, which passed unnoticed in the brazen light of day, were now etched with extraordinary clarity. Distant hills, craters, gullies, and valleys sprang into view as though seen through a three dimensional microscope.

A jackal on the evening hunt trotted through the adjacent bush, paying scant heed to our presence. An early owl swooped soundlessly in front of the vehicle. And as we turned into the entrance to Mike's house, palates panting for that first refreshing rush of ice-cold lager, the first bats were already around the eaves, hawking for insects in the gathering darkness.

Wild animals were frequently kept by those with the inclination and time to look after them.

Most had been acquired as orphans, often presented by Africans, who had found them, abandoned by their mothers. Sometimes the mother had been killed by dogs or hunters. Sometimes the mother was deliberately killed in order to sell her offspring to the eccentric and sometimes ingenuous European.

An extraordinary variety of species was to be found residing in the homes and gardens of Kenya's non-African residents.

Some people preferred reptiles and lavished their waking hours on snakes, chameleons and injured tortoises. Others devoted their time to looking after birds with a broken leg or wing, or to rearing fledglings. If the bird could not be released due to lack of full mobility, it would remain a permanent guest.

The wealthier landowners had a penchant for the larger, more dramatic animals. They constructed rocky dens for leopards, erected huge enclosures for lions and built heavily timbered pens for buffalo. It was not unusual on some ranches to find a semi-tame eland grazing with the cattle or to stumble over a cheetah lolling on the verandah.

Ranchers were usually tolerant or intolerant of game. The broad acres of the former would be dotted with grazing antelope and gazelle. Those of the latter contained only livestock, from which all game had been ruthlessly eliminated by shooting, trapping and poisoning. These ranches were usually commercially successful, but they were sterile expanses, devoid of the spirit and vitality of wild Africa.

Luckily such people were in the minority. Most individuals took a great interest in wildlife, whether it was small or large, scarce or plentiful, avian, mammalian or reptilian.

Jack and Joan Sommerville of Kericho had a pet porcupine. They had acquired it as a baby and it was completely tame. Porcupines are by nature nocturnal and the Sommervilles had taken account of this when constructing its living quarters. During the day it slept snug and warm in a cosy boudoir built onto the outside wall of the Sommervilles' house. From this salubrious apartment a tunnel had been knocked through the wall into the lounge. When the time came for porcupines to be up and about the Sommervilles' spiny friend would saunter forth into their midst. Guests, myself included, were, on occasion, somewhat startled to find a fully grown porcupine strolling around the house. There was no cause for alarm. Porky, as he was called, was extremely sociable. He loved to have the top of his cranium scratched, raising the crest on his head and neck in pleasure, until he resembled an Iroquois Indian in full plumage. The dogs kept out of his way and gave him a wide berth. When they came too close Porky would shuffle smartly backwards, in their direction, giving his quills an ominous rattle as he did so. The dogs would rapidly retire.

On the shores of Lake Naivasha James and Anthea Prendergast kept a pair of cheetahs.

Anthea was slender, red haired and a very fount of knowledge and wisdom where wild animals were concerned. James professed not to know the difference between a hyrax and a hyena.

Anthea appeared one day, bearing a rather rancid offering.

'Mr Cran? How very nice to meet you! I'm sorry to trouble you. You may, or may not, know that I have a pair of cheetahs at our place at Naivasha, Tiva and Taveta, a male and female.'

'No, really?' I replied. 'Any problems?'

'Well, they're eating all right and are as active as usual, but both seem to have lost weight. I've brought you a faeces sample to check for me. Perhaps they've got worms.'

'Mmm. Could well be, especially if they're cooped up in a wee cage.'

The wrong thing to say, I knew, as soon as the words were out of my mouth. Anthea bridled, her cheeks as red as her flaming thatch.

'Wee cage, my arse!'

As she was standing on the other side of the swing door I was in no position to comment on the latter, and as for the former, I had said 'if'.

'I'll have you know they live in a large, grassed, enclosure, open to air and sun.'

'Sorry for presuming otherwise, Mrs Prendergast. OK, let's have a look at that sample.'

It smelt awful, like a long-dead polecat. Holding my breath I looked at it as little as possible under the microscope. Hookworm eggs speckled the area under view.

I turned to my lady. 'Mrs Prendergast, you're quite right. Worms they have, hookworms to be precise.'

'Yes, I do like precision. Well, what are we going to do about it? Both Tiva and Taveta are very easy to handle, if that's any help.'

'Well,' I said 'There are two options – we can starve them for 24 hours and then add tablets to their meat, hoping that they don't reject them. Or, we, or, rather, I, can inject them, twice, three weeks apart, when I'm next passing.'

This rather rash offer was accepted, but it was too late to recant. Anthea had gone.

The day duly came when I was passing.

The cheetah enclosure was indeed large, wire meshed and close to a large two-storey mansion. On all sides velvety lawns stretched down to a belt of papyrus bordering the lake. It seemed an incongruous place to incarcerate two residents of the wide and windy plains – but, I reflected, most zoos and prisons take little notice of the feelings of their inmates.

The lady of the manor appeared and together we entered the cheetahs' den. If they had lost weight, they were still very large. They did not appear to resent my presence and allowed themselves to be stroked and scratched.

'OK Mrs Pren-.'

'Call me Anthea.'

'OK Anthea, I'm going to give them a subcutaneous injection of disophenol. Might sting a little but nothing to write home about. You grab hold while I inject.'

Anthea held them firmly round the chest while I quickly injected them both below the loose skin of the scruff of the neck.

The female made no sound but the male, Tiva, uttered a low growl and leapt away as soon as I had completed the injection. He stood in a corner, watching me as I went out, his spotted and barred tail twitching from side to side.

'Well, that was easy enough, wasn't it,' laughed Anthea. 'Now do come in and have a cup of coffee. James takes absolutely no interest in this sort of thing. Coops himself up in his farm office all day, poring over what's the best fertiliser to use on his crops. What a bore!'

I followed her up the imposing steps.

Anthea's arse was worth following.

Three weeks later I was back.

Syringes primed, I blithely pushed my way into the pen.

'Well, this shouldn't take long!' I said to my lady assistant.

The male cheetah had other ideas.

As soon as the door was closed behind us he walked briskly up to me. He didn't snarl or show his teeth. When he reached me, he raised both of his fore paws and clasped my right leg between them, above the knee.

The cheetah has a number of characteristics not associated with the cat family, chief of which are the inability to fully retract its claws and the possession of a large, pointed dewclaw on the inner aspect of the foreleg. I was acutely aware of these latter anatomical aberrations as they sank in, up to the hilt in my leg. The cheetah seemed to be enjoying himself, as he held me in a close and passionate embrace. I was not. I seized his forelegs and with a tremendous effort dragged them apart.

He made no attempt to bite and made no sound.

Anthea saw me holding Tiva by his wrists, a bit like a dancing master teaching an awkward pupil the first steps of a waltz, with blood coursing down my leg.

'Hugh, what on earth are you and Tiva up to? You naughty boys! Hey, I can see blood. I hope that's not Tiva's! It had better not be! You haven't stabbed him with one of your nasty needles I hope. Oh, it's yours, Hugh. That's all right then. OK. Let's get on with the injections.'

'Right,' I said, between gritted teeth.

The look on Tiva's face suggested that he was not dissatisfied with himself.

I made a mental note to suggest the tablets next time.

As we left the enclosure Tiva gave me a feline smirk.

'Well,' said Anthea, 'it's coffee time again, perhaps on this occasion with a little dash of something else, and I'll dab your poorly leg!'

As I followed Anthea's shapely derriere up the steps I reflected that there were beneficial spin-offs to being mauled by a cheetah.

🐾✕🐾✕🐾✕

The bushbuck is a handsome, medium-sized antelope, chestnut to dark-brown in colour, its flanks enlivened by a variable pattern of stripes and spots. The average weight is 150 pounds and the height at the shoulder 36 inches. The male has short, straight, partially-spiralled horns, which he puts to good use when attacked or cornered, being one of the most pugnacious of antelopes. The bushbuck, although elusive and shy, is still to be found over large parts of Africa, living as it does singly or in pairs, lying up by day in dense bush or forest, and emerging at dusk to browse on favoured shoots or leaves.

Sooner or later, a male bushbuck kept in solitary confinement will get the urge to sow his wild oats and if not allowed to do so will express his displeasure in a manner not calculated to endear him to his carers.

Wily the bushbuck lived in a large pen adjacent to the house, in Lanet, of Pat and Sue Neylan, who had decided that the time for the

274

parting of the ways was fast approaching.

The crunch came when their garden girl, Purity, went one day into Wily's enclosure to replenish his water bowl.

In view of the fact that during her 33 years on Planet Earth unmarried Purity had borne nine children, it appeared that her contribution to Kenya's family planning programme was less than whole-hearted.

One consequence of this seemingly endless procession of pregnancies was a steady and relentless deposition of successive layers of adipose tissue, rather like the sedimentation of such rocks as sandstone over the millennia of geological time.

As Purity bent down to add water to Wily's bowl, the caudal aspect of her upper thighs came into view.

The sight was more than Wily could bear. Lunging forwards, he skewered poor Purity, who rose with a shriek which awoke slumbering herdsmen and had distant pedestrians turning uneasily in their tracks.

Fortunately Purity's limbs were sufficiently well larded to ensure that the damage was superficial.

It was enough, however, to seal Wily's fate. He had to go.

Pat Neylan was a farmer, agricultural contractor and a skilled pilot, the owner of a red and white Cessna 180, a four place tailwheel machine, ideal for operating in and out of the rough, short, dirt strips of East Africa.

He phoned me one evening.

'Hi, Hugh! How goes it?' Pat's voice was unmistakable. 'Look, we've got permission to take Wily to the Mt. Kenya Safari Club at Nanyuki on Saturday afternoon. Can you come and sedate him or knock him out so that he's a manageable proposition on the journey? I don't want him jumping out of the plane half way there!'

Pat gave a great laugh. I also gave a great laugh and, before I realised what I was doing, I had agreed.

After I had put down the phone I reflected that I was less than well acquainted with *Tragelaphus scriptus*, as I discovered the bushbuck was called in scientific circles. Indeed my only sight of the creature had been a fleeting glimpse of a retreating rump in the thickets bordering Lake Nakuru. Today was Wednesday so I didn't have much time to find out what I needed to know if Wily was to arrive at his salubrious destination still breathing and still inside the plane.

I discovered that the recommended drugs for immobilising bushbuck involved combining a tranquilliser with a narcotic. The former included xylazine and azaperone, the latter etorphine and fentanyl. I also discovered that although these were the recommended drugs, no one seemed to have actually used them on a real live bushbuck. Great!

Between calls the following morning I phoned a chemist in Nairobi. I had decided to use the azaperone/ fentanyl combo and, mirabile dictu, he had both in stock, together with, even more miraculously, a supply of the antidote, nalorphine. I had a feeling the latter might be needed. The drugs were dispatched on the overnight taxi and arrived the following morning.

Their concentrations were such that the total volume of both fentanyl and azaperone, required to immobilise an adult bushbuck, was only 2mls and that of the antidote little more. If necessary then, the dart pistol could be used, but, as Wily was accustomed to people, both in and around his enclosure, I hoped that this would not be needed.

Saturday afternoon came and, armed with my equipment, some theoretical knowledge, and little else, I drove out to Pat's property at Lanet, on the outskirts of Nakuru.

Pat was in his early thirties, tall and good looking. His hair was dark and neatly combed. His penetrating eyes were blue, but not the languorous, deep colour of a balmy tropical sea, rather the sharp, vibrant, paler blue of northern waters, sparkling under a winter sun. His sense of humour was sardonic, such that it was sometimes difficult to know whether he was joking or being serious. He was generous to a fault.

In 1912, Pat's father, Dennis, had arrived in the country from South Africa. The population then was sparse – in some places almost to the point of non-existence. On one occasion Dennis walked from Thomson's Falls to Lumbwa – a distance of about eighty miles – in an area now densely packed with farms, both large and small, without seeing another human being or any sign of habitation. On another he went hunting for elephant in the region of Lake Baringo, where elephant have not now been seen for generations. During his return to civilisation his mules, bearing the trophies of the chase, succumbed, probably from horse sickness, in the region of Lake Hannington, leaving him stranded upon its baking, inhospitable, alkaline shores. There he survived by knocking down with a stick the flamingos which paddled around in its green, greasy waters. He then parboiled them in the adjacent hot springs and ate them.

Wily was lurking in a corner of his enclosure. He regarded us with suspicion. He knew that something was up.

He also looked a bit odd. I moved a bit closer and saw that Pat had put a length of rubber hose over each horn. He didn't wish to share the sufferings of poor Purity. I was grateful – neither did I.

I estimated Wily's weight, computed the required dose, and then reduced it somewhat to compensate for the fact that he was not totally wild, being habituated to the presence of people. It has been found that such animals react favourably to a lower dose than do their counterparts in the wild. Under the circumstances I sincerely hoped that this finding was correct.

We entered, Pat seized Wily by his rubberised horns, and, after a short, sharp tussle, I injected him in the rump.

'That should take effect in about twenty minutes,' I said.

'OK,' replied Pat. 'Let's go to the house for a cup of tea. Sue's coming along as co-pilot. I've removed the back seats of the plane and you and Wily will go in there as baggage.' He laughed.

Tea over, we returned to see how Wily was faring. He looked distinctly groggy. He gazed at us myopically with bleary, half-closed eyes, took a few unsteady steps, swayed slightly and, with an audible sigh, lay down.

We waited another ten minutes and then, as Wily raised no objection, secured his legs, gently but firmly, with a pair of Sue's tights, which Pat had purloined. Next, helped and hindered by Ezekiel, the Neylan's cook, we inserted the bushbuck into a large gunny bag, securing it loosely around his neck. A light scarf was put over his eyes to act as a blindfold and we were ready to move.

A pickup transported antelope and vet to the waiting flying machine. Into this the former was lifted and deposited into the space created by the removal of the two rear seats. This space was not inconsiderable, but comfortable it was not, as I discovered when I joined my charge. In case of emergencies I had brought with me my surgical bag, together with a further supply of the immobilising combination and the all vital antidote.

The afternoon was hot and it was stifling in the plane. I was glad when Pat and Sue got in, the engine was started and we taxied to the end of the grass strip for take-off.

'You two OK in the back there, Hugh?' Pat inquired with a grin. 'Got your seat belts on?' He laughed.

Pat ran through his pre-take off checks, dropped ten degrees of flap, applied full power and we were off. The tail rose and a few seconds later we were airborne. The plane banked and turned eastwards and began climbing steeply to clear the wall of the Rift and the distant foothills of the Aberdares. Seated as I was on the floor of the plane, below the level of the windows, I could only sense these various altitudes and movements through the seat of my long suffering pants.

My pelvis was not padded and neither was the floor beneath me. As time passed my discomfort increased. Wily appeared not to be concerned by his first flight. Eyes half closed, he squatted in his gunny bag, occasionally flicking an ear. The engine droned on. From where I sat I could see a patch of blue sky with the odd, puffy white cloud drifting past. Everything was going smoothly.

Suddenly we were in turbulence. The plane dropped sharply, a wing rose. As suddenly the plane was projected upwards and then fell again to the accompaniment of loose objects flying round the interior of the cockpit. A ballpoint pen shot past my left ear and then, just beside my right ear, there was a bang, loud enough to waken the dead. It certainly awoke Wily. The right door had opened and through it I could see, rather more clearly than I wished, exactly where we were – three thousand feet above the speckled plains of Laikipia. Only later was I told that there was no risk of the door opening completely - the blast of the slipstream would see to that – but neither was it possible to close it until we had landed.

Although the roar of the slipstream and the open air view of the tops of distant thorn trees were somewhat disconcerting, I had other things on my mind.

Wily wanted to leave.

When we entered the turbulence his eyes opened wide, he flapped his ears and tried to stand up. With his legs pinioned within the gunny bag, this mild initial attempt at escape was unsuccessful.

When the door opened he went berserk. Within a second one foreleg was free and out of the bag, stabbing the air like the baton of some demented orchestral conductor, but, in view of the sharpness of the hoof, rather more dangerous. In another second the other leg would be out and, if firm action wasn't taken, he would be competing with Pat for possession of the joy stick. The rest didn't bear contemplating.

Not that there was much time for contemplation.

I seized Wily's rubberised horns and bore him forcibly to the floor. His flailing hoof just missed my left ear. Visions of van Gogh, his head swathed in bandages, flashed before my bulging eyes. Out of the corner of those eyes, as we grappled on the floor, like a pair of all-in wrestlers, I could see, with frightful clarity, the mottled floor of Africa, far below. How big a·dent would we make in that ancient epidermis, I thought. Correction – two dents. What would be the velocity of our descent? What was the formula again? Thirty three and a third feet per second and increasing?

What was I thinking about? This animal was supposed to be immobilised. It was very obvious that a substantial top-up was required.

'Everything all right in the back?' Pat roared over the general cacophony.

'Yeah, just fine!' I bellowed back.

The problem was how to fill the syringe with the desired drugs without letting go of those horns straining to be free. Pat was unable to assist. Planes of this size don't have autopilots. And it was a bit late in the day to ask Sue to undergo a crash course in contortionism in order to wriggle over the front seats to come to my aid.

Wrapping my left arm firmly round the base of Wily's horns, trying to ignore the stabbing hoof, I inched my way across the floor towards my surgical bag, dragging him with me. With my free hand I opened a drawer and found a 2ml syringe and needle. In the process of attaching the latter to the former my index finger was in grave danger of being transfixed to my thumb. Next I removed the bottle of fentanyl from the bag and transferred it to my already-occupied left hand. The contortions which followed, as I withdrew what I hoped was an adequate volume from the bottle, would have drawn gasps of admiration from Houdini. Next came the azeperone. As the total volume was less than 1ml, I injected Wily in the muscles of his neck, all of his other muscles, with the exception of those of his right foreleg, being still, I was relieved to see, inside the gunny bag.

The minutes passed. Wily's struggles grew less. His head began to loll to one side. The his tongue flopped out of the side of his mouth.

'Well, that's it. I've overdosed him. He'll be dead before we arrive!'

After about twenty minutes I could feel the plane descending and then banking in a wide turn.

We were coming in to land.

Between the seats I could see Pat yanking up the flap handle and then there was a lessening of the roar of the engine as he reduced power.

Wily looked pretty close to being in a coma, but as the wheels skimmed the grass and we rumbled up the strip, the tail finally descending to earth, he began to show signs of life, withdrawing his tongue and flicking his ears.

'Still OK in the back?' Pat shouted.

'Yeah, not too bad,' I replied.

Pat turned the plane and taxied to where a pickup was waiting. As soon as the propeller had stopped turning, everyone, except Wily, got out. My struggles with my charge and my unrelaxed position on the floor of the plane had turned me into something resembling one of the victims of the Gorgon's stare. My exit was somewhat less nimble than that of pilot and co-pilot.

Wily was lifted into the back of the pickup, I clambered painfully up beside him and, after a teeth-rattling journey, deposited him in his new, sumptuous quarters. My number one priority was to give him the anti-immobilising agent. I had the pre-filled syringe at hand and wasted no time in shooting the contents into his jugular vein.

Within a few minutes he rose in a dignified manner to his feet, elevated his nose to give us a supercilious glance and turning, ambled off to inspect his new home.

'Well, that's good then,' said Pat. Sue had a tear in her eye. She had been very fond of Wily.

As for myself, I was mightily relieved not to be delivering a stiffening corpse to such a prestigious destination as the Mt. Kenya Safari Club. The very thought made my toes curl up within my boots.

I stood up, slowly ironing out the corrugations in what was left of my spine. Poor old Quasimodo, I thought. As I rose to the upright position, my exhausted orbs traversed upwards, across leagues of dark, dense, tangled forests, belts of feathery green bamboo, moorlands, whose extent could only be guessed, until they finally alighted upon the jagged peaks and sparkling glaciers of Mount Kenya, ten thousand feet above where I stood. What a sight for sore eyes! And what a location for one of the world's most famous hostelries.

To the hostelry we now repaired. A repast of some magnificence had been prepared for us.

'Just as blimmin' well we've brought a live bushbuck,' I thought, as we tramped through the hallowed halls towards our appointed table. Our unsartorial appearance drew curious glances from the well-tailored and tastefully coifed guests, sipping martinis and Bloody Marys on their various patios and verandas. As we sullied their personal spaces, the accents of Mid and Far West hung momentarily suspended. I felt like one of Attila's Huns bursting into a session of the Roman senate.

As we flew homeward over the Laikipia plains, the sun was sinking like a huge blood orange below the rim of the Aberdares. Behind and above us the topmost towers of Mount Kenya still flashed and shone in the crystal sky.

◈│◈│◈│◈│◈

Members of the animal kingdom would from time to time affect my best endeavours in many and curious ways.

A case in point was Spotty, the unimaginatively named dalmatian owned by noted herpetologist Jonathan Leakey. Both lived a life of some eccentricity on the shores of Lake Baringo.

The spotted canine had been struck by a lorry, sustaining a fracture of the left femur. He was brought to the surgery. I operated and inserted a stainless steel intramedullary pin in the broken bone. In due course the stitches were removed and Spotty returned to his carefree life on the shores of the lake. The weeks passed, the fracture healed and soon Spotty was running around on four legs as though nothing had happened. He had yet to be returned to have the pin removed.

One hot and sultry afternoon Spotty could stand the heat no longer and went for a swim in the muddy waters of the lake.

He failed to observe the log of driftwood lying half submerged in the shallows, close by a clump of reeds a hundred yards away. He also failed to notice, as he swam contentedly in the cool, refreshing water, the slow and stealthy movement of that log in his direction – until it was too late and the crocodile seized him by the leg and tried to drag him under.

Spotty struggled madly. Luckily for him the croc was an inexperienced stripling, more used to attacking frogs and fish than dalmatians. His teeth, however, were many and sharp and after a few minutes of frantic splashing, Spotty's leg was grievously rent.

As luck would have it a young lad came wandering along, turning over stones and boulders, searching for scorpions to take to the local witch doctor. In one hand he carried a rusty tin, half full of a nightmare of rustling, venomous horror. He saw Spotty thrashing about in the ochre-coloured water and at once realised that he was in the grip of a crocodile. He carefully set his tin down on the shingle and began hurling rocks into the water.

The croc gave up and, letting Spotty go, swam swiftly back to his lair in the reed beds.

Spotty dog-paddled for the shore, dragging his ravaged limb behind him. Miraculously, he hobbled home, leaving a trail of blood behind him, followed by his rescuer, who had retrieved his can of scorpions.

Later that day Spotty was brought to me for treatment. One glance told me that the leg was beyond saving and that amputation was the only answer if his life was to be preserved.

I operated and removed the same leg I had pinned only a few short months before.

✕✖✕✖✕✖✕

Some animals, innocuous themselves, could affect the lives of others.
The burrow of the aardvark, or antbear, can be a single gallery, leading to a large chamber. Sometimes it forms a complicated network, with many openings, spread over an area of hundreds of square yards. When abandoned, they are often occupied by reptiles, warthogs or small carnivores.

Occasionally these burrows could become death traps. Their wide openings sloped steeply downwards. Inquisitive calves and young cattle would investigate the entrances to these mysterious tunnels. A calf might venture right inside, but once within be unable to turn round and because of the steepness of the entrance, be unable to back out. A larger animal might slip down the earthy door step and become wedged. If they were lucky they might be found by a herdsman, before they died of suffocation or starvation. But the aardvark burrows were often screened by vegetation and sometimes animals went missing for days before being discovered, usually by chance, by smell if dead, and if alive, by the sound of subterranean bellowing.

On Kekopey Ranch, near Gilgil, a calf, and then an old Maasai herdsman, went missing.

A search was instituted. All the ranch workers took part and after 24 hours, they were found.

The legs of the poor old herdsman were found protruding from an antbear hole. He was pulled out. In front of him, further into the hole,

281

was a young calf. This was also removed. The herdsman was dead. He had probably succumbed to a heart attack while struggling in the tunnel entrance. In trying to save the calf, doing his duty, he had died.

The calf was alive.

You either like baboons, or you don't.

Dogs don't. Perhaps this is because baboons bear too much resemblance to themselves. An adult male baboon is a formidable adversary. With his huge canines he can inflict tremendous damage on any dog unfortunate enough to be caught. He will sink his teeth into the dog and then push him away with his powerful forearms, tearing out great chunks of flesh.

Although I had many occasions to regret the strength of those teeth, as I spent backbreaking hours stitching and repairing ripped up dogs, I felt a degree of sympathy for the baboons. The dogs were almost invariably the aggressors, probably trying to kill a young animal and, intruding into the well-knit organisation of baboon life, had fallen foul of these redoubtable primates, whose intelligence they invariably underestimated.

Baboons did not need to rely solely upon brute force to overcome their canine adversaries.

Charles and Olivia Hunter lived on a small farm on the slopes of Menengai Crater on the outskirts of Nakuru, where they milked cattle and grew grapes. They also made cheese, whose consistency and flavour was such that it was possible to be eaten without teeth and, preferably, without taste buds. In huge bubbling vats, located in underground cellars, they fermented their own wine. The bouquet was such that it was difficult to decide whether to drink it before, with, or after the cheese. Whatever qualities it lacked, potency was not one.

The Hunters kept English bull terriers, tough, muscular, stouthearted, loyal and essentially brainless dogs.

Of an evening dogs and owners would, from time to time, stroll up through the fields behind the house, to the rim of the crater, there to turn and admire the view across the town to the lake and the distant hills of Eburru. One evening a troop of baboons was also on the rim of the crater, although probably not admiring the view.

The dogs leapt forwards eagerly, barking furiously. The baboons rapidly retreated, mothers, infants and adolescents in the van, a rearguard of adult males confronting their frantic piggy-eyed enemies. A battery of enormous baboon canines kept the dogs at bay, allowing the females and youngsters to disappear over the lip of the crater. Slowly the guardian males also made their retreat, until only one large daddy baboon was left.

He appeared to be in no hurry to leave, strutting arrogantly within a few yards of the enraged bull terriers.

Suddenly he turned and made a rush for the cliff edge. The dogs, maddened by their lust for blood, tore after him. Too late, the dogs saw the abyss yawning beneath them. The baboon leapt into space, landing safely on a tree growing in a crevice, twenty feet below the rim. The leading dog fell two hundred feet to his death on the rocks below. The baboons barked in triumph. The other dogs, less fleet of foot, managed to stop just in time, paws scrabbling for purchase on the loose soil.

Dogs have short memories and over the next few years two more bull terriers took their final leap into space, while baboons barked in derision from the crags.

At regular intervals dogs, which had fallen foul of wild animals, were brought in for treatment.

Buffalo hounds were gored by buffaloes. Dogs which attacked porcupines appeared on the operating table with faces, chests and legs bristling with quills. When the beautiful, sad-faced, black and white, colobus monkeys occasionally descended from the trees in which they spent the bulk of their days, they were capable of inflicting impressive injuries on dogs which came within range of their claws. Very rarely a dog, selected for supper by a leopard, escaped, and was presented with hide ripped and torn by the cat's razor sharp talons. And dogs which were foolish enough to approach adult male water buck were often carried in with coils of intestine protruding from perforated abdomens. Dogs which fell foul of hippos were not presented because they were dead.

The excitement engendered by having Man's Best Friend thus savaged by Nature Red in Tooth and Claw could result in some surprising telephone messages.

One day I came into the surgery, after a series of farm visits, to find the following alarming communiqué written on the pad by my secretary: 'Dog mauled by guinea pig' – and the name of a farm at Elementaita.

I tried hard to imagine what sort of guinea pig was capable of inflicting injuries to a dog sufficient to warrant veterinary attention. Perhaps there was a mad scientist living on the Elementaita plains, breeding a super nova race of the rodent, equipping it with teeth along the lines of those once possessed by the sabre toothed tiger.

The mystery was solved when the patient arrived.

It had been gored by a warthog.

❋

The hour was late and I was making preparations to retire to what I hoped would be a well earned, if temporary repose, when the telephone rang. It was April, the wet season, and rain was thundering on the roof. The noise was deafening. This was bad enough. What made things worse was a poor line and the fact that the caller was Luigi Costa.

'Dottore! Dottore! Jambo! Is me, Costa! I call about Benito! He has bad leg! Benito! Very bad! I is coming now to you! Wait!'

Costa was an Italian, working on machinery maintenance on a sisal estate about twenty miles from Nakuru. He spoke a language which he believed to be English, an opinion shared by no one but himself. This language he spoke with tremendous fluency, accompanied by a hurricane of gesture, mime and arm flailing.

On one occasion I was privileged to be the sole recipient of Costa's verbal expertise when he came to the surgery for advice, concerning Benito, his large alsatian dog.

Benito was suffering from vomiting and diarrhoea, but he was so wild that Costa had been unable to get him into the back of his pickup.

All this was conveyed to me in Costa's unique combination of personal grandiloquence and vivid body language. He bent double and his face went purple as he demonstrated the dog trying to pass a jet of liquid faeces. An alarming, sound-accompanied exhibition of retching told me the poor Benito was now voiding his stomach contents. When it came to showing how his dog had refused to get into the pickup Costa leapt into the air, arms windmilling, jaws snapping like castanets.

I could only understand one word in ten, but I got the message.

It was now plain to me how it was possible for non-English speakers in Gujerat or the Gobi Desert to comprehend the performed works of Shakespeare. The details might be lost amid the sound and fury, but the gist was obvious.

Costa was middle aged, of medium height, with grizzled hair and carefully tended beard. The hair on his chest was also grizzled and contrasted with the gold medallion which nestled in the undergrowth, exposed to view by his carefully unbuttoned shirt.

When Costa met you on the street he would seize you by the hand, remove the cigar from between his teeth and start talking. After a minute or so I would try to withdraw my hand. Costa, sensing an attempt at escape, would tighten his grip. When it was finally released and I essayed a few tentative backward steps, Costa would keep pace, maintaining his fearsome, all-but-incomprehensible monologue at a range of a few inches.

It was at such moments that I wished Costa was more like his compatriot, Basso, a cattle manager on a farm near Njoro. Costa came from the south of Italy, Basso from the north. Basso, when speaking to non-Italian speakers, conversed only in Swahili, slowly and with ponderous deliberation, thumbs hooked into his wide leather belt, corduroy encased legs and booted feet firmly planted to give due dignity to his utterances.

However, it was not Basso on the other end of an appalling line, but Costa, and having heard the name Benito bawled several times in succession, I assumed that the alsatian was again in trouble. I bawled to Costa to bring Benito to the surgery as soon as possible.

Costa lived twenty miles away at the end of a dirt road. I waited for an hour and then drove to the surgery.

The rain had stopped. Clouds of flying ants were swarming around the few functional street lights and little knots of people armed with tin cans and plastic bags were busy scooping up the insects as they fell dazed to the ground. When lightly fried, I had been told, they made a delicious snack. Basically carnivorous by nature, I preferred to dine on selected cuts rather than consume the entire animal, guts and all, and as a result, had thus far felt no urge to become an insectivore.

Shortly after I reached the surgery, Costa hurtled round the corner in his battered Mercedes and screeched to a stop.

He burst out of the car, cigar clenched between his incisors. Without removing it, he launched into a verbal fandango, at the same time seizing his right leg below the knee and hopping down the street on his left. From experience I understood that Benito had suffered some sort of accident to his right hind leg.

After a few minutes of these verbal and physical histrionics, I suggested that we adjourn and turn our attention to the patient, still slumped on the back seat of the Merc.

As we carried him into the surgery I glanced at his hind leg. It was enormously swollen.

Costa explained that the alsatian had been found caught in a wire snare, set to trap game. The dog had been missing since the previous evening. A search party had been sent out and when he was eventually discovered, struggling with the wire noose biting deep into his hind leg, the lower part of the limb resembled a grossly over-inflated German sausage.

I examined the leg closely. The wire had cut deeply into the skin and muscle. The foot appeared to be devoid of sensation and the skin of the toes had turned an unpleasant shade of violet. I pulled the hairs and they came away in my fingers, revealing damp, cold skin. The legs and toes were thick, oedematous and doughy. The outlook looked bleak. I mentioned my fears to Costa, who said something unmentionable about poachers.

I clipped Benito's right foreleg and gave him a massive intravenous injection of hydrocortisone and crystalline penicillin. In order to relieve his obvious discomfort I gave him an intramuscular injection of pethidine, cleaned up the wound and dusted it with antibiotic powder.

285

Because of the gravity of the damage to the leg, above all, to the circulation, I told Costa that I would have to keep Benito in one of the surgery kennels, so that I could assess his progress on a daily basis and treat him as required.

For a few moments Costa was unnaturally silent. Then he launched into a tirade of unprecedented vigour against the callousness of those responsible for the injury caused to his faithful friend Benito.

'Bastardos! Bastardos! Povere Benito!' he yelled.

Amid a torrent of Italian, English and Swahili, four-lettered adjectives preceded an extraordinary variety of insulting epithets, which were shot out with a venom which surprised even me. Then, just as suddenly as the outburst had begun, it stopped. Costa shrugged his shoulders, gave a smile of resignation and helped me to carry Benito to a kennel.

Then, seizing my hand in both of his, he thanked me profusely for all my present and future help. With a courtesy, as touching as it was genuine, he gave me an old fashioned bow and was gone. I could hear his gravel-throated Mercedes roar off onto the night.

Over the next three weeks I fought to save Benito's leg.

Although the swelling slowly subsided, a large area of skin and muscle below the hock had lost its blood supply. As the days passed the affected tissues became necrotic and sloughed away, until a large section of bone was exposed. Amazingly Benito did not lose his appetite and tucked into his daily ration of meat and milk with gusto. At one point I feared that vital ligaments and tendons might be lost, rendering the leg little more than a useless appendage. Luck was with us, however, and although the poacher's snare had cut deeply, it had not rendered all of the blood vessels to the leg null and void. New flesh crept, with agonising slowness, across the white bone, to be followed by a paper-thin layer of new skin. The day came when Benito put a tentative paw to the ground. Shortly afterwards he was able to go home to Costa, who completed his aftercare with such devotion that three months later a large scar and a slight limp were the only legacies of the hunter's noose.

※※※※※

When time permitted, which was not very often, I would escape for half an hour from the unremitting stress and strain of dealing with the never diminishing flood of patients, the halt, the lame, the quick and, occasionally, the dead, together with their variegated and sometimes demanding owners, and repair to the shore of Lake Nakuru. The lake and its environs were designated as a bird sanctuary and had yet to be given national park status. As such, no fee was required for entry and from time to time I would nip down at lunch time and munch a sandwich or samosa at the point where the Njoro River flowed into the lake. Also dining at this spot would be several thousand flamingos and pelicans, sieving and scooping the soupy waters with all the frantic haste of birds for whom there was no tomorrow. The flamingos did not feed in silence and the air was filled with their chatterings and thick with the stench of their droppings, which carpeted the shoreline and enriched the slithery, alkaline water, swarming with the blue-green algae on which they fed.

The lesser fry pottered about on the foreshore – sandpipers, stints, ruffs and plovers – while in the air above, a shuttle service of cormorants flew between their nests in the tall trees on the edge of a clump of adjacent forest and their fishing grounds further out in the lake.

Despite the clamour of the feathered throng it was a strangely peaceful place.

In the distance a family of warthog might be observed rooting for their daily crust. Shaded by thorn trees, reedbuck drowsed away the mid-day hours, oblivious to the infantile antics of a group of adolescent vervet monkeys in the branches overhead. In the velvety cool of the forest, clumps of waterbuck drifted idly from one patch of greensward to another, expending the least possible amount of energy to maintain their bodily status quo. When I thought of the effort I daily expended to maintain my own bodily status quo, I occasionally thought that a short period of time spent as a waterbuck might be singularly soothing, especially on the shores of Lake Nakuru, which were all but devoid of predators.

At irregular intervals the crapulous grunts of a surfacing hippo would penetrate the avian Babel, sounding like an inebriated Indian Army colonel who had just been titillated by a scandalous story involving a member of the opposite sex.

Wild birds were often brought to the surgery for treatment.

A flamingo with a damaged wing, a hawk with a broken leg, a hornbill with an injured beak – all these and many more found temporary residence in the kennels normally occupied by cats and dogs. Their handling and treatment required great care. Equally important, if they were to survive, was the provision of a suitable and acceptable diet. Some bore no resemblance at all to what the bird ate in the wild. A mash containing various combinations of maize, bread, barley, rice, hard-boiled eggs, dog meal and cod liver oil tickled the palates of algae-eating flamingos – which was just as well in view of their dietary peculiarities.

On one notable occasion I gave bed and board to a Ruppel's griffon vulture with an injured wing – one of a consignment destined for an overseas zoo. Its sojourn strained my olfactory cells to their uttermost limits. The smell emanating from this massive, dark brown bird, with its bare, snake-like neck, was overpowering, a combination of the aroma one would get if one mixed several pounds of rotten meat with an armful of decomposed guts and topped it off with more than a whiff of excrement. I was unsure whether the stench was an integral part of the bird itself or whether it derived from its vulturine habit of inserting its head and neck deep into the innards of well softened carcases, the better to winkle out that juicy titbit so dear to a carrion-eater's heart.

This bird, together with his mates, had been caught in a drop-net, which had been suspended from a large thorn tree, below which lay the corpse of a zebra, shot four days previously. A few birds escaped when the net fell, but the majority had been trapped, bloated with meat and barely able to waddle, let alone take off.

It always amazed me how, when an animal died on an open plain, vultures would appear out of an apparently empty sky, spiralling down one by one, hopping clumsily across to the carcase, until it was so covered by a seething mass of squabbling birds as to be almost invisible. When an outbreak of East Coast Fever killed dozens of cattle on a farm adjacent to Lion Hill near Elementaita hundreds of vultures arrived for the feast. Normally there was not one to be seen.

At regular intervals I examined large numbers of birds being exported to zoos around the world. They came from the Baringo district and from the area at the foot of Mt. Elgon on the Uganda border. The former were birds living on, or by, the waters of the lake or in the nearby bush. The latter were in the main, forest birds. They arrived in crates, fitted with bowls of food and water, perches if necessary, and mesh screens admitting light and air.

Aloof and angular herons, with their air of academic abstraction, contrasted with the frenetic activity of tiny, iridescent sunbirds, flitting constantly from perch to feeding spout and back again. In one cage might sit a beady-eyed pygmy kingfisher, only four and a half inches long, so small it was not difficult to believe that it fed, not upon fish, but on insects such as crickets and grasshoppers. In another might be a pair of Ross's touracos, from the forests of western Kenya, large clumsy-looking birds, with violet-black plumage, crimson flight feathers, a square bright red crest, an extraordinary yellow–orange bare face and a medley of throaty, cackling calls.

Finches, weaver birds, barbets, flycatchers, warblers, bulbuls – the variety was difficult to grasp. There were so many species that the non-ornithological mind, such as my own, was quite boggled. In Kenya there are more than a thousand species of birds and for anyone arriving from more temperate zones, identification can be a frustrating task.

Personally I disliked intensely seeing birds confined in this way, even though I knew that they would be kept in much larger enclosures at their final destinations. Very few, if any, of these birds were endangered.

Africans, on the whole, are very tolerant of birds, rarely killing them, even when they feed on their crops. Certain tribes, such as those living on the shores of Lake Victoria, do trap small birds for food, and others, such as the Maasai and Samburu, encourage their young men to hunt them as part of their initiation rituals, but these are exceptions, and one of the joys of living in and travelling through Kenya is to see birds in large numbers all over the country. Even in the centre of Nairobi, with the pedestrians below surging to and fro like columns of disturbed ants, flocks of redwing starlings can be seen swooping gloriously over the jammed traffic. In almost every tree can be heard the perky chirping of weaver birds and the cheerful chattering of gregarious starlings, with their brilliant metallic plumage.

While travelling through the countryside I was constantly diverted by birds of every conceivable variety. Telephone poles were favourite perching places for birds of prey, such as the long crested hawk eagle, with its lax cockatoo-like crest blowing in the wind, and its air of proud loneliness. The poles were also much favoured by African hawk eagles and augur buzzards and sooner or later I would see one of these raptors launch itself at some unsuspecting rodent in the verge on the opposite side of the road.

Over wheat fields, marsh harriers cruised at low altitude, quartering the ground for prey, while during the European winter large numbers of steppe eagles arrived. Black shouldered kites were common, hovering over farmland.

Once I saw a large bird of prey flying slowly at high altitude with a snake, several feet long, dangling from its talons. It was having some difficulty in controlling its reluctant fellow traveller, which was writhing and wriggling in a desperate attempt to free itself. Slowly the pair passed out of sight.

Snakes were not the only objects which attracted the attention of these aerial carnivores – squawking chickens were not infrequently hoisted skywards by the ubiquitous black kites, and on one occasion I was presented with a cat, which had had an unpleasantly close encounter with a martial eagle, a bird with feet and claws of such strength as to be able to kill small antelopes.

In marshy areas the curious hammerkop was common, a rather disconcerting bird, with its sombre brown plumage, thick square crest and its habit of standing alone at the edge of some murky pool, staring fixedly into the water, as though seeing something there not visible to anyone except itself.

Wherever cattle were to be found, so too was the cattle egret, a delightful bird, with its delicate, controlled flight, snowy feathers and sociable habit of feeding in small, friendly, family flocks, among, and occasionally on, its large tolerant companions.

On the wide, breezy highlands the sight of a long-tailed widow bird, accompanied by his gaggle of female followers, is something to gladden the heart of anyone interested in birds. Jet black, apart from bright red and buff shoulders and with a tail two feet long, he flies with slow, jerky wing beats, tail expanded, a few feet above the ground. Equally striking is the ground hornbill, a massive stately bird, about the size of a turkey, very often seen in threes – an avian menage a trois – stalking over open ground in search of insects. A ground hornbill's eyelashes are immensely long and would be the envy of any film star, male or female. A friend, who had once kept one as a pet, told me that the bird was so amenable and intelligent that within a very short time it was completely house-trained.

And then there is that well-known eccentric, the secretary bird, striding across the windy plains, his crest of quills tossing to and fro in his quest for beetles, lizard, mice and snakes.

＊＊＊＊＊

Fabian Fitzpatrick was the manager of a large farm at Salgaa, near Kampi ya Moto, where he lived in a sprawling wooden house with his wife, Ophelia. Both liked to cultivate an air of genteel poverty. Other than at weddings or funerals, Fabian was never known to wear anything on his feet other than flip flops, which he purchased for a pittance in Nakuru. Economy was everything. On one occasion they happened to be in town and had one of their labradors with them and noticed that it had a considerable mass, which turned out to be a benign tumour, dangling from its belly. The dog was in fine fettle and not at all put out by this swinging lump, probably having grown used to it over the past few weeks. Eager not to squander time and petrol on a return trip to Nakuru I was asked whether I would 'whip it off while they waited?' I declined, and fixed a date for later in the week. Frugality won the day however, when they finally retired, to everyone's astonishment, to a baronial mansion in the shires.

One of Fabian's cows had died and I was on the farm doing a post mortem examination.

It was mid morning, the sun was blazing and the Africans removing the contents of chest and abdomen appeared to be moving in slow motion, seemingly stunned by the heat. Rivulets of sweat trickled down faces and necks. Crickets shrilled with deafening persistence in the long grass of the field in which the animal had been found, but, despite the noise, I felt myself growing drowsy in the heat. It required a conscious effort to concentrate. I mopped my brow and moved surreptitiously into the shade cast by a small thorn tree.

A yell, which combined disgust, horror and revulsion, brought everyone sharply and unexpectedly to full wakefulness.

A huge, hairy spider had leapt, for reasons best known to itself, into the now empty chest cavity. Its body appeared, to my startled orbs, to be about two inches wide and the legs several more.

My opportunity to examine the formidable and interesting arachnid vanished when my companions, who had understandably surged speedily backwards like a retreating tidal wave, surged forwards with equal force and a stout fellow wielding a panga bisected the creature with what seemed to me a degree of unnecessary violence.

I was assured that the spider was highly poisonous and that the slightest nip would result in a nasty, painful expiry. Perhaps, but that was unlikely to happen unless it was cornered or provoked. So I regretted its death, although if I had found it nestling in my bed or bath I knew that it would have been bisected, or even trisected, with equal vigour.

One day I was myself guilty of provoking a creature considerably larger, and potentially more dangerous, than the wretched spider.

Driving back from Subukia late one afternoon, I was climbing slowly out of the valley when I saw the body of a huge snake crossing the dusty road in front of the car.

Its head was hidden in the vegetation beside the road but I knew from its size that it could only be a python.

Without a moment's thought I jammed on the brakes, was out of the car in a trice and had seized the snake by the tail. The python showed no reaction to being thus rudely handled around its nether regions. It just kept on going. Although its head was invisible it looked about twelve feet long. I hauled backwards, straining manfully. For all the effect I had I might have been trying to arrest the progress of a runaway rhino. It dragged me to the verge. I let go and it disappeared.

'You stupid bugger,' I thought. 'What the hell did you want to do that for? Do that one more time and you'll be pushing up the daisies.'

Rather more attractive to most people's eyes than spiders and snakes were the caracal and serval cat I was occasionally called upon to treat. The former, the African lynx, with its long-tufted ears and fawn coat, was the epitome of wild savagery, utterly unable to be handled. The latter, spotted and striped, was as affectionate as a kitten.

Not quite so playful were the three lions, which suddenly appeared in the lower Subukia valley. No lions had been seen there for decades and it was surmised that they had come from the ranch lands of the Laikipia plateau to the east. They were an adult male and his consort and a half grown youngster.

Once again Peter Pring, whose cattle had been poisoned en masse by arsenic, was the recipient of bad luck. During the course of one week, five of his milking cows were killed by the lions. Another was mauled and sustained a punctured trachea, together with several lacerations and bites. This was probably due to the clumsy efforts of the unskilled adolescent, attempting and failing to make his first kill.

I repaired the various wounds and the cow made a good recovery.

Soon afterwards the lions killed another cow on a nearby farm and then disappeared, presumably back to their regular stamping grounds.

I was disappointed not to have been favoured with a face-to-face meeting with the perpetrators. But, not long afterwards, however, I was able to come whisker to whisker with some other lions, which helped to redress the balance.

I was asked by Marchesa Stephania Bartoluzzi of Naivasha to examine her four lions, due to be exported to the USA.

Two of the lions were mature adults, a male and a female. A few years previously they had been the unfortunate and presumably, unwilling, participants in a wildlife feature film, which had a strong anthropomorphic bias. The result, as far as the lions were concerned, was a strong anti-human bias.

The Marchesa, who was plump, personable, voluble and the wrong side of forty, led me to the lions' den, which was in a sort of grotto below her massive, castellated, mansion.

Encased in a totally unsuitable, mid-thigh, sheath dress, she sashayed down the steep, rocky steps, which led to the carnivores' dwelling – a large open-air cage with a rocky den in one corner.

'Now, zey are not so friendly as before. Not too bad, but...'

She left the word hanging in the air for me to digest.

As soon as I made my appearance before the bars, I was greeted with a snarling roar, as the two lions launched themselves in my direction. A frightening close-up of enormous yellow canines, exposed gums, flattened ears and pin point pupils had me stepping smartly and involuntarily backwards, almost onto the Marchesa's luridly painted toes.

'Right, Marchesa,' I said, with a light laugh. 'I think I can safely say that neither is suffering from caries, gingivitis or tonsillitis. What are you feeding them on? Their halitosis is awful!'

The Marchesa also laughed.

'Ah, we give zem offal, dead cows, we shoot ze warthog for zem as well. Sometimes horsemeat. Zey are loving it.'

'I'm sure they are.'

The rest of my examination was conducted at long distance.

The other two lions were almost too friendly.

'Zey are on Crescent Island,' said the Marchesa. 'If you will excuse me for one momento, but I must change.'

She returned, having changed from the skin-tight dress into skin-tight slacks. I assumed there was purpose to the change of raiment.

Crescent Island was joined to the southern shore of Lake Naivasha by a narrow causeway, and when we arrived the lions were nowhere to be seen.

As we got out of the car my companion informed me that, as soon as the lions saw or smelt us, they would appear. They, she assured me, were very fond of her. Having just peered into the very maw of the beast I sincerely hoped so.

As we moved through the open bush, the Marchesa would, every now and then, stop, raise her head and give a loud woof, rather like a Great Dane with laryngitis. This, I assumed, was meant to simulate a lioness summoning her wayward children.

It seemed to work, because shortly after an especially loud woof, delivered in a strong Italian accent, there was a sudden rush of tawny bodies, bursting through the vegetation. I stood my ground, fearing the worst.

I was ignored in favour of the Marchesa, upon whom they pounced. I didn't know whether to feel offended or relieved. Together they rolled and wrestled on the ground in what I hoped was a friendly tussle. Lion tussling was much easier, seemingly, in slacks than in a skirt.

Eventually the Marchesa surfaced from beneath her feline friends, to be almost immediately knocked down again. I had to admire her pluck. On the other hand, I thought, perhaps she was satisfying some sort of inner masochistic drive – you never knew with Italians.

Finally she staggered to her feet and gained some semblance of control over her charges. I examined them and pronounced both to be healthy and fit to travel.

But to what a fate – sentenced to incarceration for life in a chilly animal prison which, even if open-plan, nonetheless deprived them of freedom and activity. And in the main, they would be gawked at by bored, ignorant people with little interest in wildlife, having a day out and getting a cheap thrill and a snide sense of superiority over magnificent animals captured and brought from distant lands for their enjoyment and entertainment.

More fortunate were the groups of semi-tame antelope I helped to translocate from one part of the country to another. The duiker, reedbuck, oribi, impala and steinbok I darted, remained to live their lives beneath the wide, blue skies of Kenya, amid the sounds and scents of Africa.

293

CHAPTER SIXTEEN

Work! Work! Work!

There was no end to it.

The phone rang before I got out of bed in the morning. It rang after I had gone to bed at night. It rang during breakfast and during the evening meal. And, of course, all day long in the surgery. It got to the stage that, if the phone failed to ring for a couple of hours, I began to be concerned, to wonder if my standards were slipping, to worry about loss of income, until finally I could see myself peering out through the grating of the poorhouse or through the bars of the debtors' prison. Then the phone would ring again.

I was frequently exhausted, hungry and stressed. Mid-day meals were a rarity and it was a red-letter day if I arrived home before the onset of darkness. The social functions to which I was invited were marked, or marred, by my being, almost invariably, the last guest to arrive. Often, as I was arriving, the early birds were leaving, peering disapprovingly at me as I gave way to them on the road. As a result I found myself drawn, not unwillingly, towards the small remaining hard core, to be found at the end of every party, putting the world to rights amid a dense fog of beer and whisky fumes. Returning home in the small hours could be a hazardous exercise if the roads were muddy and slippery, but I found that with a few gins under my belt any piffling restraint vanished and I was able to tackle well-nigh impassable sections of turnpike with cavalier and reckless abandon.

My car, now a Peugeot 504 saloon, was robust, roomy and, by the modest standards of the day, fast. It was tailor-made for the highways, and more particularly, the byways, of Africa and was popular with participants in the annual East African Safari Rally. Spare parts were readily available and, for the non-mechanically minded, such as myself, it had the all-important asset of being reliable in all sorts of adverse situations. I had a sump guard and a petrol tank guard fitted and had the door pillars strengthened. It was good in mud and could almost, if not quite, be driven under water.

I had the opportunity of putting this surprising attribute to the test when travelling early one evening between the farms of Cyrus Morral and Captain Hugh Barclay.

While I was on the former, a thunderstorm of monumental proportions had broken. Rain had fallen to such an extent that all the fields were soon flooded. Having finished my work for Cyrus, I set off to attend to a sick cow on the Captain's farm, next door. The rain was still hissing down. As I came over the brow of an insignificant bump on the farm track, a stream which I had not seen before was coursing with some violence across my path. It was about a foot deep and ten yards wide. A slow and careful crossing with judicious use of the throttle to prevent water from entering the exhaust pipe soon had the vehicle on terra, which if not firm, was at least more solid than water. And it was visible, seen somewhat darkly through a windscreen obscured by rain and approaching darkness.

By the time I had dealt with the cow on Captain Barclay's farm the darkness was almost, if not quite, absolute. A few minutes later I was back at the newly formed torrent, which, to my concern, had risen during my brief absence by another eighteen inches.

I stopped to take stock of the situation. I studied the waters, whose surface was broken by whitecaps surging theatrically past in the gloaming. I could have turned around and returned home by an alternative, longer, route. But, stimulated by the challenge, and by the double dram of Glenfiddich forced upon me by the hospitable Captain, I decided to take the plunge and entered the flood at a speed equivalent to that of a lifeboat rushing down the slipway into a sea churned up by a force eight gale.

Like a destroyer burying her bows in a twenty foot high wave the car hit the water with a spectacular splash. She shuddered, temporarily knocked back onto her metallic haunches. Water surged over the bonnet and windscreen. The headlights were now under the surface, shining eerily in the depths. To my gratification the car kept on going, until she – and here the nautical ' she' was well deserved – reached the other side, where she rose from the flood like a surfacing submarine.

A couple of spark plugs were slightly dampened during these sub aqua manoeuvres but that was all. The car kept on motoring and they soon dried out.

Less fortunate was Jack Norton, who asked me to accompany him one weekend to Lake Baringo, where he proposed we did a little fishing and swimming.

Jack was a Baringo fetishist. He lived, slept and breathed Baringo. He could talk about nothing else. He spent all his spare time there, rushing down to water-ski, bird-watch, fish, sail and camp.

I knew I was in good hands, the hands of an expert, a local expert.

Saturday mornings were no less busy than the rest of the week so I told Jack that I would follow him in my own car and meet him at an agreed rendezvous on the lake shore in the late afternoon.

This, as it turned out, was a wise decision.

The road from Nakuru to Lake Baringo was all dirt and rock.

By getting up earlier then usual and missing lunch I managed to get away by mid afternoon and set off on the 75 mile drive to the lake. The road surface was dry and as I rattled through the double line of tin roofed shacks which made up the hamlet of Mogotio I reckoned on getting to my destination well before dark.

Hornbills, with their curious dipping flight, swooped across the road in front of the car. A pair of dik dik scuttled into the nearby bush, which grew more and more desiccated with each passing mile. The country was arid and uninviting, the vegetation dense and thorny. People were few. A solitary, snowy-toothed child minding a herd of goats gave me a tremendous wave as I crept cautiously across a rocky lugga. An old woman, carrying an immense load of firewood on her back toiled towards her distant home. A pair of lads, dogs at heel, bows in hand, strode swiftly and purposefully along the road.

On my left the craggy, wooded heights of the Tugen Hills marched northwards. To my right, viewed over endless miles of undulating thorn and rock, rose the eastern wall of the Rift Valley.

Lake Baringo was more than three thousand feet lower than Nakuru and the road very gradually descended towards the distant waters. Such being the case, I was surprised that after thirty miles I felt no perceptible increase in temperature.

I raised my eyes heavenwards in search of an answer and found it in the distant skies. They were an unpleasant purplish-black, the colour of an over-ripe grape. I had been so intent on avoiding the various irregularities in the road that I had not glanced above the horizon for the past half hour. As I now examined the as-yet far off firmament, the stygian skies were split by a sudden flash of lightning.

I still had some considerable way to go and optimistically hoped that a sudden bend in the road might bear me away from what looked like the mother and father of all storms. Perhaps a strong cross wind might blow it out of my path.

The road continued, straight as an arrow, homing in on the brute. The wind rose. Soon I could hear the mutter of thunder and the first huge drops of rain spattered themselves on the windscreen. A few seconds later forward visibility was virtually eliminated as I entered the storm. Great sheets of rain swept over the sodden bush, driven by a fierce gale. The ditches on both sides became rushing torrents but the road was rough and stony, so there was little chance of getting bogged.

So I pelted on, nose glued to the glass in an effort to see where I was going, wipers in overdrive, fountains of muddy water bursting out to left and right. A few goats stood miserably in the pouring rain, backs hunched and tails turned to the icy wind. I caught a glimpse of the youthful goatherd, crouched beneath a leafless thorn tree, soaked to the skin, grey with cold.

After a few miles the rain eased, lessened and finally stopped. The sky grew lighter and a few shafts of weak sunlight shone on a saturated landscape. The volume of water tearing down the sides of the road and lying in wide pools in the bush suggested that it had been raining here for some considerable time.

I bumped down the steep, gravelly incline to the suspension bridge spanning the Perkerra River, just south of the township of Marigat. I stopped the car and peered over. The river was in full spate, a roaring, brown flood, pouring through the gorge upstream from the bridge and overflowing the banks lower down. The noise of the water slapping against the banks and bursting over boulders was deafening.

Thoughtfully I carried on, wondering what had happened to Jack and if I would see the lake that night. Further on there were no more bridges, but there were several luggas, normally dry, to cross. But, with all this rain, who knew what I might find.

I did not have long to wait.

I passed through the suburbs of Marigat, a process which took mere seconds, consisting as they did, of only a few tin roofed dukas.

A mile further on I drove over a hump in the road and down the incline which led to the first lugga, and found that I had caught up with Jack. He was sitting in his car, a Peugeot 504 like mine, in the middle of a torrent, which was at least thirty yards wide. The windows were open and water was flowing in through the front left window and out via the right rear window.

In the back of the car I could see a seated figure, which I recognised to be that of Jack's daughter, Jenny, seated, like him, with water up to her armpits. The car had been partially slewed round by the force of the current and the front end was further up stream then the rear. From my privileged position it looked as though Jack had attempted an unsurveyed crossing and had driven into a depression or hole in the bed of the lugga, which was normally as dry as the proverbial bone.

I parked my car and advanced into the flood. As I did so, Jack opened his door and stepped out and was almost swept away. He stumbled, slipped and groped his way along the side of the car. With an effort he floundered like a gunshot walrus in my direction, finally reaching a spot where the water was only knee deep.

I was relieved to find that the water was quite warm. It was obvious that the extraction of Jack's car would be the work of more than a few minutes.

By this time a considerable collection of interested dwellers of the local area had materialized, as if from nowhere. On my arrival, apart from a couple of incurious rustic swains studying the scene with non-committal and casual indifference, the river bank was deserted. Now there was a colourful crowd, chattering and laughing and generally having a good time. It was Saturday evening after all. The occasional whiff of pombe drifted in my direction. Now and again one of the mob stumbled and almost fell into the river.

Jack gave me a brief and rather terse summary of the situation.

'I've crossed this bloody lugga scores of bloody times, I tell you. Never had any trouble before. In and out. The bottom's usually hard and stony. There must be a hole half way across. I bet some bugger's been digging for sand and dug a bloody great pit, right in the middle of the bloody road! Absolutely bloody well typical! Now look what's happened!'

We waded back to the car and from the flooded boot, Jack, with some difficulty, extricated a rope. It looked rather frail to my inexperienced eyes, a bit like the thing you would use to suspend your laundry from, not the hawser I imagined would be needed to haul out vehicles embedded in rivers. But who was I, a mere tyro in such a situation, to argue with a local expert? He fastened it to the metal ring below the rear bumper. This was not easy because of the shifting sand and gravel. The whole river bed seemed to be on the move.

While Jack directed operations, about fifteen muscle-men, including myself, seized the rope and began pulling. The water where we stood was about knee deep and it was hard to maintain balance on the unstable gravel. Nothing happened. The car obstinately refused to budge. We strained until our eyeballs bulged.

Jack showed signs of irritation. It was obvious that we weren't putting our backs into the job. His language became a trifle peremptory and peppered with those words not normally used in polite society.

We tried again, heaving with might and main.

There was a sharp crack as the rope parted. Fifteen bodies staggered backwards and fell with a communal splash into the river.

We rose from the river bed cackling with laughter, looking like a gang of half drowned, inebriated rats. Our involuntary immersion in the tepid water was no shock to the system.

Suddenly, above the roar of African laughter, I heard a curious rumbling sound. All heads, including mine, turned upstream. Round a bend in the lugga poured a miniature tidal wave. Not big by international standards, only about a foot high, but enough to unbalance an unsuspecting wader and to cover a bit more of Jack's unfortunate car. It made one wonder what might come next. I could see the car being borne into the bosom of Lake Baringo, together with daughter Jenny, who still sat on in the rear seat, as though in a sort of mobile Turkish bath.

Jenny was persuaded to vacate her watery couch and we waited and watched to see what would happen next.

To general relief there were no more tidal waves and the water level began, very slowly, to drop.

'Right, Hugh,' declared Jack. 'Man has failed, so I suggest we now try horse power in the shape of your car. The level's low enough for you to reverse in and hitch up to my car.'

As Jack's tow rope had been found to be wanting, I produced my own, a lengthy home-made affair, constructed from a defunct parachute, and virtually unbreakable.

The level was still falling, so I turned my car round and backed gingerly into the water, which was now only ankle deep. We hitched up, I shoved the gear stick into first, raised the clutch and applied power and then some more. The rope held firm but so much sand, gravel and stones had built up, around and under Jack's wretched car that nothing short of a bomb, tractor, or four wheel drive vehicle was going to shift it. All I was doing was digging myself into the bed of the lugga.

By now twilight was well advanced and in a very few minutes it would be pitch dark.

I cast off and drove back to Marigat as fast as I dared.

Through the open doorways of some of the dukas lining the solitary street I could see the flicker of hurricane lamps. Outside one of the larger establishments I spotted a parked Land Rover. I turned and stopped beside it. The building, which had mud walls, glass-less windows and a corrugated iron roof, proclaimed itself to be the Marigat Hillton Hotel. This was inscribed on a large yellow board, which in the fading light, looked positively faecal. The signwriter had misjudged his letterings somewhat, and the last two letters of 'hotel' were jammed almost illegibly beneath the first syllable. One side of the mud wall entrance was enlivened with a painting of a well-dressed gentleman, seated at a table and raising to his lips a tankard of gargantuan proportions. On the other side of the doorway another painting depicted what appeared to be a female version of the Laughing Cavalier, although less flamboyantly attired, leering suggestively at her male counterpart downing his beer a few feet away. The artistic style was strong and vigorous with no wastage on extraneous detail.

As I approached the simple portals of the Marigat Hillton Hot I could see that its dim interior was jammed with a mass of shadowy figures. A radio was blaring Zairean dance music, people were shouting and the smell of roast goat hung strongly on the evening air.

With some trepidation I stepped inside.

For a few moments my entry went unnoticed.

Then every head swivelled in my direction and the shouted and spoken word abruptly ceased. This is not to say that there was silence. The rural ghetto blaster continued to pump out its hypnotic rhythm at maximum decibels.

I approached the bar counter, which was covered with beer bottles and awash with their contents. The surface was innocent of glasses and mugs.

Selecting a large, jovial, prominent looking fellow, with an abdomen to match, I explained my, or, more correctly, Jack's predicament. He gave a great roar of laughter, in which he was joined by his drinking companions. Throwing his arm round my still soaking shoulders, he ordered me a beer, told me that his name was arap Sang, revealed that he was the owner of the Land Rover, and that of course he would help, but there was no need to hurry. By the time we had drunk a couple of Tuskers the water in the lugga would have fallen as rapidly as it had risen and then it would be a relatively simple matter to pull the vehicle out.

'Bloody good thinking,' I concurred.

'Yass, and no hurry in Africa as well!' he laughed.

Half an hour later, feeling rather warmer if not much drier, I followed my companion out to his somewhat dilapidated Land Rover, into which, with some difficulty, he heaved his beery bulk.

As only one of his headlights was working I drove ahead in my 504 back to the lugga.

Jack was striding up and down the shingle like a guardsman on parade. Jenny was sitting on a boulder, drawing on a languid cigarette. How it, and the match which lit it, had escaped immersion, was a mystery.

'Where in hell's name have you been? What took you so long? I was beginning to think you'd bloody well shoved off back to Nakuru!' Jack was on serious edge.

I raised an admonitory finger.

Seconds later friend arap Sang roared and rattled to the rescue.

As he had said, the water level had indeed fallen – to such an extent that there would be now no difficulty in my being able to cross by car – provided I drove upstream and avoided the hole into which Jack had so precipitously driven.

Arap Sang reversed his Land Rover, backed up and, with the aid of my despised piece of parachute, hitched up. With a crunch he inserted four wheel drive and then, with an unpleasant grinding of metal against rock and gravel, he dragged Jack's Peugeot out.

Once on the bank Jack did everything he could to get his car to start. It was hopeless. Sand, grit, gravel and water had invaded its very vitals.

The silence which greeted the turning of the ignition key sounded very expensive indeed.

Jack, was, by this time, not surprisingly, close to the end of his tether, with Jenny not far behind.

Together, with the assistance of proffered largesse, they persuaded arap Sang to tow their stricken vehicle to the lake. He agreed, but pointed out that there were further luggas ahead to be crossed before sanctuary could be reached.

We set off. Arap Sang led the way, with Jack closely attached behind. I followed at a discrete distance. The lugga now presented no major difficulties – a short rush upstream, followed by a rapid turn downstream and I was across and following the rather sad hindquarters of Jack's car along the track lined by dense, dark vegetation.

A shallow stream appeared and was easily forded. We rounded a bend and in front of us was yet another lugga. In the darkness, with our headlights flashing on the dark water sliding past, it looked deep, too deep for any car to cross unaided. Arap Sang drove slowly into the water, pulling Jack behind him. The exhaust pipe of his 504 dipped and disappeared below the surface, to be followed by the bumper. Soon the water was half way up the doors. This, I thought, wasn't doing the car much good. Both vehicles reached the father bank, but, with the possibility of yet more watery obstacles ahead, I decided to call it a day, or, rather, a night. Whatever Jack was using his vehicle for, mine was primarily for work, and wouldn't be of much use submerged in the environs of Lake Baringo.

I conveyed my decision to Jack and turned for home, which I gained at about midnight, after a journey which strained my powers of concentration to the utmost.

Jack reached the lake, but his poor car never fully recovered from its ordeal. A lorry had to be summoned to tow it back to Nakuru, and during this seventy five mile succession of bashing and bumping my unbreakable tow rope finally sundered. Jack had the engine overhauled and sold the car shortly afterwards.

An expensive weekend.

In the dark and tangled highland forests of East Africa there lurked a disease yet to be discovered elsewhere in the world.

This was Bovine Petechial Fever, or Ondiri-itis, so named after the farm on the outskirts of Nairobi, on which the first case was discovered. The cause was a rickettsia, endemic in wild animals, and in particular the shy and secretive bushbuck.

Cattle grazing in forest or along its edge were liable to contract this disease via an as yet unidentified insect vector, probably a tick. The main symptoms were widespread haemorrhages throughout the body.

The forests above Njoro, those at the head of the Subukia Valley and those on the southern slopes of Mt. Londiani were all danger zones. As were the margins of Lake Nakuru, where many bushbuck were to be found, favouring the cool, wooded margins of the lake. I saw many cases in these areas. It was one of those diseases which, once seen, was thereafter unmistakable. The scattering of pin-point haemorrhages on the mucosa of the vulva, the bleeding into the anterior chamber of the eye and the swelling and eversion of the conjunctiva producing the colourfully named poached egg eye, the black tarry dung, all helped in making a diagnosis.

Unless treatment using double doses of tetracyclines was started very early, death was a common outcome to an attack of Ondiri-itis.

Before the true nature of the disease was discovered some bizarre treatments were advocated, including the intravenous injection of liquid paraffin and turpentine. Why this concoction should have worked was beyond my comprehension but several old timers swore by it.

With the relentless encroachment of human settlement, the destruction of the forests and the resultant decline in the bushbuck population, the disease has latterly become much less common.

Personally I found this rather sad.

After all, here was a rare organism, endangered itself, doing its bit to preserve the environment by persuading cattle farmers to keep their stock away from the forest edge and thus save vital areas of water catchment. The threatened extinction of this fascinating disease, together with its host and its forest refuge were pointers to a future full of looming calamity.

A disease which has shown no signs of declining is Three Day Sickness, otherwise known as Ephemeral Fever. A viral disease of cattle, carried by midges and mosquitos, it causes a muscular stiffness, lameness and sometimes an inability to stand. Because of difficulty in swallowing, the animal often drools from the mouth. There is a rise in temperature and a drop in milk yield, but most animals recover spontaneously without treatment after a few days.

Epidemics would sweep the country at regular intervals, sometimes affecting many thousands of animals. It seemed to me to occur more commonly on open plains, perhaps due to involvement with wild animals.

Because of its superficial similarity to many other diseases, when outbreaks occurred I would be inundated with calls for assistance. One Sunday I visited 18 farms to examine cattle affected by various forms of the illness.

On the whole it was a benign ailment and death was very rare. Recovery was virtually assured and one left the farm with the self-satisfied feeling of having done some good without actually having done anything more than make a simple diagnosis.

Other diseases were not quite so accommodating.

Kim Mandeville was a belted earl, a duke no less, a gentleman farmer with oceans of blue blood surging through his aristocratic veins. He was no ordinary mortal. But, despite having ancestors dating back to the time of King Alfred, Beowulf and Sir Bedivere, he wore his ermine lightly and was as friendly and as easy going as you could wish. With his charming wife he lived on a small farm in Subukia. For some reason his lovely partner found it necessary to fortify her existence with numerous daily draughts of mother's ruin, a practice which did nothing for her physical and mental wellbeing.

Kim had been, for a while, an amateur rally driver, competing in the East African Safari Rally. On one occasion he had been involved in an accident, which had resulted in a head injury. This, although serious, had healed well, with the exception of damage to one tear duct. As a result he had to frequently mop one weeping eye, a disconcerting habit, which had the uninitiated wondering what had been said or done to have thus stung poor Kim to the very quick.

A number of Kim's cattle were unwell.

'Sorry to trouble you, Hugh, old chap, but I wonder if you could pop out and cast a glance over a few of my calves. They just don't look right, not eating, losing weight, reluctant to move.'

Kim gave the impression that I would be doing him the most tremendous favour by visiting his farm, whereas I felt the opposite was the case.

A fresh breeze was stirring the branches of the thorn trees as I drove down the narrow, dirt road to Kim's farm. The sky was a perfect turquoise blue, fading slightly towards the horizon. A few small clouds floated high over distant hills, whose ridges and contours stood out with extraordinary clarity in an atmosphere washed clear by overnight showers.

A black-headed heron stood motionless in the shallows of a small reed-fringed dam. A pair of ring-necked doves flashed, twisting and turning, through the branches of nearby trees. Nesting weaver birds twittered and chuckled in the thorn trees.

It was difficult to imagine disease and death, whether animal or human, occurring amid such idyllic surroundings, but alas, such conditions seemed to positively promote outbreaks of plague and pestilence.

Kim was sitting in state, partaking of a solitary late breakfast. He asked me to join him. Over lemon tea, sipped from cups as large as porridge bowls and poured from an antique silver teapot, worth more than my annual income, nibbling wafer-thin shards of brittle toast, well larded with home made butter and Chivers marmalade, we discussed the outbreak of disease affecting the calves.

'Yes,' said Kim, 'Several calves are unwell. They're all between four and six months of age. They're not keen to graze, they're salivating, and some have got diarrhoea. And they don't like being in the sun. They always seem to be lying under trees. And another thing I've noticed. Their skins are sticky.'

'Sticky?' I said.

'Yes, sort of moist and tacky.'

'I see,' I replied. I didn't really, although I had a vague idea what this might be.

We had another mammoth beaker of tea and then strolled across an acre of velvety lawn, crossed the dam wall and climbed a style into a small paddock where a small cluster of black Aberdeen Angus calves was grouped under a tree. Sitting on the grass beside them were two muscular Turkana men. The elder of the pair had a large metal plug protruding from his lower lip. It pulled his lip downwards slightly, exposing his splendid teeth, glistening with saliva. The younger man, who had no lip plug, had several rows of small scars encircling his brawny biceps.

The calves were depressed and apathetic. Dried dung, evidence of chronic diarrhoea, clung to their hindquarters. A cloud of protesting flies rose as we approached. A sour, foetid smell hung in the air.

The younger Turk seized a calf for my inspection.

The calf was emaciated and dehydrated and had a marked rise in temperature. I looked in the mouth. The gums and palate were reddened and inflamed. The coat felt wet. I felt the skin in the groin and axilla. It was damp and, as Kim had said, sticky. I pulled at a tuft of hair and it came away in my fingers, exposing a raw, square, patch of skin. The calf flinched in discomfort.

'Kim,' I said. 'This is sweating sickness. There's nothing else it can be.'

'Really, tell me about it.'

'Well, I've only seen a couple of other outbreaks, as it appears to be quite localised, confined to small isolated areas.'

'Just my luck, then, that it decided to pop up here. Murphy's Law I suppose.'

'Yes, it's an odd disease, a tick-borne toxicosis, difficult to prevent and difficult to treat. So it's not an infection. The toxin develops in the tick and the longer the tick remains on the calf the more severe the symptoms. A short period might produce no symptoms and no immunity. A bit longer, moderate symptoms and reasonable immunity. And a bit more, severe symptoms and death.'

'Which is what I've got,' said Kim.

'Looks like it. All we can do is give the calves some antibiotic to combat secondary infection and the rest is tender loving care, keeping them out of the sun and rain, giving them an easily-digested diet and removing all ticks. Even so, some will probably die.'

After I had injected the calves we walked back to the house.

'It's bloody difficult,' I said, 'to induce immunity without killing the calves. You can't eradicate the ticks, because they have alternative hosts, such as birds and wild animals. So you have to try and dip or spray the calves in such a way that the ticks can feed on the calves for about four days and produce a mild reaction, followed by immunity. Got it?'

Kim gave me a wry smile.

'Damn Murphy's eyes!' he said.

🏛✕🏛✕🏛✕

Emergencies took many different and manifold forms.

Shona Penn was the wife of Ken, headmaster of Nakuru Secondary School. An attractive, willowy ash-blonde with a barbed sense of humour and a penchant for smoking her favourite brand of nicotine through a cigarette holder of extravagant length, she maintained a modest string of mounts in stables adjacent to her house on the school compound.

One afternoon Shona phoned the surgery.

There was an unusual note of panic in her otherwise well-modulated tones.

'Hugh, can you come! Now! Please! Something terrible has happened to Ngorare. He's my favourite horse and Kiplangat, my syce, has just come rushing up to the house to say that he's collapsed. He can't get up! He's struggling to rise but he seems to be paralysed in both hind legs.'

From where Shona was standing, telephone in hand, she could see the wretched Ngorare in his rather overgrown paddock, flopping about on the ground like a tethered elephant seal.

'What the hell?' I thought.

'Right, on my way,' I replied.

The school was only a couple of miles from the surgery, so I had little time in which to cudgel my overtaxed brain as to what on earth was on the agenda this time. Before I had got my cerebral cortex into first gear I was on the premises.

Ngorare was in a fearful state, as was Shona.

The former was covered in sweat, his nostrils were dilated and his eyes rolled in terror as he struggled to gain his feet, his hindquarters hidden in a luxuriant growth of waist-high weeds.

The latter was pacing up and down like a caged tigress, inflating and deflating her shapely superstructure as she puffed on the local equivalent of a Balkan Sobranie.

'Hugh! Thank God you've come! Thank God!'

305

I wished people wouldn't say that. It made me feel that I was there as an emissary of the Almighty, expected to work a miracle on His behalf.

'Poor Ngorare! Look at him! Can you help him? What's happened to him?'

'Well, let's have a closer look at him. I can't see his hind legs in all this undergrowth.'

I forced my way into the weedy thicket.

'Curious,' I called out, 'I can see his tail and his pelvis, but his legs seem to have vanished.'

'What?' Shona's voice rose several octaves.

'Yes, no sign of them at all!'

By this time Shona was almost hysterical.

Kiplangat was close at hand, anxiously watching the proceedings. I dispatched him to fetch a grass slasher, that indispensable length of bent metal, used all over East Africa to cut away rank and unwanted herbage.

Rapidly and expertly he cleared a wide swathe around the unfortunate Ngorare's rear end, which appeared to have sunk into the earth.

Ngorare made another violent attempt to free himself from whatever had him in its grip, and as he did so, I caught a glimpse of a wooden edging.

I returned to the car for my longest and strongest rope and requested Shona to summon assistance from the school. When a small posse of excited workers had assembled I drew the rope around and below Ngorare's tail and gave the order to pull.

Ngorare emerged from the clutches of Mother Earth like a cork from a bottle. Or, rather, from an abandoned lavatorial long-drop, which had lain hidden in the weeds, until Ngorare had tumbled into it. It was fortunate that its dimensions were such as to have prevented any more of his person from entering, or the logistics of extraction would have been nightmarish.

Both Ngorare and Shona looked a trifle sheepish as I accompanied them to their respective quarters. Over a welcome cup of tea Shona at last was able to enjoy a hearty laugh.

There was nothing laughable about the predicament of another patient I saw a few days later.

Major Freddie Jones farmed at Njoro. An elderly bachelor, with a distinguished military record, he had served in three wars – World War I, World War 11, and the 'Mau Show'. Whenever I visited his farm he would invite me in for a glass of port or a mug of beer and regale me with tales of life in the trenches. He had fought in the battle of the Somme, in which he had earned a DSO and an MC and in which trench foot had almost carried off his lower extremities. A yellowing photograph of himself as a young hussar, resplendent in frogged jacket, stared down at us from the mantelpiece.

Freddie's constant companion was Simba, a large yellow labrador.

As Freddie limped round the farm, leaning on his stick, clad in voluminous 'empire builders' – the baggy, knee length, khaki shorts he always wore – Simba seemed to be constantly at his heels.

Now both Freddie and Simba, neither particularly steady on their pins, were in the surgery. Accompanying them was Kimani, an ancient retainer, who served Freddie with a mixture of devotion, resigned tolerance and the respect reserved for someone even older then himself.

Leaning on his stick and peering at me earnestly with his faded blue eyes, Freddie explained that when Simba had returned home earlier that afternoon, after a solitary run, he had a minor fit or convulsion. This had only lasted a few seconds, but half an hour later he had another. The latter was more violent and lasted longer. Simba did not fall down, but the Major, wisely, thought that he should seek help.

On the journey to Nakuru, Simba had yet another fit, in the car, his limbs, head and body racked with violent, uncontrollable convulsions. By the time the party reached the surgery Simba appeared to be rather better and he was able to totter, albeit rather unsteadily, inside.

As Simba wandered rather apprehensively round the surgery, sniffing at various objects of interest, I watched him carefully.

Suddenly he stopped in his tracks, became completely rigid and jerked violently backwards, juddering and twitching, almost falling down. This lasted about thirty seconds and then stopped. Simba resumed his inspection of the surgery. Ten minutes later he had another fit. This one was so severe that he fell onto his side, limbs thrashing wildly, head and neck bent backwards.

Moses was in attendance and together we lifted Simba, struggling madly, on to the table. I filled a 20ml syringe with the anaesthetic sodium pentobarbitone. While Moses held Simba's right foreleg, which was jerking backwards and forwards like an uncoordinated piston, I clipped the hair over the cephalic vein. Not an easy task. By the time I had finished jerking backwards and forwards in sympathetic rhythm, I felt almost in convulsive mode myself. After episodes like this I often thought that I would acquit myself rather well as a surgeon in an open boat in a full gale, going with the flow, so to speak. With difficulty, slowly and methodically, I injected a few mls of the solution into the vein, then trickled in some more, until the labrador relaxed, the convulsions stopped and he lay on his side, breathing slowly and deeply.

'Freddie,' I asked, 'what cattle dip do you use?'

'Beg pardon?'

'I said, what cattle dip do you use?'

'Kimani,' said Freddie, 'sisi na safisha ngombe na dawa gani?'

'Toxaphene, bwana,' Kimani replied.

'Major,' I said, reverting to formalities, 'I'm pretty sure that this is toxaphene poisoning.'

'Really? Explain yourself, sir!'

'Well, the symptoms, severe though they are, are not severe enough for, say strychnine poisoning, and I've seen toxaphene poisoning before, and what Simba did just now is very typical. The stuff is very toxic and will kill dogs and jackals, even hyenas. There's no antidote but provided one gets the convulsions under control by giving the dog a general anaesthetic there is a good chance of recovery, which is not the case with strychnine poisoning. It seems not to have an unpleasant taste and so hungry or thirsty dogs will lap it up. Perhaps Simba was hot and thirsty and near the dip and had a drink or perhaps some swine dropped a piece of poisoned meat near your boundary.'

'Yes, they used to do that during the Mau Show. Evil buggers!'

Kimani, who for all I knew might have played a leading role in the Mau Show, remained impassive, gazing intently at the unconscious Simba, who was breathing slowly and steadily – a good sign. If his respirations had been fast and shallow the outlook would have been poor.

Farmers wishing to rid their properties of stray dogs, jackals and hyenas would often inject toxaphene into small chunks of meat, dropped at strategic points. But this did not always work out as planned. One farmer left out pieces of poisoned meat, trying to kill a stray dog. The intended victim ate the meat, which it vomited shortly afterwards. The farmer's terrier, out for a nocturnal stroll, came across the ejected offering, swallowed it, went into convulsions and promptly died.

'Right, Freddie,' I said. 'You had best leave Simba here for the night. I think he should recover all right. I'll check him later this evening.'

'All right, Cran, if you say so. Give me a ring if he gets worse.'

I returned to the surgery at just before midnight and Simba was still out cold. But his membranes were a healthy pink so I remained confident. The following morning he was walking round the surgery wagging his tail.

Freddie was delighted beyond measure, beaming from ear to ear as he hobbled out to his waiting car, Simba once again at his heels.

When two emergencies occurred simultaneously I could be caught unpleasantly in a cleft stick, with the manure and feculence whistling at high speed in my direction.

Late one Saturday morning Peter Brown phoned from Marmanet Estate, Subukia, some thirty miles from Nakuru. Peter Brown used to be Peter Braun, and he was German, tall, lean, blue eyed and blond haired, as one expects Germans to be. Scurrilous rumour had it that he had been an S.S. officer during the war and that his number was tattooed in his armpit. Peter did not exactly goose-step or click his heels, but he had that slightly intimidating camp commandant manner which made one decide that it might be better not to mention the war after all.

'Iss zat you, Herr Doktor Cran?'

I just stopped myself from answering 'Jawohl, mein officer,' when he continued. 'My Cherman Shepherd Dog, Rommel, iss very badly injured. He chased a rabbit, und ze rabbit under a gyro mower did run, being pulled by a tractor. Ze tractor was cutting ze grass by ze farm road. It has now chust happened. Can you vait until I arrive? By ze way ze rabbit escaped.'

I was glad to receive this post-scriptum.

I asked Moses to prepare the instruments for the lengthy job which I knew lay ahead.

At about 1.30 Rommel and his Teutonic owner arrived.

The former, weak from loss of blood, was carried in on a sack. He was carefully laid on a table and I carried out a thorough examination. He was covered in a mass of cleanly incised wounds. The blades of the gyro mower had done their work well. He had a compound fracture of the left radius and ulna. His right carpal joint had been slashed open. Except for one foot all of his toes had open fractures. In some the joints were exposed. In others the bones were partially or wholly severed. In addition there were several skin wounds of varying length.

He looked as though he had been attacked by a madman with a butcher's cleaver.

Clearly it was going to take me all afternoon to repair Rommel. Luckily the wounds were all clean, sharp edged, uninfected and very recently inflicted.

'OK, Mr Brown, leave him with us and come back in a couple of hours or so and see how we're getting on.'

'Tanks, Doktor, he's a gut dog.'

Herr Braun marched smartly away in the direction of the Men's Bar.

I gave Rommel a sedative and began to shave the wound edges. In view of the massive blood loss I did not dare give him a general anaesthetic. After about half an hour I had all the wounds exposed. The trickiest ones were those involving the toes.

As Rommel was well sedated I cleaned and disinfected the various wound edges and injected local anaesthetic into the muscles and skin adjacent to the incised radius and ulna. In spite of the fact that the two bones were cut clean across, the extraordinary sharpness of the wound made me decide that the insertion of an intramedullary pin or the application of a plate was unnecessary.

Just as I was starting to insert the first stitches the phone rang.

As I was otherwise engaged I asked Moses to answer it.

At the other end of the line was a local potentate well known to me. Physically he looked a bit like a cross between the Roman emperor Nero and the Zulu king Chaka and he often behaved like both.

One of his Friesian heifers was stuck calving and could I come right away? I asked Moses to explain that I was, at that very moment, endeavouring, with some difficulty, to piece together a badly injured dog and that I would come to his farm at Rukongo, some fifteen miles away, as soon as I was finished.

I had just completed the repair of the radius and ulna and had applied a light cast when the phone rang again. It was our mutual friend, inquiring if I was finished yet and when might I be expected. Moses replied in suitably tactful vein and I turned my attention to the repair of foot number one, stitching tendons, realigning severed bones and closing skin.

Half an hour after the second call came another. This went on throughout the afternoon. I could set my watch to them. They were accurate to the minute.

I clenched my jaws and restrained the urge to temporarily abandon Rommel, seize the phone and inform my caller, in well-chosen one syllable words, that it was impossible, even for me, to deal satisfactorily with two emergencies simultaneously, especially when they were fifteen miles apart. Instead, after an obligatory mental count to ten, I requested Moses to ask our impatient chum to leave the heifer strictly alone and to wait until I came.

Several toes, a number of skin wounds and two phone calls later and Rommel looked almost dog-like again, instead of resembling a mangled carpet.

As I was inserting the final stitch the phone rang yet again. Ye blimmin' Gods! This was too much - and he was out of phase, having rung only ten minutes previously. I seized the receiver in a blood-stained hand and was just about to let rip when I heard the reasoned tones of Jeremy Roache, the Provincial Veterinary Officer, on the other end of the line.

Jeremy told me that he had just received a call from our feverish friend, who sounded as though he was hopping around like an enraged jumping flea. Because of my general slackness and tardiness in dealing with his distressed animal, Jeremy had now been asked to rush to the scene of suffering.

'I'm afraid you're not his favourite person at the moment, Hugh. You're not the flavour of the month, old chap, certainly not today, anyway. He thinks you're sitting on your hands in your surgery, fiddling around with your tweezers and thread while his beast is out there straining its guts out trying to give birth. I haven't calved a cow since I left college and besides, I've no equipment, so I'm bound to make a hash of things. You'd better give me the benefit of your superior knowledge and feed me some basic info on bovine obstetrics before I foul things up.'

Jeremy was an excellent fellow, dependable, efficient, available and easy to deal with, but he was basically a desk-wallah, an administration expert, who knew, with alarming efficiency, how to move coloured pins about on the huge map of Rift Valley Province, hanging on the wall of his spacious office. He was in his element when it came to rushing a vaccination team to the remotest regions of Turkana-land to control an outbreak of Contagious Bovine Pleuropneumonia or throwing a quarantine cordon around an epidemic of Foot and Mouth Disease in distant Masai-land. This was his forte and he performed it to perfection. Getting down on his grey-flannelled knees to winkle out a log-jammed foetus was not.

Even so, as Jeremy was a good deal older than me, I felt I was teaching my grandfather to suck eggs. I passed on a few treasured words of hard won wisdom and told him that I would be on my way as soon as I had cleaned up and returned my patient to the waiting stormtrooper.

'OK, Hugh, wish me luck!'

Forty five minutes later I was on the road to Rukongo and Rommel was on his way back to sylvan Subukia.

At about 6pm I crept into the farmyard. The place seemed deserted. The cattle crush was near the farm entrance and the adjacent road sloped down a slight incline. I turned my car round and left it facing downhill, ready for a quick getaway should it be required. The owner of the heifer was made of easily combustible material and the merest spark could ignite and inflame his wrath.

I climbed a style and walked across a field to the crush. I found the heifer lying close to its entrance, a dead calf beside her. I gave her ribs a prod with my knees. Her hindquarters rose a few inches and then flopped down. The dead calf was large and its head and forelegs were swollen. The mother was small and undersized.

She had obturator paralysis, caused by damage to the nerves which innervate the inner muscles of the thighs. This can occur when a calf becomes jammed in the pelvic canal for an extended period or when uncontrolled force, usually in the shape of an excessive number of men, or even a vehicle – so called 'Toyota Traction' – is employed to drag the calf out. The nerves get crushed between the calf and the mother's pelvis. Recovery is dependant on the degree of damage.

This did not appear to be too bad, although the vulva was markedly swollen, suggesting that the calf had been stuck inside for a long time.

'Where was everyone?'

Then, above the soughing of the wind in the gum trees, I heard a low, rasping noise, the unmistakable sound of the human snore. Walking softly, I rounded the bole of an extra-large gum tree, whose parchment-like bark was peeling off in long strips, and there, sleeping the sleep of the inebriated, lay the herdsman who had presumably assisted, or otherwise, in the birth of the dead calf.

I gave a loud cough, and, with an alacrity surprising in one so firmly clasped in the arms of Morpheus, he scrambled to his feet, grinning inanely.

Extracting an accurate case history from one whose immediate vicinity was in all probability spinning wildly before his ochreous eyeballs was not easy, but I was given to understand that the heifer had been observed to be in difficulties at about midnight. Why then, I asked, was the request for assistance not made until some fourteen hours later? A foolish question, to which the stock answer was given: namely, that it was thought that she would calve by herself. By the time Jeremy Roache arrived, the heifer had been down and unable to rise for several hours, with partial paralysis already present.

His choice of action was limited. A Caesarian section might have helped, but Jeremy had neither the tools nor the know-how to carry one out. And as time passed the belligerent owner became more and more insistent on immediate action, which was indeed required in order to resolve a situation brought about by his own initial inaction.

By the time the gentleman in question appeared, strutting towards me like a displaying turkey cock, I was ready for him

Before he could open his mouth to speak I got my oar in first, asking why he had left his heifer in difficulties for fourteen hours before seeking help, why had he not phoned me in the morning, and so on. By the time I had finished he had shrunk to almost human proportions and he even went so far as to apologise for the succession of phone calls with which he had plagued me, when he knew full well that one was enough.

As is always best in such situations we finally parted on friendly and understanding terms.

And, as an added bonus, a few days later the heifer struggled to her feet and eventually made a full recovery.

☆☆☆☆☆

Single, or even double, emergencies – equine colics, prolapses, road accident cases, poisonings – could be taxing enough, but multiple emergencies could be even more testing. When they did occur I always thanked my lucky stars for my formative training in the local Boy Scouts troop and school Cadet Corps, which had prepared me for just about anything life could throw at me. Ex-lance bombardier Cran was ready.

A large farm owned by a landowner even more important than the princeling of Rukongo, in fact the most important in the country, Jomo Kenyatta himself, lay within the orbit of my daily endeavours.

To this farm one day came 300 Dutch Friesian heifers.

These heifers had left the land of their birth, Holland, at the tender age of eighteen months, and journeyed to their destination via the Cape now known as one of Good Hope, but originally called the Cape of Storms by knowledgeable mariners. And storms there were. The vessel in which the unfortunate animals were confined was small and it rolled abominably in the heavy seas. Life aboard was far from happy. All suffered from the effects of sea sickness and from the steamy, sweltering heat of the tropics on both sides of the continent, and before the port of Mombasa was reached five of the bovine passengers had expired and their carcases consigned to the deep and to the following sharks.

Following disembarkation the weary travellers were moved by train to a farm near the town of Kitale, at the foot of Mt. Elgon, on the Uganda border, some 550 miles from the coast. Here, thanks to an altitude of 6,500 feet, the climate was more temperate, and rendered bearable by the cool air flowing down from the huge mountain, dominating the horizon to the west, and from the Cherangani Range to the east.

Unfortunately, the meteorological improvement was not matched by one in diet. The farm was grossly overstocked, had little grass and less water. As a result the Dutch Friesians, instead of gaining weight, shrank in size, until their total poundage was considerably less than it had been at the time of their departure from Holland several weeks before.

It continued to fall.

No cognizance was taken of their bodily diminution, however. The experts back in Europe issued a decree that the heifers be inseminated on a particular date – according to their growth rate in Holland. The miracle was, in view of their stunted growth, that any conceived at all. Unfortunately the vast majority did, and so the scene was set for a parturition problem of major proportions and one which landed, fairly and squarely, in my lap.

The first hint that trouble was afoot was when I was asked to assist with a small rash of calving problems on another farm, which had been in receipt of a much smaller number of Dutch heifers. Out of twenty animals I had to personally calve five – two embryotomies, two Caesarian sections and one forced extraction were my lot.

This, I thought, was a bit too much.

It was, however, a mere flurry before the main storm.

The evening of Saturday 16th June saw me reclining peacefully, if not gracefully, in a steaming bath, tankard of cold Tusker at my elbow and perusing the pages of a humorous novel. I was well-established, having been immersed for the better part of half an hour. The upper lids were just beginning to slide over the orbs. It had, after all, been a heavy week. Bed beckoned and therein, if still awake, I would complete the remainder of the chapter.

The phone rang.

As I was alone, the oath, which in polite society would have remained unspoken, or at the very most, been ground out between clenched teeth, was vented with the full vigour that the privilege of solitude allowed.

Dripping, I raised the receiver.

It was Kamau, the stout, ebullient cattle manager of the Presidential farm in receipt of the 300 Dutch Friesian heifers. I knew him well, from many visits to the farm at Rongai and it was he who had assisted me most nobly during the notorious prussic acid poisoning episode.

'Jambo, Bwana Kamau,' I said. 'What's the problem this time?'

Kamau explained that one of the heifers was labouring under no misapprehension that she was in serious difficulties in trying to give birth.

'She is on time to deliver and she is straining and straining with all her might and main. Of the calf there is no sign. This is one of Mzee's most valuable heifers. You are coming to help us, isn't it?'

I knew this to be a rhetorical question. The owner was of such a stature that no refusal or hesitation was to be entertained.

'Right,' I said. 'Give me a few minutes to get dressed and I'll be with you shortly. Can you have some hot water and soap ready?'

After having redonned my doffed garments, I drove with as much speed as was possible in the interests of safety to the farmyard, where the heifer stood awaiting my ministrations.

Like an ebony Falstaff, Kamau emerged from the surrounding darkness. Whether his melon-sized grin was one of relief at my arrival, or the appreciation of some private joke, was difficult to determine under the circumstances. Close at his heels clustered a knot of rustic minions.

As I observed the scene in the beam of my car headlamps, the Friesian abruptly bent herself into the shape of a half moon, gave a tremendous backwards strain, and uttered a hollow groan.

From my vantage point I groaned silently in unison.

Because of her intense preoccupation with her internal affairs, she was easily persuaded to enter a crush, which a cursory glance suggested had been built sometime during the previous century. A bucket, whose upper perimeter resembled the jagged arete of an Alpine ridge was produced. It contained, despite my modest request, a modicum of well chilled water. With a morsel of proffered soap I lubricated my strong left arm and proceeded to inspect the patient.

'Well, Bwana Kamau, we have problems here, my friend. This heifer is small, much smaller than average and her pelvis is still immature. I can just feel the nose of a calf on the other side of the cervix, which is only partially dilated. But there's no way it's going to come through and be delivered normally, not a hope.'

'Then you will have to cut her?'

'Yes, that's right. So let's get her out and get on with it.'

314

We backed her out of the crush and I began making preparations for an immediate Caesarian section.

My normal procedure was to shave and disinfect the left abdominal area between ribs and pelvis and administer local anaesthetic and an epidural, if needed. I next laid out all my instruments on the bonnet of my car, had the animal gently cast with ropes and then, having stripped for action, made, as the textbooks so graphically have it, my first bold, sweeping incision.

It was often at this point that those about to faint, did so.

Invariably they were male. Women appeared to possess the stamina to gaze unblanched as muscles were incised, as arteries spouted, veins gushed and intestines and other organs were exposed to view.

As far as men were concerned, age or race appeared to have no bearing on who should crumple unconscious to the ground. The stitching of a small wound in a dog's hind leg one day had a six foot, six inch, denim-clad American folding himself into a figure of eight knot beneath the surgery wash basin. A similar procedure had an Asian youth pole-axing himself against the fridge door.

Out in the field the monotonous slump of falling bodies kept pace with those falling down indoors. The steady drip, drip, drip of blood from a half inch wound made during an operation to correct upward fixation of the patella in a pony, resulted in the syce, who was holding its head, spread-eagling himself on his back, dead to the world, while his companions, unsympathetic to a man, convulsed themselves with laughter.

And on one memorable occasion, while doing a Caesarian section at night in an antediluvian cowshed, whose only illumination consisted of a flickering hurricane lamp, my attention was briefly disrupted by a loud, solid, woodenish clunk. Turning round, I observed the headman being dragged away. He had passed out cold, fallen backwards and had struck the back of his skull with full force on the edge of the wooden manger. When I returned the following morning to examine the cow, I fully expected to find that the man had been hospitalised or, at the very least, confined to his bed. Not a bit of it. He greeted me as cheerfully as usual, and was going about his daily tasks as though nothing had happened.

The manger also appeared to be unscathed.

To my relief everyone considerately refrained from fainting as I cut deep into the Presidential heifer.

Accustomed as I was to operating under primitive conditions, with sub-sub-standard facilities, the operation went smoothly. Attracted by the car lights, I had the active participation of several thousand buzzing, flying, crawling and hopping insects and beetles, several of which entered into the spirit of things by doing their utmost to get right inside the opened abdomen.

315

The participation of my human assistants was enthusiastic, if unskilled, and more than once I had to make a peremptory request that unwashed hands be removed from the vicinity of the wound.

The difference in degree of risk of infection from unwashed insects and unwashed hands was, to my mind, a fine one.

The calf, when eventually extricated, was huge. It was, much to the gratification of myself, the workers and the mother, alive. By the time I departed, looking forward with keen anticipation to the comforts of bed, it had managed to stagger to its feet and was floundering about the yard, searching for its mother's teats.

Three days later, while my major domo was on the point of dishing up the evening repast, his specialité de la maison – stew, potatoes and peas, followed by rhubarb crumble, the phone rang. It was my too cheerful friend Kamau again.

Once more I sallied forth into the night and once again the Caesarian scenario was repeated.

Five days later another summons was received.

For a change this one came during daylight hours and my workload was relieved somewhat by the presence of assistant Moses. And, as an added bonus, this particular calving required no surgical intervention. The calf, although very large, as usual, with retroflexion of the head and neck, was able to be removed intact from its undersized dam.

June was now drawing to a close.

If I had had any inkling of the horrors which lay in store during the months of July, August and September I would have made immediate arrangements for a long and pleasurable vacation – anything – confining myself to a Cistercian monastery on a diet of dry bread and water for three months, walking nude, backwards over the Himalayas, swimming up the Amazon from mouth to source, playing footsie with piranhas and anacondas.

The first of July was a Sunday and darkness saw me once again Caesarian sectioning yet another luckless heifer. The second of the month was a bumper day, and had I been a lecturer in obstetrics at a veterinary school I would have been over the moon, with a wide spread of problems to puzzle through. Three calvings came my way – one Caesar, one embryotomy and one forced extraction, all during the hours of daylight. I could scarcely believe my luck.

The remainder of the month followed suit – thirteen calvings, eight of them at night, five of them embryotomies, three Caesars, four forced extractions and one involving an episiotomy.

August, a holiday month for some, was one neither for myself, the farm staff nor the parturient heifers. An average of one every second day was trundled forth, mainly for surgery or embryotomy and of these, one third were so unkind as to present themselves either at night or on a Sunday.

During the hours of daylight my ministrations were complicated, assisted or hindered by a gang of convicts who laboured daily on the farm. Clad in off-white shorts and shirts, they were a cheerful crowd. The NCOs wore pill box caps and boots. The rank and file, neither.

And of course, in daytime there was always the added frisson of excitement in knowing that at any moment Jomo himself might appear, like Zeus descending from Mt. Olympus to mingle among mortals. Not that he mingled among these lowly mortals and their blood-bedaubed leader as they wrestled with yet another parturient heifer. The boma in which the action took place was mere yards from the road leading to a presidential pleasure dome, built beside a tree-bordered dam. As the stream of gleaming Mercedes sped by, I would glance up from my labours to see the noble profile of the great man and feel touched by the hand of history.

September, season of mists and mellow fruitfulness, was a fruitful one as far the Dutch Friesians were concerned, but not one calculated to make me feel particularly mellow.

The first eight calvings of the month were all done at night, four of which were either on a Saturday or a Sunday. My social life, such as it was, went out of the window.

By the first week of October the flood of calvings had subsided, dwindled to a trickle and finally stopped.

Between mid-June and early October I had visited the farm 79 times, had personally calved 47 heifers, 25 at night, on Saturday afternoons or Sunday, and had carried out 16 Caesarian sections, 17 embryotomies, twelve forced extractions, one episiotomy and one sacrificial Caesarian section.

It was a signal example of the application of inappropriate, 'expert' advice from outside the country going disastrously wrong.

And to rub salt into my personal wounds, five years were to go by before I would be paid for my contribution to the salvage of the fiasco.

CHAPTER SEVENTEEN

The pursuit and the running to earth of non-payers was a never-ending task. Sometimes it took the form of a flanking movement. Sometimes it was a full frontal assault. At other times it required stealth and guile to bring the miscreants to book.

Often the worst offenders were those who could most easily afford to pay – the wealthy absentee landlords living in sybaritic splendour in Nairobi mansions, from where they ran their enterprises, fuelled, in part, by my honest toil. They employed managers, who for the most part had no access to cash or cheque book, but who thought nothing about phoning for a credit service at all hours of the day or night.

At the other end of the spectrum were the proletariat, the sons of the soil and *sans culottes* who, although they might wish to pay, seldom had the means to do so. Sacks of mealies and clutches of eggs wrapped in cabbage leaves, welcome though they might be, did not help to balance the books.

Until I formulated a firm policy of deposits, cash before work from new clients and the ending of credit facilities for defaulters, things had reached such a pass that I had insufficient funds with which to purchase a new Peugeot when the life of its predecessor had come to the end of its allotted span.

Fortunately a well meaning farmer, Mike Weatherseed, who had an interest in retaining my services for the wellbeing of his cattle and horses, came to the rescue and gave me the use of an elderly Ford saloon.

This allowed me sufficient time to accrue cash to purchase a new vehicle and to redress the dire financial situation.

'She may look ould 'n' decrepit, but she's a goer,' roared Mike, a large, blunt Yorkshireman of indeterminate shape, banging the driver's door several times in an effort to close it.

'She'll never let you down!' he shouted. 'Sound as Sheffield steel! Got 'guaranteed' stamped all over 'er, she 'as!'

As I drove away the door reopened and I had to repeat the banging process, unsuccessfully.

The three months I spent at the wheel of the Ford demanded a degree of vigilance hitherto unrequired when cruising in the Peugeot.

The vehicle was elderly and regular maintenance obviously had not been uppermost in Mike Weatherseed's mind, judging by the anvil chorus coming from its tortured bodywork. But bearing in mind the litany of proverbs which my old grandma was always exhorting me to follow, such as not looking gift horses in the mouth, beggars can't be choosers and so forth, I pressed on.

One morning I was en route to a farm near Turi to carry out some routine pregnancy tests on a herd of Jersey cattle.

Just before the saw-milling township of Elburgon was a long, very steep hill. I approached it at speed, roaring up the lower slopes in third gear. Forward momentum slackened markedly as I reached the crux and I changed down to second. As I did so I found, to my consternation, that the gear stick had come away in my hand, parting company with whatever held it attached to the mechanism beneath.

Luckily the gears had already passed the critical divide from third to second and I was able to grind upwards and come to a halt on a level spot. A certain amount of juggling and sleight of hand enabled me to slot the nether part of the stick into a transverse groove and I was able to continue on my way.

This mechanical shortcoming did confer certain distinct advantages. Whenever I wished to go to the cinema or go into a shop I would remove the gear stick, take it with me and leave the car in the street, secure in the knowledge that any potential thief would be nonplussed by this lack of vital equipment and pass on to a more lucrative choice.

Not that I could imagine anyone wanting to steal the wretched thing. I had had a narrow shave. The brakes were almost non-existent. A techni-coloured vision of the car, gearless and brakeless, hurtling backwards down the hill at ever increasing speed, stayed with me for several days.

Not long afterwards I had occasion to put those brakes, such as they were, to the test.

I was on a large farm, near the township of Kampi ya Moto.

Within the farm a dirt road bisected the property. I was driving along this at a not unreasonable speed when I surmounted a small rise and there, directly in front of me, transecting the road from side to side, was a freshly dug ditch.

There was no possibility of avoiding it. It was about three feet deep and about six feet wide, just about right for containing a platoon of soldiery and their accoutrements in some comfort and also concealing them from an approaching enemy.

I applied the brakes with some force and zero effect and shot into the ditch, hit the opposing side with a fearful crash and soared up the other side like an out-of-control Cresta Runner. The steering was almost wrenched from my grasp as I also soared upwards within the uncomfortable confines of the car, all but braining myself on the roof. The car made a violent and unpredictable right-hand swerve, moving rather like a startled wildebeest scenting a lion. To the right was a near-vertical bank. The car surmounted this with appalling ease and roared, virtually out of control, along the top for fifty or sixty yards until it came to a standstill through lack of momentum. I drove gingerly along for a few hundred yards until a sloping ramp allowed me to descend.

Once back on the road I found considerable difficulty in driving in a straight line. Inspection of the right front wheel and attachments revealed serious structural deformities. When I eventually reached the manager's house it was found that the only way to drive the car back to Nakuru was by reversing the wheel.

The wheel turned all right, but not silently. The screeching noise it made could be heard half a mile away.

It was heard by a couple of policemen, taking their ease beneath a wayside tree. As I approached they rushed into the road, waving their arms and brandishing their weapons.

I ground to a noisy halt and glued on my most winning smile. The gendarmerie warily circled the car.

'Eee! What is this terrible kelele (noise) you are making on thee highway? You must be knowing you are committing a most serious offence!'

'Jambo, inspector!' I addressed myself to the more senior of the duo, a large flabby fellow, with an intimidating glare, an impressive paunch and sporting sergeant's flashes on his shirt.

He brightened momentarily at the unofficial promotion. It was as though a brief ray of sunshine had shone through a thundercloud.

'Habari ya kazi?' I asked (How's the job going?)

'Mzuri tu,' they both agreed. (Pretty good)

Talking earnestly, I explained that I had been on an errand of mercy when the problem arose, speeding – well, not really speeding – to the aid of a sick animal. At this point I inquired about their own stock, knowing that both would have cattle somewhere, either nearby or at the ancestral home. Within no time we were deep into the niceties of bovine disease, frequency of dipping, milking procedures and the reason for my being stopped had been almost forgotten.

Five minutes later, although the sergeant muttered something about 'chai' (tea i.e. baksheesh) and 'njaa' (hunger), I was waved on my way.

I saluted respectfully.

The vehicle was dispatched forthwith to a garage for repair and brake correction.

While I was waiting to collect it, an urgent message was received from a large Cistercian monastery on the forested heights above Kipkelion, some fifty miles from Nakuru. From the monastery it was possible, on a clear day, to see the Kavirondo Gulf of Lake Victoria, yet another fifty miles away. Cattle were dying and would I come? Brother Bernard was on the line, the immensely tall, dignified and kindly Dutch monk who ran the dairy. He was the only member of the order given dispensation from their vow of silence.

By late afternoon the car was retrieved from the garage. I inquired of the foreman whether the job had been done properly.

The foreman, an unprepossessing individual who appeared to have an unfortunate affliction involving his eyelids, such that he had to throw his head back in order to see properly, scrutinised me rather like a camel being offered a plate of fish and chips.

'The vehicle is now pafect,' he told me. 'Our customers are always being completely satisfied with our wak.'

'Well, I hope that I will be numbered among them,' I thought as I departed in the direction of the monastery.

As I headed westwards into the setting sun, the distant crest of Mt. Londiani was etched black against a lilac sky. By the time I reached the base of the escarpment leading up to Molo and Mau Summit it was quite dark and I switched on the headlights.

I ground up the seemingly endless hill, peering along the meagre cones of yellow light at the uprising tarmac, pitted with holes and cavities like a strip of decaying Gruyere cheese.

It was still warm and I had the windows wound down.

Every now and again a whiff of something hot and *je ne sais quoi* assailed my nostrils, reminding me of the time when major domo Njoroge fell asleep in the kitchen and let a saucepan of soup boil dry. On this occasion I assumed the smell arose from overheated tarmac. It had been a very hot day.

Half way between Mau Summit and Kedowa I drew into the side of the road to relieve bladder pressure under cover of darkness. As I placed my foot on the brake it sank without resistance to the floor and the car coasted for an inordinate distance before finally deigning to come to a halt.

'Hell's teeth! What now?' I thought.

As I got out of the car my attention was caught by an eerie light emanating from the right front wheel. I wasted no time in investigating this phenomenon.

The brake drum was glowing cherry red. As I bent to inspect this unwelcome sight I could feel my eyebrows curling from the heat. By the light of a torch I found the brake pipe to be on the point of final disintegration. Its dissolution was clearly the source of the peripatetic smell.

I opened the bonnet and found the brake fluid reservoir to be as I expected it to be – empty. I was in a spot. So far I had been climbing all the way from the foot of the escarpment and had had no occasion to make serious use of the brakes. Now there was no question of continuing to the monastery. It involved a precipitous descent to a palm-fringed river, followed by an ascent of more than a thousand feet around several hair pin bends to the forest edge, all of which had later to be reversed – in the dark. A motorised form of Russian roulette.

I bayed my frustration to an unseen moon.

I would have to return another day.

As I snailed my way back to Nakuru in bottom gear, white-knuckled digits clamped to the hand brake, right foot madly and ineffectually pumping the foot brake, my thoughts concerning the heavy lidded foreman were not of a charitable nature.

I also made a conscious decision to learn to fly at the earliest possible opportunity.

⚐⚑⚐⚑⚐

Anne-Marie Esseline's elderly alsatian bitch, Swara, had broken her leg.

Some years previously she had fractured a femur, which I had pinned. Healing had been excellent. Now she had been run over by a tractor and the other femur had been smashed. The old dog was partially deaf and had not heard the approach of the tractor being driven at high speed round a corner by a young mechanic.

In view of her advanced age and the extent of her injuries, it was decided that a peaceful termination to her sufferings was the most humane solution to her problems.

The Esselines were Belgian.

Anne-Marie's husband Alain was a farming contractor with a fleet of combine harvesters and tractors, which regularly fanned out over countryside far and near, ploughing, sowing and reaping for those prepared to pay and because of his expertise, many were. Alain, a sardonic individual with a fondness for large cigars and cognac, was not one who believed in soiling his hands unnecessarily. He paid others to do that. As a result of this personal squeaky-clean policy, he was always immaculately attired in the casual, yet expensive garb, of an English country gentleman, exuding an aura of wealth and the time in which to spend it.

The Esselines lived in a large, rambling old house near Elburgon and had several other dogs in addition to Swara. Two of these were boisterous, young black labradors.

I arrived to be met by Anne-Marie. Alain was nowhere to be seen.

'Bonjour, Hugh, vous etes arrivé, alors. Aujourd'hui, c'est un jour triste, n'est-ce pas?' Anne-Marie was understandably upset at the imminent demise of her old dog.

I agreed with her sentiments entirely. It is a sad business ending the life of a faithful companion, even when it is in the pet's best interests.

Swara was lying on the stone veranda, hind leg grossly swollen.

'Now, Anne-Marie,' I said, 'can you please take the two labradors away? They'll just get in the way. Thanks very much.'

Anne-Marie disappeared with them round the corner of the building to, I presumed, either tie them up or lock them in a room.

Meanwhile I filled a 10ml syringe with Euthatal – triple strength pentabarbitone. When Anne-Marie returned I asked her to hold Swara while I clipped the hair over the old dog's foreleg in order to visualise the cephalic vein.

I asked Anne-Marie to hold the leg and I knelt down, the better to administer the injection.

I was in this supplicant, genuflecting position when the two labradors burst round the corner.

Like a crocodile seizing an antelope at a waterhole the startled Swara rose up with a snarl and sank her fangs into my nose. Uttering a justifiable expletive I threw myself backwards and detached my proboscis from the alsatian's jaws.

I clapped my hand to my face in order to determine how much had been removed. I felt no pain. In fact my nose, or what I assumed was left of it, felt so numb as to be non-existent. I was certain that the dog had bitten it right off.

With what I considered to be admirable restraint I asked Anne-Marie for directions to a bathroom containing a mirror.

Anne-Marie was horrified at what had happened.

'Ah, je suis tellement desolée! It's all my fault!'

The general brouhaha brought Alain forth from wherever he had been lurking. Puffing on an evil-smelling cheroot, he surveyed my countenance in silence, before giving a wicked grin.

'Mon Dieu! Maybe you should have a stiff whisky before you have a look at yourself.'

Great! Thanks!

In fact, to my surprise and relief, my nose, although punctured and by now multicoloured, was still attached to my face. It appeared to be swelling with alarming speed. Within a very short time it was a carbon copy of that organ which disfigured the features of the late Charles de Gaulle, a most unpleasant sight.

Satisfied that I was not going to be deformed for life, I returned to complete my distasteful task.

But first I made personally sure that both labradors were securely confined behind locked doors.

◎◎◎◎◎◎

Although, to the unseeing, ignorant eye, parts of the Kenya highlands seemed to resemble certain areas of Europe, a closer inspection would soon have shown that they were as African as the Congo or the Kalahari.

The huge landscapes, whether forested or densely cultivated and packed with small holdings, the vast skies peppered with soft fluffy clouds or blackened with driving rain, the heavily laden buses swaying at high speed along the pot-holed roads, the peasants pecking at their fields in preparation for planting, a black-shouldered kite hovering in search of prey, a pi-dog gnawing at a dead zebra lying beside the road, above all the sun, burning bright and fierce on the people, animals, mountains, plains and valleys, showed that this was indeed Africa at its most equatorial.

That sun, seemingly so benign at cool, high altitudes, could be a dangerous enemy, when encountered so close to the equator, especially to people and animals not of Africa.

Northern Europeans, particularly those of Celtic origin, who failed to protect themselves from the sun's ultra violet rays with hats, long sleeved shirts, dark glasses and blocking creams, did so at their peril. Sooner or later, many, if they lived in the tropics long enough, would develop unsightly skin blemishes, which, if left untreated, could develop into a horrid array of epidermal cancers, basal cell carcinomas or even squamous cell carcinomas, all of which had the cash registers of the Nairobi dermatologists ringing a merry and profitable tune.

Animals were not spared. White cats were among the most susceptible. Repeated exposure to the sun would result in the condition know as feline solar dermatitis, which affected in particular the ears, and to a lesser degree, the nose and eyelids. The initial insult frequently worsened until a carcinoma appeared. Keeping cats out of the sun was well nigh impossible. In many cases surgery was eventually required, usually involving amputation of the affected ears. This van Gogh-ian procedure was surprisingly cosmetic, once the hair had re-grown, giving the patient an attractive teddy bear look.

White bull terriers were a disaster in Africa. Within a few months of birth or importation, pre-cancerous skin lesions would appear, mainly on the abdomen. Constant medication and protection from the sun would then be required to stave off the day when the first ominous lesion would

324

arise like an ugly volcanic eruption. From then on surgery, and yet more surgery, would be needed, until in some cases it became difficult to find enough spare skin to close the necessarily large incisions. My advice to those who favoured the breed was to always choose a black and tan animal. But the dictates of canine fashion meant that my words were often ignored – to the detriment of the poor animal.

Collies fared little better. They frequently suffered from nasal solar dermatitis, so common in this breed as to be named 'collie nose'. The poorly pigmented skin of the nose became hypersensitised to sunlight and the intense light of the equatorial highlands was especially dangerous, causing irritation, ulceration and sometimes the development of yet another squamous cell carcinoma. The only effective control was protection from sunlight and the tattooing of the susceptible area with black ink, a messy but effective business.

White faced cattle were prone to the development of cancers in the tissues surrounding the eyes, and I was constantly employed in the sanguineous task of enucleating bovine eyes or dissecting out affected conjunctivae or nictitating membranes. Another area of bovine anatomy under continuous bombardment by the actinic rays was the skin of the vulva and thereon, in exotic cattle such as Friesians and Ayrshires, tumours were wont to grow like mushrooms. Occasionally even the haired skin was affected. Ayrshires, in particular, seemed to be prone to develop large, unsightly, evil smelling growths on the middle of the back, much favoured by flies for the laying of their eggs. In this area, no operation, cosmetic or otherwise, was possible.

✕✖✕✖✕

I awoke with a start.

I could have sworn that I had heard the roaring of lions. But that was impossible because was I not abed in suburban Nakuru? Then it came again, louder and seemingly closer. The massive, threatening, overpowering sound filled the air with its message of forlorn savagery and wild sadness. The hair on the back of my neck rose. I opened the window. The bedroom was so small that I did not need to get out of bed to do this. I merely reached up and undid the window-catch. Yes, there was no doubt at all. Lions were close by, somewhere not far away, giving tongue, roaring at the moon. Safe in my little house, it was pleasantly exciting to lie listening to the king of beasts letting the world know that he was who he was.

But – lions in Nakuru?

All was revealed the following morning when I received a call from an Indian circus encamped in the Afraha Football Stadium in Nakuru, sited a mere half mile from my modest dwelling.

The ringmaster was on the phone.

'Doctor sahib! Doctor sahib!'

My professional thorax swelled with pride at this appellation.

'I am calling from Indian circus. We have problem of the most serious magnitude, which I am calling upon your worthy expertise to solve. We are having three lions – Indian lions precisely. Two are female and one is male. One female is now receptive to the male and he is a most ardent fellow, so much so that the lion tamer lies in much danger. There he is, in the cage, in the very centre, a hot lioness on the one side and a very frantic male on the other. You can imagine his danger! Can you administer drugs to stop her season, before we have bloodshed? As you know, the show must go on!'

The Gemeni Circus, from Tamil Nadu in southern India was a modest establishment, with a threadbare big top, a few clowns, a clutch of girl gymnasts, a duo of tightrope walkers, a couple of performing dogs, some horses, a couple of bears, a tiger – and three lions.

'Right,' I said. 'Give me a few minutes to think about this and I'll come down to see what I can do.'

I cudgelled my brains.

The only drug available to me was Ovarid tablets, which I occasionally used to terminate oestrus in the bitch. But would it work on a lioness? Would there be any undesirable side effects? How much should be given. A double dose? A triple dose?

I drove to the circus, wondering what to do.

I parked my car and walked round the back of the big tent to where I expected the animals to be. I smelt the lions before I saw them – the rank reek of large, confined cats. The male was in one cage, the two females in another. The male was pacing up and down. Every now and again, before he turned, he would jump up against the side of the cage in apparent frustration.

A small, dark, Indian was standing watching him, a worried frown furrowing his forehead.

'Good morning!' I said. 'I've come about the lions.'

'Ah good, good,' he replied. 'I am lion tamer and because of womanly affairs in lioness I am in much danger! Oh dear me!'

Another Indian hurried up. This was Mr S. P. Ragunathan, the ringmaster, who was very black and also small, with well oiled hair. I explained the limited options available.

'Ah, doctor sahib, needs must be when the devil drives, eh? We must be doing what we can. Let us go for the drug and hope for the best. The last four performances we have had to tie rope round the belly of the male to prevent access to the female. This does not give good impression to the paying public.'

326

So I gave him several Ovarid tablets, telling him to crush them into powder and mix them with the lion's next meal of raw meat.

'Most grateful, doctor sahib. Now you are here please to examine our tiger. He is limping a little. When jumping through the hoop he stumbled and hurt his right front leg.'

The tiger was a splendid beast, pacing up and down in his cage. He came towards us and rubbed himself against the bars. He was well fleshed and obviously very fond of Ragu, who scratched him behind one ear. With his attention thus diverted I examined his leg. A middle toe was swollen and tender.

'It looks like an injury to this toe,' I said. 'He probably landed badly and over extended it. A few days rest should see it right. I don't think drugs are required.'

'Thank you, sahib,' said Ragu, conducting me to where the bears were kept. There were two of them, big and black with a white V on the chest. They swayed from side to side. Dangerous animals, their huge claws were capable of inflicting terrible injuries. Their distress at being continually confined was all too apparent.

Ragu turned to me.

'Doctor sahib. Thank you for coming. I am most grateful and as token of my thanks I am giving you complimentary tickets for you and your friends for our last performance on Saturday evening. Please come!'

'Many thanks,' I replied. 'I will do my very best to be here.'

Although grateful, I was also worried. I did not particularly want to have a ringside seat to the rending of the lion tamer limb from limb, subsequent to my shot in the dark treatment.

Saturday came and with it a call to a farm near Mai Mahiu, at the foot of the Kikuyu Escarpment, beyond Naivasha, eighty miles from Nakuru, to treat a lame bull and stitch a badly tusked boar. By the time I had completed these tasks it was mid-afternoon. With a bit of luck I might miss the performance and the messy termination of the lion tamer.

It was dusk by the time I rolled into Nakuru, but I had not reckoned on my friends to whom I had allocated the tickets. They were desperate to go. They were my guests and were waiting outside the surgery.

'Dammit!' I thought.

'Hi, everyone!' I called as I opened the door of the car. 'Look's like we're too late. The last performance started half an hour ago. Sorry!'

Some smart alec piped up. 'Let's just drive down anyway!'

'Yes let's!' yelled everyone else.

'Dammit again!' I thought.

So we drove down and into the car park, adjacent to the big top. As we did so, a turbaned flunkey came rushing across to us, and to me in particular.

'Doctor sahib! You've come! Wonderful! Wonderful! We have held up the performance waiting for you. Come this way sir, and your friends. This way sir!'

I felt an utter louse. Here I was, smelling of ripe pig, unwashed and unchanged, still in my shorts and boots and here they were, ushering me and my friends to the best ringside seats.

We sat down, a band struck up a wailing oriental tune and the show began. Gymnasts, clowns, tightrope walkers, performing dogs, bareback riders, all had their part to play. It was pretty low key stuff. It was not Bertram Mills by any stretch of the imagination, but it had the local audience hooked and riveted.

I was waiting for the lions.

At last the cage was erected, the tunnel was attached and in they came. The small lion tamer stalked into the arena, turned in my direction, gave me a wink and a grin and I gave a sigh of relief. He opened the cage door and went in and cracked his whip. The lions leapt onto their tubs and did their stuff, raised their paws, jumped through their hoops and behaved impeccably.

It was a wonderful performance. It knocked Bertram Mills into a cocked hat.

✼✼✼✼✼

Gerald and Josephine Southey owned a small farm at Turi, called Cheviot Ltd. Here, at an altitude of over 8,000 feet, they grew pyrethrum, raised Ayrshire cattle and ran a small flock of sheep for mutton and wool. Gerald was crippled and as a result the bulk of the farm work fell onto Josephine's shoulders. Their wooden house was modestly furnished and it was evident that they had little money to spare for personal luxuries. They were, however, the most hospitable of people and a visit to the farm never passed without my receiving an invitation to partake of some home baking, fruit from their garden or, depending on the time of day, lunch or dinner.

Josephine had phoned to report that one of their cows was behaving oddly, stamping her hind legs, swishing her tail and seeking the shade.

The dirt road from Njoro to Turi paralleled the railway line to Kisumu, the Uganda Railway, which beyond Elburgon, spanned a number of streams in a series of spectacular viaducts.

Just before Turi village I turned left up a narrow road. The farm track leading to the Southey property was one of those with a prominent hump in the centre, clearance of which was just possible by their ancient Land Rover, but not by my newly acquired Peugeot, whose exhaust pipe lay some inches below its summit. So, with one wheel on the crown of the hump and the other half way up the adjacent verge, an arm wrenching and spine jarring approach was made to the farm. In wet weather it was accepted that at some point during the ascent one would slip back into the ruts with a resigned crash and from there on progress was a series of noisy wallaby-like leaps, which became progressively louder as the exhaust pipe and other parts of the vehicle's nether regions became detached from the main structure.

Once committed to such a road there was no turning back.

At least, I thanked Providence, it wasn't as bad as a track I once had the misfortune to ascend in the Mau Narok area. That was steep, narrow and greasy with mud, its sides bounded by vertical banks, against which positive contact was impossible to avoid. So much so, that, on the way up, two hub caps were ripped from their moorings. I collected them on the way down.

Josephine Southey had heard my approach from afar and was waiting when I lurched to a halt. She was a small, homely, friendly person, who reminded me of a contented, preoccupied little bird, such as a thrush or a robin, hopping through life, doing this and that, helping people and harming no-one.

She led me through a wicket gate into a paddock. In one corner stood a small, wooden dairy and into this the patient, an Ayrshire cow, was being driven by an aged retainer. As her head was being secured in the yoke, she stamped her feet several times. Josephine told me that the cow had cut her milk yield during the past couple of days and was very difficult to milk as she kicked whenever her teats were touched.

I ran my hand down the cow's flank. Her skin felt dry and hard, like parchment. I looked at it more closely. Only the white skin was affected. The brown areas were normal, soft and smooth. I walked round the cow and lifted her tail. The vulval skin was a dark, reddish purple colour. I looked at her muzzle. It was also abnormal, a brownish, reddish colour and, instead of being moist and covered with a patina of dewdrops, was quite dry. As were her teats, which were stiff and hard. She lashed out when I bent to touch them.

Despite all of these defects she had not stopped eating and her temperature was normal. But she had been seen to spend most of her time grazing in the shade beneath the many trees dotted over the farm.

And she was the only animal affected.

'Well, Josephine,' I said. 'She's got photo-sensitisation and, as she's the only cow with this problem, the cause is most likely a plant.'

I explained that, unlike sunburn in which lightly or non-pigmented skin becomes inflamed following exposure to rays in the ultra violet range, photo-sensitisation is a reaction to sunlight due to the presence of a photo-sensitising agent in the skin. Most are derived from plants and involve some degree of liver involvement.

'But what sort of plant?' Josephine wanted to know.

'Could be any of many – ragwort, lupins, crotolaria, lantana. Sometimes it can be a by-product of a disease such as leptospirosis.'

Josephine was one of those people with an insatiable curiosity about anything of a remotely scientific, biological, medical or veterinary nature. She was also totally unconcerned about the passage of time. She plied me with question after question of an increasingly abstruse nature until my brain whirled. I glanced covertly at my watch, wondering how best to make a tactful exit.

Josephine was relieved when I told her that individual, isolated cases of photo-sensitisation were rarely life-threatening and even more so when I told her that no expensive medication was required. All she had to do was to move the cow to an alternative, shady paddock, apply plenty of soothing milking salve to the teats and, if necessary, healing oil to the dry cracked skin and let nature do the rest.

By this time the hour was so advanced and my brain so numbed by the barrage of questions that I succumbed and let myself be persuaded to partake of a slice of homemade bread, larded with farm butter and wild honey, harvested from the adjacent forest, washed down by a glass of tangy lime juice. We sat on the sagging wooden verandah, Gerald in his wheel chair, surrounded by a pack of dogs of varying degrees of odoriferousness and ourselves in a couple of equally sagging camp chairs. In the overgrown garden iridescent sunbirds flitted to and fro, dipping their long curved needle-like beaks into tangled clumps of multi-coloured flowers. My eye was attracted by a fluttering, darting movement in a nearby tree. It was a little bird, chestnut, grey and white, with a tail of extraordinary length. It was a paradise flycatcher. Whether it had been named after its own stunning appearance or after its delectable earthly surroundings I never discovered.

❧❦❧❦❧❦

My own earthly surroundings were a little less delectable not long afterwards when I was asked to carry out a post-mortem examination of a cow on an African smallholding.

The tiny farm was one of several, carved out of a former European property and the grass access road wound and twisted between dozens of two acre plots before reaching its destination.

The owner, a grizzled yeoman wearing oversized gum boots, emerged from his thatched home as I drove into his yard. At his heels clustered a knot of pre-teenaged children. The door of the earth-walled house was open and I could see the beaten earth floor and the bed in one corner.

'Wapi ngombe likufa?' (Where's the dead cow?) I asked.

'Huko,' he indicated with an upward jerk of his stubbly chin, gesturing towards another house I hadn't noticed before. It was built in a European style and had probably been that of the manager of the farm before the property had been sold and broken up. It was in a bad way, unpainted, the windows gaping emptily, weeds growing waist high up against the walls, the stonework cracked and crumbling.

'Fuata mimi,' he said. (Follow me)

Wondering, I followed the old man into the dilapidated house and into what had once been an acceptable bathroom and there, reclining in the tub, lay the viscera of the recently dead cow, ready for my inspection and judgement as to the cause of death. It was indeed a novel place in which to conduct a post mortem, only marginally lessened by the swarms of bluebottles buzzing through the broken windows and by the absence of water in the taps.

A few weeks later a well dressed African businessman asked me to come to his house near the centre of town to examine a flock of chicks, some of which had recently died.

His house was a substantial structure, with neo-colonial overtones. I was impressed.

'Come along, daktari,' The Saville Row suited grandee ushered me in to what I assumed would be a genteel tea and biscuit nibbling ceremony before the strenuous business of dealing with the ailing avians.

I was denied this pleasure as mine host led me through a well furnished lounge, down a corridor and into what I took to be the master bedroom.

This was devoid of furniture and its floor was a moving mass of chicks, whose incessant cheeping pierced the ammonia-filled atmosphere.

My companion appeared to think there was nothing unusual in keeping large numbers of domestic fowl within the confines of his house and, in the African context, there wasn't. Although many Africans live in towns and cities, their hearts are in the countryside, in the family homestead. The presence of a cow, a couple of goats, a flock of chickens or even a few pigeons kept in the backyard of an urban dwelling helps to maintain that rural link so vital to African life. Every Easter and Christmas tens of thousands of people living in Nairobi pour out of the city, en route to their family homes. Often these are many hundreds of miles away. People travel by bus, taxi, train and car and not a few perish as sleep-sodden night drivers career into unlit lorries, over-laden buses swerve into ravines and kill-me-quick taxis, bursting with passengers, smash into each other at break-neck speeds. At the end of the holiday the exodus is reversed with similar homicidal results.

Everyone seems to think that it is worth it, this brief return to the ancestral roots, this supping at the tribal spring. Such quondam stimulants are not to be found within the dwellings of former colonial settlers. Hence the abandonment of the European house on the old man's farm.

Although traditional customs and practices and values have been so eroded by Western influences, from time to time I was afforded the rare privilege of a glimpse into a vanishing past.

While examining cattle in the dry, bush country, between Nakuru and Baringo, a party of young, male initiates came into view, clad in the garb appropriate to their particular stage of life, and, without looking either to right or left, passed across my field of view and disappeared. Afterwards I wondered if I had actually seen them. It had been like opening a window into a secret room, looking in, and then, suddenly closing the shutters.

The first time I saw Kipsigis girls wearing their post-circumcision skin robes I almost drove off the road. I was on a murram highway somewhere between Kericho and Sotik, travelling from the estate of one tea baron to that of another. The surrounding countryside was delightful – gentle, rolling green hills, meandering streams, wooded valleys, and everywhere the small, neat, hedged fields of the Kipsigis. The air was balmy, the sky a soft blue, dotted with soft white clouds. I was reminded of sepia photographs of an England before the mania for economy, amalgamation and mechanisation ripped out the hedgerows and reduced a green and pleasant land to a mind-numbing vista of monocultured wheat, potatoes and sugar beet, and fields full of cloned sheep and cattle.

Turning a corner I was galvanized out of my soporific state of semi-slumber by a group of sinister, hooded figures standing by the road side.

They wore dark brown skin cloaks, which completely covered them from the top of their heads to just above the ankles. Their arm were free. The figures silently watched me through small brown eye holes cut in the skins which covered their faces.

Despite the summery surroundings I felt the hair on the back of my neck rise as the proverbial cold shiver ran down my spine.

I had, however, no cause for concern. These were recently circumcised Kipsigis girls and before I reached my destination I passed several other groups of similarly clad maidens, poised on the threshold of womanhood and a possible lifetime of servitude and drudgery in a male dominated society.

❀ ❀ ❀ ❀ ❀

As a boy I had conceived an intense interest in what was known as the Great Outdoors. I was fascinated by the inhabitants of this often bizarre

332

world. I was held spellbound by tales of Canadian trappers padding on their snowshoes through wintry northern forests, timber wolves snapping at their heels, of Dinka tribesmen, standing stark and stork-like in their Sudanese swamps, of South Sea islanders skimming from atoll to atoll in their outrigger canoes, accompanied by a large, dark triangular fin or two, of Dyak headhunters slipping silently, like phantoms, through dense steaming jungle, the trophies of the chase dangling carelessly at their belts.

One asset which I most admired about these people was their ability to make do with what they had, to live off the land, to utilise their surroundings, without destroying it, to merge into the background, something virtually lost to Modern Man.

Another attribute which really caught my imagination was their expertise in making fire without matches, by using a flint, or the rays of the sun or even by rubbing two sticks together.

One day, while on a farm on the edge of the Mau Forest above the little town of Njoro, I encountered a Ndorobo nightwatchman. His native tongue was a dialect of Nandi, but he also spoke some Swahili. He was a small man, clad in an ex-army greatcoat, and he carried a bow, a quiver of arrows and a simi in a red leather scabbard.

The sun was declining behind the bambooed heights of the Mau, throwing them into deep shadow. By contrast, the summits of the Aberdares – Satima and the Kinangop, some forty to fifty miles to the east – stood highlighted and golden, seemingly still basking in warm sunshine.

I had been treating a cow with anaplasmosis. As I returned my drugs to the car, one of the farm workers drew a scrap of newspaper from one pocket and a pinch of tobacco from the other and rolled a crude cigarette. He fumbled in his pocket for matches and found none. His companions were unable to help.

Before I could tell him that I had a cigarette lighter in the car the Ndorobo had intimated that he could supply him with a light.

From his quiver he produced two pieces of wood. One was a round rod about eighteen inches long. The other was about the same length, but flatter and about an inch wide with three round holes at one end.

The Ndorobo removed his simi from its scabbard and laid it flat on the ground. Then he placed the wood containing the holes at right angles across the blade and sat down. From his quiver he extracted a small handful of dry moss, which he arranged next to the holes. Placing his left foot on the outer part of the wood to hold it firm he inserted the rod into one of the holes and began to roll it at high speed between his palms.

Within a few seconds a wisp of smoke appeared.

The Ndorobo fed a little moss into the hole and continued with his task. The moss began to smoulder and then caught fire.

The man with the unlit home-made fag dangling between his lips bent down, picked up a tuft of the now blazing moss and inhaled deeply.

I was most impressed.

The whole process, admittedly in the hands of an expert, seemed considerably easier and faster than the exercise in applied frustration which constituted the attempt to find a combustible match in a box of locally manufactured lucifers. As match after match failed to ignite, snapped in half, or fizzled out after a momentary spark, the air would become blue, not with smoke, but with cries of rage and the ground would be littered with discarded match sticks.

❋ ⅄ ❋ ⅄ ❋

The very mention of Foot and Mouth Disease is normally sufficient to send a cold shiver down the spine of any self respecting vet living and working in the British Isles. Visions of bulldozers tipping great mounds of bovine carcases into gigantic pits inevitably spring to mind, coupled with scenes of ruined farmers shooting themselves within the confines of their quarantined properties.

In Africa, where this viral disease is endemic, an outbreak, although serious, does not result in squads of slaughterers, armed with humane killers, hastening to perform their grisly task. In the humped cattle of the Boran or the Nandi breeds the disease may be so mild as to be hardly apparent.

In large parts of Kenya most cattle are vaccinated twice yearly. Nevertheless, outbreaks occur with monotonous regularity, due to viral mutation, to the arrival of a virus other than that incorporated in the vaccine, to the illegal movement of unvaccinated stock or to shortage of vaccine.

Of the seven serotypes, six occur in Africa. Plenty to choose from.

The lesions caused by Foot and Mouth Disease are mainly confined to the tongue, lips, dental pad, nostrils, feet and teats. Severely affected animals, usually those of the European dairy breeds, may take weeks or months to recover, or may remain permanently damaged. This is often due to secondary infection of the udder or hooves resulting in chronic mastitis or lameness.

The virus, one of the most contagious known, is one to which most, if not all, cloven hoofed animals are susceptible. Man, although not usually cloven hoofed, is occasionally infected.

My first introduction to this malady of such ill repute was on a ranching property, lying on the saddle between the forested heights of the Eburru range and the Mau escarpment. The place was called Kiambogo after the large black buffalo which periodically would leave their forest home to sample the meticulously preserved grass leys and fields of wheat,

334

much to the irritation of the Macdonald family, whose hard work and dedication had turned rank bush into prime pasture and carefully cultivated paddocks.

Macdonald pere, in particular, would turn puce with fury when one of his Maasai herdsmen reported yet another incursion from the jungle. Having given a detailed description of damage wreaked on crops, fences and water troughs, the herdsman would listen impassively while his employer, eyes bulging, neck muscles standing out like knotted twigs, spittle spurting from his lips, would vent his verbal spleen on buffalo in particular and wildlife in general.

When I received a call one Saturday afternoon to examine a group of sick steers, I was relieved to learn that the peppery patriarch was enjoying a weekend's fishing at the coast, laying waste the denizens of the deep. I had no wish to be present during an attack of apoplexy brought on by a diagnosis on my part.

As I drove the 20-odd miles to the ranch, I pondered, not for the first time, on the extraordinarily high number of emergencies and disease outbreaks which occurred on Saturday afternoons, Sundays and public holidays.

The affected steers were grouped in the corner of a large field. Half a dozen Maasai lay at their ease in the long grass nearby.

I shook hands with the neopara, or headman.

Clad in a red shuka and a hairy blanket, wearing car tyre sandals as big as small water skis on his large feet, copper ornaments swaying from his pendulous ear lobes, his face bisected by a nose of Romanesque proportions, he was an imposing figure.

Several of the affected cattle, cross-bred steers, stood motionless, ropes of saliva suspended from their muzzles. From time to time one would move its jaws and smack its lips. The animals appeared to be reluctant to move and when one did, it was markedly lame.

I didn't like the look of this at all.

I asked the headman to catch one for me.

He said something in Maa to a young fellow, who produced a long stick from which was suspended a rope noose, the end of which he held in his hand.

Stealthily approaching an affected steer from the rear he whipped the noose up a hind leg as soon as it began to move and in an instant had drawn the rope tight. The steer, despite being unwell, took off as though a red hot brand had been applied to its backside, bucking and kicking. Before it had gone very far, however, the rest of the Maasai, shukas flying, had rushed in and seized the rope, bringing the animal to a standstill. One man grabbed the tail, another the head, and in a trice the steer was thrown onto its side, ready for my inspection.

By this time I had a fairly shrewd idea of the nature of the disease confronting me, so, wishing to reduce the possibility of its spread from the ranch to a minimum, I asked one of the Maasai to open the animal's mouth. He at once seized it by the nostrils and inserting his hand into its mouth, withdrew its tongue.

To my horror the entire anterior half of the epidermis came off in his hand, rather like a glove being pulled off, leaving the denuded tongue flapping about in the wretched animal's mouth like a piece of live raw steak.

Now I was in no doubt. This was Foot and Mouth Disease at its ugliest.

We roped and examined several more steers. Some had unruptured vesicles on their dental pads, some ruptured blisters between their hooves, a few lesions on the margins of their nostrils. None, fortunately, was as bad as animal number one.

I discussed with the headman the possible source of the infection. He was of the opinion that cattle being illegally moved at night along the ranch boundary were the most likely origin. He was familiar with the disease, which I was not, and suggested that, because of its excessively contagious nature and its almost inevitable spread to the rest of the cattle on the ranch, it would be best to mix infected and uninfected animals together in order to get it over with as soon as possible.

I agreed that if the disease appeared in another herd this should be done.

Two days later another herd was affected, all the cattle were mixed together and after three weeks the vast majority had recovered.

I told the headman that, as this was a notifiable disease, I would have to inform the district veterinary officer, who would impose the statutory quarantine restrictions on the farm. These were usually kept in force until six weeks after the last recorded case.

In the corner of the field was a large water trough. I drove across to it, and, using a towel and a bottle of disinfectant retrieved from the boot, feverishly scrubbed the car wheels and my shoes. It was less than ideal, but it was better than nothing. I would get Njoroge to do the job properly when I got home.

When I did get home I found Njoroge in merry mood. Even when I requested him to set to and scrub the car as he had never scrubbed it before, his bonhomie did not desert him.

I was puzzled by this freakish deviation from character, by his apparent goodwill to the world at large and to me in particular. The was not the Njoroge I knew.

The week had been an exhausting one and the Foot and Mouth outbreak had been the last straw. I was feeling decidedly ragged round the edges. A good stiff G&T was what was needed to restore the inner man.

Having consigned my garments to a bucket of near boiling water, I changed, and, with palate tingling in anticipation and whetted by the delay, withdrew from the sideboard what I knew to be an almost full bottle of Mr Gilbey's best.

It was empty.

Hadn't this happened once before?

I glanced through the window at the figure toiling over my car, directing a jet of water from the hose-pipe with what now appeared to be less than accurate precision at the windscreen. Snatches of song reached my ears through the portable Niagara at his command.

I felt that I was paying considerably over the odds for this startling burst of energy, but decided to let it run its course. With the volume of water cascading onto my car it should, at least, be well cleaned.

The cleansing of the chariot completed, I tackled my butler about the mysterious case of the now non-existent gin.

Had I never heard of evaporation? That had a familiar ring about it. Had I not studied science at school and university?

Njoroge shook his head in mournful disappointment at my discreditable lack of common knowledge, staggering slightly as he did so. A whiff of Gilbey's floated in my direction, to be immediately sampled and identified by now sensitised nostrils.

My observation that the bottle top had been firmly screwed down failed utterly to dent his argument.

I gave up. Life was too short. Besides, his meat pies and rhubarb crumbles were in a class of their own.

I settled for a couple of warm Whitecaps.

‍

Another viral disease was regarded with understandable dread by horse owners. This was African Horse Sickness, a seasonal, non-contagious infection transmitted by night-flying midges. The virus, of which there are nine serotypes and over forty antigenic strains and which, on its home ground, cycles silently in zebras, in which no symptoms appear, usually makes its presence felt after the rains, when midge multiplication is in full swing. The symptoms which appear are due to impaired function of the circulatory and respiratory systems, the virus increasing the permeability of the inner lining of the capillaries, giving rise to a transudation of plasma into the tissues and body cavities. In severe cases the horse literally drowns in its own fluids.

There is no specific treatment and, although nursing and the use of cardiac and respiratory stimulants and corticosteroids may be of value, any recovery is due to the degree of virulence of the infecting strain of virus and the immune status of the horse affected. Attributing success to any particular drug is sheer wishful thinking.

Most people endeavoured to vaccinate their horses once yearly, a few weeks before the anticipated onset of the rains in March or April. But, as the only manufacturing source in the world was South Africa, with periods of frequent high demand, vaccine was not always obtainable.

Since the Second World War the disease has appeared in various areas outside zebra stamping grounds, due to the spread of infected midges, or in some cases, to the importation of zebras to zoos. It has appeared in various parts of North Africa, the Iberian peninsula, the Middle East and even in India and Pakistan. As a result of this viral invasion, the then-Shah of Iran instituted measures to have a vaccine manufactured on Persian soil, presumably primarily to protect the pampered prancers of the Royal Stables, but also as a source of supply to other countries in need. Since the rise of the ayatollahs and Islamic fundamentalism vaccine from this source is no longer available.

The South African vaccine was one mainly made for the local market. It contained a limited number of virus strains and so did not confer complete immunity. As a result, anyone relying on vaccine alone to protect their horses was living in a fool's paradise. Protection from midges was also essential, by stabling from dusk till dawn and using insect repellents.

'Some horse owners are imbued with an insufferable sense of superiority over the infantry. This can be especially so in the case of women, particularly if they also ride – something to do with the feeling of power these individuals acquire when in control of a physically stronger creature clasped between their thighs.' So I had read somewhere, and there were occasions when I readily believed it.

Cynthia Jackson, fortunately, was not one of these. If anything, she was rather the opposite. Although addicted to horses – indeed, her massive haunches and vast thighs bore an uncanny resemblance to those of a medium sized Shetland pony – she was far from being starry-eyed about them. To her they were expendable, and if they did not come up to the mark they were either sold or led out to face the firing squad, of which I was the one man member. On an annual basis a select group of the chronically lame and barren, unproductive drones, would be brought forth for execution, when it would be my disagreeable task to dispatch them in an expeditious, humane manner.

Cynthia was the manageress of a large stud, of over 150 horses, sited on the windy Kiwi Plains due south of Lake Nakuru. Most of her charges were breeding mares and their offspring, colts and fillies, and a small number of mollycoddled stallions, kept in cloistered quarters. From these, at the appropriate time, they would be led out, neighing and rearing in frantic anticipation, for brief and violent copulation with the mare of Cynthia's choice.

Two horses, a mare and a filly, were ill. The telephone line was, as ever, faint and distorted, so, apart from this scant information, I had no idea what awaited me.

It was late afternoon and a warm, soft light flooded the flat-topped acacia trees dotted about the paddocks. Santa Gertrudis cattle grazed contentedly, accompanied by a small cohort of snowy plumaged egrets, pecking busily at disturbed insects. An African hawk eagle launched itself off a post as I passed. An eland, huge and tawny, leapt effortlessly over a fence, while a group of zebra wheeled and turned to stop and stare before galloping off.

Cynthia emerged from her house as I drove up. Accompanying her was a mixed pack of assorted canines – a Great Dane, a bull terrier, a couple of hunt terriers and an individual of dubious parentage.

These were confined to the overgrown garden while we went to examine the horses.

The mare was very ill indeed. She stood with head extended, legs apart, gasping for breath. With nostrils dilated she shook her head as though trying to inhale more air. She coughed and a white froth appeared at her nostrils. Then, to my astonishment, she bent her head, seized a tuft of grass between her teeth, and began to chew it.

With my stethoscope I listened to her chest and heard a horrid symphony of wheezing, bubbling and gurgling.

I turned to Cynthia and shook my head.

Before I examined the filly I took the mare's temperature and found it to be 41 degrees centigrade.

The filly was less seriously affected. Her breathing was normal and her temperature only slightly elevated. The main abnormalities were confined to her head and eyes. The conjunctiva was red and swollen to such an extent that her eyelids were everted, while the indentations above her eyes – the supraorbital fossae – were filled and bulging above the adjacent skin.

I lifted my stethoscope to listen to her heart.

As I did so there was a sudden crash and I turned to find the mare thrashing on the ground, her legs flailing like those of an exhausted finalist galloping towards the finishing line of the Grand National. Only this mare was galloping towards Death. She uttered a series of long drawn out gasping groans, bent her head backwards and stopped breathing. A foamy flood gushed from her nostrils.

To my relief Cynthia did not burst into tears or throw herself on the body of the deceased as others of her gender might have done under similar circumstances.

Instead she hitched up her shapeless jeans, which had sunk to well below the pelvic plimsoll line, wiped her hands on her backside and gave a relieved grunt.

'Well, that was quick. Horse Sickness, wasn't it?'

'Yes, the hyperacute pulmonary form – almost always fatal. The filly has the less severe heart infection. She might recover.'

'They should have been vaccinated two months ago but there was no vaccine in the country then.'

'Yes, I remember. Well, let me do what I can for the filly. I really don't have much faith in drugs for Horse Sickness but we have to try. I'll give her a diuretic to try and clear away any fluid, a corticosteroid to reduce the swellings above the eyes, an antibiotic to cover secondary infection and an antihistamine, which a horse vet in South Africa claims to be helpful, heaven knows why. Get her into a stable, she must have total rest, give bran mashes and cross your fingers!'

The filly did make a complete, if slow, recovery.

We cut open the mare's chest and removed the lungs. I cut into them with a knife. A torrent of white, frothy liquid poured out. The mare had drowned in her own juices.

As the sun was by now inclining towards the yardarm I allowed myself to be persuaded to partake of a glass of something more potent than afternoon tea. This was in order to discuss preventive measures with regard to African Horse Sickness and at the same time to anaesthetise myself from my immediate surroundings, namely Cynthia's drawing room. Herein I presently found myself seated upon an appropriate horsehair sofa, whose upholstery was such that my gluteals were virtually in contact with the floorboards. On my left the Great Dane nibbled at my ear, on my right the bull terrier salivated over my shorts, while at my feet the terriers fought over a discarded biscuit.

An offer of a refill was accepted with alacrity.

By the time I came to leave I was pretty well numbed to my proximate environment and was able to weave my way with casual ease through the heaps of saddlery, dusty piles of 'Horse and Hound' and mounds of ancient jodhpurs, discarded footwear and half chewed dog biscuits, which littered the room.

Outside, the night sky was clear and black and sparkled with the points of a million stars. Twenty miles away the lights of Nakuru glowed beneath the dark mass of Menengai.

As I drove towards those lights along the dusty road the eyes of the innumerable kangaroo-like spring hares, which inhabited this area, shone red in the headlamps as they hopped away into the darkness.

CHAPTER EIGHTEEN

The time had come, I decided, to take to the air, if only to escape for a few brief moments from the stresses and strains encountered on a daily basis on the bosom of Mother Earth. And if, at the same time, the ability to pilot an aeroplane could be incorporated into my work, so much the better.

Accordingly I enrolled as a student at the Nakuru Aero Club, whose nerve-centre was a wooden shack, the main feature of which was the bar. Flying and non-flying members gravitated to it like iron filings to a magnet.

The instructor was a skinny, bespectacled fellow called Clive Yelland, which seemed rather appropriate as he spent a large percentage of his time yelling at me to keep the wings level, to watch the altimeter, to keep an eye on the compass setting, to raise or lower the flaps, and so on.

The amount of time and effort involved in obtaining a private pilot's licence was daunting – a minimum of forty hours at the controls was required, of which at least ten had to be as pilot in command. Then there was a three hour cross country exercise, an hour long flying test, written exams in aviation law, airframes and engines, navigation and meteorology and a separate test to obtain a flight-radio telephone operator's licence.

Trying to fit hour-long flying lessons into a long working day was no less difficult. For the first three months these were scheduled for 7am. I would get up at 6am, be back on the ground by 8am and be in the surgery by 8.30, ready to start work.

After three months of this, however, Captain Yelland had had enough of rising with the lark, or whatever corresponded to the lark in East Africa, and decreed that 8am was a more civilized time to start yelling at his new pupil.

The club aircraft was a Cessna 172, a comfortable four man high wing monoplane.

Initially I found taxiing the plane confusing, until I learnt that this was done by using a mixture of throttle, rudder and brake, only using the joystick or yoke to keep pressure off the nose wheel by use of the elevators on the tail.

Soon I began to feel at home in this new element. The mass of dials on the instrument panel – altimeter, direction indicator, airspeed indicator, artificial horizon and vertical speed indicator – made sense. The use of carburettor heat to warm the engine at low revs to prevent icing was logical. The use of the rest of the complex panoply of controls – fuel mixture lever, rudder trim, master switch, magneto switch and flap lever – began to slot into place.

Getting the plane into the air was not difficult. After going through the take-off checks – the most important of which was ensuring that the fuel lever was switched to ON – and dropping ten degrees of flap, it was basically just a matter of barrelling down the grass strip at full throttle until a certain critical speed was reached. At this point a little backward pressure on the yoke would lift the plane off the ground. The rumble of the wheels would stop and one would be left with the roar of the engine and the whistle of the slipstream as one juggled for control.

Landing the machine was rather more complex and frequently more traumatic, certainly for the aeroplane. Various procedures had to be followed, such as lowering the flaps and gradually reducing power, before it was possible to return to terra firma. An announcement had to be made on the plane's radio to advise any other pilot unlucky enough to be nearby, indicating what it was one was about to attempt to do. This part of the flight procedure frequently had Captain Yelland's larynx stretched to its limits.

Ideally the plane should glide gracefully at minimum height over the outer edge of the airfield, with power off and flaps down, to land lightly, but positively, on the greensward, thence to proceed, with a satisfying rumble of wheels, down the centre of the strip.

One of the reasons for Captain Yelland's excitement during the landing phases in the early stages of my instruction was that a number of them were made rather too positively for his liking. Not infrequently the plane would bound back into the air like a startled antelope and then proceed to catapult its way down the runway in a series of giant kangaroo-like leaps, veering from side to side, with my feet pumping madly on the rudder pedals in an effort to keep it moving in a straight line.

I had to admire the good captain. The plane had dual controls, as do nearly all aircraft. Despite facing imminent annihilation every time I was at his side, never once did he take over. Thanks to his massive forbearance, my confidence grew apace.

Occasionally I would indulge in a sort of reverse landing, when I failed to reduce power sufficiently on the approach. When it became alarmingly evident that a hard landing was imminent I would raise the nose to drain off a bit of speed. The plane would then float for anything up to a hundred yards down the runway before coming down with an unedifying crash. The embarrassing quiet as the plane levitated, power off, a few feet above the ground, allowed my long-suffering instructor to give full vent to his pent up feelings.

'Give me strength! Give me strength! Thank God you weren't in the Battle of Britain! We'd all be speaking German and eating sauerkraut!'

On one occasion my approach on finals was far too high and in an effort to get the plane on the ground I ended up like a kamikaze pilot aiming his Zero at the deck of an American warship.

'On the other side again!' groaned Yelland.

On another occasion I was far too low and roared along at tree top height for what seemed like a couple of miles before flopping onto the runway.

Despite these deviations, however, after twelve and a half hours of instruction, Captain Yelland decided that I was competent enough to go solo.

This is the moment when the cockpit feels uncomfortably empty and one realizes, as the instructor disappears towards the cosy confines of the clubhouse, that one is on one's own. For the next ten minutes or so, during the solo circuit there won't be anyone in the right hand seat bawling out one's mistakes.

My first solo was devoid of any hairbreadth escapes from injury or death. It was, boringly, totally, incident-free. Minus the weight of Captain Yelland, the plane, after a short ground run, sprang into the air. I raised the flaps, trimmed the elevators, roared round the circuit, downwind, base leg, finals and executed a perfect landing.

'Well done!' yelled Yelland, after I had tied the plane down.

I drove to the surgery.

As I did so, I could not but regard the passing motorists with a mite of condescension, mere earth-bound mortals, scurrying here and there, like ants or migrating lemmings, mindlessly pursuing their petty errands.

After ten minutes of solo flight I had acquired an overblown vision of myself. I saw myself, stern visaged, helmeted and goggled, long scarf streaming in the wind, swooping over crowds of open-mouthed admirers in my vintage Tiger Moth.

I could fly!

After that first solo I felt I was getting somewhere, although much remained to be learned and many hours of instruction and study lay ahead.

I loved the smell of hot oil and the cracking of the engine as it cooled down, the roar as the engine burst into life, rocking the wings with the blast from the propeller, the feeling of exhilaration as the plane left the ground and the sense of satisfaction in a landing well done. I loved the sense of space when aloft and the immense views, brown and yellow and green, mountain, plain, river and lake, encircling the plane below, while above, the sky seemed so close one could almost touch it. There was a feeling of freedom, of being in sole control of the situation, in command, something seldom encountered at ground level.

Meanwhile, back on that mundane ground, where I toiled for my daily crust, death and disease were seldom so obliging as to hang fire while I swooped and soared across the firmament. I frequently returned to earth with a bump in more senses than one.

◎◎◎◎◎◎

Dr Keys was a tall, elderly, rigid, stiff-backed buffer, who had spent the bulk of his working life in India. His upper lip was adorned with what looked like the faded remnants of a military moustache. He had a limited sense of humour but his nature was basically kind and tolerant.

Since leaving the sub-continent in the mid fifties, he had worked in various government hospitals in Kenya. As a result he was still working in them, having failed to amass sufficient funds to support himself and his wife in their declining years, such was the miserable salary offered by these establishments.

Mrs Keys had considerably less humour than her husband. She was a lean, leathery creature with a physiognomy resembling that of a prune which had been discarded in Death Valley for several years. This may have had something to do with the fact that their union had borne no fruit. Looking at her, I found it impossible, even at the furthest stretch of my imagination, to envisage what she might have looked like forty years previously, and what had attracted her to the young, and possibly dashing, Dr Keys.

Whatever the cause, it certainly didn't make dealing with her an easy task.

On my return from an early morning aerial exercise therefore, when I saw the rusting hulk of the Keys' Ford Zephyr parked outside the surgery, my heart sank rapidly bootwards. It speedily ascended when I perceived the vehicle to be occupied only by Dr Keys and a canine companion. The latter I recognized as Buster, a rather beaten-up boxer of indeterminate years.

Dr Keys levered his angular, arthritic frame out of the car, and, looking not unlike an aged marabou stork, preceded me into the surgery.

'Hello, Cran,' he greeted me in his gravelly, aristocratic accent. 'I wonder if you'd have a look at Buster. He's had the odd drop of blood dripping from his prepuce for the past three or four days, although other-wise he appears to be quite normal. Perhaps he's got a touch of the clap!'

Dr Keys indulged in a short, hollow laugh.

I summoned Master Moses and together we hoisted Buster onto the table and laid him on his right side.

I extruded the latter's penis and immediately observed several friable, cauliflower-like growths.

'Yes, he's got the canine clap all right,' I said. 'Look at those – transmissible venereal tumours. He's been out fornicating with dirty bitches. They've transplanted their horrid tumour cells onto his penis during copulation and this is the result. But surgical excision is usually successful.'

Dr Keys nodded sagely.

'Go ahead, old chap. You know best. Must do what we can for him.'

'Right. Leave him here and collect him late this afternoon. By that time he should be ready to go home.'

Dr Keys looked tired and haggard, his complexion grey, his features drawn. His threadbare jacket hung loosely from his bony shoulders. At your age, I thought, you should be retired and at home, feet up, perusing the 'Telegraph', not slaving away for a pittance in an understaffed, under-equipped hospital, overburdened with a surfeit of impecunious patients, all suffering from illnesses few of which were in the early stages, and many of which were past helping. No wonder you look exhausted.

Buster remained behind while his master departed to advance himself a little closer to the grave.

I gave Buster a short-acting anaesthetic and, with tissue forceps and sharp surgical scissors, removed the offending growths. Operations in this area are almost invariably accompanied by a great rush of blood and this one was no exception, but artery forceps and packing brought the seemingly-alarming haemorrhage under control. I avoided using ligatures because of the risk of causing adhesions between the penis and the prepuce.

By the time Dr Keys arrived in the late afternoon, looking even more shattered than in the morning, Buster was up and ready to depart. The bleeding had stopped, but I told Dr Keys to expect to see a few drops of blood during the next few days, following which they should stop. After a month I wanted to examine Buster again, to check for tumour re-growth or for any I might have missed.

Four weeks later Buster was pronounced to be tumour-free and fit to copulate with bitches similarly free from this repugnant condition.

Shortly afterwards Dr Keys and his good lady moved to Machakos, south of Nairobi, there to labour in the equatorial salt mines of yet another government hospital.

This proved to be altogether too much for Mrs Keys, for soon after their arrival at their new post, she, poor soul, expired, and went to her Maker, dying apparently of cancer but more likely of despair.

Thus it was that when, eighteen months later, Dr Keys reappeared in Nakuru to teach potential paramedics within the confines of a building which looked as though it had been transplanted in toto from the Gorbals of Glasgow, his only companion was an aging Buster. When I saw Buster I consoled myself with the thought that whatever disease processes might afflict him during his limited future, venereal disease was not likely to be among them. The same might also be said of his master.

However, there were plenty of other diseases associated with Buster's terminal years to ensure that professional contact was maintained. Nephritis, arthritis, gingivitis, dental tartar, enlargement of the prostate, cataract, skin tumours and incontinence, all singled out the wretched Buster for especial attention.

Because his owner was at work all day and Buster was unable to walk the mile or so from his home to the surgery, I had to make several visits to the doctor's house on the hill overlooking the town and the lake. Being government quarters, it was a drab concrete box, surrounded by a patch of weeds and bare earth, all carefully and tastefully designed to uplift the flagging spirits after a stimulating day in the wards and lecture theatre attempting to instil knowledge and wisdom into the unreceptive skulls of a posse of unco-operative students.

On most occasions Dr Keys wasn't there and I was received by his butler, a placid, easy-going Kamba, who invariably greeted me with a curiously soporific smile. This benign gent drifted around the premises, beaming at nothing in particular, occasionally giving vent to a quiet chuckle, and leaning against the wall when the going got tough. He appeared to be under the constant influence of some powerful hypnotic drug. On one occasion, not wishing to offend his susceptibilities, I accepted his offer of a cup of tea. After about 45 minutes he reappeared, swaying sinuously across the room like an Egyptian belly dancer, bearing before him a tray upon which teetered a massive kettle and teapot, which for several seconds hovered dangerously above my groin before being deposited with a crash onto a side table. The tea, already milked and sugared, was excruciating. If this is the standard of the cook's cuisine, I thought, it was little wonder Dr Keys was as thin as he was. The fellow was either cultivating opium in the garden or helping himself to the doctor's supply of valium.

At weekends Dr Keys was at home, re-charging his batteries, so he told me, in preparation for the horrors of the week ahead.

One Sunday morning, receiving a summons to attend to the ailing Buster, I was met at the door by Dr Keys, wearing a long white night-shirt. With his cadaverous visage and grey locks he resembled a latter day version of Scrooge confronted by one or other of the three Ghosts. I hoped my own resemblance was to that of Christmas Present and not to those of Past or Future, or even to the wretched Marley, but having partaken rather well, if not wisely, in the Men's Bar the night before, I rather doubted it.

Finally the dread day came when it was decided by mutual consent, excluding, of course, the opinion of the patient himself, that Buster's sufferings should be terminated by humane euthanasia.

With assistant Moses I arrived at the residence to find that a deep, sheer sided grave had been excavated, presumably by some hired hand, amid the weeds surrounding the house. Certainly neither Dr Keys, nor his steward, were capable of such spectacular spadework. I peered into the shadowy depths. A couple of lines from John Webster's 'Land Dirge' rose to mind – 'Keep the wolf far thence, that's foe to men, For with his nails he'll dig them up again.' There wasn't much chance of that happening to Buster once he was down there.

Dr Keys stood rigid and silent, jaws clenched, while I clipped the hair over the old dog's cephalic vein, cleaned the area with spirit and slowly injected the triple strength pentobarbitone solution into the blood stream. Before the syringe was emptied Buster's head had slumped forwards and he collapsed slowly and gently onto his side, heart and respirations at a standstill. A merciful and kindly end, one denied to many humans.

The doctor was obviously heartbroken by the death of his pet. He knelt down by Buster's side and wrapped the body in a blanket. Then, with an audible creaking of geriatric joints, he rose and walked stiffly to the lip of the yawning pit and carefully laid Buster's mortal remains on the freshly turned earth.

To my alarm and astonishment he then scrabbled down the scree-like slope of loam and rubble and vanished into the grave.

I ran forwards and found the dome of the good doctor's skull to be about eighteen inches below my boots.

Gruffly he requested me to hand down Buster's body. This I did, following which he carried out a series of half hidden last rites, before asking for help in getting out.

This was easier said than done.

Apart from myself and assistant Moses, the only other help at hand lay in the decidedly dubious form of the doctor's somnolent steward, whose cannonball-like cranium I could see hovering over an adjacent bush, grinning from ear to ear like an inane Cheshire cat.

Despite his lack of flesh, the doctor was big of bone. Moreover his declining years had robbed him of his strength and he could give me no assistance as I struggled to haul him, single-handed, out of the pit. When his features turned an ominous shade of blue I decided that different tactics should be adopted. Visions of myself, my assistant and the cook, shovelling soil over the lifeless remains of both Buster and his master rose before me with unpleasing clarity.

I dispatched Moses to the car to fetch the stout rope we used for casting recalcitrant cattle. I then joined Dr Keys and Buster in the tomb and tied the rope securely round the former's waist, following which I gave him a leg up, while Moses, now joined by the bemused butler, hauled manfully from above. A short, sharp struggle ensued, accompanied by a fair amount of grunting, sliding and slipping and not so *sotto voce* muttering of oaths by the baser member of the team.

Once the doctor had been returned to the land of the living I turned to the task of getting myself out and found my climbing experience singularly useful in scrambling up the vertical sides of Buster's pit.

About six months after Buster's dispatch to a better world, Dr Keys himself expired after a short illness, and was, in accordance with his instructions, cremated on a pyre of logs on the shores of Lake Nakuru, a fitting ceremony being conducted with admirable efficiency and reverence by the local Hindu community.

☖☖☖☖☖

Well prior to the acquisition of these bonus points by the Grim Reaper at the expense of the Keys menage, my flying training continued to proceed, if not to flourish, under the aegis of an increasingly nervous Captain Yelland.

Certain aspects of the course of instruction, with an over-enthusiastic embryo airman at his elbow, were not designed to engender feelings of relaxation in the bosom of an inherently anxious instructor.

Stalling and spinning in particular, closely followed by forced landings without power, had Commander Yelland barking his orders in an increasingly, and disturbingly, high pitched yelp.

Although, prior to my first solo, I had received basic instruction in the essential aspects of these deviations from normal flight, we now proceeded to examine them in exhaustive detail.

These exercises were not for those with a delicate stomach. During the stall, the sudden sickening plunge, frequently accompanied by a sideways lurch as a wing dropped, had one's pylorus leaping upwards to grapple violently with one's gizzard.

The spin took things a bit further. During the spin the plane is simultaneously pitching up, yawing and rolling. Fortunately things happen so quickly that there is little time to consider what might be happening to one's recently ingested breakfast or lunch.

We would fly the aircraft to an altitude of 3,000 feet above Lake

Nakuru and there practise entering and recovering from spins. As we flew over the lake, a sharp look-out had to kept for birds, especially flights of pelicans. A collision with one of these massive birds could have terminal consequences.

After an inspection turn, to ensure that there were no other aircraft lurking in the vicinity, I would level the wings, close the throttle and raise the nose of the plane until it was above the horizon. I always found the sudden silence after the roar of the engine rather unnerving – a mute indicator that something alarming was about to happen. The only sound was the rush of air and the buffeting of the wings as the plane struggled to remain airborne. As the air speed dropped, the stick had to be held further and further back. Then, before the plane stalled, the drill was to stamp on the rudder in the desired direction of the spin and pull the stick right back. Immediately one found oneself looking straight down at the ground 3,000 feet below, with the horizon whirling round and round at ever-increasing speed and the tops of the thorn trees and the edge of the lake getting closer and closer with every passing second.

A convulsive bang on the opposite rudder, coupled with shoving the stick forwards brought the mind-bending rotation to an end and one found oneself in a forward dive, howling vertically downwards, with the instructor bellowing in your right ear to get the nose up. Fortunately the aircraft did this almost by itself and as the nose came up to the horizon I would open the throttle to climb back up to 9,000 feet to practise another spin. I would practise spin recoveries from straight and level flight, and from a turn, and, probably most important of all, recovery from the incipient spin, one which might occur at low level, when taking off or coming in to land.

I found it all quite exhilarating.

Captain Yelland just looked a bit older.

We would take off from Nakuru Airstrip to practise forced landing without power, the object of which is to enable the pilot to effect a safe landing in the event of engine failure.

This exercise demanded a fair degree of understanding of the rules of flight, and, as any significant errors would have, at least in theory, serious repercussions, a modicum of concentration and application was required in order to avoid engendering an unnecessary degree of excitement on the part of the instructor.

Engine failure occurring shortly after take off was simulated as it carried a major risk of becoming the real thing.

Once we had gained sufficient height, however, we would practise in earnest, initially within the orbit of the airfield.

On the downwind leg, without warning, the instructor would lean over and yank the throttle shut.

The first thing to be done was to raise the nose and trim the plane to its best gliding speed, so converting speed into distance. Next was to plan where to land – in this case the airfield – checking wind speed and direction, and selecting a 1,000 foot point abeam the threshold of the runway. This was the key to the whole operation and from it a gliding turn was effected onto base leg, which had to be positioned close to the boundary of the field in order to maintain sufficient height. On the way down I would run through the failure checks – fuel, mags, mixture, carburettor heat and, if time permitted, give a May Day call. By this time I would be getting pretty low and, if things were going according to plan, turning over the 1,000 foot point onto base leg. Here the crash checks were started, switching off everything likely to cause a conflagration in the event of a crash – fuel off, mags off, fuel mixture cut – and tightening harnesses and opening doors.

During this exercise I had to take care not to get carried away and take things too literally. Hence the nervous aroma exuded by the instructor. I had to remember to give the engine a warming burst for every 500 feet of descent to keep the engine warm. Failure to do so might result in the carburettor icing up, bringing the fan at the sharp end of the plane to an abrupt and exciting stop.

Depending on the strength of the wind I would lower ten to fifteen degrees of flap, aim to land well into the field and switch off the master switch when a landing was assured.

The tricky bit was getting the altitude and distance right, the latter being dependent on the former. One could do something about being too high, but, in the event of an engine failure, nothing at all about being too low. Except pray. Or, as that doughty pilot, Pat Neylan, once told me – 'put your head between your legs and kiss your ass goodbye!' Yes, indeed. Initially my simulated forced landings without power were invariably undershot into the gum trees near the adjacent army camp or into the small-holdings on the wrong side of the runway threshold. This did not please Captain Yelland, who would voice his displeasure with a falsetto shriek.

Finally things seemed to gel and we went out into the country, where things were not quite so regulated.

A good deal more initiative and imagination were required in order to decide where a landing might be made without writing off both plane and occupants. There was little point in effecting a text book approach onto a lava flow or into a swamp, when a perfectly satisfactory lake shore, open paddock or road lay close at hand. One had to think one's way right down to the ground.

It was exciting, whistling silently earthwards, scanning the ground, scrutinizing the instruments, turning onto base leg and approach, bringing the machine almost to touch down and then opening up with a roar, to burst away over the tops of the acacia trees.

When, as occasionally happened, we went flying in the late afternoon, there was nothing more pleasant than cruising homewards in the soft evening light. The air was generally still and gust-free. Below, the shadows lengthened as the plane's own extended shadow rushed silently over the ground. A close watch might reveal flocks of birds returning to their roosting places – ducks, geese, egrets, pelicans.

Then came the ordered, seemingly leisurely descent to earth, followed, if I was favoured by more than a modicum of skill, or luck, by the gratifying whoosh of wheels brushing grass before they contacted terra firma with the soft, satisfying thump and rumble so beloved of aviators.

The next port of call was the Aero Club, a pleasant, homely sort of place, small and intimate, with a bar at one end, a map table at the other and a few easy chairs and a fireplace in-between.

Perched on a stool at the bar, the Whitecaps slid easily over the tonsils, served with distinct lack of style by Elijah the barman, whose chunky form seemed to be a permanent fixture. Almost equally permanent was Abdul, a non-teetotal, non-flying Muslim member, who would sit for hours tossing neat whiskies down his throat. A wealthy businessman, generous to a fault, with a paunch of impressive proportions, he would eventually totter out to his Mercedes and roar off into the night.

It was always my hope not to be disturbed during these post-flying sessions, and this was indeed frequently the rule, mainly because the telephone seldom worked. One evening, however, just as I was settling down to a shandy and a plate of sausages and eggs, presented by the versatile Elijah, the phone rang.

At the other end of the line was a frantic Asian.

He was from Nairobi and, with his family, had spent the day at Lake Bogoria, on whose west shore are numerous hot springs, geysers, steam jets and deep pools of boiling water. With them was their German Shepherd Dog, Simba.

Here they had a picnic in the shade of a clump of mimosa trees. After the meal they went to view the hot springs, accompanied by Simba.

Simba sprang ahead, barking joyfully, revelling in his unaccustomed freedom.

Suddenly he vanished from sight.

Drawn by frantic yelping his owner ran forwards and discovered that Simba had fallen into a huge pool of bubbling, boiling water. Paddling madly, Simba reached the bank and scrambled out, steaming from every pore.

His owners bundled him into the Merc and drove at the speed of light to Nakuru, rocketing over the unsurfaced road, oblivious to the damage being inflicted on the suspension.

In one mighty gulp I downed my sausage and egg and flushed them stomach-wards with the remainder of my shandy.

My passage from Aero Club to surgery was swift, although not to be compared to the grossly overloaded buses which swept past like jet propelled tanks, with a roar like a cyclone and a blast of wind which almost blew me off the road.

The main street of the town was relatively quiet. In shop doorways night-watchmen were bedding down for the night, their repose undisturbed by the glare of long-defunct street lights. A couple of garishly made-up whores scuttled into an alleyway on the approach of a pair of patrolling policemen, accompanied by an eager-looking alsatian on a short leash. A solitary matatu, bursting at the seams with shadowy occupants, lurched drunkenly round a corner, the turn boy's backside protruding from the rear door as he scrabbled for adhesion within the packed interior.

The Mercedes was waiting at the surgery door.

The dog had been virtually parboiled. The miracle was that he was still alive. Over almost his entire body the hair could be pulled out in tufts, revealing the red weeping surface beneath. Even the inside of his mouth had been scalded by the boiling alkaline water. The eyes alone appeared to have been spared, eloquent and pleading for release from the torment engulfing the body.

Fluids, cortocosteroids and antibiotics were immediately given intravenously to maximum effect. All was in vain. The damage done was beyond the power of mortal man to rectify and, half an hour later, Simba slipped into merciful oblivion.

⚡⚡⚡⚡⚡

It was a Sunday afternoon and I was doing a Caesarian section on a Boran heifer. Assisting me were the owner, local landed aristo Rupert Littlejohn, and a Maasai herdsman.

The former had already incurred my suppressed wrath by performing an amateur episiotomy with his penknife. Now I had to stitch up his botched butchery as well as operate on the heifer.

I was halfway through the operation. I straightened up to ease my aching back.

In the azure sky to the south west I noticed a cloud, no bigger than the proverbial man's hand.

I drew the attention of the herdsman, as a local expert, to this small blemish in the firmament and inquired of him whether, in his opinion, it was advancing or retreating.

He assured me that it was of no significance and I bent once more to my task.

Twenty minutes later, with the heifer's abdomen incised and exposed to the elements, the heavens opened with a crash of thunder and the roar of falling water.

Hailstones bounced painfully off my bare back. I raised my eyes and caught those of the herdsman. Over his shuka he was wearing a raincoat. I looked at it pointedly. Wordlessly he took it off. Even if he had spoken I wouldn't have heard a word above the general cacophony. I motioned with scalpel and forceps for the raincoat to be held over the wound as an impromptu umbrella.

By the time I had inserted the final stitches we were all standing up to our ankles in a stream of icy water rushing around the perimeter of the recumbent heifer.

As I repaired Rupert's miserable efforts, the sun re-appeared.

We released the heifer, she scrambled to her feet and immediately charged us.

I sympathised. I felt like charging the herdsman.

Rupert Littlejohn seemed to attract rain like a carcase attracted flies.

He rented grazing in the spectacular Hell's Gate gorge from its Maasai owners. The gorge lay a few miles to the south of Lake Naivasha.

One afternoon he phoned to say that one of his Boran cows grazing in the gorge had prolapsed her uterus. I asked him to have a square pit dug next to the animal and to have help at hand.

As Hell's Gate was about sixty miles from Nakuru it was late afternoon by the time I wound my way beneath the beetling cliffs which overhung the flat floor of the gorge. Groups of kongoni, eland and zebra grazed peacefully on the short, wiry grass. A lammergeyer, wings motionless, swept majestically along the face of the cliff.

I drove up a short hill to where a group of Maasai men and Rupert stood clustered around the patient. A large Land Rover was parked a few yards away.

The cow was lying within the circle of an old manyatta. The ground was thickly littered with dry, desiccated lumps of cow dung. 'At least the stuff's dry,' I thought. On the perimeter an Egyptian vulture hopped away, looking a bit peeved at having its territory invaded.

As I approached, the light began to fade and a strong wind to blow. I glanced at my watch. It was only five o'clock – at least an hour and a half before sunset. Clouds of dust billowed thickly across the floor of the gorge.

Rupert looked up as I got out of my car

'Hello, Hugh,' he said, in his Old Etonian accent. 'How are you?'

He drew on his cigarette.

'I've had a pit dug as you asked and I've covered the prolapse with a tandarua (tarpaulin) as it was getting covered in dust, not to mention flies. And I've brought plenty of water. It's warm too!'

'Good man,' I replied. 'We can use the tandarua to line the hole. It'll lend a spurious air of cleanliness to the disgusting surroundings. I'd wear a mask if I had one. It might keep the flies out of my nose!'

Rupert threw back his lordly head and gave an upper class whinny.

'Right then,' I said. 'To work!'

I prepared my equipment, secured the cow's legs with ropes, gave her an intravenous infusion of calcium borogluconate and removed my shirt, the better for close-quarter prolapse grappling. I cleaned the uterus with the proffered water and then instructed the attendant Maasai to begin lowering the cow's forequarters into the tarpaulin-lined hole.

As they did so, it began to rain. With a clap of thunder and a flash of lightning the rain hissed down with frightening force. Out of the corner of my eye I saw Rupert scuttling sideways, like a hemiplegic crab, towards his Land Rover.

For the rest of us there was no shelter. The hillside was soon awash with running water, which began to pour into the pit. I worked with frantic speed, hands and fingers slippery with water and obstetrical lubricant. Soon I was so cold that I began to shiver like a man with St. Vitus's dance.

By now the pit was half full of water. The tarpaulin held every drop, effectively preventing any seepage. The uterus finally slipped into position and I thrust my quivering arm up to the shoulder into the cow's abdomen to ensure that it was fully inverted.

I glanced at the cow's head. Her nostrils by now were only a couple of inches above the silty surface. Her chest was almost completely submerged.

It was time to get her out.

Although slightly better clad, the Maasai were almost as cold as I was. Another problem was that many Maasai, although prodigiously strong in the leg and powerful walkers, are weak in the arm, the majority being herdsmen unused to carrying anything heavier than a spear or club.

The men heaved and struggled, the wet ropes slipping through their numbed fingers.

I had visions of the cow drowning before my eyes.

'Harambee!' the men began to chant, as they strained and tugged.

The cow's pelvis teetered on the edge of the pit, slithering in the mud. The Maasai staggered backwards and the cow was out. I inserted a couple of stitches into her vulva and, as I did so, she rose slowly, as if in slow motion, to her feet. She tottered off down the hill, heading towards a clump of acacias where the rest of the herd was sheltering.

During all of this aquatic activity Rupert had remained snug and dry within the cosy confines of his Land Rover, occasionally switching on the wipers, the better to see how we were getting on. I made a mental note to add an extra charge to his bill for this piece of upper class arrogance. Although awash with wealth, Rupert was the sort of person who made a point of never using a new envelope for sending mail if he could use a used one. Perhaps that was how he made his money.

🌷🌷🌷🌷🌷

My flying training was fortunately free from the downpours which seemed to be drawn to Rupert Littlejohn. This was mainly due to the fact that most of my flying was done in the mornings, whereas in East Africa, rain, when it falls, mostly does so in the late afternoon or evening.

The day for my solo triangular cross-country exercise dawned bright and clear, the sky devoid of clouds.

I was to fly firstly to Kisumu, on the shores of Lake Victoria, then to Kericho and finally back to Nakuru, a total of rather more then two hours' flying time.

Never having flown this distance on my own before, I was, prior to my departure, a trifle nervous. As usual, once I was airborne, my anxieties fell away, engrossed as I was in the complexities of flying the plane, maintaining my course, keeping a look-out for other aircraft and birds and announcing my position from time to time on the radio. Initially there was a slow, steady climb to clear the heights above Molo, followed by a swift descent towards the distant Kavirondo Gulf and Kisumu. My estimated flight time was just over an hour.

Kisumu was a manned airport with a long tarmac strip capable of handling large passenger aircraft. Consequently, as I rushed ever lower, over the steaming fields of sugar cane and flooded rice paddy fields surrounding the unsavoury township of Ahero, my anxieties resurfaced.

I switched on the hand held mike, tuned to the Kisumu frequency and advised the tower that I was approaching from Nakuru and announced my estimated time of arrival.

I was greeted with a storm of static of which I understood not a word. I tried again. Once again the cockpit was filled with an unintelligible racket, crackles, whistles and whines, interspersed with the odd syllable which sounded as though it was being transmitted from Outer Space.

By this time I was over the stubby forefinger of water separating Kisumu town from the airport.

Within a couple of minutes I was over the tower and runway. I

355

looked down. The building looked deserted. I could see no sign of life. No red or green lights flashed upwards. The parking apron was a blank square of tarmac.

I searched for the windsock and saw it streaming westwards towards the lake. Turning onto downwind leg I scanned the sky for other aircraft. Nothing. The sky was empty.

Chattering into the radio I executed an elegant curving turn onto finals and touched down just beyond the threshold.

'Rats! Rats!' As soon as I was down I saw what seemed to be several miles of level tarmac stretching ahead of me. I should have landed at least halfway down the strip. I had been so obsessed with the microphone that I had failed to notice the vast acreage of bitumen below.

As I trundled along, hoping that there were no planes coming in to land behind me, I was sorely tempted to take off again, but felt the airport authorities might not approve.

After what seemed like an age, I at last turned off the runway and taxied to the tower.

I switched off the engine, stepped out and walked to the two-storey building. 'Where the hell was everyone?' I pushed open the door and was just starting up the wooden staircase when I heard a familiar voice – '…an' my headquatters will be in de foma white settla town of Nakuru. De new boundary of Uganda be stretchin' as per de demarcation prior to 1902, as laid down by my good friends de British. It will be takin' in de wold famous Masai Mara Game Reseve, Lake Naivasha, de tea estates of Kericho, de Rift Valley stretchin' up to Lake Rudolf and of course de Lake Victoria pot of Kisumu. Long live Uganda!'

It was Al-Haji Field Marshal Idi Amin Dada, VC, DSO, MC, D.Litt, President of neighbouring Uganda, broadcasting details to his people and the world, of a minor unilateral territorial adjustment.

I clattered up the stairs and pushed open a door labelled Flight Controller. A couple of figures crouched over a transistor radio whipped round as I burst in.

'Jambo, gentlemen! So, where are we? Uganda or Kenya? Do I need an international flight plan or a local one? Which one do I need to fly to Nakuru via Kericho? Or are we all in Uganda now?'

They looked at each other and grinned.

'That man! Ha! He is a nothing but a black colonialist! A mass murderer! Throw him to the crocodiles!'

'Yes, indeed. Now, can I fill in a flight plan so I can get back to Kenya?'

'Yes, sir! Right away sir.'

I was glad they had been so absorbed by Idi's expansionist ambitions and had not seen my amateurish landing, demonstrating to all and sundry that I was an inexperienced student pilot.

I filled in the form rapidly and departed.

I had been fed with stories about how impossibly hard it was to find the airfield at Kericho, a grass strip so perfectly camouflaged by the tens of thousands of acres of green tea bushes surrounding it as to be almost invisible. Some pilots had apparently failed totally to find it and had ended up in Narok, eighty miles away. I was luckier and to my pleased surprise arrived right over the strip, rather spoiling the effect by landing downwind and downhill. Fortunately there was no-one around to see me execute these major gaffes.

Only 45 minutes later I was lowering flaps and reducing power as I came in to land at Nakuru, easterly outpost of Idi's new Uganda.

✳ ✳ ✳ ✳ ✳

'When you keep livestock, you've got to expect deadstock!'

So spake Charlie Robertson, farmer and breeder of Jersey cattle and thoroughbred racehorses. It was a dictum he was fond of repeating to tyro farmers and apprentice managers, as though to forestall any connotation of failure associated with the demise of any of his own stock, for whatever reason.

It was not a view to which I personally subscribed, although I had to admit that it did allow one a certain degree of latitude when dealing with Charlie's animals. Where animals were concerned Charlie was a DIY fanatic and had invariably had a stab, usually in the dark, before summoning the vet. As a result, those disease processes, which failed to respond to his nostrums, were often far advanced, as was not infrequently the hour, by the time he admitted defeat and reached reluctantly for the telephone.

Dragging cattle and horses back from the brink was an uphill task on Charlie's farm. Most infuriating of all was to be plucked from one's hammock in the early hours of the morning to go to the aid of an unfortunate parturient mare or cow, on whose travailing, birthing offspring Mr Robertson's rude hands had been laid, to their frequent detriment and not infrequent death. On such occasions, as I struggled in the darkness, with a chill wind soughing across my unshirted shoulders, trying yet again to render a silk purse out of a sow's ear, I sometimes felt that my own demise was not far off.

Dogs also did not escape the long arm of Charlie's homespun enthusiasm to satisfy his overblown opinion of himself as a local expert in the animal field.

On one memorable occasion, wishing to eliminate stray dogs which were visiting his farm at night and troubling his cattle, he laced chunks of meat with toxaphene. These he scattered at strategic points frequented by the unwelcome canines. Unfortunately he failed to lock up his own dogs and he also failed to take into account the sensitive palates of their feral cousins. The result was that the latter promptly regurgitated the poisoned meat, which was immediately consumed by Charlie's favoured terriers, attracted by the scent of fresh meat and by the whiff of their free-ranging relations.

Luckily I was at hand and spent an active hour, endeavouring to simultaneously anaesthetise three violently convulsing dogs, closely observed by the ever-watchful Charlie. In this task I had a modicum of success and the following day all three returned to the bosom of their master's family.

Charlie was one of those annoying Scotsmen who are constantly parading their kiltly assumptions as though the rest of humanity has seriously lost out in not being born to the north of Hadrian's Wall. To drive the point home his farm bore the pretentious title of 'Bahati Braes', as though it were a family seat in the Highlands of Scotland and not the highlands of Kenya.

Bald and middle-aged, Charlie's small blue eyes were constantly darting hither and thither, never ever quite meeting one's own. His shoulders were slightly stooped and, with his overly short shorts hoiked up into his groin, and his mincing gait, he resembled a short sighted heron that had seen better days. Whenever he wished to emphasise a point, or announce his presence, he would clap his hands together like a schoolmaster trying to bring order to an unruly class. Little wonder he was known as 'Clap Hands Charlie'. A couple of decades earlier he had been briefly married, but his wife had left him. If she had found him half as irritating as I did now, I could well understand why.

Another of Charlie's dogs, his labrador retriever Ranter, was ill.

From time to time Charlie would sally forth with like-minded cronies to slaughter the innocent water fowl on a nearby dam, into whose murky waters Ranter would be dispatched to retrieve any downed birds.

Now Ranter was unwell, losing weight and vomiting. As he had been ill for about a month when Charlie finally made contact, I had reason to fear the worst.

When the phone rang and I realised that Charlie was on the other end, I briefly excused myself, dragged over a chair, and sat down. Charlie was nothing if not loquacious and I knew I was in for a long session.

'Is that you, Hugh?' The accent was strong.

'Aye, it is.' My response rose unbidden.

'A'm phoning aboot Ranter. The puir fellow is no' weel at a' and a'm getting a wee bit worriet. He's no been right for aboot a month. He's eating all right but for the last two weeks he's been throwing up after eating. Then he re-eats the expelled offering and it stays doon. But now he's losing weight. His ribs are showing and what's more curious is that I've noticed that his legs are getting bigger. An' a' this despite the fact that I've been filling him full of vitamins and minerals and such-like I get frae yon drug peddler chappie who comes tae the farm once a month. I must have spent a fortune on him.'

'Right, Charlie, can you bring Ranter in tomorrow morning? I need to see him and we'll probably have to take an X-ray as well.'

'Can ye no' prescribe something over the phone? It's a lang way into Nakuru frae here, ye ken.'

'I know, but no, bring him in.'

This he did, and as poor Ranter staggered into the surgery my heart sank. He was just a bag of bones, covered by what looked like an old, moth-eaten rug. As he swayed through the door he gave a convulsive cough and collapsed.

'Look here, Hugh, I ken the old chap's a bit weak and underweight, but see what ye can do for him. There's a shoot at Ol Bolossat in three weeks time and I'd like tae go. I dinna fancy plunging intae they hippo-ridden swamps tae retrieve ma own birds!'

Charlie rubbed his hands together. I was relieved that he didn't clap them.

'You miserable shit!' I thought.

Aloud I said 'I don't think Ranter will be doing much retrieving for a while, by the look of him.'

I lifted Ranter onto the table, a fairly easy task in view of the fact that he must have lost about half of his bodyweight.

He was in an appalling state. Apart from his skeletal appearance, the most striking feature was his legs. The bones of the radius and ulna, tibia and fibula, metacarpals and metatarsals were all about twice their normal size. I ran my hands down them. They were all overlaid with new bone, while the adjacent soft tissues were swollen and tender. Little wonder poor Ranter had difficulty walking.

I had seen this condition before and knew that Ranter was suffering from pulmonary hypertrophic osteoarthropathy. This tongue tangling disorder is usually associated with a long-standing lesion within the chest. Such being the case the prognosis was bleak.

Ranter's breathing was fast and shallow. I listened carefully to his lungs. Judging by the ghastly chorus of gurgling, wheezing, scraping and rasping, it was a miracle he was still alive.

I quizzed Charlie long and hard.

Regurgitation after eating, gradual, but inexorable loss of weight – 'and, aye, noo that Ah think back, he's had this wee bittie cough and a struggle drawing breath frae time tae time' – these were the main features. I examined blood smears and a stool sample and found nothing remarkable.

I turned to Charlie.

'Well Charlie, I think Ranter's probably got tumours in his lungs and that the source of these tumours may be a spirocerca nodule in the lower part of his gullet.'

I saw little point in breaking bad news gently to such as Charlie.

'Spiro what?' he said.

I gave Charlie a brief synopsis of the lifecycle of this rather unusual worm, which spends its time within nodules located in the walls of the lower oesophagus, stomach and aorta of the dog. Eggs passed in the faeces of the unfortunate canine host hatch only after they have been consumed by a suitable coprophagus beetle – dung beetles to the laity. Following ingestion by the beetle, the hatched larvae become encysted within the body of the beetle, chiefly, for reasons which I was unable to explain to a frankly skeptical Charlie, within the insect's tracheal tubes. If such beetles are swallowed by a host other than a dog, for example by a chicken, a rodent or a reptile, the larval worm becomes encysted yet again. The final host becomes infected by ingesting an infected beetle or one of the so-called transport hosts, at which point the larvae emerge, to migrate via the walls of the thoracic aorta to their final destination in oesophagus or stomach.

By the expression on Charlie's pinched and narrow face it was obvious that he didn't believe a word I was saying.

I could read his mind – 'This young bugger is trying to pull the wool over my eyes wi' a' his book learnin', the arrogant know-all.'

I ploughed on in the face of his disbelief to explain that, if the oesophageal lesion is very large, the dog, obviously, has considerable difficulty in swallowing and that the passage of food over the nodule will stimulate a vomiting reflex, which leads to loss of bodily condition.

'Right, Charlie? Are you with me?'

Charlie just stared at me.

I proceeded to elaborate.

The nodules, due to their position, not infrequently become infected, may give rise to reactive granulomas and in many cases turn into oesophageal sarcomas, a particularly nasty tumour, which often contains cartilage or bone and which may spread to nearby tissues, including the lungs. When this does happen it is often accompanied by the gross thickening of the lower leg bones as exhibited by the unfortunate Ranter.

Charlie pursed his thin lips and wrinkled his nose, as though I had just broken wind.

'In the early stages of the disease, the adult worms can be killed by an injection of disophenol. If not, things go from bad to worse to incurable...'

Charlie clearly thought all of this was a load of horse manure. It was all too fanciful for words.

'OK, then,' I said. 'What we have to do to confirm this is to take a chest X-ray in conjunction with a barium meal.'

I could see Charlie's mind ticking over, as he mentally counted out the bawbees. More money disappearing down the drain.

Eventually, after a great deal of snorting and sighing, he agreed, and the following day the emaciated form of Ranter was borne off to the X-ray department of the War Memorial Hospital, where, incredibly, Miss Brown still held sway. Fortunately, though not overly fond of her fellow man, she doted on dogs.

The result was as I expected. The X-ray showed a huge mass in the posterior thorax, while others, smaller in size, peppered both lungs.

At last, Charlie was convinced and agreed that humane euthanasia was the only answer to Ranter's terminal predicament. He consented to a post mortem and the diagnosis was confirmed.

Charlie would have to take his chance with the hippos.

⚱⚱⚱⚱⚱

After dealing with the intense close-up work associated with small animal medicine and, more especially, having to cope with such unlovely specimens as Charlie, and others of his ilk, it was always a relief to be able to escape to the wide open spaces which lay beckoning over the blue horizons which edged the margins of the Rift.

So, when I received a request to castrate a group of camels on a ranch near Maralal, I was overjoyed. No doubt the camels would have been rather less enthusiastic had they known I was coming.

An invigorating surge of life, spiced with a dash of adrenalin, seemed to suddenly surge through my veins.

One afternoon I set off for the ranch, following the dirt road which wound its way through Charlie's stamping ground, Bahati, before dropping steeply down into the Subukia Valley. The eastern side of the valley, along which the way to Thomson's Falls crept and clung like a thin brown thread, was even steeper.

At its foot a stark sign needed no words to alert the non-bookish wayfarer to the perils ahead. It showed in graphic outline a right angled triangle with mammoth, house-sized boulders leaping down its fearsome slope. At the summit stood a similar warning, generally ignored by the majority of motorists, especially if they were also drunk.

The sign was probably not even seen by one bus driver, who, several sheets to the wind, set off with his complement of passengers from Thomson's Falls.

I was on a farm in the valley below when the bus plunged over the edge of the road, nose diving vertically into the forest below.

Peering upwards from where I stood, I could just espy the vehicle, which seemed to be suspended by vegetation, about a hundred feet below the road.

Fearing the worst I drove up the narrow dirt track. To my astonishment no-one had been killed or even seriously injured. The tattered survivors, covered in dust, some minus their footwear, others with torn raiment, came tottering down the road, carrying their now rather battered baggage. They seemed to regard the whole thing as an acceptable hazard to be mutely borne by those obliged to use public transport. Almost an Act of God in fact.

The driver had been drunk when the bus had left Thomson's Falls. Shouting and singing and waving wildly to bemused pedestrians, he swung the vehicle around corners with such violence that on one occasion a basket of windswept chickens was catapulted into a nearby field. As, with ever-increasing speed, the bus approached the edge of the valley, the terrified passengers crowded forwards in a last ditch effort to persuade the driver to slow down. He seemed to regard this unwarranted interference as a slight on his manhood, and as a result it goaded him to jettison whatever little caution he still retained.

By some latter day miracle he negotiated the initial right hand ninety degree bend which overhung the five hundred foot drop into the valley and thereafter it was all downhill, howling and skidding round bends and leaping over bumps and boulders.

The passengers knew that an accident was about to happen. It was only a question of how serious it would be.

There was no effete retaining barrier so a short period of wingless flight seemed inevitable before journey's end.

There was a fearful crash as the bus hit an inappropriately sited tree, detrunking it as it did so. For a second, which to the passengers seemed to last several hours, the bus hung poised on the brink, before slowly toppling into the forest below. This convenient lack of forward momentum saved the passengers' lives. Although the bus dropped about a hundred vertical feet, it became advantageously entangled in a mass of closely-meshed trees.

The bus driver, inebriated though he was, departed at high speed into the adjacent vegetation.

For several months the bus remained where it was, unable to be winched up the vertical slope above it. Finally a gang of labourers hacked a track through the forest below and it was eventually dragged by oxen and tractor to the nearest section of road.

On my present journey I was spared such vicarious excitements.

The less than obvious attractions of Thomson's Falls were soon left behind and, within minutes, I was ploughing my way through deep drifts of fine dust in the forest beyond.

The trees suddenly ended, the road dropped sharply and there, stretching before me, was the Laikipia Plateau, named after the Maasai who once owned it, before they were forcibly evicted by the brutish hand of British imperialism. A vast, greenish-grey plain, covered in wiry grass, thorn trees and rock, it was now divided into large ranches, owned or managed by characters of varying degrees of individual eccentricity.

The plain was immense, seemingly flat but in reality undulating, riven by dry gullies and studded with low hills. Far to my right the speckled peak of Mt. Kenya broke the horizon. To the north, far beyond the point where sky met earth, and a hundred miles from where I now was, lay the tiny town of Maralal and from then on it was mountain, scrub and desert all the way to Lake Turkana and the Ethiopian border.

A bone-jarring ride through a desiccated forest brought me to Rumuruti. A rutted road lined by a few nondescript dukas, a police station and a stockaded prison, there was little else to catch the eye. Miniscule though it was, the place had the atmosphere of being on a frontier, perched uneasily between the highlands and the plains. Knots of tribespeople from the wild north clustered outside the unpainted shacks, squatting, sitting or lying under the withered acacias. They charged the quivering afternoon air with an almost tangible vivacity, a feeling of life lived unsnared by the mind-numbing entanglements of the present age, free from the miasma of petty and major restrictions which have settled over the life of so-called modern man from pre-parturition to post mortem.

Perhaps, I thought, these people were equally hedged around by their own tribal codes of jurisprudence which limited their own activities to a similar degree.

Still, at least they looked the part.

A Samburu warrior strode past, red cloak flapping in the hot wind. For all the attention he paid to me or my car, only a few feet away, I might not have existed.

A Turkana, whose craggy features looked as though they had been bluntly carved from obsidian, lay stretched out in the shade, his neck resting on his small carved stool, his mud-packed hair and jaunty ostrich feather well clear of the dust. Under a separate tree sat a group of Pokot women, so black and so sombrely clad as to be almost invisible, were it not for the flash of red amid the mounds of bead necklaces surrounding their necks and resting on their shoulders. Although the two tribes look superficially similar, there is little love lost between them. The Pokot men are circumcised. The Turkana are not. The Pokot speak Kalenjin. The Turkana speak Turkana, and used to call the Pokot the Suk, a derogatory word which did not please them, and which until recently, to their intense annoyance, found its way into popular usage.

From one of the dukas stepped a Somali. Tall and slim, with fine boned features, his small arrogant head surveyed the scene like a cheetah scanning the plains for prey, seeming to ignore entirely the lesser mortals gathered in the dust below him. Clad in a long green kikoi, his sandaled feet seemed to glide across the ground. In many of the remoter parts of East Africa the Somali, due to his enterprise and ability to survive and thrive in adverse situations, has taken over the role of the former Indian dukawallah, selling and trading and running transport services to places where no-one else will go, although such pioneer activity, like that of his sub-continental counterpart, is unlikely to be impelled by altruism.

Two hundred yards and two minutes and I was through Rumuruti, its short-lived urban delights hovering tantalisingly in my trail of dust.

The road, gravelly, rocky and rutted, ran through low, thorn-covered hills. For the first ten miles it was bounded on the right by the Rumuruti swamp, a papyrus-choked playground for hippo and buffalo. Through it flowed the Easo Narok, which later joined the Easo Nyiro, a river which, like so many others in Kenya, fails to reach the sea, ending its run in the Lorian Swamp in the wastelands of the Northern Frontier.

I pressed on, anxious to get to the ranch before dark. I still had another forty miles to go and my speed, thanks to the conditions under wheel, had dropped dramatically.

As I trundled along, I noticed that all the wire in the boundary fences through which the road passed had been torn out and lay looped and tangled on the ground. Many of the posts had also been broken. This, I later learned, was caused by the herds of elephant which roamed at will across Laikipia. Such was the damage they caused that most ranchers had given up the endless task of trying to repair their flattened fences.

By now it was late afternoon and the air was growing cooler.

At last I began to relax.

Far from the maddening shrill of the telephone and out of range of manic bus drivers, I allowed my gaze to range over the near-by bush, now sharp and clear in the softening rays of the declining sun, every branch and twig, each slender grass stem and jagged boulder, picked out in sharp relief.

An early jackal slipped across the road, looking over his shoulder at the car, quickening his stride as I approached. A half dozen tawny kongoni antelope materialised in a clearing, wheeling and rocking through the open bush. A group of giraffe gazed benignly down as I passed, their huge, mild, doe-like eyes, fringed with impossibly long lashes, registering neither surprise nor alarm at my presence. In the distance, small groups of Thomson's gazelle skittered to and fro, glad to be free from the crushing weight of the malignant sun. Their larger, more heat-resistant cousins, the dignified Grant's gazelle, trotted slowly away when they heard the crunch of stones beneath the wheels of my chariot.

A short rocky escarpment, a long stretch of black cotton soil, thankfully dry, and I passed through a gap in a dry stone wall and onto the ranch.

I looked around.

I seemed to be in a gigantic rockery. Everywhere I looked there were rocks – black, brown, yellow, grey and even orange. How could anyone, I asked myself, raise stock in this blighted wilderness?

As if in answer to my question, a long, trailing, procession of cattle materialised out of the bush, heading towards a distant, thorn-enclosed boma (corral). Their coats were glossy and sleek, their ribs well covered. Following them was a small flock of black-headed Dorper sheep and behind them sauntered a thin, narrow faced herdsman. Over one shoulder he carried a long, slender, leaf bladed spear. At his waist the slanting rays of a reluctantly vanishing sun shone like a spotlight on the red scabbard containing his simi (short sword). He raised his hand in greeting as I passed. Animals and man, suddenly, did not seem alien to this wilderness, but part and parcel of it.

The sun sank below the horizon and at once the world was plunged into brief tropical twilight. The slow passage of the car generated a deliciously cool breeze. I inhaled it with pleasure.

The main ranch buildings were atop a rocky bluff and by the time I had picked my way over the boulders at its base it was quite dark. Headlights on, I ground up the last mile in low gear. By a sharp turn in the track, a massive overhanging rock seemed to block the way. As I squeezed past, a huge shadow moved in front of the car. Startled, I stalled the engine and found myself eyeball to eyeball with a very large buffalo bull.

He seemed displeased by my presence.

Frantically I turned the ignition key, forgetting that the car was still in gear.

It lurched forwards like a drunken kangaroo. Just when violent contact between beast and machine seemed inevitable, my hand, greasy with sweat, slipped off the steering wheel and onto the horn. Startled by the sudden blast of noise, the buffalo swerved to the left, crashed into the bush and was gone.

I waited until my heart-rate had subsided to something approaching normality before drying my palms on my shorts, re-starting the engine and creeping uphill once again.

I knew I had arrived when I heard the thud of a generator churning out electricity to the ranch buildings. I drove into a rocky clearing and switched off the engine.

As I did so a pack of enormous dogs rushed out of the darkness, barking furiously and leaping up at the vehicle. Between their howling I could hear strips of paintwork being gouged out by their claws as they launched themselves at my defenceless car. My recent encounter with the buffalo seemed positively benign by comparison.

'Go home, Panya! Shove off, Chafu! Down, Tumbo!'

A shadow, almost as large as that of the bull buffalo, loomed up beside me, thrusting an ice-cold bottle of Tusker through my open window.

'God, thanks, Piki, man. I need that. Just met a chum of yours at the bottom of the hill. Almost as big as you with bloody great horns sticking out of his head!'

Piki van Reenan laughed.

'Old Pembe! That old buff's been hanging round here for weeks. He had a couple of my blokes up a tree the day before yesterday. Hope he shoves off soon or I may have to get rid of him permanently and make him into biltong!'

Piki was the manager and an old friend. He was an Afrikaner and ran the ranch for the owner, a wealthy Arab sheikh, who flew in from time to time with a posse of his well-heeled friends and an entourage of nubile camp followers to enjoy a week of sybaritic indulgence, before returning reluctantly to the strictures of Islam.

Piki's round face grinned down at me. With his closely cropped head and ragged moustache he looked like a Prussian castaway. Although not tall, Piki was large, very large. From his sockless feet, thrust into scuffed and battered veldtshoen, his legs sprang upwards like giant oak trees, following which his body seemed to spread out in all directions. His vast paunch made a mockery of the Laws of Gravity and hung suspended in mid-air, perched on the belt which encircled Piki's upper pelvis and lower abdomen and which also served to prevent his crumpled, khaki shorts from falling down.

'Come on in, man! The sheikh's down at the coast, so we won't be disturbed by him or his friends.'

Piki, his own Tusker firmly clasped in a massive hand, directed me along a path which meandered through a minefield of cunningly sited boulders. It led eventually to his modest dwelling, which lay at some distance from the sheikh's palatial quarters.

In the fullness of time, Piki's cook, a snaggle-toothed, crouch-backed Samburu of indeterminate vintage, lop-eared, bent and gnarled, creaked out of the kitchen and laid before us a couple of chops, carved from a Thomson's gazelle, shot earlier in the day. They were delicious, made more so by the inordinate wait for their presentation, which kept salivary glands and stomach juices stimulated to a high degree of expectation.

I was woken next morning by the cooing of doves in the trees outside my room, by the chattering of starlings and the chuckling of weaver birds. I got up and went outside. The air was cool and refreshing. I walked a few paces through the dry, grey bush and stopped. The ground fell away steeply, almost vertically. In a valley below, bounded by barren, rocky hills, coiled a river, its waters glinting like gun metal in the early morning sun. Its distant course could be traced by following the serpentine loops of tall, green trees which lined its hidden banks. Then the valley broadened out into a bush-covered plain, already beginning to shimmer in the rays of the infant sun. Beyond, distant blue mountains were etched against the pale morning sky.

I tore myself away. I was here to geld camels, not to gaze at the scenery.

Stimulated by Piki, the Samburu cook produced an edible breakfast of coffee, eggs and toast in record time, following which we drove to the cattle yards where the camels would be waiting.

There was no sign of Pembe.

The camels, a dozen in all, were waiting with their handlers as we drove into the yards. I was mightily impressed.

On many ranches the workers, and management, were affected by a condition in which all notion of time, or its passage, was absent. Meals were moveable feasts, usually moved several hours into the future. Breakfast might be consumed around 10am, lunch, if any, sometime between four and 6pm, and dinner anytime from 9pm onwards. Visitors from more ordered regions often found considerable difficulty in adapting to such casual gastronomics. Most ranches were so large and their roads and tracks so rough that it might take a couple of hours to drive to an outlying camp. As a result any rigid time schedule was an impossible goal, which was why I usually visited ranches at the weekend, knowing full well that a large percentage of my time would be spent driving in ever-widening circles, searching for cattle which should have been ready and weren't, or waiting in the dust and flies for a slowly moving herd to appear on the distant horizon, driven by herdsmen who rarely knew which day of the week it was. To waste time in that manner on a weekday, when I would have to return to a full surgery, would be even worse.

'Jambo, jambo, watu wote!' said Piki to the men. 'Hi, everyone! Now listen. The daktari here is not like you. Look at that big round watch on his arm. He is looking at it all the time. He has to get back to Nakuru before dark. He cannot lie around in the shade like you! He has more work to do! Bring the camels and let's get to work!'

Piki turned to me.

'Bloody good chaps these. Samburu, Pokot, Turkana, even the odd Boran. The best. The old sheikh uses the camels for taking his friends on safari around the ranch, carrying their tents, food and, most important, their drink. Sort of gets him back to his roots. Where he comes from no-one uses camels any more and everyone drives around in air conditioned Cadillacs.'

Although not as strong as entires, camel geldings are more desirable for working purposes. Being lighter in build, they may be more suitable as riding animals. They are more tractable, can be worked with females and do not come into musth, that period of heightened seasonal sexual activity in the male camel, when bulls can become markedly anti-social, sometimes downright dangerous, towards other bulls and man. At this time they frequently froth at the mouth, grind their teeth, swallow air and belch it out with the soft palate, which protrudes from the mouth like an obscene pink balloon, before disappearing back into the mouth with a horrid slobbering sound. The poll glands at the back of the skull secrete a dark reddish fluid with a disagreeable smell. And they often have diarrhoea, which they spray around with a constant flapping of the tail. As the season may last for some months, by the time it ends the camel in question may be in pretty poor condition as a result of all this accessory activity, quite apart from that expended in actual copulation.

Knowing all this, I fervently hoped that none of the camels I was about to castrate were in musth. I had no desire to have an arm ripped off, or to be deprived of the top of my skull as had happened to some unfortunate camel men.

I scanned the camels with an anxious eye. Apart from sneering down their noses at me, I could detect no overt signs of anti-social behaviour.

I asked the nearest handler, a curly headed Boran, to couch his camel, a huge, fawn-coloured monster. The Boran tugged on the animal's head rope, at the same time tapping on the camel's shins with a light stick and grunting the secret mantra – 'Toh! Toh!' The camel grunted in return, bellowed, bared his jagged, black and brown teeth, bubbled in his throat and, with a final exasperated groan of resignation, sank to his knees and lowered himself onto his chest and hindquarters. The Boran quickly hobbled a foreleg with a short length of rope and I injected the camel in the rump with xylazine, a powerful sedative.

The other handlers followed suit and I went round the seated animals, injecting them all. At the same time I checked each animal's age, examining its teeth to ensure that it was over four years. Castration under the age of four results in an underdeveloped, weak animal, unable to carry heavy loads, such as present day tourists.

I then allowed the camels to get to their feet and prepared for business – laying out scalpel, emasculator, scissors and catgut, local anaesthetic, antibiotic and tetanus antitoxin.

After about fifteen minutes most animals were showing distinct signs of being under the influence – staggering slightly, salivating profusely, pendulous lower lips drooping and eyes closed. I had seen similar sights in the Men's Bar.

As soon as the first camel sat down I moved in. Two or three men expertly rolled the feebly bellowing beast onto its left flank and in a trice had the fore and hind legs well secured with rope. The hind legs were drawn far forwards. I had no desire to have a foot the size of a dinner plate remodel my face. With a towel, I covered both of the camel's eyes, to protect them from dirt, dust, flies and sun. After swabbing the scrotum with methylated spirits I injected local anaesthetic into each testicle and spermatic cord. Within a few minutes adequate desensitisation had taken place to allow me to proceed.

An incision of suitable length exposed one testicle, which I withdrew, clamping the emasculator around the spermatic cord. Despite having used the instrument times without number, I always looked at it carefully before applying it, to ensure that the crushing part was uppermost. If placed the other way round, the immediate and spectacular haemorrhage which would ensue would speedily dispatch the victim to greener pastures and myself from the premises. I requested a camel man to hold the emasculator while I ligated the cord with strong catgut, trying to ensure, as I did so, that his grimy fingers did not stray into the wound. I applied a ligature, mainly because of the size of the animals I was dealing with and hence the size of their blood vessels, and also because, within a very few hours, the sun would be well up, causing maximum dilatation of superficial veins and arteries. Trying to stem a rush of blood in this area would be like attempting to stop a tidal wave with your bare hands. Having tied off the cord, I removed the emasculator and repeated the process on the other testicle, extracting it through the same incision. I left the wound open. After cleaning it with cold water and antiseptic, I sprayed it with gentian violet, gave the camel a shot of antibiotic and tetanus antitoxin and instructed my helpers to untie the ropes and sit the patient up.

With an irritated grunt he lurched drunkenly to his feet, and, giving me a filthy look, tottered off.

I looked around me. All the other camels were well sedated by now. Most were still standing, but one or two had obviously found this required rather too much effort and were sitting down, heads resting on the ground, in an attitude of listless lassitude. All looked like Bowery bums trying to pretend the world didn't exist.

I picked out the most comatose of the group and dealt with him first. From then on it was a matter of random selection until finally the last victim, with a roar and a belch, staggered off into the bush.

It had all been a bit too much for Piki. After observing the first operation from a tentative distance, he suddenly informed me that he had pressing business back at base, muttering something about a Toyota and

369

a broken main leaf spring. Looking somewhat green about the gills, he hurried off. He reappeared, judging it rather nicely, I thought, just as I was cleaning up. By now it was late morning.

'Time for a Tusker, Hughie, man! You've done a powerful amount of work this morning. Shit, man! I don't know how you can cope with all that blood and stuff! Really turns me off!'

'Right-o. Thanks, Piki. I've got a powerful thirst. But I'd better go easy. It's a working day and I've got to be back in Nakuru by late afternoon at the latest. And it's a bloody long way from here.'

'Ach, come on man, you can manage. I'll give you some buffalo biltong to chew on the way back.'

'Thanks, Piki.'

I had sampled Piki's biltong before and it was like fossilised wood, guaranteed to fracture the strongest of teeth and keep me chewing from Rumuruti to Nakuru.

Three Tuskers later, I departed.

I did not get far before the familiar sideways lurch and the whop, whop, whop of a punctured tyre brought me to a stop.

Changing a tyre under a fierce equatorial sun and under the influence of even only three Tuskers is guaranteed to open the finest of pores, and by the time I had finished I was fairly saturated.

Somewhat bedraggled, I pressed on.

A couple of miles from Rumuruti the road crossed a rivulet, spanned by a crude, wooden bridge. As I was negotiating this structure, which was devoid of any restraining barrier to prevent the passing motorist, fuelled or unfuelled by Tuskers, from slipping into the swamp below, the engine lost power and my foot flopped limply to the floor.

'What now?' I thought, throwing in a few unprintables for good measure.

Perched on the bridge, I hopped out and investigated the situation. The engine was ticking over normally and it took little time to discover that the accelerator pedal had broken. Luckily it was still connected to its cable. As a result I was able to drive the car by leaning down and exercising a modicum of backward pressure on the detached pedal with my right hand, while with my left I steered and changed gear. When changing gear I had to abandon the steering wheel. Consequently all gear changes were executed with some dispatch.

As I eased the 504 off the rickety planks which held the bridge together, the first vehicle I had seen since I left the ranch came roaring down the hill towards me, swaying alarmingly from side to side. It was a grossly overloaded lorry, groaning with excess weight, probably bound for Baragoi, or Loyengelani on the desiccated shores of Lake Turkana. Roosting precariously on top of mounds of baggage were several laughing

Africans, men and women, their eyes and teeth flashing in dark, dusty faces. As the lorry jolted past, gears grinding and springs creaking, they cheered and waved.

Unable to reciprocate with both hands juggling with accelerator, steering wheel and gear stick, they must have wondered why this white man looked so grim and unresponsive.

By the time I reached Thomson's Falls my pores were wide open.

The dirt road to Nakuru had never seemed so long. It went on for ever. The steep, winding descent of the Subukia escarpment took on the qualities of a nightmare.

I reached the surgery two hours later than my anticipated arrival time. The waiting queue of animals and clients seemed endless. All were doing a lot of serious bit champing. I gritted my teeth and hurried in. My cup was filled when I discovered that in addition I had three farm visits to do. One was a calving and one of the others was a horse, which had run into a barbed wire fence.

I phoned a friend, who came round to the surgery and did a jury rig repair on my broken pedal.

I finished work that night at 11.30pm.

CHAPTER NINETEEN

I was in the ditch again.

Peggy Sullivan of Mau Narok had phoned up. The time was 6pm and she had a Shorthorn cow unable to calve. Peggy was temporarily managing a large farm at an altitude of just under 10,000 feet, so when she rang my heart sank several metaphorical inches from mid-thorax to lower abdomen. It would be cold, very cold. And wet, as the month was April, the height of the rainy season.

I told Peggy I would be on my way shortly and could she please endeavour to have the cow in some sort of shelter. She said she would do her best.

Mau Narok was a high altitude enclave, farmed by a close-knit number of European settlers of widely differing backgrounds. Most were of British stock, but they included a Frenchman with an Irish name, an aristocratic Greek, an ex-Indian Army major and a German tycoon. I found Mau Narok to be an infinitely friendlier and more hospitable place than the geographically similar Molo area, whose climate, landscape and inhabitants – with certain notable exceptions – always struck me as being singularly bleak.

There were two ways to Mau Narok.

The longer, more travelled road was via Njoro.

The shorter, steeper road was via Elementaita.

I chose the latter.

All went well until I had left the shacks of Elementaita behind. Elementaita was the place which looked like an equatorial mock-up of the scene in *Shane* in which Alan Ladd guns down Jack Palance in a welter of mud in the one and only street. Elementaita didn't really have a street. The road just ran through it. There was a wooden police station on stilts on one side and a few dukas on the other. That was all.

Almost at once it began to rain. The road was not smooth. Craters filled with chocolate-coloured water appeared in my headlights. Ruts zigzagged crazily from side to side. Soon I was fighting to keep the car moving in a straight line. I hit a flat section at speed. It was greasy with mud. The back of the car broke away and I headed sideways for the ditch. I whipped the wheel into the skid and somehow regained the crown of the road. The suspension was taking a fearful pounding. I could hear the shock absorbers banging up and down as I crashed over the mass of holes, all now filled with mud and water. To have slowed down would have meant instant immobilisation.

I slithered down to a river and over a wooden bridge. A couple of miles further on, where the road began to rise steeply into the forest, I passed a pickup. The two occupants, seen briefly and dimly in the darkness and the mud and rain, were fitting chains to the tyres.

I should have been warned, but in the arrogance of ignorance, I pressed on.

The road, the first to have been built to Mau Narok, followed the line of an old elephant track. To my jaundiced eye, it looked as though little improvement had been done since it had been pounded out by the pachyderms. Higher up, it ran, tunnel-like, through dense vegetation, overhung by high banks and sunk below ground level.

For a while I appeared to be in some sort of control. Then the road entered the forest proper and at once I knew I was in trouble. It was steep, very steep, and extremely slippery, with huge ditches yawning on either side. The crown of the road resembled the back of a great blue whale, slick with water pouring down its sides. Once off that crown and I knew that my journey would come to an abrupt end.

I hadn't long to wait. After a couple of hundred yards I could feel the rear of the car slipping crab-wise to the right. Desperately I tried to force it back into the middle of the road. It was hopeless. With a horrid crunch the car slewed into the ditch and hit the bank, which at this point was about six feet high. Now the car was wedged solidly against it, lying at an angle of about thirty degrees.

I tried to drive up the ditch in a vain attempt to extricate myself. I gained a few feet. I tried alternate reverse and forward gears until the smell of singed clutch advised me to desist. I hadn't improved the paintwork either.

Switching off the engine I contemplated my situation. As I did so the lights of a vehicle appeared from behind me. In a shower of mud the pickup, its chains flapping and chewing up the road, ground past and disappeared up the hill. In their position I would have done the same.

'Well,' I thought resignedly to myself, 'that's that. It looks like Shank's pony from now on.'

Being unable to open the driver's door, jammed as it was against the bank, I struggled out of the passenger door, stood up and immediately fell down. The road surface was like glass. With some difficulty I put on my wellington boots, found a torch, locked the car and set off up the hill. The nearest farm was four miles away. The rain had stopped, and apart from the dripping of sodden vegetation, the squelch of my boots and the odd oath as I measured my length in the mud, all was silent.

The beam of my torch was less than powerful, barely strong enough to show me where I was putting my feet.

There was a harsh crash of breaking branches, a maniacal cackle and a large shape leapt into the road and plunged into the forest on the other side.

I froze in my tracks.

It was a hyena.

I waited until I could hear above the thunder of my pounding heart, before continuing gingerly up the road.

Something hit me on the head and I leapt as though stung by a hornet.

In view of the conditions underfoot this was no mean achievement.

It was a hailstone about the size of a gooseberry. Then there came another and another until with a whoosh and a rush the storm burst. The noise was deafening. Now I could hear neither my heart nor the sound of any hyena foolish enough to venture into the open.

Not that I particularly cared. By now I was soaked to the skin and my body temperature felt as though it had fallen by several degrees. The hail struck like shot gun pellets. Bruised and battered I plodded on. After about a mile the storm slackened and cleared. Drifts of hail shone eerily in the gloom.

The road descended to a shallow valley. Banks of mist lay in the hollows. The feeble glow of my torch was reflected from the swirling tendrils of clammy vapour.

Two hours after leaving my car, be-mired from head to foot, I sloshed up to the farm house owned by the ex-Indian Army wallah, Major Peter Buckley-Brown, more commonly known as Purple Pete. The derivation of this colourful appellation was the owner's flamboyant nose, which had been subjected, along with the rest of his body, to the excesses of port and whisky for most of his adult life.

I skidded up to the front door and gave it a good battering with my fist. I was in no mood for finesse.

After a couple of minutes the stentorian voice of the major could be heard demanding identification. As we were on first name terms I bellowed out my predicament.

The door opened, shedding a yellow beam of light on the foetal form of a great-coated night watchman, slumbering beneath a hedge. Displaying about as much agility as an inebriated sloth, he scrambled to his feet and gave a ragged military salute. The major gave an exasperated snort and beckoned me in. We were roughly the same height, but I was half way down the corridor before I realised that I was now towering over him and that I was on a level with the stuffed tigers' heads which glared down from the walls. About two inches of compressed mire were closely adherent to the soles of my boots.

Swiftly discarding my footwear I followed my host into his bachelor sitting room. This was sparsely furnished. On the walls were hung a number of ancient hunting prints and more heads, gleaned from the Indian jungle. But best of all was a large, roaring, wood fire and towards this I hastened with all possible speed.

'Sorry to trouble you like this, Pete,' I said, as steam rose moistly from my shirt. 'My car's stuck in the ditch half way down the escarpment and there's a cow stuck calving on Cobb Farm.'

'We'll have a burra-peg first, old chap, and then we'll plan how to get you out.'

So saying he thrust a glass containing what looked like several fluid ounces of neat whisky into my hand. I took a swallow and had a fit of coughing as the fiery fluid flowed over my tonsils.

'Let's see if we can raise Peggy. Two Land-Rovers might be better than one. Mine's getting a bit long in the tooth.'

On a side table sat a couple of plates containing the congealing remains of the major's evening repast. Surrounding them was a litter of books, papers and bits of machinery. Shoving these aside he revealed, nestling beside a defunct car battery, a telephone which looked as though it might have been hand crafted by Alexander Graham Bell himself.

'I wonder how long it'll take to rouse the operator?' the major grunted, pouring himself another massive tot. After about fifteen minutes of frantic cranking, contact was made, and the call put through.

The major put the phone down.

'Peggy'll be down in about twenty minutes. We'd better have one for the road.'

By the time Peggy arrived we were well oiled and ready for anything the night might throw at us.

Peggy was a plump, good looking blonde. She exuded toughness and competence. Her battered Land-Rover was indescribably filthy, with long stalactites of mud hanging from the wheel arches.

I enquired after the welfare of the cow I had come to assist.

'Straining like billy-oh! Still, now that you're here all will be well.'

Peggy laughed. Being unable to think of anything better to do, I laughed as well, somewhat less enthusiastically.

The major threw a coil of rope into the back of his Land-Rover. It looked strong enough to tether the Queen Mary.

To it he added a shovel and a jembe.

The major's Land-Rover was an early fifties model and as we rattled along his farm track behind Peggy's rather more modern version, I pushed open the side window to clear the air and aerate my brain. I leaned my elbow on the door sill. The door immediately burst open and I found myself three parts outside, scrabbling wildly to maintain contact with the vehicle.

'Sorry, old boy. Forgot to warn you about that door. Hasn't shut properly for years.'

The major followed the tail lights ahead.

It was just as well they were there because, although Pete's Land-Rover had windscreen wipers, it lacked windscreen washers and within a very short time mud thrown up by the wheels had reduced forward visibility to almost zero.

Every now and again we crashed into an unseen pothole with a fearful metallic bang.

I expected the major to respond to these seemingly mortal blows to his vehicle's suspension with a series of equally fearful oaths. However he remained mute, all but invisible in the darkness, his senses presumably mercifully dulled by his most recent alcoholic infusion.

We arrived at the point where my own combustion engine had failed to make the grade. The car lay forlornly in the ditch, snuggled up against the bank. Perversely, I felt slightly surprised and insulted at seeing it there, a testament to my own incompetence.

A couple of twenty point turns saw both Land Rovers facing uphill. Peggy hitched up first as hers was the more powerful of the two. Threading a two inch hawser at ten o'clock at night through the towing eye of a Peugeot half buried in mud was not without its difficulties, but at last it was done.

I clambered in and Peggy took up the strain.

The vehicles moved a couple of reluctant feet before the Land Rover began to slide, imperceptibly at first, and then with increasing momentum, into the opposite ditch.

Peggy made an unladylike remark.

We untied the rope and Peggy tried to drive out. Low ratio four wheel drive merely served to force the vehicle ever deeper into the hillside. I began to feel a bit better. After all, if a Land Rover couldn't make it, what chance had I?

After about twenty minutes of an unedifying spectacle, fortunately cloaked in darkness, of man's inhumanity to machine, we decided to call it a night.

Pete's vehicle took no part in the proceedings. There was no point in getting his roadster stuck as well.

I loaded my drugs and equipment into the back of Pete's Land Rover. The two abandoned vehicles were locked and with the three of us jammed into the front seat we churned back up the hill.

Peggy was sitting in the middle, straddling the gear stick, which, surmounted by the major's knobbly fist, weaved a sinuous dance between her substantial thighs. My own position was one which afforded me little comfort. My seat was half occupied by Peggy's left buttock, whose insistent pressure edged me ever nearer to the dodgy passenger door, threatening to eject me into the night. Whenever I tried to regain a couple of lost inches, I received a playful nudge in return. It was like doing the hokey-cokey with a young elephant.

Purple Pete seemed to be not unaware of my predicament as every now and again I glimpsed a flash of false teeth in the gloom.

He drove on past his own farm for another three miles, up a steep hill, past a stone church nestling in a clump of trees and up a long farm track.

The altitude now was well over 9,000 feet and the temperature was no longer one which could be ignored by the lightly clad, such as myself. I fervently hoped that Peggy had taken cognisance of my request that my patient be sheltered from the night air.

We passed the massive stone farmhouse, built in the 1920's, and entered a field which contained the cattle crush. As Pete's now barely functional headlights swept over its wooden posts I was astonished to see that about twenty yards of its length were covered by tarpaulins.

I turned my head in wild surmise to Peggy. By now my seating space had been reduced to about six lateral inches and further movement was out of the question.

'Yes, she's in there,' she said. 'Must be pretty warm by now!'

We stopped at the tunnel entrance.

From the rim of outer darkness a couple of figures materialised. Swathed in a fantastic collection of rags and tattered blankets they looked like the last survivors of Napoleon's winter retreat from Moscow.

These were the night herdsmen.

With these gentlemen in tow, carrying a torch and a bucket of frigid water, I entered the tarpaulined tunnel.

At once the temperature rose by about twenty degrees and by the time I arrived at its furthest point where the cow was ensconced, the atmosphere was like that of a sauna bath. Sweat cascaded down my brow. By the light of the torch I could see my overdressed companions visibly wilting in the heat.

A quick inspection revealed the offending calf to be in breech presentation and dead. Foetal fluids were almost non-existent. An explora-tory manipulation indicated that extraction was unlikely to be achieved without the aid of obstetrical tools, except at the cost of severe physical trauma both to the patient and myself, which scenario I wished to avoid at all costs, especially to myself.

I returned to the Land Rover and gave a brief report to Peggy and the major. Their teeth were beginning to chatter in the unheated cab.

Shedding my shirt, I seized my embryotome and re-entered the delivery room.

After a short, sharp tussle I brought both of the calf's hocks over the rim of the maternal pelvis, following which I sawed off both hind limbs below the joint. This allowed me to slip a rope noose round both joints and to instruct my assistants to commence extraction by pulling judiciously on the ropes. Thus doing, they extended both hind legs.

Above the grunting and panting of my companions in the near total darkness, and the grating of their feet on the stone floor of the crush, I could hear a sound like the clatter of miniature castanets.

Peggy and the major, impatient at the delay, were at the entrance to the tunnel, monitoring my progress.

'For God's sake, get a move on!' the major stuttered. 'We're bloody well freezing out here!'

I could hear his dentures rattling together like porcelain peas on a drum.

Fifteen minutes later, the calf was delivered and the cow released into the chilly darkness.

Soaked in sweat, I followed her.

'Well, you did a good job there, Peggy,' I gasped, my breath smoking in the frigid night air. 'I can't begin to say how grateful I am. I'd never have survived if that cow had been outside.'

Peggy nodded numbly, trying to smile. She was so cold she could hardly speak.

Pete dropped Peggy off at the door of the baronial mansion and we continued downhill through the mud to his own farm. It was now 1am.

I spent a chilly night in a narrow bed in Purple Pete's spare room, shivering beneath a couple of threadbare blankets.

The following morning both quagmired vehicles were dragged out by a tractor. That night I slept solidly for twelve hours.

The flying lessons continued, until finally, towards the end of 1976, I sat my flying test. Appropriately, the examiner's name was Dickie Bird.

To my relief I passed. But this was not the end of the affair. I still had the written exams to sit.

Having not sat an examination for over thirteen years, I found this imposed a severe strain on what was left of my cerebral hemispheres, especially as there was no Ground School in Nakuru.

In an idle moment I had read somewhere that one's brains cells begin dying in large numbers soon after birth, and continue doing so throughout life. At the time I had greeted this information with the derision and scepticism I reserved for reports from scientists, whose overheated imaginations I believed could be more profitably employed. Now, as I feverishly struggled with a mass of indigestible data, I began to think otherwise. How much productive brain matter had I left? As the wick of midnight oil burned low, I would brew myself a cup of black coffee, in the hope that another tankard of concentrated caffeine would stimulate the remaining cells to greater effort.

The material on Aviation Law, Airframes and Engines, and Meteorology was relatively straightforward – merely a matter of cudgelling and dredging the memory. The multiple choice papers ensured virtual success for all but the mentally retarded.

That on navigation was rather different. More than a modicum of intelligence and expertise was required, an essential prerequisite if one was to be able to pilot a plane from A to B and not end up in Y or Z. The test for the Flight Radio-Telephony Operator's Licence needed something else – a good ear and the ability to transmit, and respond to, messages received from other aircraft and from the ground, through the whine and howl of the invariable static.

The exams were held at Wilson Airport, on the outskirts of Nairobi.

Here, to the accompaniment of the whistle and thump of departing and arriving aircraft, a small group of aspiring pilots, myself among them, spent a couple of mornings in a cramped, wooden room, writing down what they hoped were the correct answers to the posed questions.

Two weeks later, in December 1976, the results arrived by post.

I had passed.

I had my wings. And a licence, if I was not careful, to kill myself.

Rumuruti, latter day Happy Valley, favoured haunt of remittance men, was home to the Khaki Highlanders, as the hybrid offspring of the area's numerous mixed marriages were called.

It also included the residence of Brigadier Rodney Nugent, formerly of the Khyber Rifles and latterly of Turi in highland Kenya. His low rambling house was located on the eastern edge of the great swamp which ran northwards from the township. From it he supervised the running of his 80,000 acre ranch, the practicalities of which were left in large part to his manager, a lowly paid Seychellois, called Patrick Jean-Louis.

Jean-Louis bore the vicissitudes of his life in semi-bondage, subject to the daily whims of his employer's uncertain nature, with remarkable passivity. Mrs Nugent had not entirely given up her own struggle, her temper being no less volatile than that of her husband. Seeing them together was like watching two equally matched and mutually hostile terriers, circling each other, snarling and backing up, hackles bristling, but never actually breaking into open warfare.

When they lived at Turi they made frequent visits to Nakuru to restock their capacious gin cabinet. After completing this vital and onerous task they would repair to the Club lounge to recuperate and catch up on news from Blighty via the spinnaker-sized pages of the 'Daily Telegraph'. This they seemed to do by a process of osmosis. They would sit opposite, pages upraised, effectively obscuring each other. The pages remained unturned for what seemed to be hours on end.

It was all too apparent to an impartial observer, such as myself, that the love that once might have been between the two, had long since withered on the vine.

Mrs Nugent possessed, in addition to her admirable conjugal fortitude, another debatable asset in the shape of a cast iron backside.

She was a large woman, with what can only be described as a formidable presence. Her antecedents were all from India, and apparently did not exclude the odd Pathan irregular. Having spent the bulk of her life in the sub-continent being cosseted, and fawned upon by a veritable battalion of servants and flunkeys, all claiming descent from an array of magnificos, from Alexander the Great to Ghengis Khan, the transfer to Africa came as something of a shock. As did the more recent shift from the moated grange at Turi to sweltering exile in the East African equivalent of Siberia at Rumuruti.

Although imperious and autocratic, her manners were those of a true aristocrat, and she extended courtesy and consideration to everyone she met – her husband always excepted.

One day she entered the surgery, clutching a pekinese to her ample bosom. She always wore large, floppy hats, and these materially added to her larger then life appearance.

I had just completed a major operation and my surgical bag lay open upon a chair.

Mrs Nugent sailed in like a schooner coming in to harbour.

Thrusting the animal into my hands, she about-faced and, before I had time to shout, 'Hold it! Stop right there!' she had lowered her massive posterior into the only chair in the room, that bearing my bag and an exposed assortment of scissors, forceps, probes, scalpels and needles.

I shuddered and briefly closed my eyes.

Mrs Nugent made no reaction. She sat as if seated in the most comfortable arm chair in her own home. For the next twenty minutes she leaned back and discussed the finer points of her own pekinese in particular, and those of the breed in general, while I palpated and prodded in an effort to discover, what, if anything, was wrong with Chairman Mao, as she was pleased to call her own specimen.

Finally, after a short, but savage tirade against her husband, she rose, received Chairman Mao, and strode out, without a mark upon her escutcheon. My surgical bag was less fortunate. Its encounter with thirteen stones of female flab had left it so bent and buckled as to be barely usable.

Perhaps the Pathan in the family cupboard had been a fakir, whose feats of physical prowess and masochistic propensity had been handed, intact, down the female line.

Now, not for the first time, I had to deal with her husband's animals. While farming in Turi, he was notorious, in my books at least, for never, ever, presenting me with a calving cow which had been in labour for less than three days. As a result I was pretty sure that he regarded me as an incompetent oaf, in that, to date, I had failed totally to deliver a live calf from any of his animals. However, he was seemingly prepared to give me a second chance.

Several cattle from a herd grazing on the edge of the swamp had died and a diagnosis was urgently required.

Jean-Louis took me down to the swamp in his open plan Land Rover, which was devoid of both doors and roof. It was little more than an engine, a chassis and a couple of seats.

By the time we got to the spot where the animal in question, a steer, had died, I felt in urgent need of spinal surgery.

En route Jean-Louis briefed me on the problem. No rain had fallen on the ranch for several months and as a result the cattle had been obliged to enter the swamp to find water. Since then seven animals had died.

Jean-Louis was a good-looking, middle-aged man, light brown in colour, dressed shabbily in worn corduroys and a tattered shirt. His manners were exquisite and his softly modulated speech was peppered with numerous 'sirs', 'doctors' and 'thank yous'. I warmed to him immediately.

The dead steer lay in a small clearing in the sea of papyrus, which bordered and covered the swamp. A knot of lean and hungry-looking Samburu and Turkana lay around the carcase, eyeing it proprietorially. They eased themselves to their feet as we rattled up.

Knives and simis appeared and the men began to skin the steer. Although it was mid-day, very soon I had been singled out for especial attention by huge numbers of voracious mosquitoes. They were so large that I swore I could see their wings flapping as they emerged from the swamp, proboscides erect and aimed at my exposed mzungu flesh. None of the Africans appeared to be being bitten, or, if they were, they gave no sign of it.

The headman, a leathery Turk, with legs like a couple of fire-blackened sticks and who was probably capable of walking thirty miles before breakfast without breaking sweat, cleft the steer's sternum with a panga. With each stroke he gave a soft grunt.

When everything had been removed I squatted down with my entourage of grazing mosquitoes to examine the internal organs in detail.

At a superficial glance they looked pretty normal. The carcase was perhaps a trifle anaemic, but that was all. However, the liver was larger than usual so I asked for a knife. The Turkana, rather aptly I thought, handed me something resembling a medieval Turkish scimitar. With a dramatic sweeping slash, I cut the liver in twain.

There was an astonished gasp from the watching Africans as a veritable volcano of wriggling flukes erupted from the cut surface. They poured through the severed bile ducts in their hundreds, twisting and turning, expanding and contracting, writhing and squirming. In the pathological thrill of the moment I briefly forgot my insectivorous entourage, busily slaking their thirst at my expense.

These were Fasciola Gigantica, a species of liver fluke found in the tropics, which, naturally, is about twice the size of that which frequents the temperate zone.

'East Africa wins again!' I thought.

'Well, we know what's been killing your cattle,' I said to Jean-Louis. 'All we've got to do now is to give a brief synopsis on treatment and control to the brigadier.'

Jean-Louis looked decidedly nervous.

'If you say so, boss.'

I laughed. 'Just point me in the right direction and I'll go and see the old buffer.'

I found the brigadier at ease on his verandah, slumped in a cane chair, asleep, snoring and surrounded by the litter of what he obviously considered to be essential to life in the tropics – a bottle of gin, a scattering of tonics, ice and a tumblerful of lemon slices. The cold corpse of a half smoked cigar lay in a chipped ash tray, which bore the faded outline of regimental crest. This, at a casual glance, appeared to depict an elephant surprised in *flagrante delicto* with a tiger.

As I bent to examine this phenomenon more closely, there was a sound at my elbow like an aardvark clearing its nasal passages.

The brigadier awoke with some violence, the tufts of hair jutting from his ears and nostrils quivering like wind-blown heather as he made an apparently unwelcome transition to consciousness.

Upon seeing me in his immediate vicinity he closed his eyes and appeared to count to ten, at the same time holding his breath.

When he opened his eyes he exhaled forcibly.

'Well? What have you found?'

As concisely as I could, I gave him a potted version of the life cycle of the fluke, one which I hoped would be suitable for a lay brain long steeped in alcohol.

I mentioned control of the aquatic snails, which are the intermediate hosts, by drainage and drugs, the use of troughs and bore holes, and treatment with anthelmintics.

I thought I did rather well.

The brigadier seemed to think otherwise.

'Costs, Cran! Have you stopped to think just how much all this is going to cost? What do you think I am? Some sort of ruddy millionaire? You chaps are all the same. Think because I'm sitting on 50,000 acres of bloody Africa I can just snap my bloody fingers and I'm like a goose laying a golden egg! Well, it's not so I tell you! Not so at all!'

His hand shook as he poured himself another drink.

All of a sudden he mellowed.

'Have a drink, old boy.'

I easily persuaded myself that it would have been churlish to refuse.

'This is not like England. Never will be! Europe in the Middle Ages perhaps. We're farting into the wind here. My cattle die of disease and the few drugs available cost a bloody fortune. Those that don't die are liable to be pinched by stock thieves. Those buggers run rings round the police. How can you expect otherwise when the coppers start off weighted down by hobnailed boots and khaki jerseys?'

He sighed.

'What profit I do make is gobbled up by the Income Tax Department – our bloody taxes are among the highest in the world and we're constantly being harassed to pay even more. As for debtors – well, you've been in the country long enough to know that most people here seem to think it a point of honour not to pay their bills. At least you don't have to pay regular homage to the local big-wig like I do.'

He swallowed the last of his gin.

He was a fast drinker.

'I suppose you're wondering why I've spent the last thirty years of my life here?'

I admitted that the thought had crossed my mind.

'Well, it's because, despite all its multitudinous drawbacks, I've yet to find anywhere better. Which perhaps doesn't say a lot for all the other places, but there it is. I love the country.'

And so do I.